July 2011
Go Pistons!

Public Workers

Public Workers

Government Employee Unions,
the Law, and the State, 1900–1962

Joseph E. Slater

ILR Press
an imprint of
Cornell University Press
ITHACA AND LONDON

First published 2004 by Cornell University Press

Printed in the United States of America

Library of Congress Cataloging-in-Publication Data

Slater, Joseph E., 1960–
   Public workers : government employee unions, the law, and the state,
1900–1962 / Joseph E. Slater
      p. cm.
Includes bibliographical references and index.
   ISBN 0-8014-4012-2 (cloth : alk. paper)
   1. Government employee unions—United States—History.   2. Collective
bargaining—Government employees—United States—History.   3. Government
employees—Legal status, laws, etc.—United States—History.   1. Title.
   HD8005.2.U5S58   2004
      331.88'1135173'09041—dc22
                              2003020656

Cornell University Press strives to use environmentally responsible suppliers and materials to the fullest extent possible in the publishing of its books. Such materials include vegetable-based, low-VOC inks and acid-free papers that are recycled, totally chlorine-free, or partly composed of nonwood fibers. For further information, visit our website at www.cornellpress.cornell.edu.

Cloth printing   10   9   8   7   6   5   4   3   2   1

Contents

Acknowledgments

In writing this book I received a tremendous amount of support. The University of Toledo College of Law was generous with research grants, and my colleagues, particularly William Richman, Rebecca Zietlow, and Llew Gibbons, provided valuable advice. Kymberlee Vining was an excellent research assistant. Lin Whalen worked wonders with formatting. Archivists and librarians in Boston, Seattle, Madison, the U.S. Department of Labor, the George Meany Center (Silver Spring, Md.), the Library of Congress, the Tamiment Library (New York City), and the Walter Reuther Archives (Detroit, Mich.) were very helpful. The partners in my old law firm, Jon Axelrod, Alice Bodley, Hugh Beins, and Barbara Kraft, allowed me to practice part-time when I began writing this book. Public sector unionists I have worked with, especially those in AFSCME Council 26, were inspirational. Timothy Sears taught me a lot about the labor movement. Chris Hayward assisted in New York. Gary Lizzio and Megan Dorsey provided keen editorial assistance, and Megan also helped with research in Seattle.

I have profited from comments from many people, including my graduate student classmates at Georgetown, Dan Byrne, Peter Cole, and June Hopkins; others exploring public sector labor history, especially Mark Wilkens and Edna Johnston; Lawrence Friedman and the participants in the first Willard Hurst Legal Institute, in Madison, Wisconsin (with special thanks to Ajay Mehrotra); and other remarkable scholars, such as Melvyn Dubofsky, Gary Gerstle, Abner Greene, Allan Hyde, Deborah Malamud, Joseph McCartin, and Christopher Tomlins. Thanks also to the editors of *Labor History* (http://www.tandf.co.uk), of the *Seattle University Law Review*, and of the *Oregon Law Review*, where earlier versions of chapters 1–3 appeared, respectively; to my copyeditor Ann Hawthorne; to Frances Benson, Louise E. Robbins, Susan Barnett, and others at Cornell University Press; and to anonymous reviewers for the Press. I was very lucky to have as mentors Dorothy Brown of the Georgetown University History Department and Daniel Ernst of the Georgetown University Law Center, both of whom gave very generous help; Professor Ernst's aid in revising the manuscript was invaluable. My wife, Krista Schneider, deserves credit for adding substance to the book, along with the standard thanks for being patient. Faults and errors, of course, remain my responsibility.

Finally, my parents, Harold and Carol Slater, were role models and sources of every kind of aid. My only true regret about what follows is that my father died before I finished it. This book is dedicated to his memory.

Public Workers

Introduction

The fundamental idea ... of organized labor ... has been the assumption—a correct one, in the main—of an antagonism of interest and of purpose between employer and employee. ... That situation cannot be applied to public employment.
SENATOR CHARLES THOMAS (D–Colorado) (1920)

Nothing can be gained by comparing public employment with private employment; there can be no analogy in such a comparison.
Perez v. Board of Police Commissioners
of the City of Los Angeles (1947)

Incorporating public employees into labor history shows that a good deal of the conventional wisdom and academic theory about unions in the United States is either misleadingly incomplete or simply wrong. Are American workers too "individualistic," divided by race and ethnicity, or otherwise culturally disinclined to organize as their European counterparts have? From the mid-1950s to the early 1990s, union density in the private sector declined from more than 33 percent to less than 12 percent; but in the public sector, from the early 1960s to the early 1990s, union density rose from less than 13 percent to nearly 40 percent. Today, about 40 percent of all union members are public employees.[1] Counting those who, for example, clean public schools as "workers" reveals an American working class quite receptive to the labor movement.

Nor have the struggles of public employees been distinct from those of private sector workers. From the Boston police strike of 1919 to the debacle involving the Professional Air Traffic Controllers Organization (PATCO) that signaled the beginning of the employers' offensive in the Reagan era, the fates of public and private sector unions have been intimately connected. But the fact that public and private sector unions were strong in different eras has had a profound effect on the nature of the labor movement. Understanding this changes the periodization of labor history, generally depicted solely as a rise and decline of private sector unions. Taking serious notice of public sector unions up to the 1960s also provides a clearer view of the factors that inhibit union growth and the factors that facilitate it. Further, it demonstrates another way in which American labor has been "exceptional." In comparable countries, public workers have long been accorded most or all of the same rights as private sector workers. The severe and enduring distinctions between all government and all private employees in U.S. law and policy are neither natural nor inevitable. Most broadly, the history of public sector unions alters our sense of what American labor actually was, why it evolved as it did, what it might have been, what it is, and what it could be.

Yet even as public sector unionism has moved into the mainstream of the labor movement, people who want to know about its past discover that it is still at the margins of history. After John Commons gave public sector unions a brief mention in 1913, the field has essentially ignored them. In recent decades, historians of the unions and the working class have gone far beyond the "Wisconsin school" that Commons founded, greatly expanding the subjects they study and the theoretical tools used in their investigations. Public workers, however, are excluded both from the new narratives and the descriptive models of labor history. As a result, revealing comparisons have been missed, and the pictures of "labor" and "workers" are incomplete to the point of inaccuracy. This trend has continued to the present day. In an article published in 2002, Robert Shaffer bemoans the fact that not only labor historians but historians in general have ignored public sector unions.[2] It is my hope that this book will help bring public sector unions into this historical discussion.

"Should public employees organize as trade unions?" John Commons asked. His answer was a qualified yes, but he made distinctions between the public and private sectors of the type that would continually haunt public sector unions. While their organization was inevitable and could be positive, he wrote, government employees should not be allowed to strike, use the closed shop, or exert excessive political pressure. These unions could have posed an interesting paradox for the industrial pluralists in the Wisconsin school. Primarily interested in how labor's larger institutions functioned as a countervailing economic power, they might have wondered why public workers, whose wages and hours of work were typically set by statute, were organizing at all. Advocates of voluntarism, they might have considered the implications of highly political public sector unions. They could have explored what tactics were appropriate for public workers. But the "old labor history" ignored these unions.[3]

That they were ignored cannot be attributed to the size of public sector unions in the first half of this century. Of course they were smaller and weaker then than now: their density of organization held roughly steady at 10 to 13 percent from the late 1930s to the early 1960s. Still, by 1934 public sector unions had grown to represent 9 percent of the nearly 3.3 million government workers in the United States, who in turn constituted 12.7 percent of all nonagricultural workers in the country.[4] Historians have studied and gleaned valuable lessons from workers in smaller, less organized industries in this period. In fact, in the early 1930s the rate of unionization in the private sector was not much greater than that in the public sector.[5] And although public sector unions had few, if any, statutory rights before the 1960s, the analogous dearth in the private sector before the New Deal has not deterred historians. Nonetheless, even recent "institutional" overviews of the labor movement examine only the private sector.[6]

The "new labor history" also has ignored the public sector. One trend of this school was to study shorter-lived or smaller groups such as the Knights of Labor and the Industrial Workers of the World (IWW). Historians found these groups to be significant both on their own terms and as examples of "lost alternatives" to what the labor movement became.[7] Public sector unions also present an alternative to the path of the mainstream private sector unions that are typically presented as normal. Government workers functioned under different institutional constraints from those affecting their counterparts in the private sector, and adopted different strategies to match. Some large public employee organizations, such as the National Education Association and the Fraternal Order of Police, have always been outside the American Federation of Labor (AFL) and the Congress of Industrial Organizations (CIO). Yet, in searching for other possibilities and traditions in the nation's past, historians have not investigated what public sector unions were doing, why their unprecedented growth took place only in the last forty years, or what the consequences of that delay have been.

Other new labor historians emphasized "worker control." In their view, labor's battle against management was not merely for better wages and hours; it was also over who would have the knowledge and skills to determine the duties of workers and the operation of the facilities.[8] Had these historians looked at the public sector, they could have seen additional examples of how concerns over the daily work process had much to do with why workers sought to organize. Although their wages and hours were often set by law, government employees still formed unions, often to agitate for greater worker control.

The new historians also examined workers who were not organized in unions, and an increasing interest in women and African Americans pushed labor history further away from its original exclusive focus on unions as institutions. Scholars also went beyond the workplace, finding explanations for much worker activity, and its successes and failures, in homes, communities, and culture. But these trends toward broadened scope and inclusion have not been extended to government employees.[9]

Initially, the liberal to leftist approaches found in most studies of labor history from at least the 1960s to the 1980s owed much to neo-Marxist conceptions of class. These conceptions stressed relationships and conflicts created by the capitalist mode of production. Such theories did not consider public workers.[10] Perhaps this omission occurred because, as some contemporaries noted, public sector unions did not contest the distribution of profits within private businesses. Or more generally, perhaps it occurred because collective actions by public employees were thought not to be battles against capitalists and capitalism, but rather merely disputes over how to provide services to the public. In this view, the makeup of government could reflect the results of the class struggle in private industry, and the government's acts might be influential in that struggle, but the organization of government itself was not seen as a site of the struggle.

But class need not be understood only in these terms. A recent study defines class largely on the basis of "the power and authority people have at work." While this approach could be applied to the public sector, no historian has yet done so. E. P. Thompson has explained that "Classes arise because men and women, in determinative productive relations, identify their antagonistic interests, and come to struggle, to think and to value in class ways." Certainly the goods and services government provides through its employees involve productive relations, and certainly these relations, which involve managers and subordinates at work, create class issues.[11] If historians had debated how government employees fitted into a class scheme, they could have weighed the implications of public employers' importing management processes developed under early capitalism (Taylorist time-management techniques, for instance) and the struggle of government employees for more voice in the work process. To the extent that these historians attributed certain conflicts in labor relations specifically to capitalism, they might also have wondered what types of labor relations existed or could have been possible in government employment, where at least some imperatives of capitalism were arguably not present. Further, historians interested in battles against capitalism could have pondered the role of public sector unions as allies or direct participants in this contest, noting that the prime opponents of public sector unions were typically private sector business interests.

In the late twentieth century, some labor historians deemphasized class analysis.[12] Still, none of the postmodern approaches tries to find a place for public workers. The "linguistic turn," which originated in the writings of

French theorists such as Michel Foucault, has asserted that language is central in "constructing" reality.[13] This school has missed an opportunity to show how important the constructions of "worker" and "union" have been to public employees. Only by implicitly or explicitly excluding public workers from these concepts could influential contemporaries, such as judges, treat public sector unions as they did.

Even today, scholars and others too easily accept the idea that the public sector does not contain "real" unions and workers. An analysis of labor and women appeared to dismiss a steep rise in female membership in unions because this rise occurred mostly in public sector unions—as if such unions were not a legitimate part of American labor. Nelson Lichtenstein portrays public employees as performing something less than authentic work. "Unlike the blue collar working class," he writes, "public employees often sat behind a desk . . . and kept their fingers clean." This would be news to the police, firefighters, street cleaners, highway construction workers, janitors, and other manual laborers in the public sector described in this book. Indeed, to use the American Federation of State, County, and Municipal Employees (AFSCME) as an example, a large majority of its members were blue collar.[14]

In recent years, some labor historians have looked increasingly to the state to explain labor's fortunes. This is part of a broader movement by historians and political scientists to "bring the state back in" to their analysis, stressing the interests and capacities of particular units of government in determining policy. This model has been applied to the development of private sector law. Surprisingly, though, works that stress the role of the state in labor matters generally ignore the state as an employer of labor. Studies have shown that the very structure of American federalism, with its myriad layers and exceptionally strong courts, fundamentally affected labor and labor law in the private sector. But no one has described how state structure played out with an even greater vengeance in the public sector, although a few scholars have noted that this void should be filled.[15]

Even modern labor historians who emphasize the significance of the state ignore government workers. Melvyn Dubofsky's *State and Labor in Modern America* barely mentions public sector unions in a chapter covering the period from 1947 to 1973, despite the fact that membership in such unions jumped from just over one million in 1960 to over 3 million in 1976, accounting for more than 80 percent of total union growth in that period. Similarly, Nelson Lichtenstein's recent *State of the Union,* an otherwise excellent overview of labor since the New Deal, discusses public employee unionism on only about three pages. Ira Katznelson, suggesting that labor historians should take greater notice of the state and political theory, mentions neither public sector unions nor their political role.[16]

Many historians studying the state and labor have singled out law as having been especially important. Perhaps the most striking disregard of the public sector is in the numerous works that use labor law to explain the size and character of unions and, by extension, American politics. Karl Klare, Christopher Tomlins, and Katherine Stone, among others, have argued that aspects of the National Labor Relations Act (NLRA) have weakened labor. Melvyn Dubofsky, conversely, sees the NLRA as a vital, unambiguous victory for unions. William Forbath and Victoria Hattam—implicitly addressing the "Sombart question" of why there is no socialism, or at least no labor party, in America—attribute the voluntarism of the AFL, in good part, to court decisions. These and other scholars have made a wide range of claims about the ways in which labor law has had a crucial impact on unions and politics in the United States. Yet none has addressed law in the public sector.[17]

This omission is especially surprising because the public sector presents an excellent opportunity to test claims about the effect of private sector laws by making comparisons with unions in the United States that were not covered by them. The NLRA, state labor relations acts, and (at least until recently) employment laws such as the Fair Labor Standards Act (FLSA) have all excluded government workers. Throughout this century, the rules of public employment have been set by a diverse assortment of state, county, and municipal laws and regulations, state court decisions, and departmental fiat. These rules have always been different from and much less generous than private sector law. Before the 1960s, the law everywhere in the United States prohibited strikes and almost all collective bargaining in government employment, and courts also routinely upheld bans on union membership. Moreover, the growth in the public sector since the 1960s occurred under labor relations statutes patterned after but more restrictive than the NLRA.[18] Yet historians of labor law have never contrasted the impact of these different rules on otherwise similar American workers and unions. Nor has any scholar probed the disabling impact of public sector labor law on the labor movement as a whole, or on American politics.

Court decisions concerning public sector labor law also help illuminate questions of causation in legal history. What types of reasoning and other influences caused judges to rule as they did? Private sector labor law has long provided examples in such inquiries. The early legal realists, objecting to the idea that law was a science that used neutral, internal rules, frequently cited labor and employment law to argue that judges often simply favored employers over employees and unions.[19] The fact that judges still strenuously objected to public sector unions even after largely coming to terms with private sector labor raises questions that should be explored. The "law and society" approach identified first with Willard Hurst and later with Lawrence Friedman agreed that politics mattered, but saw a need to look beyond the "mandarin texts" of appellate court decisions and to examine the records of administrative bodies, litigants, and social trends.[20] Public sector labor law traditionally was created by local officials, and it provides a rich field for this type of examination. The more recent approaches of critical legal studies, while finding that law is "biased," also criticize "socio-economic" models and stress the independent significance of legal forms and discourse. Labor law now is used to support claims that law and its language "construct" reality.[21] Examples from the public sector can help scholars explore and refine such claims.

More generally, these differing approaches have left notions of causation in legal history rather confused. In his first volume on American legal history, Morton Horwitz suggests that "law is autonomous to the extent ideas are autonomous." In his second volume, he ruefully asks, "how does one *explain* anything objectively in a world of complex, multiple causation?" Christopher Tomlins and Andrew King, introducing a book of essays on the history of labor law, characterize "legal forms" as "concepts" that have "multiple avenues of realization but in practice [are] conventionally realized in official discourse in ways that most accord with, or least depart from, prevailing structures of power."[22] Assuming this is correct, one might still wonder what structures are most crucial in what contexts.

The history of public sector labor law shows that combining the tools of all these different schools can yield at least an example of a more precise explanation of causation: judges were hostile to labor, they were constrained by particular state structures and accompanying legal doctrines, and they constructed the term "union" in a critically inaccurate manner.

In sum, none of the fields of history that one might expect to include public sector unions has done so. Some books examine individual unions or unions within a particular type of government employment, but few attempt to link their subjects to the broader labor movement, or even to other public sector unions. Rarely do these studies use the theoretical insights or methodological techniques of modern labor history.[23] Works in the "industrial relations" style have emerged since the 1970s, but they are typically present-minded and practitioner-oriented, usually ignoring history, state theory, and the study of social movements. And even as of this writing, there is no up-to-date treatise that discusses all or even most current public sector laws; overviews of the law that examine the rules of more than one state are rare and often hard to find.[24] Nearly fifty-five years ago, Sterling Spero's still-useful *Government as Employer* argued that unions of government employees had profound common bonds both with each other and with the rest of labor, but practically no historian has made either connection since.

This book examines public sector unions in America from the beginning of the twentieth century to the passage of the first state collective bargaining law in 1959 and its amendments in 1962. Chapter 1 begins with a "false dawn": a boom of organizing by government employees from 1915 to 1919, which culminated in the AFL's embracing police unions. The horrified reactions of employers led to bans on police affiliation with labor. Such a ban caused the Boston police strike of 1919, cutting short this first boom. Notably, even in this situation, involving the difficult case of police, public and private sector employees proclaimed their common interests, just as government officials, courts, and private employers tried to deny them. But the crushing defeat of the strike—and the fears it caused—cast a debilitating shadow over public sector unions for decades to come.

Chapter 2 is the first of three case studies that demonstrate the range of strategies that public sector unions used. In 1928 the Seattle School Board imposed a yellow-dog contract on high school teachers, forcing them to leave the American Federation of Teachers (AFT). The teachers fought back through both the courts and the ballot box from 1929 to 1932, with enthusiastic aid from the local AFL. This episode presages both the difficulties public sector unions would have with the law, and the strategies available to them, given that their employers were often elected officials. The results were intriguingly ambiguous.

Chapter 3 analyzes the law of public sector labor relations through the early 1960s. Inescapable and highly restrictive, the law was central to the experiences of all public sector unions. This chapter explores the reasoning of judges and explains why public sector labor law rights came so much later and in so limited a form by comparison with rights in the private sector or rights of public sector unions in other nations. It also highlights the impact that the failure of public sector unions to win institutional rights had on these unions and on the labor movement as a whole.

Chapter 4 surveys what these unions did in the absence of any formal legal rights. Reviewing the activities of the public school janitors and other service workers of the Building Service Employees International Union (BSEIU) in Chicago and elsewhere during the 1930s, it demonstrates that public sector labor's strategies focused on politics, behind-the-scenes deals with officials, lobbying, appeals to the public, and other kinds of informal activities. Public sector locals in the BSEIU adapted to a wide variety of local contexts, encountering political machines and civil service systems, elected and appointed officials, and a myriad of different employing agencies.

Chapter 5 describes how the powerful, left-wing, and formerly private sector Transport Workers Union, CIO (TWU), reacted after its main local in New York City was converted into a public sector union in 1940, once the city bought the subways. The TWU's political action involved mass protests and huge publicity campaigns, but it could not escape legal restrictions. Nevertheless, through both its own efforts and a gradually increasing toleration of public sector unions, the TWU managed to win about as much as could be won by such a union in this era.

Chapter 6 describes the events that ended this "pre–collective bargaining era": the battles for and eventual passage of the first state statute permitting collective bargaining in the public sector in Wisconsin in 1959 and 1962. This law was enacted after AFSCME had struggled for more than a decade to pass similar bills. Before achieving this victory, union advocates had to address the entire history of objections and obstacles to public sector unions: fears of police strikes, legal doctrines concerning government sovereignty, policy objections to unions bargaining with government, and opposition from conservative political leaders. The types of compromises and debates that took place in Wisconsin have remained live issues across the country in debates about public sector rights to this day.

This book is not a comprehensive treatment of all public sector labor. Rather, it focuses on specific unions and events, and gives additional examples and information to support the claim that these events were significant and representative. The chapters study a range of types of public employees: police, who perform a uniquely governmental job; the white-collar and "professional" teachers; "unskilled" janitors, who could just as easily have been in the private sector; transit workers, who at one time actually were in the private sector; and road crews and other county and municipal workers. The chapters also cross the country, span the period from before World War I until 1962, and address both the AFL and the CIO.

To some extent, the decision as to which types of public workers to discuss and which to omit was based both on numbers and on contemporary circumstances. Federal workers make only brief appearances in the following pages, both because they were a distinct group, governed by different laws and political conditions, and because in the period covered there were fewer of them. Between the wars, civilian federal employees were only about one-fourth of all the public workers in the United States. By contrast, school employees (the subject of chapters 2 and 4) constituted from 33 to 50 percent of all state and local government workers, who in turn were nearly 75 percent of all public employees. Thus, in 1940 there were just under 4 million public workers; almost 2.9 million were employed by state and local governments, and more than 1.1 million worked in public schools. In the twenty-five years after World War II, government at the state and local levels expanded at up to twice the rate of government at the federal level. For the period covered here, workers in the protection services of police (discussed in chapter 1) and fire were the largest category of municipal employees aside from school employees. For example, in 1940 protection service workers made up 28.2 percent of municipal employees outside the education system. Today the highest rates of unionization in the public sector are in local government employment (43.2 percent in 2001), with police, teachers, and firefighters leading the way.[25]

This book is also in part an attempt to answer Howard Kimmeldorf's call for a "new old labor history."[26] Its approach is "old" in that it studies unions as institutions, their struggles over workplace issues, and their impact on politics. It is "new" in that it focuses on locals and their members, champions a heretofore-overlooked segment of the working class, and highlights the role of law and state structure. It even borrows from the linguistic turn to suggest that the manner in which courts and others (falsely) constructed the concept of "union" influenced the history of labor.

The focus on the workplace stems first from a belief that the conditions of waged labor were a central part of life for the large portion of the population that engaged in it, and that battles over these conditions with employers profoundly influenced American society and politics. While uncovering vital truths, too much of the new labor history has found reasons for success or failure only within the working class itself, ignoring critical outside factors, or, as Dubofsky puts it, "who rules whom." The state is one such influence; employers are another.

In this respect the following analysis heeds the call of Brian Kelly (in his fine study of race and class) to bring employers back into labor history. Throughout history, the attitudes and powers of employers have often been dispositive of labor struggles; they certainly were for public sector unions. The 1980s confirmed how damaging hostile and aggressive employers can be to labor and working people, yet historical theorizing is lagging behind. Studying the public sector workplace shows what a crucial role public and private employers played in restricting the rights of public workers.[27]

The protagonists here are primarily members and representatives of local unions, not leaders of international unions, the AFL, or the CIO. Samuel Gompers appears in the background of chapter 1, and Philip Murray lends a hand in chapter 5. But in this book the gears of history start moving when individual police officers, high school teachers, janitors, subway workers, highway workers, and others organize to demand more control over their jobs, an end to arbitrary treatment and discrimination, a fair grievance system, and better wages, hours, and conditions. Among the local protagonists are the stoic John McInnes in Boston, the frustrated Walter Satterthwaite in Seattle, the skillful Elizabeth Grady in Chicago, the colorful W. K. Jones in San Antonio, the fiery Mike Quill in New York City, and the persistent and precise John Lawton in Madison. The narrative that follows is the story of what ordinary workers and their generally small and struggling locals did and did not accomplish, and why.

This book also follows the tradition in labor history of stressing commonalities among different groups of workers. Three recent trends have combined to make this approach less popular. First, the new labor history found that race, gender, and culture were often divisive. Second, postmodernism cast doubts on whether any general explanatory theory, of class or otherwise, could be applied over time and space. Finally, increased specialization among historians has caused researchers to focus on smaller areas.[28] This trend has produced a wealth of valuable detail; but the methodology of studying (for example) one set of workers, in one city, in a discrete period is by its very nature likely to produce an interpretation that finds pivotal causal factors that are specific only to those workers in that city at that time. It is less likely to discover that their struggles (their goals and the obstacles to those goals) were similar to and related to the struggles of a broad class of people, including those living in other regions of the country and in other decades.

Thus, contrary to previous interpretations, chapter 1 contends that the Boston police strike was *not* caused primarily by ethnic and religious tensions peculiar to Boston, but rather can be understood only as part of a nationwide surge of public workers affiliating with the AFL and opposition to this trend. Chapter 2 shows that ten years after these eastern, male, mostly Irish cops unionized, a group of Seattle teachers, many of them women, organized for largely the same reasons and were opposed on the same grounds. In both cases, political and business leaders feared that AFL affiliation by public employees would lead to "class domination" of the state. The janitors in Chicago, Texas, and elsewhere (many of whom were women and/or ethnic minorities), subway workers in New York City (including many blacks), county and municipal workers in Wisconsin, and other government employees also shared goals and strategies and faced common obstacles. This approach in no sense involves a rejection of culture or difference. One lesson to be learned from fine works of modern labor history in the tradition of E. P. Thompson's *The Making of the English Working Class* is that dictatorial, alienated workplaces that pay meager wages and demand long hours offend the values of a wide variety of people and cultures, and provoke resistance.[29]

It is through common obstacles and strategies that public sector labor emerges as a coherent category. Although government workers had many of the same complaints as those in the private sector, their unions had far fewer legal rights, and their range of practical action was much more circumscribed. Throughout this book, a wide variety of public workers are forced to confront the fact that they had no right to strike, to bargain, or, in many cases, even to organize. These constraints made them turn to political tactics.

How well did these strategies work? This book attempts to balance two competing notions. First, public sector unions fought hard and won victories for their members, despite limitations on their rights. While these unions could not formally bargain, they devised methods of coming to effective "agreements" with their employers. They represented workers in civil service and other administrative forums and pushed for the expansion of such mechanisms. They shared information and resources. They prevailed on public officials at all levels and appealed to the public. Through activism and persuasion, they saved jobs, improved skills as well as pay and conditions, and generally made life better for workers.

Nonetheless, the lack of rights was crippling. Public sector unions often failed to accomplish moderate goals or even to survive, largely because of the legal climate and the attitudes of employers. The failures are important in their own right. Public sector labor law, and the state structure that helped this body of law remain so restrictive, created a significant core of highly political unions in the American labor movement, at the same time keeping the size of this core artificially low during the decades when labor in the private sector was largest and most powerful. This timing sheds light on labor's strength and its very nature, up to and including the "Sombart question."[30] What if government workers had continued to organize after 1920 at the rate they had before? What if labor had contained a much larger politically active and savvy component before, during, and directly after the New Deal?

Analyzing the goals and tactics of public sector unions, the forces supporting and opposing them, and their victories and defeats illuminates a large but ignored segment of the working class. It also changes our understanding of the labor movement as a whole. Further, this history underscores the importance of law in determining the size and character of all unions, with related implications for American politics. Simultaneously, this history provides an opportunity to synthesize disparate theories about how and why judges make decisions. It also buttresses recent scholarship that argues that the structure of the American state itself had a major impact on the development of labor, political movements, and government policy. Finally, it shows how men and women employed by the government organized, against considerable odds, to fight an uphill battle for dignity, better pay and conditions, and a voice in workplace decisions. Their struggle was in some ways different from the struggle of other American workers. In other, more fundamental ways, the two were inseparable.

1

The Boston Police Strike of 1919

[A] police officer is not an employee but a State officer. . . . The following rule . . . forbid[s] him . . . from coming under the direction
and dictation of any organization which represents but one element
or class of the community.
Boston Police Department General Order 110 (1919)

Leaving out all the pretty theories and grandiloquent phrases about
their duty to the State, can a man . . . even live on such a wage?
Boston Labor World (1919)

When practically all of Boston's police officers went on strike in September 1919, they did so for reasons similar to those that have motivated other
workers then and since to do the same, but with unique consequences for
the history of American labor. Although the strikers were concerned with
wages, hours, and working conditions, it was immediately and ominously
clear that this event would be like no other job action. Even as the officers
were leaving their posts, crowds of over 1,000 gathered to attack them, vol-
unteer substitute policemen, and others. For three days following, many
denizens of the city engaged in a variety of criminal acts, including assaults,
public gambling (with attendant thefts and violence), robbery, and destruction of property. Parts of the city were frighteningly lawless. Rioters in
South Boston stoned a group of reserve park police, chanting "Kill them
all." Later, a crowd of over 5,000 formed in Scollay Square in downtown
Boston and then went on a looting spree. Property of the unpopular rich
was targeted and damaged. On the second day of the strike, mounted
troopers confronted a crowd of around 15,000. The next day's paper reported: "All Day Fight with Mob in Scollay Square—Cavalry Useless. . . .
From 7 last night almost complete anarchy reigned . . . until early in the
morning." State guards finally intervened, firing point-blank into the

crowds, killing 9 and wounding 23 others. Hundreds more had been injured in the previous days. Property damage was estimated to be in the hundreds of thousands of dollars. The *Boston Herald* explained that the rioting was "suppressed by the rigorous rule of 7000 patrolling soldiers, their authority backed by loaded rifles, fixed bayonets, [and] mounted machine guns." Ostensibly to prevent further violence or even a general strike, Governor Calvin Coolidge then called out the rest of the state guard and told the federal secretaries of war and navy to be prepared to send troops. With peace finally restored, all 1,147 strikers were fired.[1]

Unfortunately for public sector unions, the most searing and enduring image of their history in the first half of the twentieth century and beyond was the Boston police strike. The Boston strike was routinely cited by courts and officials through the end of the 1940s. Even in later decades, opponents of public sector unions would invoke the strike as a cautionary tale of the evils of such unions. Labor was doubly cursed in that this event involved police. First, the Boston debacle provided alarming evidence that strikes by government workers were dangerous and destructive. The fact that the particular employees involved had jobs uniquely related to civic safety was often lost in future debates, as the strike was used as precedent to support bans and restrictions on all types of government workers. Second, the example of police heightened the difficulty of seeing all public employees as "workers": the type of people who should have the right to form unions. After all, the interests of police and labor had often been opposed, and the paramilitary structure of police departments did not seem a good fit for democratizing bodies such as unions. Thus, although the Boston police strike was as atypical as it was dramatic, it contributed far more than any other single event to the peculiarly American view that public sector labor relations were something entirely distinct from private sector labor relations.

Despite the fact that the Boston police strike was a central event in the history of public sector unions and thus a central event in the history of all American labor, historians have rarely portrayed it as such. Fundamentally, though, the events in Boston can be understood only as part of the larger narrative of contemporary labor history. From 1916 to 1922, David Montgomery explains, "workers' demands became too heady for the AFL . . . to contain . . . and too menacing for business and the state to tolerate." During and directly after World War I, the union movement was growing in both the public and private sectors. In 1919 police unions were affiliating with the AFL at an impressive rate. That year, a new police local led the Boston strike without express approval from the AFL. The underlying issues were common for the day: wages eroded by postwar inflation, long hours, unsanitary conditions, a weak company union, and supervisor favoritism and reprisals. The precipitating event of the strike was also typical: management suspended union leaders and announced it would not tolerate an AFL union. The police strike involved over 1,100 workers, led to considerable violence and several deaths, and achieved national notoriety, not unlike other prominent labor actions of that year such as the Seattle general strike and the steel strikes. Despite all this, the Boston strike is rarely seen for what it was: a vitally important moment in the history of labor and workers. The reason that historians generally ignore the impact on labor is almost certainly because the strike involved public employees, specifically police.[2]

Police are the most difficult kind of public worker to envision as part of labor, but one must do so in order to understand the Boston police strike. Unionists and their advocates have traditionally been wary of police, in good part because they often broke strikes. Analyzing the place of police in a system of class structure can be complicated. Still, cops on the beat typically have come from working-class backgrounds, they perform rigidly disciplined wage labor, and in many other ways they share the identity of "worker."[3] Indeed, the unionization in Boston was part of a national trend of police affiliation with the AFL, which in turn was part of a national boom in the organizing of a broad range of public employees around World War I. In 1919 the AFL extended this vision of worker solidarity to police, chartering thirty-seven locals.

Opposition to police affiliation with the labor movement caused the Boston strike, and a central issue debated before, during, and after the strike was whether *any* public employees should be allowed to organize. Nonetheless, studies of the event have traditionally concentrated on ethnic and political factors specific to Boston and its police department, contrasting elite Republican Protestants, such as Massachusetts governor Calvin Coolidge and his appointee Police Commissioner Edwin Curtis, with the largely Democratic, Irish-Catholic police force and Democratic mayor Frank Peters.[4] The strike is also well known for having launched the national political career of future president Coolidge. But the cause of the walkout was Curtis's ban on police affiliating with the AFL, and the broader trend on which contemporaries focused was the nationwide increase in public workers, including police, joining the AFL. In fact government officials, businessmen, union leaders, and socialists all predicted that public sector unions would shift the balance of power in all labor relations. The AFL maintained that government employees were members of the working class. Opponents insisted that they had nothing in common with labor and that AFL organizing in the public sector would lead to domination of the state by union interests.

In early and mid-1919, these debates increasingly centered on police. Would AFL police unions refuse to break strikes? Would they themselves strike? Neither side dealt with these issues successfully. Across the country, government officials ordered police officers to leave the AFL, prompting numerous confrontations, including the Boston strike. Labor leaders never reconciled their support of public sector unions with the alarming possibility of a police strike. The disastrous conclusion of the Boston dispute ended the first, false dawn of public sector unionism, and reverberated for decades. Still, the labor movement in 1919 understood the common interests of public and private sector workers, and historians should do the same.

Public employee unions had a history before the Boston strike. In the United States, as well as abroad, some government workers had been unionized and active since at least the 1830s. Distinctions between the public and private sectors were, however, more blurred in the nineteenth century than in the twentieth. Government at all levels was smaller then. Organized public employees were typically members of predominantly private sector unions, such as skilled tradesmen working in naval yards. When unions first appeared in the federal service in the 1830s during Andrew Jackson's presidency, the government claimed no special status distinct from other employers. It did not challenge the rights of employees to unionize, demonstrate, use political pressure, or even strike. Government opposition to the unionization of its employees did not really begin until postal workers began to organize in the late 1880s and 1890s. The kernel of the idea that public workers should be treated differently (as well as the beginning of highly adversarial labor relations in the U.S. Post Office) can be seen in an order in 1895 by President Grover Cleveland's postmaster general, William Wilson, which forbade any employee, on pain of removal, to visit Washington "for the purposes of influencing legislation before Congress."[5]

Like private sector unions, much of the activity of public sector labor in the nineteenth century centered on hours legislation. Public workers in Philadelphia won the ten-hour day after a major protest in June 1835. According to union leader John Ferral, "Each day added thousands to our ranks. We marched to the public works, and the workmen joined in with us; when the procession passed, employment ceased, business was at a standstill." Also in the 1830s, the National Trade Union (NTU) sent a request to Congress for the ten-hour day on federal works. "We do not . . . demand anything from the government but one's rights which have been acknowledged by the generality of employers throughout the Union," the NTU maintained. While this move brought no immediate results, in 1840 President Martin Van Buren signed an executive order that established the ten-hour day for workers on federal projects. Two years later, workers in the shipbuilding crafts began fighting for the eight-hour day. By 1854 this workday was the standard for caulkers. In 1861 Congress passed a prevailing hours and wages law for the navy.[6] As these examples indicate, exactly which workers were "public" was not always clear, as much work for the government was done by employees in crafts organized by private sector unions.

The first organized municipal employees were also skilled workers in craft unions with both public and private sector members. These early public sector unions often attempted to act like private sector labor. As early as 1867, the National Labor Union unsuccessfully called for the closed shop in public employment; labor would have almost no success in bringing any form of union security to the public sector until the late twentieth century. Public sector unions in the nineteenth century also sought to negotiate contracts. The Chicago Electricity Department signed the first known formal agreement between a municipal agency and a labor organization in 1905. Public sector unions sometimes used the tactics of private sector unions, and public employers sometimes responded in kind. During strikes of street cleaners and garbage and ash collectors in 1906 and 1911 in New York, police attacked the workers, and both strikes ended when the city imported thousands of strikebreakers. In the second decade of the twentieth century, public employers also began to form "employee associations"; these were equivalent to company unions in the private sector and often included managers.[7] Nonetheless, legitimate public sector unions organized with increasing fervor.

The impetus to unionize among municipal employees in the later nineteenth and early twentieth centuries was in part a desire to confront a growing problem in government employment: political machines and their corporate allies. Generally, labor did better in the absence of machines. John Commons reported that where government reformers were in power, local officials would consult with labor in setting wages, hours, and working conditions, but where machine politicians or business cliques controlled city hall, there was hostility to unions of city workers. Therefore, Commons called the organization of municipal employees "the most important practical contribution that has been made to civil service reform in a democratic government." Public employers should officially recognize unions, "to give them a part in the administration of the department and then to hold them to that responsibility." Labor's enemies also included those who profited from association with machine bosses. For example, the Chicago Teachers Federation (CTF), a forerunner of the AFT, waged a long struggle against notoriously corrupt influences in the government of Chicago. The CTF's lawsuit in 1902 against wealthy tax evaders brought a million-dollar increase in revenues to the schools and a raise for teachers.[8]

Public sector organizing continued in the early twentieth century, and by January 1918 the AFL's *American Federationist* could proudly announce that public employees had "come forward voluntarily in recent years in large numbers" to join the AFL. After fitful starts in the first decade of the century, the movement took off around World War I. In 1906 the AFL created its first national union of government workers, the National Federation of Post Office Clerks. In 1902 the CTF affiliated with the Chicago AFL, and the national AFL directly chartered a teachers' local in San Antonio. After a few abortive attempts to create a national teachers' union, in 1916 the AFL formed the AFT. In the year before the Boston strike, the AFT grew from 2,000 to 11,000 members. In 1917 the AFL established the National Federation of Federal Employees (NFFE). That same year, the National Association of Letter Carriers (NALC), founded in 1889, affiliated with the AFL, as did the Railway Mail Carriers. The AFL chartered its first firefighters' local in 1903 and created the International Association of Fire Fighters (IAFF) in 1918. The IAFF soon grew from about 5,000 to over 20,000 members. From 1918 to 1919 alone, the number of its locals more than tripled, from 82 to 262.[9]

The overall rate of unionization in the public sector reflected this activity. From 1900 to 1905, union density in government employment was less than 2 percent, increasing to only around 3.5 percent in 1910. But from 1915 to 1921 density rose from 4.8 percent to 7.2 percent, an especially impressive increase given that the total number of government employees in these years grew by more than one-quarter, from 1,861,000 to 2,397,000. Thus, from 1915 to 1921 the total number of public workers in unions nearly doubled. Given the fact that these unions lacked even the limited ability to organize and exert economic pressure that private sector unions had won by this time, these gains are striking. Also, at least some commentators seemed prepared to accept them as part of the broader labor movement. Charles Beard wrote in early 1919 that if "public employees are denied the right to organize and to use coercive measures, they must then leave their fate entirely in the hands of a benevolent legislature; and . . . the wages and hours of many public servants are not such as to commune a close observance that the government is always a benevolent employer."[10]

Unionists repeatedly equated the concerns of public and private sector workers. After Postmaster General Albert Burleson argued that government employees should not be allowed to join an "outside organization"—meaning a union—the *American Federationist* replied that in "every kind of employment" workers needed a representative that supervisors did not control. "Public employees must not be denied the right of organization . . . and collective bargaining, and must not be limited in the exercise of their rights as citizens." The AFL stated that it sought the same goals for government and private sector employees: collective bargaining rights, improved wages and hours, and an end to Taylorist management practices. Simultaneously, leaders of public sector unions affirmed their links to private sector labor. "The teachers are at last realizing that as workers their place is with the other workers of the country, and that it is their duty to the schools to align themselves with the labor movement," AFT president Charles Stillman wrote. NFFE president Ernest Greenwood credited AFL-assisted lobbying for recent improvements in federal pay scales. With "millions of labor voices" added to their appeals, Greenwood claimed, NFFE had been as effective as a private sector union. He was optimistic enough to add that the public now believed that government workers had the "same right to . . . bargain collectively" as those in the private sector. Gilbert Hyatt of the National Federation of Postal Employees (NFPE) also cited AFL lobbying and new attitudes toward public employees. "The old delusion . . . that any government job is a sinecure, has been thoroughly exploded." He urged the government to become as good an employer as the average private company.[11]

No one factor explains the heightened interest of the AFL and public workers in each other, but several developments in law, politics, and the state clearly contributed.[12] First, in 1912 the AFL helped pass the Lloyd-LaFollette Act. This legislation gave federal workers the formal right to organize, spurred growth in their unions, and seemed to inspire unions of employees of local governments such as the IAFF and the AFT. Second, the battle against political machines had led to campaigns for civil service laws that state and local government workers joined through their unions. Third, the war had enlarged both the size of government and the potential scope of its activity. Total public employment leaped from 1,861,000 in 1915 to 2,461,000 in 1918.[13] This trend prompted the *American Federationist* to argue that public workers needed the right to organize because "government activities are being extended into every industry," putting many workers either in or potentially in the state's employ. Indeed, by November 1918, 9 million Americans worked in war-related industries. Government involvement in labor relations—most prominently through the federal War Labor Board (WLB)—also undercut the distinction between the private and public sectors. In addition, World War I, like World War II to follow, helped decrease attacks on labor because of political and social pressure to collaborate for the war effort. Scholars have focused on this phenomenon in the private sector, describing the need for uninterrupted industrial production, but these attitudes also affected the public sector. For example, Sterling Spero notes that during World War I, the War Department greatly modified its attitude toward unions of its own employees, virtually recognizing them and practicing the "utmost cooperation." In this spirit, although the WLB did not have authority over the public sector, it took jurisdiction in at least one case because both parties (the city of Pittsburgh and a firefighters' union) had consented.[14]

With the public sector movement in full swing, repeated requests by ordinary officers finally convinced the AFL to accept police unions. Until 1919 the AFL had refused to charter such locals. The 1897 AFL convention rejected an application from a police group in Cleveland, despite the endorsement of the application by the Cleveland Central Labor Union and the AFL's regional organizer. The AFL explained that it was "not within the province of the trade union movement to specially organize policemen, no more than to organize militiamen, as both . . . are too often controlled by forces inimical to the labor movement." Of course relations between law enforcement and labor had often been adversarial, as police broke strikes and attacked worker protests. In his 1925 autobiography, AFL president Samuel Gompers described violent encounters with law enforcement, providing vivid details of an attack by mounted police on a crowd of union supporters that included women and children. Even though the incident had occurred decades earlier, Gompers wrote that "to this day I cannot think of that wild scene without my blood surging in indignation at the brutality of the police." In 1917, prompted by more requests from police organizations and a request from the St. Paul, Minnesota, delegation, the AFL convention voted to reexamine the prohibition on police locals, but in May 1918 the AFL Executive Council (EC) let the old rule stand, stating that it was "inexpedient to organize policemen at the present time."[15]

A year later, however, faced with yet more applications from police, the EC referred the issue to the June 1919 AFL convention, and that body reversed the prohibition. The resolution doing so simply stated that since police in various cities had organized and requested affiliation, the AFL would go "on record as favoring" the organization of police unions and would grant them charters. The response was immediate: by September 1919 the AFL had received sixty-five requests from police organizations and had chartered thirty-seven locals. Gompers remarked that in his thirty-six years as AFL president, he had never seen as many applications in as short a time from any other trade. The enthusiasm was mutual. Frank Morrison, secretary of the AFL, instructed organizers to give "particular attention" to police.[16]

The few AFL statements on police unions attributed the change in policy to the large number of applications, but also stressed the common status of all public and private workers.[17] Days before the Boston strike, Gompers spoke to the commissioners of the District of Columbia about a rule they had recently issued that required D.C. police officers to leave a local AFL union they had formed. Gompers explained that despite numerous requests over many years, the AFL had "held off" on chartering police unions. But the "requests and applications became so wide-spread and from so many sources" that the AFL had altered its practice. In support of this claim, Gompers provided a list of thirty-three police locals, noting that they were in twenty-one states from all parts of the nation and that almost all had a membership of 100 percent of the eligible officers.[18]

Moreover, Gompers portrayed police as public employees, and public employees as workers. He compared the ban on AFL affiliation by the D.C. commissioners to President Theodore Roosevelt's repudiated "gag order" of 1902, which had prohibited federal workers from seeking to influence legislation on their own behalf. Arguing that the end of war-related production had hurt public and private workers equally, Gompers stressed that the police officers themselves had chosen to join the AFL to combat low wages and poor working conditions. He denounced "opposition to the attempt to organize the policemen who seek organization." Again emphasizing that all workers should have the right to organize, Gompers argued that if "working people . . . policemen included" had the right to join "any lawful organization" before the war, they should not be denied that right after it.[19]

Ominously, though, Gompers's testimony displayed the unresolved tensions between the AFL's declared moderation and the radical prospect of a police strike. He stressed that the AFL was responsible, patriotic, and law-abiding, unlike the IWW—to which, Gompers implied with no evidence, police might turn if they could not join the AFL. Indeed, the AFL would be a "stabilizing influence." New members were told that the membership "obligation" of a police local contained nothing contrary to police duties. When pressed on the strike issue, he replied that the Lloyd-LaFollette Act barred federal employees from joining groups that imposed a duty to strike, and this restriction had not been applied to the AFL. Also, the AFL itself could not order strikes, and police could not join private sector affiliates that could.

These assurances implied a distinction in the ability of public and private workers to strike that was clearer in theory than in fact. Formally, the AFL held that the "final remedy" for government employees was legislation, not the withholding of labor. Yet public sector unions in the AFL had struck, as had unaffiliated police unions in Ithaca, New York, in 1889 and Cincinnati, Ohio, in 1918. In both cases the striking officers were immediately replaced, and the strikes ended quickly and with little disruption; but the issue was not imaginary. The question was whether organization or affiliation with labor increased the chances of strikes. Believing that it did, and foreshadowing the battle in Boston, the mayor of Cincinnati had forbidden police officers to join the AFL after they had voted to do so.

Thus, while Gompers asserted that the police unions in the AFL would bring greater stability, and while no AFL police union had struck, when Gompers proclaimed that police wanted the "great mass of four million workers" to support them, nothing in his testimony indicated exactly what that support could involve.[20] Such ambiguities would be devastating in

Boston, where labor leaders would have to confront the contradiction implicit in Gompers's position: insisting that public workers had the same rights as private sector workers, even while worrying that strikes by at least certain public employees—notably police—would lead labor into a deeply damaging confrontation in which labor's demands would be opposed to the public interest.

In addition to fears that police themselves would strike, union opponents were also extremely concerned about how police officers in the AFL might act during strikes by other unions. The D.C. commissioners claimed that they welcomed unaffiliated police organizations but had barred AFL organizing to assure the "independence" of the department. They spoke of "divided loyalty" and "charges of favoritism" if police officers who were members of an AFL union were called on to handle strikes by members of other AFL unions. This was a concern voiced later in Boston and elsewhere, often by private sector business interests. Ironically, this concern seemed to assume a greater set of common interests among public and private sector workers than that side of the debate would normally admit. Gompers parried that the AFL merely wanted the police to be neutral and "not throw their full weight" against workers. Unconvinced, the D.C. commissioners suggested that AFL-affiliated police would attack strikebreakers, and insisted that the ban on affiliation was needed to prevent "even the charge of partiality."[21]

Although the AFL never boasted of any advantages that affiliated police unions would bring to labor, it probably saw some. The behavior of local police was often critical to strikes and pickets, so much so that some unionists had joined police reform movements. Just months before the AFL reversed its policy on police unions, IAFF president Thomas Spellacy had reported to the AFL's EC that the mayor of Colorado Springs, Colorado, had threatened to destroy the local firefighters' union by locking out its members and using police to replace them. Spellacy added that several police officers had told him that they would not act as strikebreakers if they were organized. The AFL never publicly discussed such considerations, but labor's advocates on the left were less discreet. In July 1919 the socialist *New York Call* announced that it viewed "policemen on the beat as members of the working class" who would soon be "solidly lined up beside the rest of the country's wage earners." Days before the Boston strike, the *Call* predicted that unionized police might not evict tenants or attack strikers, and that someday even soldiers might unionize. "In that day strikes might not be necessary," the paper prophesied, and "the worker could and would be lawful in his enterprise for the simple reason that he would be the law."[22]

Such visions may have contributed to a spate of nationwide attacks on police unions by local government employers before the Boston strike. In

Portland, Oregon, mayor George Baker fought unionization, claiming that it would cause divided loyalty in labor disputes. Portland police officers countered that joining the AFL would help them understand the views of workers. Los Angeles mayor Frederick Woodman raised wages and formed a police relief association to impede union organization. Officials in Terre Haute, Indiana, and Norfolk, Virginia, ordered police officers to leave the AFL or resign; Norfolk's director of public safety threatened to use soldiers to patrol the city if the officers refused both options. Typifying much opinion in Congress, Senator H. L. Myers, a Republican from Montana, proposed that police officers in the District of Columbia who had joined a union be denied pay. In Jersey City, New Jersey, Mayor Frank Hague prohibited police from joining the AFL, alleging it was "subversive of discipline." In Detroit the police commissioner ordered the dismissal of all 400 members of a police association: "As long as our organization often has to be the fence between employers and strikers, it must be neutral and it certainly could not be that and have union affiliation." Officials in Lynn, Massachusetts, barred "allegiance of any nature" by police to any group which required "a greater loyalty" than that owed to the government. "If the cap fits the American Federation of Labor," Lynn mayor Walter Creamer added, "it can wear it."[23]

In no sense, however, were these attacks limited to police unions. Public and private employers opposed other public sector unions as well, focusing on those affiliated with the AFL. Ironically, in the 1919 AFL convention proceedings, the entry after the resolution authorizing police unions stated that all the members of a firefighters' local in Cincinnati had been fired to discourage affiliation with the IAFF. In 1918 and 1919 resistance to the IAFF prompted seven strikes in the United States and Canada. As chapters 2 and 3 show, many school boards in this period prohibited teachers from joining the AFT; teachers responded with political campaigns and lawsuits. All types of public employee unions came under attack. In August 1919 former Massachusetts attorney general Albert Pillsbury offered legislation that would have made it illegal for any government worker in the state to join a union. "Every . . . public service is now being conducted at the sufferance of organized labor," he complained.[24]

The leaders of the AFL (all from private sector unions) tried to resist these attacks, as did local AFL bodies and the police officer members themselves. The EC advised police that they had the right to organize, and the labor press across the country supported police unions. The New Jersey Central Labor Union declared it would fight for the Jersey City police local. The District of Columbia police local won a temporary restraining order that blocked the commissioners' ban on AFL affiliation on the grounds that the rule was not "needful" and the commissioners' authority extended only to "needful" rules. (The Boston police union would later unsuccessfully make a similar claim.) President Woodrow Wilson then asked that the D.C. case be held in abeyance and resolved at an upcoming general labor conference. In the wake of the Boston strike, Congress settled the issue with laws barring strikes and AFL affiliation by police in the District of Columbia.[25]

The Boston Police Union was born in August 1919, amid the increasing controversy over AFL police unions, but also amid increased militancy by public workers in that city. In August 1918 the Boston Firefighters Union, a charter IAFF local, won raises after threatening to resign en masse. In August 1919 hundreds of city engineers and stationary firemen threatened to strike unless they received raises. The Boston Central Labor Union (BCLU) and its newspaper, the *Boston Labor World,* consistently supported public sector unions generally and the police union specifically. In August 1919 the BCLU, which was dominated by private sector unionists, warned Boston mayor Frank Peters that it supported the demands of city workers. The BCLU also backed the wage requests of an NFPE local; the *Labor World* claimed that the board of health would close a private business that was in as poor a condition as the main post office. The *Labor World* also championed the AFT locally and nationally. Generally, the BCLU welcomed the new Boston Police Union and cheered rumblings of police organizing in other Massachusetts cities such as Wellesley and New Bedford.[26]

Massachusetts and Boston had even faced public sector strikes before. Workers struck over Taylorist management methods in the Watertown arsenal in 1911 and in the Charlestown navy yard in 1914. Moth workers (exterminators) struck at least four times in Massachusetts between 1907 and 1917, and gravediggers in Milford struck in 1913. The Watertown workers went out again in 1918. Boston carpenters struck army and navy worksites in 1918. Garbage and ash collectors walked out in Springfield in 1917, in Lawrence and Lowell in 1918, and in Newburyport in 1917, 1918, and 1919 (the workers suffered defeats in all but the first action). The Fall River City Employees Union won pay hikes after striking in July 1919. On a larger scale, in April 1919, 20,000 employees of New England Telephone and Telegraph, then under government control, waged a six-day illegal strike and gained significant raises. But like the national AFL, the BCLU was concerned about the consequences of public sector strikes, and thus seemed to equivocate on this issue. Former BCLU president Edward McGrady told a meeting of over 2,000 postal workers that the AFL did not want them to strike "except as a last resort." Indeed, the BCLU was often cautious about strikes of all kinds, reproaching employees of the Bay Street Rail Company for threatening to stop work over dissatisfaction with a WLB award.[27]

In contrast to labor's approach, leaders of the Boston Police Department distinguished their employees from other workers. The conflict began in 1918 when Police Commissioner Steven O'Meara learned that Boston police officers were considering AFL affiliation. O'Meara issued an order stating that even rumors of unionization were "likely to injure the discipline, efficiency and even the good name of the Force." If officers had obligations to an outside organization, he stated, they would be "justly suspected of abandoning their impartial attitude." He claimed that he did not dispute the "wisdom or even necessity" of unions in the private sector. Public sector unions, however, were "of doubtful propriety," and police in particular should not be allowed to organize because they were responsible for impartial law enforcement. On July 29, 1919, in response to more talk of affiliation, the new police commissioner, Edwin Curtis, promulgated Rule 102, which stated that Curtis was "firmly of the opinion that a police officer cannot consistently belong to a union and perform his sworn duty," and that a police officer "should realize that his work is sharply differentiated from that of the worker in private employ."[28]

Undeterred, police in Boston affiliated with the AFL on August 9, 1919. Their complaints were typical of all workers: low wages, long hours, unhealthy conditions, and despotic supervisors. Police had been voted a raise in 1898 that was not put into effect until 1913. Over this period, the cost of living had doubled. After that, pay had remained at the 1913 level until a small increase was granted in the spring of 1919. At the time of the strike, officers in their second to fifth years earned $1,200 a year; the most any officer could earn was $1,400; and officers had to buy their own uniforms, which cost over $200. "Leaving out all the pretty theories and grandiloquent phrases about their duty to the State," the *Labor World* reasoned, "can a man . . . even live on such a wage? No, he manages to exist, that is all." Officers worked regular weeks of seventy-three hours (day shift), eighty-three hours (night shift), and up to ninety-eight hours for some assignments. They were sometimes required to remain on duty seventeen hours in a single day. Supervisors also limited where they could go on their days off. "Such men are deprived of enjoying the comforts of their home and family," Boston Police Union president John McInnes insisted. Station houses were so unsanitary that the men frequently found vermin on their clothes when they went home. "If the board of health made an investigation as they do in the case of private houses and stores . . . there would be court prosecutions," McInnes lamented. He also complained of many indignities caused by authoritarian management, such as supervisors' requiring their subordinates to run menial errands unrelated to work.[29]

Patrolmen had received little help from the Boston Social Club, a company union that Police Commissioner O'Meara had organized thirteen years earlier. McInnes called it a "weak-kneed organization, controlled by police officials." Police supervisors, McInnes explained, had ignored the club's requests and fixed its elections. Further, McInnes charged that the club representatives were "marked men" and were given less desirable assignments. Notably, he listed strike duty as such a penalty. Instead of this hapless organization, the officers wanted a "red-blooded" union to "formulate their own policies and not be subject to the dictates" of management. In frustration with the impotency of the club, its president and vice-president, Michael Lynch and John Harney, joined the Police Union before the strike.[30]

Police Commissioner Curtis would not allow a union affiliated with the AFL, and this position, coupled with the refusal of the police officers to leave the AFL, caused the strike. On August 11, two days after the union affiliated, Curtis issued General Order 110, which barred officers from belonging to almost any organization with ties outside the police department.[31] According to the order, a "police officer is not an employee but a State officer" and must be prevented "from coming under the direction and dictation of any organization which represents but one element or class of the community." There was no doubt that the directive was aimed squarely at the AFL. On August 20 Curtis summoned union leaders to his office to tell them they could not organize an AFL local. On August 21 over 800 officers met and defiantly installed the officers of the local whom they had elected the night before. Frank McCarthy, regional organizer for the AFL, announced that the union had been formed to give "assistance within legal lines" to police and to establish "collective bargaining in all matters" affecting their working conditions. The local now claimed over 1,300 members. Leaders of the BCLU met with Governor Coolidge and told him that this was not only a police matter but a fight of organized labor; Coolidge rebuffed them.

On August 26 Curtis tried union president McInnes and seven other policemen for violating Order 110; on August 29 he held a ten-minute hearing for eleven others. Of these nineteen men, seventeen were union leaders, and Curtis mistakenly thought the other two were as well. Further confirming the nature of the dispute, Mayor Peters stated that the question was "clear cut": police did not have the right to affiliate with the AFL.

On September 7 Curtis suspended the nineteen men for violating the antiunion policy. The next day the union voted to strike by an overwhelming 1,134 to 2, and on September 9 more than 1,100 officers walked out, leaving about 400 on duty. Curtis fired the suspended men on September 13. During the strike police department officials left no doubt about the centrality of the AFL, distributing circulars that stated that the department opposed "Divided Authority" and identifying labor affiliation as "the Real Issue." Well after the event, Curtis maintained that the "sole issue" of the strike was police membership in the AFL.[32]

The events of the strike have been well recorded. Curtis claimed to be prepared, with substitutes ready, but although he had a day's notice before the strike, no replacements were deployed for over twenty-four hours after the work stoppage. The first two days saw petty crime escalate into looting and violence, especially in South Boston. The state militia eventually restored order, using 4,768 troops, but nine people were killed and hundreds injured. Labor blamed Curtis and Coolidge for being unprepared and not reacting properly, but it was the union that was broadly condemned. The striking police were vilified by the press, public officials, and employers. In one of the more temperate responses, the *New York Times* editorialized on September 10 that a "policeman has no more right to belong to a union than a soldier or sailor."[33]

More broadly, however, before, during, and after the strike, the debate over the Boston Police Union turned on a central issue in American labor history: the extent to which government employees, including police, could be a part of organized labor. The *Labor World* consistently supported police and other public sector unions throughout the country, affirming that they were part of a public sector movement and a larger struggle for workers' rights. "Theoretically, no injustice is ever perpetrated on servants of the public," the paper editorialized, but police had "grievances just the same as men in other walks of life." All workers should have the right to bargain collectively, and thus Curtis's ban on the AFL was "un-American" and threatened the rights of labor generally. On September 20 BCLU president Michael O'Donnell and AFL organizer Frank McCarthy issued a statement that justified the organization of police in part on the grounds that they were "among the lowest paid workmen in the city, and the longest worked." They also cited AFL unions in the city's firefighting, water, and other agencies that were working well with management. The BCLU pointedly criticized local newspapers of "pronounced capitalist tendencies" for one-sided coverage of the strike.[34]

Similarly, opponents of the Police Union made objections that applied to all public sector unions. The heads of many private businesses wrote to Curtis recommending that no government employee of any kind be allowed to join the AFL. Using logic that could be extended to any public worker, Governor Coolidge declared that police were not "employees" or even "holders of a job," because no private concern made a profit from their efforts. Police "are not in any sense labor bodies," the *Buffalo Courier* protested; "their duties do not constitute a trade." Curtis's Orders 102 and 110 similarly asserted that police were public officers, not employees. The *Labor World* rejected this designation by focusing on class: "Does a policeman's daughter marry the son of a chief justice or do the sons of a policeman and of a chief justice play on a Harvard football team together?" It added that even "public officers" had to eat. Meanwhile, some opponents of the Police Union ironically imitated the rhetoric of the industrial labor relations they were trying to distinguish. Taking a page from private sector employers, O'Meara and Curtis claimed that "agents of an outside organization" could not help police.[35]

Attempting to deflect criticism before the strike, the BCLU echoed Gompers's testimony in the District of Columbia, asserting that AFL affiliation would have a moderating influence on the Boston Police Union. BCLU business agent P. Harry Jennings told Mayor Peters that an unaffiliated, independent group "would be under the control of nobody but the members and they could do as they liked." But if the police were in the AFL, "the guiding hand of this organization would be over them, and no action . . . could be taken without its sanction, which would be granted if they were right and withheld if they were not." The *Labor World* reprinted the contention of the *Rhode Island Labor Press* that AFL membership would make police less susceptible to corruption from powerful elites and the claim by the *Midwest Labor News* that only AFL unions could raise police pay enough to ensure the retention of an adequate force.[36]

The officers fought to remain in the AFL, insisting on their affinity with other workers despite their employer's attempts to distinguish them. At the August 26 disciplinary hearing, police department representative James Devlin argued that government workers were "not employees in any sense of the word" but rather were "public officers." A public officer "is not employed, he is appointed; he is not discharged, he is dismissed; he holds office, but he does not hold employment." The attorney for the members of the Police Union, James Vahey, replied that the officers had organized for "the same three reasons that actuate and inspire every man who wishes to join a union—to increase wages, to shorten hours, and to improve working conditions." In any job in which workers faced "closely-knit, powerful corporations," Vahey continued, an employee acting alone would be forced to accept the employer's terms. Increased costs of living had hit policemen as hard as anyone else, yet police pay was half that of a carpenter or mechanic and less than that of a streetcar conductor. Vahey insisted that unionized police would perform their duties during strikes without bias. Just days before the strike, McInnes vowed that the Police Union would not renounce its right to affiliate. On the day of the strike vote, he proclaimed that the AFL "has once and for all come to stay," and in mid-September he declared that the AFL charter would "never leave my hands." Well into the strike, the police officers voted to remain in the AFL.

The two sides also sparred over the legal rules applicable to unions in government employment, an issue that would remain central to public sector labor relations for the rest of century. At the disciplinary hearing, Vahey argued that a Massachusetts statute prohibited "yellow dog contracts"—agreements not to join unions as a condition of employment—and that this principle should be applied to police. Devlin parried that the U.S. Supreme Court had held such statutes unconstitutional in *Coppage v. Kansas* (1915).[37]

Despite Vahey's assurances, opponents of the Boston Police Union spotlighted the issue of "divided loyalty," as had opponents in the District of Columbia and elsewhere. Even before the local affiliated, the *Boston Herald* editorialized that it would be "a long step toward 'Russianizing' ourselves" if police were "the servant of a special interest." Curtis's Order 102 asserted that officers could not be impartial if they were "subject to the direction of an organization existing outside the department." Order 110 admonished that a policeman should not be controlled by "one . . . class" because in attempting "to serve two masters" he would fail either as an officer or "in his obligation to the organization that controls him." Noting that the "chief argument" against the local was that it supposedly forced police to choose "between two unions—the United States or the AFL," the *Labor World* responded that police should simply have the same right to organize that other workers enjoyed. Order 102 had a less benign interpretation of labor's motives: "It is difficult to see . . . what a policeman can hope to gain by the proposed affiliation, although it is easy to see how the other affiliated bodies may gain a great deal."[38]

Business leaders were even more explicit that the "divided loyalty" charge reflected concern over greater power for organized labor. A statement by the Boston Chamber of Commerce on August 27 raised the specter of sympathy strikes by police to support other AFL locals. The chamber announced that it would make its building available as a recruiting station for strikebreakers if the police walked out. This declaration, one speaker at a Police Union meeting said, made the dispute "a class issue." Hundreds of businessmen wrote Curtis to support his policies and to express horror at the prospect of police joining the AFL. The Boston Bar Association and the Boston Fruit and Produce Exchange, among other organizations, also opposed affiliation well before the strike. The heads of many companies wrote to Curtis repeating that "officers of the state cannot serve two masters." One Boston firm denounced the "traitors" whose "first consideration" was the AFL; others accused the AFL of trying to control the government. Private employers across the state and country advised Curtis that police had nothing in common with labor and worried about the spread of pro-union police. For example, the Employers' Associations of Worcester County and Eastern Massachusetts attacked affiliation before the strike; and both the Businessmen's Association of Pawtucket, Rhode Island, and the rather distant Exchange Club of Indianapolis, Indiana, made the divided-loyalty objection.[39] Even the comparatively moderate Storrow Commission, a group of thirty-four businessmen whom Mayor Peters had appointed to try to avert a strike, opposed affiliation on the grounds that it would create bias in labor disputes.[40]

Union advocates, not surprisingly, denied that police had a tradition of impartiality in dealing with labor. The *Labor World* noted that the Boston police force had frequently been deployed against strikers. It also described a steel strike in Pennsylvania in which police, "(non-unionized, of course) rode down a crowd of union workers, injured several, and arrested 19 at the behest of the company. Did someone say 'neutral?'" Of course, union supporters understood the anxiety of the complaining employers. The *New York Call* published a cartoon boasting that "a union cop won't club another union worker." The *Call* added that organizing campaigns in police departments and the newspaper industry would, if successful, restrain two of the most significant opponents of labor. Before the Boston strike, the *Call* even claimed that police unionization would cause "a complete reversal" of the positions of capital and labor. "Organized force, for the first time in history," would be aligned with unions, the paper enthused.[41]

In 1919, the year of the "red scare" and unprecedented militancy by workers, such radical visions of union power stiffened opposition to the Police Union and placed organized labor in a difficult position. The seemingly socialist Seattle and Winnipeg general strikes earlier in the year had alarmed portions of the nation, including many AFL leaders. Businessmen across the country echoed the New Hampshire Manufacturing Association's appreciative description of Curtis—two weeks before the Boston strike—as "the Ole Hanson of the east" (a reference to the mayor who defeated the Seattle strike). The Boston Police Union and labor in general were denounced as "Bolshevik," much to the chagrin of the AFL and BCLU, both of which vehemently opposed communism. For example, the *New York Sun* expressed fear that unionized police could lead to "virtual Soviet rule." The "whole movement was the very essence of . . . Bolshevism," echoed the *Newport Daily News,* and various Boston businesses also warned of "Soviet rule." The prospect of police striking or supporting others who did was a particularly emotional issue in 1919, a year that saw 3,600 strikes involving 4 million workers in the United States. Massachusetts alone experienced 396 strikes in 1919, the most since records had begun being kept in 1887. More broadly, from 1916 to 1922, levels of strike participation were greater than ever before. Compounding the bad timing for the Boston Police Union, in August 1919, just as the controversy in Boston was heating up, police in London and Liverpool led highly publicized strikes.[42]

The BCLU soon became trapped between its support for public sector unions and its fear that radical acts such as a police or general strike would end badly. Following the somewhat contradictory course that Gompers had set in the District of Columbia, the BCLU made threats while simultaneously arguing that the AFL and the Police Union were moderate and responsible. Before the strike, the *Labor World* insisted that the AFL preferred peaceful settlements and struck only when employers forced them. McInnes denied that union membership would interfere with police duties. AFL regional organizer McCarthy and BCLU president O'Donnell sent Coolidge and Storrow copies of the AFL's organization manual and constitution to show that affiliation was not inconsistent with police work. McCarthy and O'Donnell also repeated Gompers's argument that other unions would not control the police. On the other hand, in mid-August the BCLU announced that it had named a seventeen-member committee to work with McCarthy to prepare to "fight on aggressive lines if a single policeman is suspended or discharged for his union membership." Moreover, on August 23 the BCLU declared its willingness to call a general strike to back the police. Ultimately it would refuse to take this step. This failure was partly due to the risks inherent in joining an unpopular and losing strike, but it also resulted from the inability of the BCLU to work out the contradictions between its genuine support for public workers and its legitimate concerns about the results of an actual police strike.[43]

In early August the *Labor World* tried simply to wish the problem away. "Suppose . . . as a protest against unfair wages, officers of the law would abandon their posts. What would happen? . . . Imagination runs rife at the prospect." It concluded, too easily, that "one cannot imagine a striking police force, and so long as they are treated properly there is no necessity for such." Public opinion would also be a deterrent. Other police unions, such as the Jersey City local, had promised not to strike. Weeks later, the *Labor World* reiterated that strikes would not occur if management was fair. The BCLU's public pronouncements never clarified what would happen if management was unfair, a disturbing omission given that police, like other workers, often joined unions because they felt mistreated by management. Nonetheless, the *Labor World* blithely speculated that because of "their high conception of duty, it is doubtful whether the staff would abandon their posts in any case."[44]

As tensions in Boston grew, the BCLU showed more concern that police might use the tactics of private sector unions. On September 6 the *Labor World* allowed that "the police differences as to the right to organize seem to have endless possibilities for trouble with dangers of unbridled crime in the city." During the strike O'Donnell and McCarthy actually proposed a system that many police and other public sector unions use today: settling disputes over pay and other matters by using a mutually agreeable arbitration board that would make a binding decision. Such a system, they presciently argued, would eliminate the need for work stoppages. But with the strike raging, the door was closed to their suggestions. By September 27, with the damage mostly done, labor bizarrely tried to minimize the crisis. Quoting AFL secretary Frank Morrison that other police locals would not walk out in sympathy and that the Boston strike was a unique matter of union self-preservation, the *Labor World* asked, "What is there to be afraid of?"[45]

The inability of the BCLU to deal effectively with its competing impulses to support the police and to avoid a police strike led to disastrous inconsistencies on the crucial question of whether to call a general strike in support of the police union. Up to September 20 labor leaders talked tough. On August 23 the *Labor World* reported that the BCLU had "manifested its readiness to call a general strike of all the organized labor in this city," and that three unions had already agreed to this plan. Although the Massachusetts Attorney General's office quickly declared sympathy actions illegal, on September 12 the Massachusetts Federation of Labor ordered Boston locals to vote on a general strike. It was widely reported that many unions had voted yes, and on September 13 the *Labor World* claimed that there was a "probability" of sympathy strikes by Boston elevated rail employees, stationary firemen, firefighters, and others, including building trades workers. On September 20 the *Labor World*'s headline proclaimed: "UNIONS EXPECTED TO VOTE FULL SUPPORT TO THE POLICE STATION." The article declared that the telephone operators, Hebrew trades, and other unions had voted to strike, and described plans that would allow vital services to continue. Various other sources claimed that the Plumbers, Machinists, Boilermakers, Bartenders, Electrical Workers, Cooks and Waiters, Garment Workers, Machinists, Typographers, Sheet Metal Workers, and Teamsters were prepared to strike. McCarthy asserted that the AFL, from Gompers on down, backed the right of police to affiliate, and that nine-tenths of the BCLU unions had voted to support them.[46]

A central motivation driving labor leaders was their continuing conviction that police and other public workers should be treated as part of the labor movement. O'Donnell and McCarthy's statement of September 20—well into the strike—maintained that the Boston police officers "simply wish for the same liberty of action in promoting their economic interests . . . as is enjoyed by all other employees of the city of Boston and the State of Massachusetts." The officers were following "the same course as is being pursued by all workers of our nation."[47]

This belief in the common interests of private and public sector workers was, however, not quite enough to cause the BCLU to undertake what would in fact have been one of the most daring and radical acts in the history of the AFL. At its meeting on September 21, the BCLU delayed its decision on the general strike and refused to release the results of a vote on the issue. The *Labor News* reported that some felt this was a "tacit confession of defeat." On October 5 the BCLU met again and made a final decision not to stage a mass work stoppage. Remarkably, its leaders barely averted a vote in favor of striking at the October 5 meeting after two Police Union members appealed to labor unity. Policeman Charles McGowan singled out unions involved in the press, asserting it was "high time that newspapers being run by the brains of union men stopped rapping the unions. These men took an oath not to injure union men, but they are doing so every day by writing stories, setting the type and printing the newspapers." But McCarthy, O'Donnell, and BCLU business agent Jennings, while promising support, all spoke against a general strike. Significantly, Stephen Kitchell of the Lithographers Union recounted the manner in which the Winnipeg and Seattle strikes had been crushed before advising against a Boston general strike. The *Labor World* explained the BCLU's decision: "With prejudice fanned so astutely by certain anti-union interests, any further demonstration is bound to react on the laboring class as a whole." Showing remarkable faith after the BCLU had been indecisive and misleading, the Police Union still voted confidence in the BCLU at the union's next meeting. Conversely, the AFL's behavior caused one historian to call organized labor "the nearest thing to a villain in the piece."[48]

Nonetheless, locally and nationally, labor exhibited some real solidarity. The Amalgamated Clothing Workers refused to sew uniforms for police replacements. Members of the Theatrical Stage Employees gave free benefit performances for the strikers. Locals of the Carpenters, Railroad Station Employees, Sheet Metal Workers, Bartenders, and Freight Handlers voted financial support, as did the Massachusetts Federation of State, County and Town Employees. The BCLU placed a weekly strike assessment on its members. The Massachusetts AFL called for Curtis's removal and reinstatement of the strikers, and the BCLU also pressed hard for rehiring strikers. Gompers wired Coolidge and Peters on September 12, offering to end the strike if the matter could be resolved along with the District of Columbia police dispute at President Woodrow Wilson's labor conference. Coolidge countered that only Curtis could make such a decision. Gompers blamed Curtis for the strike and demanded his removal.

Overall, however, the AFL did not know how to respond to a police strike. Gompers told Coolidge that when police took AFL charters, "it is with the distinct understanding that strike action will not be resorted to." AFL vice-president Matthew Woll insisted that all workers had the right to organize, but that the AFL opposed strikes by public workers. With a police strike already in progress, such assurances accomplished little.[49]

Still, even after the strike was clearly lost, labor voices throughout the country continued to equate police officers with other employees. Police work "may be a sacred trust," the *Detroit Labor News* argued, "but the landlord will not accept it in lieu of . . . rent, nor does the grocer consider it as a medium of exchange." Police strikes were novel, but "are we not living in a new day?" The *Labor Advocate* decried Curtis's "organize and you're fired" attitude. The *Wheeling Majority* claimed that the justness of the union's cause was not being reported: "Editors won't do it, because they don't want policemen to organize. The statesmen and office holders and union-hating employers won't do it . . . for the same reason." The *Midwest Labor News* insisted that the public should be loyal to the police. In a speech to the Boston Chamber of Commerce in January 1920, Gompers blamed Curtis for the strike and argued that AFL affiliation "was perfectly natural and normal" because police in most cities "were most oppressively and unjustly treated."[50]

The final defeat of the police was their failure to win reinstatement after the strike was over. The *Labor World* strongly advocated rehiring the strikers; it sponsored and publicized a petition drive and quoted the few local leaders who supported the idea. It denounced the mainstream press for urging Curtis "to make the wholesale discharges permanent and to create a new force that shall be spineless as far as organizing for their own protection is concerned." It argued that "the men desire to resume their work at once and nothing stands in the way but violent prejudice and lack of understanding. . . . Put the men back to work!" Early in the strike Mayor Peters had requested an opinion from the state attorney general as to whether he could reinstate officers whom Curtis had removed; the reply was that he could not. Labor briefly took heart when the campaign manager for Democratic gubernatorial candidate Richard Long announced that Long would bring back the strikers if he beat Coolidge. Nearly a hundred members of the Police Union campaigned around the state for Long. Trumpeting his leadership during the strike, Coolidge was victorious, although notably he lost in the city of Boston by over 5,000 votes, despite support from every mainstream newspaper.[51]

Curtis and Coolidge opposed reinstatement, and their position was widely popular. A letter to Curtis from the Cameron Appliance Company was only slightly more emphatic than average: "Recruit a new force, if it takes twenty years and costs a billion." A fund of $471,758 was collected to pay state guards until replacements were found. Those who favored rehiring, including the Dorchester American Legion (which stressed that many of the strikers were veterans), were an ignored minority. The nineteen men whom Curtis had suspended and discharged tried to regain their jobs through a lawsuit. They alleged that the anti-affiliation rule was not "needful" and thus was beyond Curtis's authority, that yellow-dog contracts were impermissible in public employment, and that the rule was unconstitutional. On November 7, 1919, the court ruled for Curtis; the union filed exceptions, but on December 16 the court dismissed the case. In May 1920 McCarthy wrote Gompers that he could "see nothing that would give me the right to believe that there is any chance for the restoration of the strikers to their old jobs." He also noted that all but fifty had found other employment.[52]

Ironically, the strike resulted in wage increases for Boston police. The minimum pay for patrolmen was quickly boosted from $1,100 to $1,400 per year. Neighboring jurisdictions also saw improvements. Melrose, Massachusetts, police received a $200 raise to $1,600 per year. "We hope they will show some appreciation for the work the striking Boston patrolmen did for them," the *Labor World* commented. "If it did nothing else, the much criticized strike improved conditions all over the country." Indeed, in the District of Columbia, New York City, and elsewhere, police were given pay hikes and other benefits soon after the strike. Boston teachers also received a salary increase in the strike's wake. On the other hand, in the 1920s the new Boston police force developed something of a reputation, at least among unions, for violent treatment of strikers and picketers.[53]

The AFL's final description of the event once again linked police to all other workers. Its convention in 1920 passed a resolution declaring that the strike had proved that the natural aspirations of all mankind for a "just share of self-respect" could not be denied. Only through "organization, solidarity and unity" could "the rights and welfare of wage earners" be protected. The resolution concluded that the "Boston police situation is but one more sacrifice in the human struggle against autocracy . . . out of which has grown a better and brighter day for their successors and fellow workers."[54]

The aftermath of the Boston strike significantly postponed the coming of this better day for public sector unions. All police locals affiliated with the AFL were soon destroyed. The Boston Police Union ended as it had begun, with the language of union solidarity. The local's last statement, in mid-October 1919, rejected Coolidge's label of "deserter": "We went out because we were not deserters, because we would not desert the comrades punished for our fault." The police local in Knoxville, Tennessee, which had been the first to affiliate, surrendered its charter soon after the strike. Congress quickly prohibited police and firefighters in the District of Columbia from striking or affiliating with the AFL, and a number of local governments and police departments followed suit. The Macon, Georgia, local resisted but was eliminated when the city council installed a more anti-union police commissioner. The Oklahoma City, Oklahoma, local proclaimed its strength at the AFL convention in 1920 but collapsed soon thereafter.[55] At its 1920 convention the AFL authorized exploring a national police union, but this venture came to naught. There would be no AFL-affiliated police locals until the 1930s and 1940s, and these too would meet strong opposition. A national AFL-CIO police union would be proposed only in 1969 and not created until 1979.[56]

Although other public sector unions tried to avoid association with the Boston disaster by emphasizing or adopting no-strike policies, many were still devastated. In November 1919 the National Federation of Post Office Clerks voted down a proposal to remove a constitutional ban on strikes. The AFT reaffirmed its no-strike rule in 1920. The number of strikes by IAFF locals decreased sharply after the Boston strike, and the IAFF ratified a no-strike clause in its constitution in 1930. National public sector unions formed in the 1930s, such as AFSCME and the American Federation of Government Employees adopted similar no-strike rules. Into the 1960s, neither the AFL nor the CIO would approve of any strikes by government employees. Still, in the year after the Boston strike the IAFF lost fifty locals, including its Boston affiliate; twenty-three had disbanded by February 1920. The strike also led to losses in the membership of the AFT and other public sector unions. The rhetoric after the strike often did not distinguish among types of government workers. In Lynn, Massachusetts, Mayor Walter Creamer warned an IAFF local that "no man can serve two masters." In an unsuccessful attempt to bar the organization of all federal workers, Senator Henry Myers of Montana argued that such employees were like soldiers and should not join groups "which might put them in an attitude of antagonism to the Government."[57]

Thus, the strike cut short this false dawn of public sector organizing. After years of increases, the number of unionized government employees fell from 172,000 in 1921 to 171,000 in 1922, despite an increase in total government employment from 2,397,000 to 2,455,000. Such trends continued, and the rate of unionization in the public sector, which had risen rapidly in the preceding years, now stagnated, hovering just below the 1921 rate of 7.2 percent for nearly all the 1920s. It finally inched past 8 percent in 1929 and 1930, but the momentum that was once so strong had been dissipated.[58] Beyond the numbers, as subsequent chapters show, memories of the Boston strike inhibited the growth of public sector unions for decades. It became too easy to equate any form of public sector unionism with the calamitous strike. Also, the strike helped separate government employees from the labor movement. Rules against affiliation with the AFL forced public workers into "associations" that often resembled company unions. The national AFL also took less of an interest. For example, the Boston strike ended attempts by the AFL to form a council of unions of city workers, called the Municipal Employees' Association. One study concludes that the Boston strike gave public sector unions "a nearly fifty-year set-back."[59]

Surprisingly, those who study workers and labor have mostly ignored the intimate connection between the Boston strike and public sector organizing, almost as if they accepted Coolidge's demonstrably false assertions that the Boston strike was "not a question between employer and employee" and that it had "absolutely nothing to do with wages or conditions of labor." In 1920 Commissioner Curtis, while denying that the officers had any real work-related grievances, claimed that the movement had been an attempt by the AFL to control the police force. But Coolidge then rode his performance during the strike to national office with Warren Harding. Harding's "return to normalcy" made the strike seem part of the abnormalities of the war years and ensuing radicalism.[60]

Still, the strike became an enduring symbol. In 1957 a study of public sector labor relations observed that "even today, in the defense of their opposition to public employee unions, officials refer to this strike as embodying all of the evils of unionism for government employees." In 1968 Ray Wachs, city attorney for Eau Claire, Wisconsin, wrote that union opponents would quote Coolidge to denounce all public sector unions. Labor tried to derive a different moral, with AFSCME president Jerry Wurf arguing in 1969 that the Boston strike demonstrated the need for collective bargaining, since it was Curtis's "obdurate denial of all compromise and mediation proposals which precipitated the strike." But President Reagan cited Coolidge and the Boston strike as a precedent for firing striking PATCO workers in 1981, and the PATCO dispute also prompted the *Wall Street Journal* to publish a tribute to Coolidge's actions in Boston.

In such renderings, much of the truth of the strike was lost. A publication by an organization of police chiefs in 1958 mischaracterized the strike as having been over the question of whether police should have the right to strike. All these and similar references have reinforced a particular interpretation of the strike by certain contemporaries. President Woodrow Wilson famously called the strike an "intolerable crime against civilization." More specifically, the *New York World* separated the police from other workers. "Properly refusing to consider the Boston revolt a part of the great American labor movement, the . . . authorities have penalized it as it deserves."[61]

This refusal to confront the issue of AFL affiliation obscures the broad solidarity that public and private workers had begun to establish by 1919. "The policemen, firemen, street cleaners, and other employees of the municipality are part of the working class, with the same interests, the same rights and wrongs, as men in the building trades, the garment industry, or any other field of private employment," the *New York Call* asserted. The AFL's Frank McCarthy even predicted that the militia would not act against striking police: "The time when a soldier takes orders to work against his brothers and sisters is past."[62] Such visions may have been idealistic, but they had intriguing implications in the context of contemporary labor militancy and radicalism. At a minimum, police in Boston showed that many public "officers," even police, were also workers, both in their own minds and in the minds of the labor movement.

The strike also proved that although public workers had problems in common with their brothers and sisters in the private sector, their unions would have to use different tactics. Public sector unions had in the past officially disapproved of strikes, but in fact used them. The Boston debacle forced a change in practice. For example, although the IAFF called strikes "inadvisable" in 1918, in 1918 and 1919 firefighters were involved in thirty strikes, mass resignations, or lockouts. After Boston, such activities substantially decreased. The police strike also hindered efforts by public sector unions to use other tools of private sector labor. President Wilson's second labor conference, in March 1920, issued a report that concluded that governments could not enter into binding arbitration with unions of their employees. This policy contrasted with the use of arbitration in public employment that England adopted around the same time.[63]

Simultaneously, public employers across the nation issued rules barring all kinds of public employees from even organizing. The fight against these sorts of restrictions would be central to public sector labor through at least the early 1960s. But after Boston, what kinds of tactics could unions use in this fight?

2

Yellow-Dog Contracts and the Seattle Teachers, 1928–1931

> If the organization's purpose and ends are attained, it will mean a determination of school policies and affairs by a class organization instead of by the duly elected . . . representatives of the people.
> Seattle School Board Resolution (1928)

> When . . . the voters of this city . . . have the opportunity to speak to Dr. Sharples, they will tell him, as they have Mr. Thorgrimson, that there is no room for reactionaries on the School Board.
> King County (Wash.) *State Labor News* (1929)

The 1920s witnessed a weakened and conservative labor movement. The postwar strikes had been crushed, Republicans were ascendant, and employers pressed for the "open shop." Under William Green, who had replaced Gompers, the national AFL was often almost passive. The voluntarist model of avoiding the state and instead using economic pressure on discrete employers seemed ubiquitous. These trends affected many local AFL bodies, including the once-radical Seattle Central Labor Council (CLC).[1] Yet at the end of this decade, when the AFL's opposition to political involvement seemed at an all-time high, a primary concern of the Seattle CLC was local school board elections. These elections were part of a conflict that stretched from 1928 to 1931 between a Seattle local of the AFT and anti-union school board members, and their respective supporters in the community. The fight, which drew national attention, took place in the courts, municipal and state elections, and the press. It led to a Washington Supreme Court decision in 1930, *Seattle High School Teachers Chapter 200 v. Sharples*. It involved what the *Seattle Post-Intelligencer* called "probably the biggest labor question ever raised in the state"—a remarkable statement, given that Washington had in the past decade been home to the Seattle general strike and considerable activity by the IWW.[2] Public sector unions were turning to law and politics, and they were taking their private sector allies along.

The events in Seattle had important similarities to those in Boston, even though they took place a decade later, across the continent, and featured a very different type of worker. Again, a local government employer prohibited affiliation with the AFL; again, local and national partisans of labor defended the public sector union; again, local and national business interests attacked it; and again, the meaning of the "neutrality" of the state was hotly debated. The teachers, however, did not strike. Instead they challenged the rule in court and also attempted to take advantage of an aspect of state structure not present in Boston: their employers, the members of the Seattle School Board, held elective office, and thus could be voted out. This fact placed the dispute in the court of popular opinion as well as in courts of law. Thus, labor undertook what would become staple tactics for public sector unions: appealing to notions of the public good and fundamental rights, and focusing on elections of employing officials. The results were much more ambiguous than in Boston. After the parties alternated victories in school board elections, the *Sharples* decision in late 1930 seemed to settle the matter by upholding the yellow-dog rule. Nevertheless, the board dropped the rule soon after this decision, and the Seattle AFT local ultimately reemerged.

These events also highlight the general and continuing problem of yellow-dog contracts in the public sector. The use of such contracts in the private sector is well documented. Yet the practice was much more devastating to public workers. First, although such contracts were made illegal in the private sector in the 1930s, they remained legal and very much in use in the public sector into the 1960s. Second, private sector unions could fight back with various economic tactics that, after Boston, were unthinkable in the public sector. Contemporaries understood the impact on government employees. When the AFL paper, the King County (Wash.) *State Labor News,* observed in 1928 that the "past year has seen more publicity on the subject of . . . 'yellow dog contracts' than ever before," it was referring to the Seattle teachers. This chapter shows how yellow-dog contracts kept the numbers of organized government employees much lower than they would otherwise have been. It also shows how public sector unionists articulated a belief in a fundamental, constitutional right to organize that they would continue to urge, despite decades of judicial disapproval, until it was finally adopted by courts in the 1960s.[3]

The AFT was chartered in 1916, and by 1919 it had nearly 12,000 members. By 1923 the effects of the Boston police strike, the red scare, and opposition from public and private employers as well as from the National Education Association (NEA, then essentially a company union) had reduced the total to 3,000. From 1929 to 1933, the period of the Seattle struggle, the organization began to rebound, with membership growing from 5,000 to 7,000. While major gains in the mid-1930s boosted the figure to 40,000 in 1938, this was only a small fraction of the approximately one million public school teachers in the country. But the AFT always had influence beyond its size as a result of prominent activists such as John Dewey, its strength in major urban centers such as New York and Chicago (70 percent of Chicago's public school teachers were in the AFT in the late 1930s), and its ties to organized labor. Undoubtedly, though, bans on affiliation had repressed the union's size and power. Most famously, the "Loeb rule" barred the AFT in Chicago schools from 1915 until 1922, when years of political agitation finally led to its repeal. Such bans were constant thorns in labor's side. For example, in 1913 officials in Peoria imposed a yellow-dog contract on teachers, instantly killing an AFT local; in 1927 Superior, Wisconsin, adopted such a rule; and Saint Louis, Los Angeles, and other cities also barred their teachers from joining the AFT in the late 1920s.[4]

Relations between the national AFL under president Green and the feminist and leftist leaders of the AFT were often strained. Nonetheless, in November 1927 the *American Federationist* proclaimed that the right of public school teachers to organize was "fundamental." That same month, after a meeting attended by nearly half of the nearly 500 high school teachers in Seattle, the AFT announced the formation of the High School Teachers Union, Local 200. Interest in the union had been keen for some time. Florence Hanson, the AFT's national secretary-treasurer, reported that in mid-1927 she had spoken to a group of 350 teachers in Seattle who "almost pushed me off the platform in their eagerness to put their signatures on that charter application."[5]

This enthusiasm was prompted in part by the failure of the Seattle High School Teachers' League, an organization affiliated with the NEA, to win raises in 1927. Pay rates had been a bone of contention since 1922, when the school board had cut wages. Also, class sizes and extracurricular obligations were expanding. Local 200, which soon had a majority of the city's high school teachers as members, quickly affiliated with the Seattle CLC and the Washington State Federation of Labor. "With these connections," the local believed it could "command the respect of society," which the Teachers' League never had. W. Earl Miliken, temporary president of Local 200, explained that the teachers "expect to encounter opposition—discrimination has been shown against members in other cities . . . but they have won out in the long run and we expect to do the same."[6]

The local soon elected permanent officers. Reflecting the composition of the teaching force, three of five were women. Lewis Morrow became president and Lila Hunter vice-president. The union drafted a constitution that called for the promotion of good teaching; better wages and working conditions; tenure; participation of teachers in school administration; an end to discrimination based on sex, marital status (the Seattle board, like many in this era, would not employ married women teachers), race, religion, or political beliefs; cooperation with organized labor; and protection of teachers' civil liberties. Consistent with AFT and trade union philosophy, but unlike the NEA, the local did not permit school superintendents or principals to be members.[7]

Dr. Edward Smith of the Seattle School Board welcomed the local with a veiled warning. The board "will certainly not discriminate against members of the union. . . . Their affiliation couldn't conceivably make any difference . . . unless it should develop that it interfered with their efficiency in the classroom." From this statement the *Post-Intelligencer* deduced that "there will be no controversy until the union presents its first demand to the Board." The *Labor News,* a paper jointly published by the Seattle CLC and the Washington Federation of Labor, accented the positive. The "public as well as the teachers are glad to hear the members of the Board so express themselves." This interpretation was undercut by the board's immediate refusal to allow the union to meet in a high school room, although it typically allowed other groups to use school facilities.[8]

The union soon became a subject for public debate. In December the *Seattle Star* ran a series of articles questioning the propriety of an AFL-affiliated teachers' union. The head of the local Parent-Teachers Association (PTA) "regretted" the organization of the local, distinguishing it from the Teachers' League, which was not part of the "union movement." The PTA "has paid slight attention to the union movement because it deserves slight attention." W. C. Dawson, president of Associated Industries in Seattle, asked the board to fire all AFT members, as the local allegedly would seek to "replace teachers' certificates with a union card." The local replied that teachers had as much right to join a professional organization as did Mr. Dawson.[9]

On the other hand, as in Boston, the local central labor council enthusiastically embraced government employees in the AFL, and its newspaper consistently commended local and national public sector unions. The *Labor News* praised the national efforts of the AFT, NFFE, NALC, and IAFF; it was a strong advocate of public sector locals in Seattle; and it advocated collective bargaining for city workers. Unlike the Boston police, the Seattle teachers had an effective national union, and the AFT lauded Local 200 in its journal, the *American Teacher.*[10]

Local 200 immediately collaborated with the Teachers' League in an unsuccessful attempt to improve Seattle's relatively low pay rates. The organizations requested a wage scale with a maximum salary of $3,000 per year, instead of the current $2,400. Of the thirteen American cities with populations of 250,000 to 500,000, the maximum compensation for high school teachers was lowest in Seattle. Indeed, for the school year 1926–27, the median salary nationally for high school teachers in cities with a population of at least 100,000 was $2,583. This problem was compounded by growing enrollments in Seattle, which led to increased class size and teaching loads throughout the 1920s. The teachers wanted the board to authorize more pay or, in the alternative, to put a millage increase on the ballot for the March 1928 city elections.

In early January 1928 the board rejected both requests. Board member Ebenezer Shorrock said that the public was not competent to pass on salary matters. The *Labor News* replied that the people "who pay the bill" should be allowed to decide. The board's position was "at radical variance with the democratic principles underlying our system of free schools." At the board's next meeting, member Otis Thorgrimson repeated that the issue should not be put to the voters. James Taylor, the president of the Washington State Federation of Labor, told the board that it should either grant a pay hike or allow a vote on the issue, but the board reaffirmed its position on January 27.[11]

On February 18 the board did adopt a new salary scale. It increased the maximum to $2,600 ($2,700 for teachers with a master's degree), but it also lowered pay for new teachers and lengthened the time it would take to achieve the maximum. Walter Satterthwaite, then president of the Teachers' League and future president of Local 200, criticized the move. Local 200 described the new pay schedule as "ornamental." The teachers were "not satisfied"; the maximum salary should be $3,000. Adding fuel to the fire, on March 2 the board granted raises averaging $200 a year to principals and other school executives, but on March 9 it denied substitute teachers more pay.[12]

Even so, the local remained optimistic. On March 3, president Morrow wrote to AFT secretary-treasurer Hanson that "we have the most courageous, industrious, and harmonious group that can be found anywhere." The April 1928 *American Teacher* contained five articles by Local 200 members, arguing that AFL affiliation was desirable because it provided "contacts" outside the schools, and claiming that the press in Seattle, "although not enthusiastic" about the local, had "manifested no unfriendly spirit" toward it. Local 200's program for the coming year would include finding new sources of funds for the schools, lobbying the state legislature for a tenure law, and lobbying for a statute that would improve pensions. The local pledged solidarity with the labor movement and sent clothing to striking miners in Pittsburgh. "What we attempt for our own group, we shall as faithfully strive to assist all other laborers to attain." It was a "dawning of a new day."[13]

The teachers' demands also included more worker control. The local would "call to the attention of the public the right and duty of class room teachers to direct, in a larger way, the affairs of the school." The union wanted "to assist in determining length, number, and size of classes; in adjusting room conditions; in revising courses of study; in limiting extracurricular activities; and in shortening the working day." Administrators were not "closely enough in touch with school life." The "ideal of Unionism," the local concluded, was giving workers "a larger share in management" and its rewards. Individual union members agreed. "Let the school board look after the physical needs of the schools," urged teacher Ralph Upton, "but let the teachers look after education." After all, the Seattle superintendent of schools was not an educator (as had been the practice in earlier times) but was "simply an executive officer."[14]

With no right or practical ability to bargain, the AFT now turned to a tactic unique to the public sector: an effort to unseat employers through politics. In the school board elections of March 1928, the local and the CLC supported candidate John Shorett against incumbent Dr. Caspar Sharples. The race was nonpartisan, but the lines were sharply drawn on the labor issue. The CLC strongly backed Shorett, and Local 200 said it would do all in its power to elect him. Sharples claimed that the budget could not bear higher pay, but the union was not convinced. A member of the local characterized the school board race as representing "the age-old conflict between democracy and autocracy." The board had shown contempt for the public as well as for the teachers. In contrast, the "American ideal of education is democratic," as was the ideal underlying the labor movement.[15]

Sharples narrowly defeated Shorett, by fewer than 1,700 votes out of 84,600 cast, the only close result of the municipal elections. Turnout was surprisingly high: in previous years it had averaged around 20,000. Commentators attributed the heightened interest to the participation of labor. Shorrock, who remained on the school board after an unsuccessful bid for city council, became president of the board. He read Sharples's victory as a vindication of the board's policy and "a public condemnation" of those who hoped the election would be "the first step toward securing" a board "committed beforehand to their personal monetary benefit." The board's members, Sharples, Shorrock, Thorgrimson, E. B. Holmes, and Edward Smith, had been incumbents since at least the mid-1920s. None was friendly to labor. Also apparently boding ill for public employees, Frank Edwards, a union opponent, defeated incumbent Bertha Landes in the mayor's race. Edwards would, however, play no role in the dispute over the teachers' union.[16]

Local 200, which now had 250 members, remained enthusiastic. On March 20 former Local 200 president Miliken told Florence Hanson that the union was growing and considering expanding into the junior high schools. While he was disappointed that Shorett had lost, and that the unaffiliated Grade School Teachers' Club had backed Sharples, he predicted future successes for the local.[17]

Miliken, however, did not realize the extent to which the local's activities and goals had alarmed the board. On April 27, 1928, the board voted to defer reappointing high school teachers. The *Post-Intelligencer* took this act as an indication that the board "intends to fight unionism in Seattle schools by disciplining leaders of the movement." Local 200 charged that the purposes of the delay were to intimidate teachers and to permit the board to weed out AFT members. Shorrock did not actually deny this, averring only that the board "might have had other reasons." When asked if the board would refuse to rehire certain teachers because of their role in the wage debate, he replied, "We haven't come to that yet." Sharples curtly advised the press to "draw your own conclusion." In fact the minutes of the board's meeting on April 4 reveal that it had already approved a "revised" contract for teachers. The CLC appointed a committee to support the teachers at the next board meeting, in early May. "Are the High School teachers of Seattle to be jobbed for exercising their inherent and constitutional rights to organize for their own protection?" asked the *Labor News*.[18]

It was increasingly clear that the board would move against Local 200. On May 4, the day of the board's meeting, the *Post-Intelligencer*'s headline read: "Showdown on Teachers' Union Today." The article cited fears that AFT members would not be rehired. It quoted Shorrock that the board had "no obligation to re-employ any teacher" who did not measure up to the board's standards "in the class room or out of it." If that was not explicit enough, Shorrock added that the board viewed with concern "any movement, either individual or collective, which threatens the efficiency of the schools." Still, according to Shorrock, the board had not made any decision on the union.[19]

"Board Bars All Union Teachers," the *Post-Intelligencer*'s headline announced the next day; school officials were "delivering a body blow to unionism in the teaching corps." On May 4 the board had adopted a report condemning Local 200. The union had "aims and methods which the Board regard as conflicting with the best interests of the schools." It was the local's "purpose to secure control of the Board." This would "mean a determination of school policies and affairs by a class organization instead of by the duly elected and appointed representatives." The local was "prejudicial to the best interests of the schools." This was true, first, because its organization was "carried on in secrecy, not even its membership having been disclosed." Such conduct "is obviously un-American." Second, the board alleged without specifics, the local's drive for members had been "coercive." Third, the local advocated "the replacement of constituted authority" by the AFT.[20]

The board then unanimously passed a resolution reappointing all the high school teachers, but requiring each as a condition of employment to sign contracts containing a yellow-dog clause. The clause stated, "I hereby declare that I am not a member of the American Federation of Teachers, or any local thereof and will not become a member during the term of this contract." Notably, this new rule applied only to the AFL-affiliated AFT, and not to the independent or NEA-affiliated groups in Seattle, such as the Teachers' League, Grade School Teachers' Club, Principals' Association, or Association of Intermediate School Teachers. Indeed, the board announced that it would still meet with these organizations, but, echoing language from Boston, added that it could not tolerate "divided allegiance." The board noted that Thomas Cole, the Seattle superintendent of schools, and various high school principals agreed with its stand.[21]

Local 200 and the CLC immediately sought a temporary restraining order (TRO) against enforcement of the yellow-dog rule, alleging that it would violate the constitutional rights of teachers. On Saturday, May 5, superior court judge Charles Moriarty granted the TRO. Union attorney George Vanderveer had actually gone to Judge Moriarty's home, where he found the judge mowing the lawn, to present him with the pleadings. David Levine, president of the CLC, and Charles Doyle, CLC secretary, supplied affidavits for the union. Moriarty's one-page order held that there was probable cause to believe that the board would "arbitrarily and unlawfully deny employment" to AFT members. The TRO restrained the board from either denying employment to teachers or firing them because of union membership, and from mailing contracts with the yellow-dog clause to the teachers.[22]

The school board remained adamant. Its attorney, Henry Pennock, vowed that the board would establish the validity of the yellow-dog rule in the courts. Shorrock called the TRO "childish" and said that the board's policy would not change. He was "not at all alarmed by the suit. . . . We can handle the situation if they get fifty injunctions against us." Already anticipating a political war, Sharples insisted that not even the threat of recall elections would alter the board's position. The board soon enlisted lawyers from two separate law firms to assist Pennock: John Powell and Otto Rupp. On May 19 Judge Howard Findley, to whom the case had been transferred, extended the TRO until a full hearing could be had.[23]

While the case was pending, the Seattle AFL began a crusade for the teachers that would last more than two and a half years. Its goal was to influence public opinion and thus political action. Such activities are contrary to many depictions of labor nationally and of the CLC specifically. Dana Frank writes that the halcyon era of the Seattle general strike of 1919 had ended in the early 1920s. In the later 1920s the historically conservative building trades represented almost 40 percent of the Seattle AFL's approximately 18,000 members; conservatives led the CLC in 1929. Frank even states that after 1920 "labor's political stance became very much like the conservative business interest."[24] It is all the more remarkable, then, that a new, struggling public sector local managed to rouse the CLC into sustained political action opposing the area's most formidable business interests.

Labor supported Local 200 publicly and behind the scenes. The CLC announced that the board was denying teachers "their inalienable and constitutional right to belong to a legally constituted organization representing their calling." The CLC ridiculed the board's statement that individuals could still join the local as long as they did not work as teachers; the point of the rule was to prevent teachers from joining the AFT. The CLC linked the ability of all workers to organize with the notion of citizenship. Denying teachers the right to unionize violated a "fundamental principle of democratic republican government." The slur on the AFT was a slur on the AFL. If it was wrong for teachers to belong to the AFT, then it was equally wrong for "every member of organized labor to belong to his or her respective branch" of the AFL. With Sharples and other board members in mind, the CLC added that it would be equally "wrong for doctors, lawyers, merchants, etc., to belong to organizations of their own choosing."

At the same time, the CLC attempted to mollify possible fears over affiliation. The *Labor News* noted that Local 200 sought the same objectives as had the Teachers' League, and that the league, whose membership overlapped significantly with that of Local 200, had also resolved that the yellow-dog rule violated civil rights and democratic ideals. Further, the local's constitution barred strikes, and it was not a "secret" organization: its meetings and governing documents were public. More aggressively, CLC president Levine alluded to "the war for Democracy in the Seattle schools," arguing that Sharples wanted to ban Local 200 because the union's support of Shorett had nearly cost Sharples the election. In May the business agents of a dozen local AFL unions, along with CLC leaders, held a special meeting to plan aid for the teachers; the CLC and member unions gave considerable financial assistance to Local 200, and many union leaders wrote to the board in protest.[25]

The national AFT also swung into action both behind the scenes and in public debates. In a series of press releases, the AFT denounced the yellow-dog rule as, among other things, "a direct denial of the rights of citizenship." The *American Teacher* reprinted messages from labor supporters across the nation attacking the board. Florence Hanson mobilized AFT officials and activists in support of Local 200, soliciting strategies and passing along contacts. She also informed AFL president Green of the situation. She told Local 200 leaders that the AFT and AFL would help the local to the "fullest extent" and reminded them that AFT locals in Chicago and San Francisco had won repeal of yellow-dog rules through political campaigns. AFT president Mary Baker pledged funds from the AFT's organizing budget. AFT national officials provided attorney Vanderveer with precedent (noting that Los Angeles, St. Louis, and a number of smaller towns had banned union teachers). Hanson even sent copies of the AFT constitution and other documents to a vice-principal in Seattle to assure him that there was "nothing secret about our organization."[26]

Linking their cause with that of all labor, Hanson and AFT president Baker convinced Green to contribute. Baker argued that it was "a matter of grave concern to people everywhere that a public school board" was using "the identical notorious yellow-dog contract being used by mining corporations against unfortunate mine workers in West Virginia." Hanson also referred to West Virginia miners in an AFT press release, adding that yellow-dog contracts were "now in evil repute" and considered "un-American." Pursuant to Baker's request, Green wrote to both the Seattle CLC and the national AFT about Local 200. On May 11, the AFT quoted Green extensively in a press release. "It seems incredible that the Seattle School Board would assume such an un-American position," Green began. "The right of voluntary association . . . is an American right which must not be abridged" and "one which every true American will cherish and defend." The yellow-dog rule was "an insult." The CLC should "employ every honorable means" to abolish the rule and "prevent the imposition of a form of involuntary servitude upon the school teachers."[27]

AFT locals and prominent members joined in the chorus. Telegrams praising Local 200's fight for "democracy in the schools" came from the three large AFL locals in Chicago. The New York Teachers Union forwarded its protest to the Seattle School Board. John Dewey, then a philosophy professor at Columbia University, sent the board a telegram cosigned by several of his associates, criticizing the ban on the AFT. In a separate message to the board, Dewey labeled the rule a limitation on the rights of citizenship, "contrary to the American spirit and also highly inexpedient as it will alienate strong and self-respecting teachers from the profession."[28]

Other labor groups across the country charged that the rule violated fundamental rights of workers and citizens. The New York City Central Labor Council sent the board a telegram disparaging the ban on the AFT. The central labor council in Portland, Oregon, called the ban "a challenge to the liberty of a group of workers" and "an assault on the fundamental liberties of all citizens." Teachers should "not be required to surrender the rights of citizenship to secure public employment." The rule was "ridiculous," the *Southwest Washington Labor Press* scoffed. The board had no more right to impose it than to tell teachers "what church they should belong to." The rule helped demonstrate that "capital is going to try to discredit labor wherever it can." If the teachers had joined the chamber of commerce, "the Board would have praised them." Since "doctors, lawyers, etc. have their organizations," the Fort Wayne Federation of Labor asked, why shouldn't workers enjoy the same privilege? Many unionists recalled the role of labor in creating the public school system.[29]

The AFT sought endorsements from other organizations and individuals, with mixed success. The New York Jewish Theological Seminary, among others, denounced the board. Rabbi Stephen Wise labeled the ban an "intolerable threat against personal, social and professional freedom of teachers, who are servants of the state but not . . . slaves of a municipality." Those remaining silent after AFT solicitations included the American Association of University Professors and the American Association of University Women. Perhaps most disheartening was a bipartisan snub from Washington's two U.S. senators. Democrat Clarence Dill demurred on the grounds that it was "unwise politically" to take a stand. Republican Wesley Jones said that he lacked sufficient information about the case.[30]

The Seattle School Board fought back in the contest for public sentiment. The CLC "says it represents 35,000 citizens of Seattle," said Shorrock. "It should be remembered that there are more than 110,000 registered voters in Seattle." The schools were operated for the benefit of the children, not the teachers. The board claimed that it had received a "mass of letters," most commending its actions. The board freely admitted that the AFL was its target. Thorgrimson distinguished between the NEA-affiliated Teachers' League, "which is a local organization and which works publicly," and Local 200, "which is affiliated with a national labor group and works more or less secretly."[31]

As in Boston, the business community strongly supported the public employer against the union. The *Post-Intelligencer* observed that most of the favorable letters to the board were from "Seattle business and professional men and large employers of labor." These included Gerald Frink of the Washington Iron Works, who opined that no public institution should be unionized. Businessman Laurence Colman insisted that "public employees should not engage in politics to further their own ends." Charles Frye, prominent in the meatpacking industry, congratulated the board for refusing to be "bluffed." The head of the Centennial Mills and Pacific Coast Biscuit Company agreed that teachers should not unionize. The *Post-Intelli-gencer* listed more than a dozen similar letters from other business leaders. On May 15 the Seattle Chamber of Commerce passed a resolution applauding the board for "refusing to turn over the education of our children and the direction and control of the Seattle public school system to any other agency whatsoever." Notably, Thorgrimson, the AFT's biggest nemesis on the board, was a member of the chamber of commerce, as was school superintendent Cole. In response, CLC president Levine wondered if the board would refuse to hire teachers who had joined the chamber.[32]

The case even drew attention from national business interests, with the *Wall Street Journal* editorializing in favor of the Seattle School Board. "If the power to unionize were conceded, the taxpayer would lose control of his own school district," the paper insisted. The goals of the AFT were "employment regardless of fitness, high salaries, pensions out of the public pocket, promotions by rote and all the rest of that deadening inefficiency which such organizations bring about." The *American Teacher* replied that teachers should have a voice in running the schools, as they were more expert in education than "politicians . . . who are interested in securing contracts for the business groups that back them."[33]

The teachers also blamed the "Power Trust"—private power companies often condemned for monopolistic practices, overcharging, and opposing municipally owned power utilities. The AFT had recently skirmished with the trust after power companies introduced materials into the public schools that praised private control of the industry. AFT leaders repeatedly posited a connection to the Local 200 case. Florence Hanson observed that the yellow-dog rule was promulgated very soon after the AFT had critiqued the trust. The rule was therefore "an effort of a branch of big business to discipline the sole organization which has persistently opposed propaganda in the schools." Dewey made similar accusations, as did Henry Linville, AFT vice-president and president of the Teachers Union of New York. Hanson complained to the Federal Trade Commission about the influence of the trust on the Seattle case. Although a smoking gun never emerged, Otto Rupp, one of the lawyers for the Seattle School Board, also represented the Puget Sound Power and Light Company, a trust member and creator of school propaganda.[34]

The injunction hearing, held before overflowing courtroom crowds, began in mid-May, before Judge Howard Findley. On May 15 Local 200 won an initial procedural victory. Judge Findley denied a motion by the board to dismiss the union's suit on the grounds that the board had unreviewable control over hiring. Findley would hear testimony on the merits. Board attorney John Powell sharply distinguished the public sector: "Unionism, however beneficial it may be to protect workers from the tyranny of private employers, has no place in public schools." Democracy was threatened if "one class of people" could insulate themselves from "the whole." Powell then switched and analogized public and private employment. He noted that laws banning yellow-dog contracts in the private sector had been held unconstitutional and argued that public employers had the same right to contract. Vanderveer, representing Local 200, replied that in public employment, the yellow-dog rule was unconstitutional, comparing it to government prohibition of a particular religion. Additionally, the Fourteenth Amendment prohibited as "class legislation" rules such as the union ban that irrationally separated out specific groups. Vanderveer also stressed the no-strike clause in the local's constitution and emphasized that the national AFT would not control Local 200.[35]

President Levine of the CLC testified briefly that neither the AFL nor the CLC had the right to call a strike, and that the AFT had a no-strike provision in its constitution. But the main witnesses were local president Morrow and board member Thorgrimson, and they offered starkly dissimilar images of the union. Both knew they were competing for public opinion as well as the judge's decision. Seattle's major dailies gave blow-by-blow coverage to the proceedings, as did the *Labor News*.[36]

Morrow portrayed the union as moderate. He was also a member of the Teachers' League, and he testified that the league had been even more active in the salary campaign than had Local 200. The AFT forbade strikes, and, contrary to the board's claim, the local had never used "coercion." He personally had friendly relations with administrators. Teachers simply wanted to settle complaints "in a more official way." The union excluded principals because teachers traditionally had been able to exert little influence, and it would be easier to present their perspective if the organization did not include managers. Affiliation with the AFL would give the teachers more clout, but the union's goals were reasonable: improved pay and leave, more say in running the classroom, and a tenure rule requiring a formal hearing before discharging any teacher who had completed probation. In contrast, Thorgrimson characterized Local 200 as "undesirable" and "strongly militant," and warned that it would use political power to achieve "class control" of the schools. He opposed measures that would give teachers more power or any tenure rights. The board needed full control over personnel and policy, he insisted. He objected to nearly every goal Local 200 had listed, including sabbatical leave.[37]

It soon became obvious that the board's chief fear was the political power of the AFL and resultant increased worker control. Thorgrimson testified that his "main objection" was that Local 200 had "affiliated with outside organizations" for "the purpose of political pressure." Affiliated teachers would "go to the polls with an increased strength . . . which would disrupt the school because it would take away the authority vested in the Board." It was "quite clear" that the local intended to "control the Board by political methods," by running candidates "who would agree beforehand to do certain things." Specifically, it would be "hostile to the best interests of the schools" if labor used "political pressure to achieve their end, particularly in matters relating to the control of courses of study, the number of teaching periods, tenure, efficiency ratings, etc." A "resort to the polls in such matters" was wrong.[38]

Also, Thorgimson insisted that the political power of labor would be used for "class control." Were Local 200 to succeed, it would "mean a determination of school policies and affairs by a class organization" instead of by elected officials. Affiliation meant control by a force that was "to a large extent outside the schools themselves." The AFL would take away the board's authority. The "aggressive" AFT would use "whatever pressure is necessary" and gain "more power" than the Teachers' League could ever achieve. It was this "power . . . through their affiliation with the labor movement which rendered their actions objectionable."[39]

Further probing from Vanderveer revealed little evidence for the board's other officially stated objections. Thorgrimson conceded that members of the local were as competent as other teachers. The local had caused no insubordination or discipline problems. The board had not investigated any allegation of coercion. It was not even concerned that the local would strike. Thorgrimson admitted that other organizations of teachers had lobbied the board for raises, and that he could think of no "obnoxious political activity" that Local 200 had undertaken that differed from the actions of other teachers' groups. The only evidence for the "secrecy" charge was that the board had not known the local was organizing until it was chartered in November 1927.[40]

Still, sounding more like a private employer than a guardian of the public trust, Thorgrimson claimed that Local 200 would "create discord in the schools in the place of cooperation that had existed." A "militant organization" would prevent "harmonious relations" with the board and superintendent. If teachers were unhappy, they should leave. Fundamentally, the board had the power to exclude teachers representing "any certain school of thought." Local 200's Miliken told Hanson that this testimony "bared the autocracy of the Board to public gaze." The *Labor News* echoed that the hearings had ripped aside "the veil of hypocritical so-called Americanism" and shown the board's action to be a "high-handed arbitrary edict."[41]

Judge Findley ruled for the board, dissolving the TRO on May 23, 1928. He used the "freedom of contract" doctrine from private sector yellow-dog cases, cited other cases that had upheld bans on unions in the public sector, held that he must defer to the school board, and rejected the union's constitutional arguments. As to the constitutional claims, Findley quoted Justice Holmes's ruling in *McAuliffe v. Mayor of New Bedford* (discussed in chapter 3) and held that teachers had a constitutional right to join the AFT, but no right to be employed as teachers. Citing private sector precedent, Findley maintained that employers and employees had "the same freedom of choice" regarding the employment relationship. Also, Findley held that he must defer to the board's discretion, as the yellow-dog rule was within the powers that the legislature had granted to the board. The board could determine qualifications for teachers, and the court could not review its "wisdom or lack of wisdom." Findley buttressed these conclusions with precedent from the public sector. In 1916, *Fursman v. Chicago* had upheld the "Loeb rule" barring Chicago teachers from AFT membership. *Fursman* reasoned that the Chicago school board had "the absolute right to decline to employ or re-employ any applicant for any reason whatever or for no reason at all," and that no person had a right to be a teacher. In 1915, *Frederick v. Owens* had upheld the Cleveland School Board's ban on grade school teachers joining the AFL on similar grounds. The board did not have to justify its criteria to the courts, and while teachers had the right to affiliate, they had no right to be teachers.[42]

Local 200 immediately appealed, espousing a very different vision of fundamental rights in employment. The day after Findley's decision, George Vanderveer filed a *supersedeas* motion in the Washington Supreme Court, asking that the TRO be kept in force until the supreme court heard a full appeal on the merits. Otherwise, Vanderveer protested, union members would be denied employment, the local would be destroyed, and the schools disrupted. The rule denied teachers their "natural right to associate," deprived them of liberty and property without due process, violated equal protection guarantees, was impermissible class legislation, and improperly regulated conduct outside the schools. School board attorney Powell replied that granting the motion would greatly inconvenience hiring. The board did agree not to mail the contracts to the teachers until the state supreme court had ruled on the union's motion.[43]

While this appeal was pending, school board president Shorrock made an unsubtle threat of retaliation, and the teachers worked on public relations. On May 25 Shorrock announced that he was withdrawing his vote for the board's previous position that all teachers who signed a yellow-dog contract would be employed. This implied that the board might refuse to hire members of Local 200 even if they signed the contracts. The press speculated that union leaders would be punished. Superintendent Cole, trying to smooth the waters, allowed that there would be no "kicking the other fellow just because he is down." Unconvinced, Miliken wrote to Hanson that the teachers were willing to fight but feared the "desire for revenge" by

Shorrock and Sharples. Hanson and AFT president Baker recommended that the teachers focus on public support. With an eye to such concerns, Morrow stressed that Local 200 would not strike over the dispute, because "our first duty is to the children and the people of Seattle." Although the teachers were being "unjustly treated," the union would "do nothing to disrupt the school system."[44]

A five-member panel of the Washington Supreme Court decided that all nine justices should hear the union's *supersedeas* appeal *en banc*. On May 28, Vanderveer began his oral argument on behalf of the union by remarking that the schools were in "no danger of perishing" if union teachers held their jobs until a full appeal could be had, and that teachers risked losing significant rights if forced to sign the contracts or resign. He labeled the yellow-dog rule "an insult to organized labor," asserted that half the children in Seattle schools came from union homes, and rather feebly attempted to distinguish the precedent permitting bars on unionized teachers as having involved strike threats. School board attorney Powell replied that if the motion was granted, the supreme court would in effect be reversing the lower court on the merits. Justice O. R. Holcomb asked how the teachers were to live while the full appeal was pending. Powell answered that they could find jobs elsewhere or conform to the rule. Vanderveer responded that if the court denied the motion, "two hundred fifty teachers will be put out of employment."[45]

The court denied the union's motion on May 31, 1928, in a short order that contained no analysis. The local decided to continue with a traditional appeal to the state supreme court; this effort would take more than two years. Shorrock, retreating from his earlier threat, said that the yellow-dog contracts would be mailed to all the teachers and that everyone who signed a contract would be reemployed. Morrow called a meeting of the local on June 1 to determine whether the teachers should sign the contracts.[46]

The local, with the blessing of labor, decided to sign the contracts, disaffiliate, and carry on the war in the political arena. AFT national vice-president E. E. Schwartztrauber told Hanson that refusing to sign would mean mass firings, and that the Seattle CLC had, reluctantly, advised signing. Schwartztrauber worried about disaffiliation. But, noting that the board had trained university students as potential replacement teachers, he told Hanson he saw no alternative and asked for her consent. The CLC counseled Local 200 that "a battle cannot be won if the army is destroyed." On June 5, after obtaining approval from Hanson and the national AFT, Local 200 disaffiliated. A small group of teachers not employed in the high schools or not in active service remained in the AFT. With Morrow's endorsement, Walter Satterthwaite, who was also president of the Teachers' League, became the president of the AFT group. The teachers and the CLC vowed to renew their campaign against the yellow-dog rule.[47]

Again, the keys to this strategy were politics and public opinion. Miliken promised a "determined effort to change the complexion of the School Board" at the next election. This meant appealing to the electorate. Hanson wired Schwartztrauber: "Few martyrs useless. . . . must have public sentiment for final battle in ballot box. . . . most important task before you is to create a favorable public opinion." She suggested that Morrow stress that the teachers were concerned about the children, while the board had been willing to place them in the hands of unqualified instructors.[48]

Unionists warmed to the task, arguing their case in the press. Schwartztrauber stated that teachers in Portland, Oregon, had been organized since 1919 and had experienced no difficulties with their school board. Morrow explained that the teachers wanted a settlement that would not harm the schools or the children and thus planned "an appeal to reason rather than a resort to economic compulsion." In signing the contracts, the *Labor News* reported, "the teachers sacrificed their own interests to conserve the best interest of the pupils and the schools."[49]

The mainstream press, however, did little for labor, expressing sympathy regarding pay but skepticism about union rights. The more conservative *Seattle Times,* in an editorial titled "School Board Must Control," stated that while it favored higher wages, union affiliation did "not relate to wages, hours or working conditions" but rather concerned "the Board's authority to direct the schools." Local 200's lawsuit "leads so far away" from the original issue of salaries that "the *Times* cannot follow with indorsement." Indeed, the *Times* approved "resistance to any form of dictation" that would alter the board's control. It praised Judge Findley's ruling as being "so clearly in accord with law and common sense that even the most ardent advocates of the cause of the school teachers may not fairly complain of it." The paper found entirely sensible the position that teachers had a right to join the union but no right to be teachers. The *Post-Intelligencer* counseled the union to accept its loss but also urged compromise for the benefit of the children. Schools were "not mere industries intended to provide employment and livelihood for teachers, nor should they be small kingdoms upon which official autocrats may obtain practice in dictatorship." The teachers and the board should work together for better pay and pensions.[50]

Not surprisingly, the *Labor News* promoted a different view of Findley's decision. It was "one of the most subversive decisions handed down by any King County court in a long time." The board could now fire teachers "for exercising a right enjoyed by all other citizens." Highlighting labor's willingness to contest the matter politically, the paper added that Findley "has overlooked the fact that he must look to the people next election to return him" and warned that he might "find them not in accord" with his decision. Meanwhile, Seattle labor would back the local's appeal to a "higher and fairer tribunal," the state supreme court.[51]

Despite the defeats and the disaffiliation, local and national labor bodies remained loyal to the teachers, emphasizing that the principle involved was crucial for all workers. "The question is one of far more importance than merely determining future conditions of employment for Seattle teachers," the *Labor News* explained. "It involves the right of persons employed in the public service to join organizations of their own choosing." The Washington State Federation of Labor, at its July 1928 convention, went on record as favoring a tenure law for teachers that would essentially override local yellow-dog rules. In August, State Federation president Taylor promised to push for state laws to reverse the yellow-dog rule and to fund court appeals to "find out whether or not a school teacher has the same constitutional rights as the students to whom they are required to teach the doctrines of human liberty." Taylor insisted that the teachers' union "will remain part of the labor movement, and it will continue to receive the undivided support of organized labor until the fight for constitutional liberty has been won."[52]

The AFL's *American Federationist* condemned the school board in equally broad terms in an editorial written by president Green. The case involved "an issue fundamental for human liberty": the right to join a lawful organization. The yellow-dog clause would establish a precedent "to justify regulation of the personal lives of public employees. Such a principle is clearly at variance with free institutions." Giving school boards such authority was "a potential menace to the spirit of education." Green even espoused political action. Seattle labor should "convince the voting citizenry that this policy must be changed." Also, AFL secretary-treasurer John Frey analyzed the Seattle case in an address to the AFT convention. Whether in the public or private sector, the ability to organize was a fundamental American right, Frey proclaimed. Employers, doctors, and other professionals were organized. This right should not depend upon the consent of those in authority. "At the bottom of everything," Frey concluded, "is this right to voluntary association for lawful purposes."[53]

The AFT publicized the case nationally. In New York on June 20, 1928, Henry Linville delivered a radio address on the topic, the text of which was made into an AFT pamphlet. Linville argued that Findley's decision exemplified what all union members were up against: "antiquated notions" of the "sacredness" of contract. The board would have hired inexperienced replacements, so for the children's sake the teachers had signed the contracts. Linville also observed that the Boston police strike had led to attacks on AFT locals by economically powerful groups. The Seattle case "will become significant in labor struggles for basic human rights," he concluded. The teachers were fighting "against the privileged few for the future well-being of mankind."[54]

The AFT understood the broad practical implications of the case. Schwartztrauber complained that the Seattle situation had caused AFT organizing in the Northwest to come to a halt. Teachers who had inquired about forming locals "are today silent in fear of their jobs." Even those who saw the AFT as "the only solution for unbearable conditions . . . are not inclined to expose themselves at the present moment to attack." In September the *American Teacher* pledged "every resource" to help the Seattle teachers. The AFT voted to pay $500 for Local 200's court costs and prepared to lobby for a state tenure law. The doctrine of "freedom of contract," the AFT warned, had been "given a new and unforeseen interpretation by the vested interests."[55]

In contrast, the NEA, at its July 1928 convention, voted down a proposed resolution condemning the yellow-dog contract in Seattle. Both nationally and in Washington State, the NEA was sponsored by public and private employers and run by administrators, and it deplored the union orientation of the AFT. Revealingly, the motion to condemn the Seattle board was first rejected by a resolutions committee that consisted of forty school superintendents and principals, and one teacher. Advocates of Local 200 forced a vote by the full convention. Satterthwaite, present in his role as president of the Teachers' League, spoke for the motion. Speakers against included a grade school principal from Seattle and a school superintendent from Oklahoma. The defeat of the motion was a "striking demonstration of being dominated by *principals* and not by *principles,*" the *American Teacher* quipped bitterly. Nearly two decades later, the AFT was still citing this vote with outrage. The NEA never lifted a finger to oppose the ban.[56]

Local 200 now promised a showdown in the school board elections of March 1929. As early as June 1928, Morrow observed that the yellow-dog rule was a "question for the voters of Seattle to settle." In "future School Board elections, the people undoubtedly will be anxious to know the attitude of candidates on this question. . . . We have no doubt about the eventual outcome." The CLC's Levine affirmed that the "fight for freedom for teachers to exercise their constitutional rights to join any organization . . . has just begun." The September 1928 *American Teacher* was even more explicit: "In the March election, Local 200 will do its very best to get two members of the Board of Education defeated."[57]

Both sides understood the importance of the March 1929 elections. In June 1928 the small Seattle weekly *Town Crier* disapprovingly reported that "the strategists of Organized Labor have served notice" that in March 1929 they would try to elect "candidates of their own choosing." Levine replied that labor, "in conjunction with other liberty loving, upright citizens," wanted a school board that "will not deny to its employees their constitutional rights." The CLC was solidly behind Local 200's political strategy. In

September 1928 the *Labor News* predicted that "sooner or later members of the Board will be elected with sufficient Americanism . . . to grant the teachers the same rights as granted to all other citizens by the constitution." And this type of strategy had widespread implications. In July 1928 Satterthwaite explained that the prospects for organizing among the nearly 12,000 teachers in Washington State would depend largely on school board races.[58]

On the other side, even after its victories, the board was not satisfied with what the *Post-Intelligencer* called the "armed truce" between it and labor. In June 1928 board president Shorrock insisted that the teachers still remained "subject to the domination" of the AFL, even though they had disaffiliated. "They are not returning to the schools in a peaceful attitude," he complained. "They are still militant." Teachers had signed the contracts only "because their labor advisors have found a way for them to retain their employment while continuing their fight." The teachers resented the law and were "bound to make their opinions felt in the classroom."[59]

Satterthwaite, now the voice of the AFT in Seattle, drew more publicity to the teachers' cause by striking out the yellow-dog clause in his contract before sending it to the board. The board returned the contract and told Satterthwaite that he had to accept it in full. He refused and was not rehired. Satterthwaite then represented Seattle teachers at the AFT convention in June 1928, where he was elected a national vice-president. This convention passed a resolution attacking the "ruthless and un-American" actions of the Seattle board and promising moral and financial aid to the Seattle teachers. Satterthwaite thanked the CLC for its efforts and expressed hope about the 1929 board elections. More ominously, in August Satterthwaite said that superintendent Cole had ordered union leaders to come to his office "and threatened them with dire things if there is any agitation of any kind. . . . Mr. Morrow was mentioned particularly as having brought the Court suit." Indeed, Morrow, the local's first president, was forced to resign in September 1928.[60]

That same month, labor used the reelection campaign of Judge Findley and other races as something of a dry run for its political strategy. The CLC attacked Findley for his decision in the teachers' case. Levine reminded his constituency that Findley had "decided that men and women may be deprived of their means of earning a livelihood" because they had joined a union. Would Findley have reached the same result if the group involved had been the chamber of commerce? Findley's supporters felt compelled to rebut labor's charges in a radio broadcast, asking that the judge not be evaluated on a single decision. Findley won, but labor showed that it was a significant force, as every other candidate it endorsed in the municipal elections was victorious. Also, labor had promoted the successful campaign of

Noah Showalter for state superintendent of public instruction. Showalter favored a tenure law and the rights of teachers to organize, and he defeated a candidate backed by the "Power Trust." Labor even heard a softening of Shorrock's position when he stated, the day after the election, that the board had never decided whether teachers would be summarily fired if they joined the union after being hired.[61]

Through the winter, nationally and locally, the AFL linked the cause of Local 200 to that of other public employees. After Florence Hanson addressed the November 1928 convention of the AFL, the convention passed a resolution calling on all unions to assist the local, so that "not only may the teachers of America be guaranteed the protection of their rights as citizens but . . . other employees of municipal, state, and federal government may likewise be protected." The *Labor News* also linked the teachers with broader worker rights. For example, in an article titled "Fine Example Here For Our School Board," it praised Canada for recognizing the right of government workers to organize. Unionists again cited the role of labor in creating public schools. During these months Local 200 did what it could to remain visible, promising to push its court appeal, elect new board members, and win a tenure law.[62]

The controversy drew international as well as national attention. On January 10, 1929, the *Social Inquirer,* a Parisian union newspaper, featured an article translated by the *American Teacher* under the title "Seattle, or an Episode in the Intolerance of Economic Power." The article accused American trusts of trying to crush unionization in the "salaried classes." The "right of association" was meaningless for teachers if it meant unemployment. Local 200's actions were "a living protest against economic dictatorship." On the other hand, *The Nation's Schools,* a journal of school administrators published in Chicago, approved of the yellow-dog rule, urging that teachers not be "allied with any class."[63]

As the March 1929 elections approached, labor became more focused. Local 200 leaders lobbied influential citizens. Satterthwaite attacked the anti-union incumbents for the amount of money they were spending on the elections and for sending a letter to Seattle's Associated Industries asking that business help "save our schools from the radicals." He warned that if the incumbents were reelected, they would retaliate against activist teachers. The *Labor News* regularly urged voters to remember Local 200.[64]

The 1929 elections were especially crucial because three spots on the five-member board were being filled. The possibility that control of the board could change was, the *Post-Intelligencer* reported, "one of the most significant features of the city wide election." This unusual situation was caused by Shorrock's death in November 1928. Dietrich Schmitz, a banker and former chair of the school board, had been appointed to fill his term until the

1929 elections. Schmitz was running head-to-head against Judge Austin Griffiths for one seat. Also, incumbents E. B. Holmes and Thorgrimson were in a pool of five candidates; the top two vote-getters would win the other two seats. The *Post-Intelligencer* endorsed Thorgrimson, Holmes, and Schmitz.[65]

Labor opposed all three of these candidates. A front-page article in the *Labor News* titled "Teachers Ask Your Support Next Tuesday" backed Griffiths against Schmitz and, from the pool of five, endorsed John Shorett and Hattie Mae Patterson. Shorett had been labor's candidate in the 1928 election; the CLC had previously endorsed Griffiths in his unsuccessful bid to become a state senator; and Patterson was president of the Seattle League of Women Voters and a former teacher. Satterthwaite remarked that while none of the candidates labor supported represented a class, "all three of the . . . incumbents represent one class—Capital."[66]

Two of labor's choices prevailed: Shorett won a three-year term and Griffiths a one-year term. Griffiths defeated Schmitz, 20,646 votes to 19,035. Shorett topped the group of five with 24,032 votes, but incumbent Holmes finished second with 19,776. Labor's nemesis, Thorgrimson, lost with 17,128 votes, but so did Patterson with 12,398. The *Post-Intelligencer* termed labor's victories "upsets," but also admitted that the outcome constituted "the most extensive overhauling" of school administration in years. The *Labor News* heralded the vote as "a direct rebuke" to the yellow-dog rule and expressed hope that the rule would now be dropped. "We trust that in a rejuvenated School Board, a little more democracy in the schools and consideration for the employees will be shown."[67]

The results were murkier than labor would admit. Shorett and Griffiths were only two members of a five-member board. Moreover, the anti-union forces took advantage of a lame-duck period to renew the yellow-dog rule. Although Griffiths was installed on the board immediately after the election (since he was completing Shorrock's term), Shorett would not be seated until early June. On April 19, 1929, the board voted to keep the union ban. It adopted a lengthy statement which concluded that it could not tolerate an "atmosphere that breeds . . . class antagonism and political activity" in the schools. Griffiths condemned the parliamentary tactic and added that the rule itself was unnecessary, unwise, a fetter upon liberty, and a dangerous attempt to stifle freedom of thought.[68]

Board member Sharples defended the rule. He was joined by Thorgrimson, who, undeterred by losing the election, submitted a lengthy statement to the board attacking labor. The AFL's "main object," according to Thorgrimson, was "to advance through political pressure . . . the selfish interests of its members without regard to its effect on the schools." Local 200 would wrest control from school administrators: "no one would be allowed to teach . . . who was not first accepted in the union"; the board would have only nominal power to hire; selection of teachers would be left to "the Federation." The yellow-dog rule was necessary "to prevent exploitation of our children from a minor group of people." Sharples added that the board must ensure that "neither the children nor the public be exploited for the benefit of anyone in any particular class."[69]

The *Labor News* countered by wondering why, given the board's logic, Sharples could keep his membership in the American Medical Association. Further, contrary to Thorgrimson's implications, the AFT did not operate a closed shop anywhere and had never sought one in Seattle. The CLC promised to repeat its political strategy. "When the time comes that the voters of this city will have the opportunity to speak to Dr. Sharples," the editorial concluded, "they will tell him, as they have Mr. Thorgrimson, that there is no room for reactionaries on the School Board."[70]

Despite the board's reaffirmation of the yellow-dog rule, labor at all levels continued to encourage teachers' unions. Among many articles on teachers and other public workers, the *Labor News* reprinted the "Teachers' Creed" of the Portland, Oregon, AFT local, which maintained that teachers should have a voice in determining school policies. Although the leaders of the national AFL and national AFT were somewhat estranged at the time, the May 1929 *American Federationist* reprinted a pamphlet from the Minneapolis AFT on why teachers should affiliate with the AFT and in a separate article argued that "intellectual workers" such as teachers should join unions. All workers "have rights as human beings and rights as dispensers of service" as well as a "solidarity of interests."[71]

The importance of the yellow-dog rule in Seattle was underscored in January 1930, when school superintendent Cole announced that he was considering resigning and would be more likely to do so if pro-union candidates prevailed in the March 1930 elections. "I will not attempt to direct the work of the Seattle public schools," he threatened, if the AFL so much as "gains a foothold." Cole, who had been superintendent since 1922 and had always favored the yellow-dog rule, asserted that the public schools in Chicago were suffering as a result the power of the AFT there. He demanded that candidates for the Seattle board make their position on the issue known, predicting that the upcoming board elections would settle this "vital question." He added that the "affiliation of a group of teachers with any one class of society which is politically organized will result in a politically-controlled system of public schools." Later in January, Cole resigned anyway; the *Labor News* attributed the move to fear that pro-union candidates would prevail in the elections. With this as background, the *Post-Intelligencer* predicted that the debate over Local 200 "promised to make the coming election one of the hottest in years."[72]

Labor continued to solicit popular support, anticipating the 1930 school board campaign. The *American Teacher* insisted that unions were not a "class movement," but rather stood for what was good for the entire public. The *Labor News* explained that unions did not seek a closed shop, but merely "the human right to join any legitimate and recognized organization without being deprived of the privilege to earn a living." The yellow-dog rule meant "enslavement of our teachers," and enslaved teachers could not teach freedom and democracy. Shorett announced that he favored pure merit among the teaching staff, without regard to affiliation in any organization.[73]

The AFT was the central issue in the March 1930 elections. Two vacancies were available: Dr. Edward Smith, an ally of Sharples, was retiring; and Austin Griffiths's one-year term was expiring. Labor endorsed Griffiths and Donald McDonald, an attorney. Opposing them and the AFT were Dietrich Schmitz, attempting to regain his seat, and Frank Bayley, an attorney. These "twins"—the most charitable term the *Labor News* used for them—ran from the same headquarters and put out joint campaign materials attacking Local 200. Their supporters formed the "Citizen's School Campaign Committee," which railed against union control of education. In a radio address its chairman, Sylvester Barker, denounced "union domination" of the schools. The "School Board, not the Labor Temple, should direct our school policies. . . . Election of Bayley and Schmitz will settle this question for all time and protect our school system." A committee pamphlet opposed the CLC and AFL's having "direct influence" over teachers. Campaign materials made pointed, if inaccurate, reference to the Boston strike: "unionism as such is no more the issue in this School Board election than it was the issue when Calvin Coolidge . . . found it necessary . . . to interpose to prevent the police officers of Boston from going on a strike." Schmitz and Bayley also received significant support from private business interests such as the Associated Industries of Seattle.[74]

Still, labor successfully created sentiment against the yellow-dog rule. The *Post-Intelligencer* reported that in a public forum on February 19, 1930, the rule was "generally repudiated." First candidates Griffiths and McDonald spoke against it. Then Schmitz "was heckled on his failure to act" against the rule. Schmitz reacted defensively, reportedly even saying at one point that while he opposed Local 200, he did not favor the yellow-dog clause. Soon thereafter, however, he issued a clarification: while he generally opposed yellow-dog contracts, he favored one in this case because Local 200 sought "control of the public schools through politics." Vowing to maintain the clause if elected, Schmitz added, "there are times when you must fight fire with fire." Around the same time, Schmitz wrote to Cole promising to oppose the attempts of "Satterthwaite and his friends" to "control and dictate the affairs" of the schools. Still, Schmitz also predicted that he and Bayley were "going to have a pretty tough fight on our hands."[75]

The race heated up in the days before the vote. Labor had helped to found public education, Levine thundered in the *Labor News,* but now some who aspired to "dictatorship of our schools" had barred labor-affiliated teachers. He also ridiculed "Banker Dietrich Schmitz and Lawyer Frank Bayley" for talk of "class domination." Schmitz and Bayley distributed a leaflet charging that the AFT in Chicago was funding Griffiths and McDonald, an oblique and arguably misleading reference to the $500 that the AFT had given Local 200 in 1928 for court expenses. In an advertisement in the *Post-Intelligencer,* the CLC denied that Griffiths or McDonald had taken any outside money. As to "group control," the advertisement noted that candidate Bayley came from the same law firm as incumbent board member E. B. Holmes. The day before the election, Franklin Cooper, the superintendent of schools in Seattle before Cole, proclaimed that teachers' unions were always detrimental to schools and that teachers should be "undisturbed by the baneful activities of agitators."[76]

The candidates offered sharp contrasts in their statements, which the *Post-Intelligencer* published. For Schmitz, the issue was "clear cut": whether voters would "officially approve" the AFT, "with headquarters in Chicago," by giving Local 200 "control" of the board. Bayley agreed that the schools should be "free from class or group control" and cautioned that a "small group of teachers" was attempting to dominate the board. Griffiths replied that "group control talk is fallacious twaddle." Teachers should not be punished "by loss of their liberty to do what is lawful." Rather, they should enjoy "the freedom of an American." McDonald denied that he was "a candidate of any group from Chicago" and said that the board should not infringe on the right of teachers to form a lawful association.[77]

On March 11, 1930, union opponents Schmitz and Bayley defeated Griffiths and McDonald. While Bayley only narrowly edged out Griffiths and McDonald for the second spot, the election was a defeat for labor. "Attempts to Unionize City Schools Fail," the *Post-Intelligencer* concluded. The race was close, but "the voters' action was decisive because the campaign had been made on such a clear-cut basis." The AFT "was virtually the only question" in the election.[78]

The CLC maintained a brave face. "Undaunted by the defeat of its candidates," the *Post-Intelligencer* reported, labor "will resume at once its fight to unionize city teachers." Levine thanked McDonald and Griffiths for "espousing labor's cause," and blamed the loss on the amount of money their opponents had spent on "misleading" campaign materials, especially concerning the Chicago AFT. Perhaps in an attempt to leave some room to work with the man who had displayed doubts about yellow-dog rules, the

CLC attacked Bayley by name, but not Schmitz. Putting as positive a spin as possible on the results, Levine offered that "practically every other person . . . has no objection to the teachers organizing." The CLC promised that as long as a yellow-dog contract was required, labor would "do all in our power to bring about its abolition." Labor was "not down hearted," and would not stop until teachers could organize. This "temporary setback . . . cannot retard progress that is bound to come with an enlightened citizenry."[79]

Labor leaders continued to champion the teachers and other public employees. Levine mocked the new school superintendent, Worth McClure, who had been selected over the objections of Griffiths and Shorett, for his leading role in the Seattle Chamber of Commerce. In August 1930 a *Labor News* editorial titled "Public Employees" emphasized the common cause of all workers. "There is only one hope for wage earners . . . and that is the Union. It makes no difference whether their employer is a private individual, a private corporation, or the municipality, County, State and Nation." It published a history of Local 200 that accused the board of imposing the rule in anger after labor's support for Shorett nearly unseated Shorrock in 1928. The 1930 campaign of Schmitz and Bayley featured "willful deceit." Regardless, the yellow-dog rule, "a blot on the name of Seattle," would "soon be removed," and teachers "will be given the right granted to other citizens," to organize. During "Education Week" in November 1930, Levine reminded the public that teachers in Seattle "are not permitted to be free men and women. . . . Unless our teachers are free, they cannot teach freedom and liberty."[80]

The battle now turned to the Washington Supreme Court. Initial arguments were made in June 1930, but in October the court set the case for rehearing *en banc*. Vanderveer pulled out all the stops. A state law allowed firing teachers only for "sufficient cause," and union membership could not constitute such cause. Unaffiliated organizations such as the Teachers' League had existed unopposed for years. Also, the board had exceeded the authority that the state legislature had delegated to it. State law prescribed specific qualifications for teachers (for example, requiring a teaching certificate), and the board could not create more. Courts need not defer to *all* board rules concerning hiring. Could the board *require* union membership, or bar Catholics or Elks Club members? Additionally, state law provided that it "shall be lawful for working men and women to organize themselves into . . . labor unions." Attempting to make the public/private distinction work in his favor, Vanderveer added that while private employers could refuse to hire union workers, a "public board" could not make rules "in contravention of the will of its creator"—here, the pro-union state legislature—and "punish" teachers who joined the AFT. Citing decisions holding regulations on business unconstitutional as exceeding the "police power" of the government, Vanderveer argued that the rule was not a valid exercise of the board's police power, because it had no relation to the well-being of the schools. Finally, the rule violated rights of liberty and free association in the state and federal constitutions by denying teachers the right to pursue their profession.[81]

In response, the board argued that courts should defer to its judgment, criticized Local 200, and asserted that unions did not belong in government employment. The court should defer to the board in this matter because state law gave the board authority to adopt rules "deemed essential to the well-being of the schools." Indeed, the board argued, it had absolute power in employing teachers, except as to three points: state statutes mandated one-year terms of employment and a teacher's certificate, and the state constitution barred religious discrimination. Beyond this, the board had complete discretion. Alternatively, the reasons Thorgrimson had given at the trial justified the rule. The union would inhibit cooperation; it advanced unwise goals; and it had affiliated with labor to derive more political power. Given this testimony, the court had to find that the rule was sufficiently related to the board's power to administer schools. Further, after the Supreme Court's decision in *Coppage,* the state law on union membership could not prohibit yellow-dog contracts, as the principle of "the employer's right to contract freely" applied in the public sector. The board also noted that *Coppage* had held that it "cannot be judicially declared" that union membership "has no relation to a member's duty to his employer." Blending such characterizations with concerns for government, the board cited precedent holding that unions were "inconsistent with the discipline which public employment imperatively requires." As to the Constitution, the board replied with *McAuliffe:* there was no constitutional right to public employment. Ironically, in citing cases involving the AFT, the board quoted the conclusion in *Frederick v. Owens:* "members of the board of education are elected by the people. . . . If the people make mistakes . . . the ballot box, and not the courts, is the place to correct these errors."[82]

The union's reply brief stressed that the rule was so irrational that the court need not defer. It was "utterly obnoxious and wholly unauthorized legislation," which arbitrarily denied teachers rights that other workers possessed, and was unrelated to their fitness. The board's power was not unlimited. Even if no individual had a right to be a teacher, a group of people could not be "arbitrarily banned from public employment *as a class.*" Many court decisions had struck down irrational groupings as improper class legislation. Additionally, AFL-affiliated public sector unions existed elsewhere in the state without problems, and the "danger of class government" was no greater in the schools. *Coppage* dealt with state statutes, not with the power of a "subordinate administrative body." Less convincingly, Vanderveer attempted to distinguish other AFT cases by arguing that in *Fursman* and *Frederick,* the legislatures had given the school boards "complete control" of the schools, sufficient to allow the bans, while the Washington legislature had not.[83]

On December 2, 1930, the Washington Supreme Court issued its *en banc* opinion upholding the right of the board to use the yellow-dog clause. "Seattle's long controversy over the rights of school teachers to belong to unions was settled," the *Post-Intelligencer* pronounced. "Supreme Court 'Pets' Infamous Yellow Dog," the *Labor News* lamented.[84]

Chief Justice John Mitchell wrote the majority opinion,[85] focusing first on deference. The "only question" was whether the yellow-dog rule exceeded powers granted to the board by the legislature, and it did not. State law did not restrict the board's authority to hire, except to require a teacher's certificate and limit the term of employment. While the law did require "sufficient cause" to discharge teachers, the court seemingly read the yellow-dog rule to apply only to the board's power to hire. Mitchell either ignored or misunderstood the fact that the contract that teachers were obligated to sign stated that they would not become members of the AFT while employed, on pain of dismissal. He asserted that the board could not banish entire classes of people from teaching, because the principle of the case applied only to hiring. This not only misread the rule, but also crucially underestimated the significance of the fact that all teachers were rehired every year. The majority next held that the right to set conditions of public employment did not involve the police power. Also, as in *McAuliffe,* a public employer's freedom to refuse to hire for any reason was not a deprivation of a public worker's constitutional rights of speech or association.[86]

The court did not stop there, however. The majority made a point of stressing the "freedom of contract" doctrine—practically the only concept concerning employment that union opponents were willing to apply equally to the public and private sectors. The court quoted entire pages from both *Frederick* and *Fursman* (decided in 1915 and 1916, respectively) to establish that bans on the AFT were permissible on these grounds. Freedom of contract applied "with equal force to public officials." Further, courts should not tell public officers whom to hire. *Sharples* approvingly quoted *Fursman*'s conclusion that it was "immaterial" whether the reason for the refusal to employ stemmed from the applicant's marital status, complexion, or union membership, or even if no reason was given.[87]

Only Justice Walter Beals dissented. He alone was concerned that the rule allowed the Seattle School Board to fire a teacher during the term of his or her employment for joining the union, or for lying about being a member when signing the contract. The statute required "sufficient cause" for firing teachers, and Justice Beals was unsure if union membership met that test. *Fursman* and the other cases the majority cited dealt only with hiring. Beals also distinguished between the board's discretion in contracting with individuals and its discretion in making a blanket rule about groups. It was troubling to exclude a class of people for reasons having nothing to do with their morals, qualifications, or ability, especially given that union membership was not illegal. Could the board bar all teachers taller than six feet? Could it *require* AFT membership? At a minimum, Beals concluded, ordering teachers to agree not to join the union during the term of their contracts was beyond the power of the board.[88]

In light of the recent elections, the *Sharples* decision seemed to resolve the entire affair. Then, somewhat surprisingly, on January 2, 1931, the school board voted unanimously to drop the yellow-dog rule. This vote occurred less than a year after Schmitz and Bayley had run successful campaigns based on opposition to the AFT and only a month after the *Sharples* decision. That same day, the board elected John Shorett, labor's ally, as its president. The board offered little explanation for repealing the rule, stating only that the "conditions which seemed to make it necessary no longer exist" and that "the issue had vanished." The *Post-Intelligencer* took this move to mean that Local 200 no longer posed a threat, as it existed "only on paper." The board "decided that [the rule] no longer is necessary," the *Seattle Times* concluded succinctly. The CLC announced that it was "gratified indeed" with the "restoration of human liberty to our teachers."[89]

Walter Satterthwaite reported to the national AFT that the board's decision was based on fear of the union's power in future elections, perhaps even on an overestimation of its strength. The board "is willing to promise almost anything to avoid a conflict," he boasted to Linville. In fact, Satterthwaite claimed, in the past half-year the board had granted key union requests, including improved leave and pay for extracurricular activities. Promotions previously withheld from members of Local 200 had been granted. Still, both Satterthwaite and Austin Griffiths felt there was an implicit threat to return to the policy should the union revive. But Shorett believed that some board members had legitimately changed their minds. Some teachers favored immediate reaffiliation with the AFT, but this could not be done because the current yellow-dog contracts ran until September 1931.[90]

The board may well have feared labor's political power. The CLC successfully flexed its muscles in the spring and summer of 1931: Seattle's anti-union mayor, Frank Edwards, was recalled; unionist Robert Harlin became mayor; and CLC president Levine was elected to the city council. Sharples retired. The back-and-forth nature of labor's electoral fortunes continued in 1932, however, when the anti-union John Dore defeated Harlin. Also in

March 1932, the last member of the school board that had originally passed the yellow-dog rule was replaced. Capturing the ambiguity of the political situation in Seattle, the *American Teacher* explained that the current board was "far from liberal, but it has felt compelled to rescue Seattle from the disgrace of the yellow dog contract." The *American Teacher* added that the "Seattle Teachers have put up the bravest fight" for the right to organize "in the history of education." Further, the repeal of the rule was due to winning the battle for public opinion, which was a "greater victory than to have won their case in the courts or at the polls."[91]

But Local 200 had been defeated, at least in the short term. Satterthwaite took a teaching job in Chicago. Over the next two years the *Labor News* praised public sector unions in the area and across the nation, including the AFT. It insisted that "government workers are like all other individuals depending upon their services for a livelihood. They are unavoidably a part of labor."[92] But no mention of Local 200 appeared in its pages. In 1933 Seattle unions with government employee members formed a "Public Service Forum"; the Teachers' League represented teachers. An attempt to affiliate the league with the AFT failed in 1935, even though former Local 200 vice-president Lila Hunter was then president of the league. In the mid-1930s professors at the University of Washington formed their own AFT local, as did adult-education teachers in the Works Progress Administration (WPA), siphoning off potential members of Local 200. Budget problems caused by the Great Depression compounded the teachers' problems. In 1935 Belle McKenzie, another original officer of Local 200, told the AFT's Florence Hanson that the union had become a "skeleton."[93]

Local 200 eventually reemerged in a somewhat chastened form. By December 1936 it had 57 paid members; a year later it had 97; and thereafter through 1945 it had 100 to 110 members. In 1946 the local finally had more dues payers than it had had in 1928, and it reached 208 members in 1947. The local did enjoy some successes. In November 1936 Stanley Atwood, one of the original members of Local 200, was elected state superintendent of public instruction, replacing Noah Showalter. Echoing the union at its creation almost a decade earlier, Atwood advocated more funding for schools, tenure for teachers, and prohibition of discrimination on grounds of race, creed, sex, marital status, or union affiliation. Also, organizing began to pick up in the Northwest. In 1935 there were only three AFT locals in Oregon, Washington, and Montana combined; by 1937 there were seventeen, including eleven in Washington, where a State Federation of Teachers was formed. That same year, Hugh DeLacy, the AFT's new regional vice-president for the Northwest, was elected to the Seattle city council.[94]

Still, yellow-dog rules would remain a serious problem for the AFT. In

1936 an *American Teacher* article subtitled "Several Boards Go on Union-Busting Rampage" described such rules in Memphis and Saint Louis, as well as the refusal to rehire union teachers in Wisconsin Rapids, Wisconsin. Half of all the teachers in Memphis were in the AFT local, but the local was still forced to disaffiliate. In Jersey City, the Hague machine that had barred a police union in 1919 did the same to the AFT in 1938. Even victories on this point consumed a great deal of the AFT's time and resources. In 1930 the AFT avoided a yellow-dog rule in Wilkes-Barre, Pennsylvania, only after interventions from local labor and the national AFT. The Saint Louis school board dropped its rule in 1937, but only after a year of intense struggle. Several months later, in San Antonio, Texas, the AFT barely withstood the combined efforts of the local chamber of commerce, manufacturers' association, and school superintendent to impose a yellow-dog rule. In 1942 the AFT had to go to the Wisconsin Supreme Court to reverse a lower court decision ordering the removal of two AFT members from the Kenosha School Board on the grounds that they could not exercise independent judgment. In 1943 the Oklahoma City School Board passed a yellow-dog rule; it took the AFT two years to have it repealed. The *American Teacher* described many other instances of discrimination against unionized teachers.[95]

Local politics were therefore crucial to the AFT, and AFL central labor councils often aided the teachers in their campaigns. Marjorie Murphy notes that the assistance of local AFL bodies with political matters was vital in keeping the AFT from joining the CIO in the 1930s. The diffuse American state structure meant that locals of the same union in the same state could have widely differing fortunes. In Chicago by 1938, a merger of separate locals and organizing successes created an 8,500-member AFT union that could boast of being the largest teachers' local in the world. At the same time in southern Illinois, school boards barred union teachers.[96]

In 1932 the Norris-LaGuardia Act made yellow-dog contracts unenforceable, but only in the private sector. The *Labor News* declared that this legislation "hangs, draws and quarters the yellow dog contract. It is deader than a doornail." The *American Teacher* optimistically speculated that yellow-dog rules would become less common in government employment as a result of this expression of national opinion on the subject. But unfortunately for the AFT and other public sector unions, public employers continued to use yellow-dog contracts, and courts would cite *Sharples* and similar cases for decades in a string of decisions that upheld rules barring public employees from affiliating with the AFL or from organizing. These rules had a devastating impact on public sector labor generally. In August 1950 AFSCME presented a report on "Unfair Labor Practices of State and Local Governments" to a U.S. Senate committee, listing numerous examples of public employers in the late 1940s banning union affiliation. Edward Cling concludes that in this era, many public employers waged anti-union campaigns similar to those in private industry before the NLRA. Indeed, bars on the right to organize in the public sector were upheld into the 1960s, thirty years after Norris-LaGuardia and the NLRA fundamentally altered private sector labor law.[97] This history raises the fundamental question of why public sector labor law in America developed so very differently from private sector law.

3

Public Sector Labor Law before Legalized Collective Bargaining

> To tolerate or recognize any combination of . . . employees of the government as a labor organization or union is not only incompatible with the spirit of democracy but inconsistent with every principle upon which our Government is founded.
> *Railway Mail Ass'n v. Murphy* (1943)

> The court, of course, knows what a labor union is.
> *King v. Priest* (1947)

The Seattle story highlights a central, ongoing, and debilitating fact of life for public sector unions that the Boston strike helped create: an almost complete lack of legal rights. Crucially, while labor in the private sector won formal institutional protections through the NLRA of 1935, analogous statutes for government workers did not even begin to emerge until around the 1960s. Up to the 1960s, under court-made law, public sector unions generally had no right to strike, to bargain, or to arbitrate disputes, and government workers could be fired simply for joining a union. Absent statutes granting institutional rights, employers—mayors, school boards, and heads of departments—issued rules and regulations that controlled labor relations. Not surprisingly, these policies were typically quite restrictive, often prohibiting affiliation with labor or organizing at all. Government workers challenged these rules, but courts uniformly upheld them, well after judges had become more tolerant of labor in the private sector. This legal regime greatly circumscribed the actions that public sector unions could undertake and often threatened their very ability to exist. Beginning in the 1960s, courts finally found a constitutional right for public workers to organize, and some states—led by Wisconsin in 1959—began to pass laws allowing limited bargaining rights. Public sector organizing then exploded. Thus legal doctrine was critical in shaping the size and character of public sector unions, and consequently the labor movement as a whole.

Yet the question of why American public sector labor law evolved as it did—separate from and much more restrictive than private sector law, and thus much differently from public sector law in comparable countries—remains strangely ignored, despite a wealth of studies of the history of private sector labor law.[1] Addressing this question illuminates several issues. First, it sheds light on the character and development of the labor movement. Public sector labor law had a major impact on the size and nature of public sector unions, and therefore on all labor. Intriguingly, the effect of labor law in government employment was in some ways the opposite of the effect of court-made law in the private sector. William Forbath and Victoria Hattam have argued that before the New Deal, judicial holdings pushed private sector unions away from politics and toward "voluntarism."[2] Law in the public sector drove unions in the opposite direction, making unions of government employees even more political than they might otherwise have been. At the same time, the law suppressed the size of public sector unions until the 1960s. This distorted the labor movement, both diminishing its political activities and repressing alternative models of how unions could represent members. Second, the history of public sector labor law is an excellent case study of how law develops. Further, it sheds light on modern issues: in the many states that still lack public sector labor statutes, key doctrines of the old legal regime still exert considerable force.[3]

Courts settled public sector labor law for a remarkably long time. Since state statutes did not begin to supplant judicial rules until the 1960s, state courts controlled most labor relations in state and local government employment for at least thirty years after the NLRA set federal statutory rules for private employment. A study of public sector law must therefore interpret and explain judicial opinions. In the public sector through at least the late 1950s, judges across the nation were unwilling to permit government employees to bargain or to strike, and courts routinely upheld bars on their organizing. This body of law was remarkably consistent over time and geographic area. It cannot be explained simply by reference to the factors driving private sector law. In the public sector, three themes recur and blend: hostility toward unions, concerns about state structure, and judicial misconstructions of the concept of a "union."

The claim by legal realists that judges in the Progressive Era were simply biased against unions (or in favor of employers) has long been influential. From the many decisions invalidating wage and hour statutes and bans on yellow-dog contracts, to the thousands of injunctions issued against unions

for strikes, threats of strikes, or boycotts, the theory that judges were imposing their own political biases seemed to explain much labor and employment law through the early twentieth century.[4] Labor historians have generally at least implicitly accepted this view. Modern legal scholars in the
realist tradition have explained these decisions as representing a "lag" period in which the law failed to deal with large-scale capitalism and its effects, or as a period in which corporate interests temporarily captured the
legal system.[5]

In public sector labor cases, judges were quick to apply anti-union doctrines and rhetoric taken from private sector decisions. The constitutional
"freedom of contract" that *Coppage v. Kansas* and other cases used to
strike down statutes outlawing yellow-dog contracts (barring employees
from joining or retaining membership in labor unions) was imported into
public sector cases simply as a matter of policy.[6] The actual holdings of the
private sector rulings were not precedent on point, because no statutory
bans on yellow-dog contracts in the public sector existed. Nevertheless, in
1915 *Frederick v. Owens* "heartily concurred" with *Coppage* and related
precedent to uphold a ban on Cleveland public school teachers' joining the
AFT. Freedom of contract "should surely apply with equal force to public
officials."[7] In 1920 *McNatt v. Lawther* upheld a ban on Dallas firefighters
joining the IAFF, citing *Coppage* and freedom of contract, and explaining
that employers must be able to decide whether union membership was consistent with satisfactory work performance. Courts cited private sector yellow-dog cases until the Norris-LaGuardia Act of 1932 invalidated them.[8]
Well after the Norris-LaGuardia Act, courts continued to uphold yellow-
dog contracts in the public sector.

Frequently courts equated union membership with disloyalty and inefficiency. In 1920 *San Antonio Firefighters' Union v. Bell* upheld the power of
local authorities to fire members of the IAFF, noting that the union had not
specifically pled that union membership would not affect firefighters' loyalty
or subject them to orders that would interfere with public service.[9] In 1917
Fursman v. City of Chicago sustained the "Loeb rule" ban on the AFT,
partly on the ground that "membership by teachers in labor unions . . . is
inimical to proper discipline, prejudicial to the efficiency of the teaching
force and detrimental to the welfare of the public."[10] In 1923 *Hutchinson v.
Magee,* approving a ban on the IAFF, quoted the assertion of the Pittsburgh
director of public safety that union membership was "inconsistent with . . .
discipline . . . subversive of the public service, and detrimental to the general welfare."[11] One judge even noted that public sector labor cases had incorporated negative views judges held of unions. In *CIO v. City of Dallas* in
1946, the Texas Court of Appeals upheld a yellow-dog rule for city employees, citing cases from eight states in support of the decision. On rehear-

ing, Chief Justice Joel Bond concurred, but added that he did not join the court's "approval of the authorities from other jurisdictions, evidencing judicial prejudice against the Unions generally."[12]

Whether "freedom of contract" ideology in labor and employment cases reflected an explicitly conscious animosity toward labor can be debated (as can the significance of the judges' understanding of their own motivations). Recent studies revising the realist interpretation suggest that judges in this era married Jacksonian, Free Soil, and anti-slavery ideology to conclude that some types of economic pressures, such as labor boycotts, were intolerable and that others, such as employers' power to fire at will, were "simply natural facts about the world."[13] Certainly, judicial views of rights in the workplace at this time were opposed not only to the views of unions and their allies, but also increasingly frequently to the views of legislators, at least with regard to laws governing private sector employment. Thus whatever the motivation, up to the mid-1930s courts frequently struck down laws that provided rights to workers in the private sector and held many actions by unions to be illegal.[14] Judges who decided public sector labor cases embodied a mindset that generally did not look kindly on rights for organized labor.[15]

Crucially, however, well beyond the "*Lochner* era" of the early twentieth century and even beyond the New Deal, public sector decisions still portrayed unions in an unflattering light. The opinion of the Texas court in *CIO v. Dallas* was one of several to quote at length the extremely hostile view of the New York court in *Railway Mail Ass'n v. Murphy:* "To tolerate or recognize any combination of Civil Service employees of the government as a labor organization or union is not only incompatible with the spirit of democracy but inconsistent with every principle upon which our Government is founded."[16] *Murphy* was decided in 1943 and *CIO v. Dallas* in 1946, by which time private sector unions had achieved significant acceptance and respectability. The years immediately after World War II saw increased concerns about union power. But not even the rhetoric from the Republican Congress that passed the Taft-Hartley Act of 1947 matched the consistent judicial denunciations of public sector unions.

Indeed, before and after the New Deal, courts in all regions of the country imposed greater restrictions on unions in the public sector than on their counterparts in the private sector. Before the 1930s, judges restricted the actions of private sector unions through common-law conspiracy and tort doctrines, antitrust statutes, and the constitutional "right to contract." Still, private sector unions managed to carve out spheres of operation in which they could organize, bargain, and strike. After passage of the NLRA, judges generally made their peace with private sector unions and with private sector labor and employment law.[17] But in the public sector, judges forged legal doctrines from the common law, arguably related state laws, and increasingly dated constitutional doctrines that were much less generous than private sector law had been *before* the NLRA.

Strikingly, this uniformity in public sector law was maintained in state courts. In contrast, state court decisions on private sector law, especially after the New Deal, displayed some variety depending on the region of the country. For example, after the NLRA and before Taft-Hartley, state courts still controlled much of the law regulating secondary activity by unions (actions aimed at pressuring employers other than the employer for whom the union's members worked, such as buyers and suppliers of the primary employer). Because state court judges in New York were relatively amenable to labor, they created more liberal rules on secondary activity than did the more conservative judges in Texas.[18] But as *Murphy* shows, New York courts were as hostile to public sector unions as Texas courts or courts in any other jurisdiction. In sum, whatever prompted judicial skepticism toward private sector unions in the progressive era cannot by itself explain the extent to which courts continued to be horrified by public sector unions after World War II.

Indeed, judges often explicitly distinguished the public and private sectors. In 1946 *City of Jackson v. McLeod* upheld a bar on police affiliating with the AFL, but averred that the case did "not involve in any way the merits or demerits of labor unions when confined to private employment. . . . Outside of governmental agencies, their merits are fully conceded."[19] *CIO v. Dallas* stressed that "the status of governmental employees, National, State and Municipal, is radically different from that of employees in private business or industry."[20] *Murphy* concluded that "we all recognize the value and the necessity of collective bargaining in industrial and social life," but "bargaining is impossible between the government and its employees, by reason of the very nature of government itself."[21] What was it about the nature of government that made public sector unions so different?

Partly, it was concerns about the division of state powers, which judges couched in terms of the doctrines of deference and delegation. While judges enforced rules requiring unwilling private employers to deal with unions, they would not impose similar direction on other branches of government. First, courts held that legislatures had delegated power over employment to local public officials and that judges should therefore defer to the decisions of these officials regarding unions. Second, courts held that public employers could not delegate any power to a private body such as a union. Delegating to labor the power to bargain or to arbitrators the power to bind governments would violate constitutional nondelegation doctrines and, ostensibly, threaten democracy. Judges therefore promoted a state structure in which they uniformly deferred to the restrictive rules of local public officials—the direct employers of labor—because such power had been delegated to them. At the same time, judges refused to allow bargaining or arbitration, on the grounds that doing so would constitute an improper delegation of power from such officials.

Courts, at least through 1946, were still sorting out the level of deference they should accord to the growing number of administrative agencies and other subordinate state bodies.[22] But in public sector labor relations, courts always took a very deferential stand. In 1917 the *Fursman* court noted that while the Chicago Board of Education's ban on the AFT was an issue of first impression, it "presents no great difficulties." The board had the statutory power to employ teachers, so the court would defer to the board in all aspects of hiring, including the board's decision not to hire union members.[23] In the 1920 *San Antonio Firefighters* case, the court denied an injunction the union sought after city commissioners threatened to fire IAFF members. It held that the commissioners had discretion in removing employees and that it would presume that such actions were lawful absent a showing of bad faith or fraud. The court acknowledged that the mayor had made a campaign promise not to retaliate against the union, but still found no bad faith. A city had the right to determine that union membership rendered its appointees unfit, the court reasoned, and the commissioners had the statutory authority to decide that the "rules of the AFL" were inimical to the interests of the city.[24]

Courts throughout the country employed this rationale for decades. In 1915, in *Frederick v. Owens,* an Ohio court held that a school board could impose a yellow-dog rule without having to give reasons "that are satisfactory to the courts."[25] In 1935, in *Carter v. Thompson,* the Virginia Supreme Court upheld a ban that applied to the IAFF but not to an employee organization that was not affiliated with the AFL, explaining that the city manager could classify IAFF membership as sufficient "cause" for discharge under a local civil service statute that required "cause" for removal. The manager "must, of necessity, be vested with a large measure of discretion."[26] Courts also deferred to civil service commissions in cases denying rights to unions. In 1946 *City of Jackson v. McLeod* overturned a unanimous jury verdict that had found the Mississippi city liable for discharging policemen who had joined AFSCME. The local civil service commission had upheld the removals on the basis of charges that AFSCME membership constituted insubordination and "acts tending to injure the public service." The state supreme court ruled that court review of the commission's decision should have been more deferential. It was "not competent" for the lower court and its jury "to convert themselves into an administrative body and to become a civil service commission."[27]

Crucially, such judicial abnegation of any role in restraining anti-union acts by public employers under the rubric of deference doomed union rights because it took place in the context of the divided and diffuse structure of governments within individual states. In effect, courts gave local government bodies, which themselves were the actual employers of labor, complete discretion to deny unions of their employees any rights. School boards issued yellow-dog rules barring membership in the AFT; fire chiefs, police boards, mayors, and heads of municipal departments barred their employees from organizing or created other restrictive rules governing their own workers to which courts would invariably defer. It is hardly surprising that these employers wrote such rules. It is arguably surprising that courts saw no troubling conflict of interest in their authors.

The second concern about state structure that judges used to limit the rights of public sector unions involved holding that bargaining, arbitration, and related activities constituted impermissible delegations of governmental power to private parties. This doctrine had its most famous expression in the New Deal case *Schechter Poultry Corporation,* which invalidated provisions of the National Industrial Recovery Act (NIRA) partly because empowering representatives of business, labor, and the public to establish industrial codes was an improper delegation of legislative functions to private parties. Public sector labor cases often relied on this branch of the nondelegation doctrine.[28] Although this doctrine was largely abandoned by federal courts after *Schechter,* in state courts, especially in public sector labor cases, it remained a live issue.[29]

Judges applied the nondelegation doctrine to public sector labor for decades after federal courts had accepted bargaining and arbitration in the private sector. In 1945 *Mugford v. Mayor of Baltimore* held that a municipality could not bargain a dues check-off provision, because "city authorities cannot delegate their continuing discretion" over labor relations.[30] In 1946 *Nutter v. City of Santa Monica* overturned a lower court ruling that permitted city workers to bargain collectively, because the authority of public officials "may not be delegated or surrendered to others, since it is public property.[31] *Dicta* in the 1949 case of *City of Cleveland v. Division 268, Amalgamated Ass'n of Street, Electric Railway and Motor Coach Employees of America* hinted that *voluntary* participation by a city in a labor arbitration might not be an illegal delegation. But the opinion stressed that public employers had no legal obligation "to set up this kind of machinery" or "to enter into any labor contract."[32] Cases holding that bargaining or arbitration in the public sector run afoul of the nondelegation doctrine continue through the present day in some states.[33]

Courts rarely faced the potential contradiction of whether to defer to a city that had decided to "delegate" authority by bargaining. As *Nutter* observed, it was not "an accepted practice for public bodies to enter into contracts with employees." A report in 1941 concluded that no city had ever signed a collective bargaining agreement similar to those in private industry, and that "legal opinions . . . are unanimous" that cities did not have the power to do so. A follow-up study in 1947 explained that the majority view was still that labor contracts with cities were "void as a delegation of public power to a private group," although a minority held that an agreement might be legal in certain cases. As chapters 4–6 show, in practice a number of cities and municipal departments engaged in informal, limited forms of bargaining, or at least discussions, with their unionized employees and came to certain types of agreements. But judges were not likely to hear such cases. When cities chose to negotiate with their employees, no logical plaintiff to challenge the practice existed.[34]

Still, some courts strongly implied that they would not defer even if local governments voluntarily attempted to share power with unions. In so doing, judges invoked the most fundamental value of state structure: democracy itself. *City of Springfield v. Clouse,* decided in 1947, refused to permit city workers engaged in street cleaning and sewage disposal to bargain. "Under our form of government, public office or employment . . . cannot become a matter of bargaining and contract." This was true because wages and working conditions involved "the exercise of legislative powers." Local officials could not bargain such power away. This opinion added another layer of the nondelegation doctrine: the state legislature had not delegated to local officials the power to determine the wages and hours of employees of local government.[35]

This reasoning made the fundamental mistake of conflating bargaining over wages, which often were set by statute, with bargaining over a host of other terms of employment, which were not. For example, *Clouse* wrongly asserted that "working conditions of public officers and employees are wholly matters of law-making and cannot be the subject of bargaining or contract." Incorrectly assuming that the statutory text was dispositive of all or even most aspects of labor relations, the court insisted that laws "must be made by deliberation of the lawmakers and not by bargaining with anyone outside the law-making body."[36] Using the same flawed approach, *Murphy* asserted that collective bargaining "has no place in government service" because working conditions were controlled by laws that could not be abrogated by agreement. Yet as AFL general counsel Joseph Padway argued, while wages in government service could be set by statute and therefore not be subject to negotiation, a union could still lawfully be allowed to bargain over other aspects of employment.[37]

Using this defective premise, *Murphy* made the "democracy" point most dramatically. Permitting any unions in public employment would "sanction control of governmental functions not by laws but by men. Such policy if followed to its logical conclusion would inevitably lead to chaos, dictators, and annihilation of representative government." *CIO v. Dallas* quoted this passage whole.[38] *Murphy* added that "nothing is more dangerous to public welfare than to admit that hired servants of the State can dictate to the government the hours, the wages and conditions under which they will carry on essential services vital to the welfare, safety and security of the citizen."[39] These judicial opinions were especially remarkable given that by the late 1940s hundreds of thousands of Americans were members of public sector unions, and such unions had broad rights in other industrialized democracies.

In applying nondelegation and deference doctrines, judges were in part using "neutral" rules that had arisen outside the labor context. As with bias toward unions, however, use of neutral rules does not explain the results in public sector labor cases. As Murray Nesbitt shows, public sector labor law was "singled out for special application" of nondelegation rules, and contemporary doctrines could have allowed public employers to negotiate. Courts were not necessarily unambiguously wrong in applying nondelegation rules, but the law was sufficiently unsettled that courts easily could have justified different results. Kenneth Davis, in a leading treatise on administrative law, concluded dryly that "identifiable principles do not emerge" from state court delegation decisions; and another review of the literature explained that "neither federal nor state courts have developed consistent principles for use in deciding when delegations to private parties are valid." Judges also varied widely in the amount of deference they gave to the decisions of administrative agencies in general.[40] Yet courts consistently held against public sector unions. Thus courts were, in part, actively promoting specific types of power relations among state actors.

Did labor cases fit the underlying purposes of the doctrine prohibiting delegation to private parties? A central rationale for this doctrine was to avoid an end run around democratic procedures by vesting legislative power in a body dominated by self-interested groups. Giving private parties legislative powers violates the principle that accountable public officials make the law. It also puts regulatory power in the hands of private parties that could regulate themselves to their own advantage. Thus, for example, a state court found an improper delegation when the California legislature empowered a seven-member board to set minimum prices for dry-cleaning, where six of the board members represented the industry. One could easily distinguish such grants of *complete* discretion to private bodies from collective bargaining in the public sector, which involves compromises between the employer and the union, or from arbitration, which involves enforcing provisions in a collective agreement to which the government employer had already agreed. In bargaining, as AFL counsel Padway observed, government officials retain significant discretion. Lee Pressman, general counsel to the CIO, also observed that bargaining involved matters "mutually determined." Judges could also have concluded, as they hold today, that arbitrators merely execute the "law of the shop" but do not actually make it.[41] Yet in the first half of the century, courts rejected such arguments.

Also, courts allowed governments to enter into contracts with *some* private entities, notably with businesses for goods and services. When the government "comes down from its position of sovereignty and enters the domain of commerce," the Supreme Court held in 1875, "it submits itself to the same laws that govern individuals there." It had long been established that states and cities could form contracts on which private parties could rely.[42] Public officials had to have statutory authorization to bind the government in this way. But although broadly worded laws authorizing states to enter into a variety of contracts were common by the 1920s and 1930s, labor cases inconsistently found that statutes governing public employment generally gave local officials complete discretion to prohibit unions but did not give them authority to contract with them. In 1942 Lee Pressman argued in vain that municipalities had the implied power to enter into labor contracts just as they did other contracts. More recently, Richard Kearney has explained that the delegation argument would have been principled only "if the various American governments could demonstrate their delegative virginity." But state and local governments "have for over two centuries negotiated contracts with private sector entities without the express permission of the electorate." Thus, "invoking the doctrine against unions [is] at best self-serving and at worst hypocritical."[43]

Further suggesting that more than a neutral application of rules motivated courts in public sector labor cases, unions of government workers failed in their attempts to rely on two aspects of the American state that potentially could have favored them: constitutional rights and the "proprietary function" doctrine. Until the late 1960s, judges repeatedly rejected claims that constitutional rights to association, speech, due process, or equal protection trumped bans on labor affiliation in public employment. In so doing, courts often cited the maxim of Oliver Wendell Holmes, then chief justice of the Massachusetts Supreme Judicial Court, in *McAuliffe v. Mayor of New Bedford*. Holding that a police officer could be fired for making statements that were within the ambit of free speech, Holmes quipped: "The petitioner may have a constitutional right to talk politics, but he has no constitutional right to be a policeman."[44] As shown in chapter 2, the *Sharples* court adopted this approach. In 1946 the union in *CIO v. Dallas* argued that the ban on affiliation violated the employees' First Amendment rights of assembly, speech, press, and petition. The court approvingly quoted Holmes's 1892 decision in reply, adding that "these rights . . . may be waived . . . by voluntarily accepting employment with the City of Dallas. . . . While they have the right to these constitutional privileges and freedoms, they have no constitutional right to remain in the service of the city." Across the country, courts relied on *McAuliffe* through the early 1960s.[45]

Since the late 1960s courts have found both that public employment constitutes state action sufficient to trigger the Bill of Rights, including the right to association, and that public employment cannot be conditioned on a full waiver of such rights. This rule in turn meant that public employment could not be predicated on a promise not to join a union. Thus, in 1969 a court found that a North Carolina law that barred public workers from joining unions violated federal constitutional rights of free association.[46] Although unionists often made this and related constitutional arguments in the first half of the century, judges invariably dismissed such ideas.[47]

Nor were unions very successful in urging a distinction between the "proprietary" role of government, in which it acted more as a business, and its "traditional" role, in which its right to avoid dealing with unions was ostensibly supreme. A few state statutes did give more rights to labor in, for example, publicly owned utilities. But in 1951 the U.S. Supreme Court struck a blow against such laws, striking down a Wisconsin statute regulating labor relations in public utilities as being preempted by the NLRA.[48] Further, courts typically resolved the question of what constituted a "government function" against allowing rights for labor. Most famously, in *United States v. United Mine Workers,* decided in 1947, the Supreme Court sustained an action against the UMW for violating an injunction against striking. The union relied on the Norris-LaGuardia Act, which banned most labor injunctions in the private sector. The Court held that since the mines had been seized by the federal government, the miners were federal employees, and therefore Norris-LaGuardia did not apply.[49] As a matter of common law, the proprietary/traditional dichotomy survived in vague forms until 1985, when the Supreme Court denounced it as "unsound in principle and unworkable in practice."[50] But judges always treated this distinction skeptically, and it rarely benefitted unions. For example, in 1946 *Nutter* rejected the distinction—which was the basis of a public sector union's claim—as being judicial legislation without legislative foundation.[51]

Public sector labor cases can be explained only by adding a third factor to the considerations of bias and state structure: judges falsely constructed the term "union." The "linguistic turn" that emerged in late twentieth-century scholarship asserts that language is central in constructing reality. This approach has been influential in some studies of labor and labor law.[52] Using a moderate version of this approach, it becomes clear that judges in public sector labor cases misconstrued the concept of "union" to exclude organizations of workers performing waged labor for the government. Simultaneously, courts rejected a competing construction of relevant terms that labor offered in word and deed. Thus, even though actually existing public sector unions had all formally renounced strikes and did not strike, and even though most were willing to forgo traditional collective bargaining and did not engage in traditional formal bargaining, courts insisted on seeing unions as institutions that inevitably struck and bargained in precisely the same manner as private sector labor did. And, with the legacy of Boston in mind, this meant that unions could not be allowed in government.[53] Also, judges refused to believe that statutes that granted rights to "labor organizations" or "unions" could possibly cover public sector unions, even in the face of legislative history that suggested they should. These judicial constructions often had a dispositive effect on the outcome of cases, and thus had a significant impact on the reality of public sector labor relations and unions.

In forming their construction of unions, judges seemed at best blind to relevant events outside their courtrooms. First, as the Introduction shows, by the early 1930s there were hundreds of thousands of members of public sector unions in the United States, and union density in the public sector began to hold steady at 10 percent or more by the late 1930s. Second, as chapters 4–6 show, these unions were active on behalf of their members, from representing them in administrative proceedings, to political actions ranging from lobbying to election campaigns, to providing benefits to members, to providing information to members and the public. Third, these unions hardly ever struck. After the Boston strike in 1919, AFL and later CIO public sector unions renounced the strike weapon, and in fact strikes by public sector unions from 1919 to into the 1960s were rare, small in scale, and short. Yet in the courtroom, unionists lacked the power to make this image of unionism real. Indeed, even though the strike wave of 1946 included some public workers, thus spurring antistrike legislation as well as judicial vitriol, the actual level of strikes in government employment was relatively minimal. In 1946—the height of public sector strikes until the 1960s—forty-three strikes of municipal employees led to the loss of approximately 88,000 days of work. But most of these strikes were one-day affairs. The time lost in this exceptional year represented only 0.034 percent of total municipal working time; that same year in the private sector, strikes cost 1.5 percent of total working time.[54]

Instead of this reality, judges clung exclusively to the private sector image of unions, ignoring the continuing existence of functioning public sector unions that did not formally bargain or strike and rejecting the sworn statements and binding documents that these unions proffered as evidence of their different nature. In 1947 *King v. Priest* upheld a rule banning an AFSCME local that more than 800 police officers had joined. The local's charter barred striking and bargaining and stated that the oath that police officers took regarding their duties came before any obligation to the union. Instead of tactics used in the private sector, the charter continued, the local would, "by publicity, direct public attention to conditions that need correcting . . . seek legislative action . . . represent individuals in administrative procedures, and prevent discriminatory and arbitrary practices."[55]

The Missouri Supreme Court would have none of it: "The court, of course, *knows what a labor union is*." (emphasis added). Defining the institution, the court took judicial notice of the "common knowledge" that "some of the most common methods used by labor unions . . . are strikes, threats to strike, [and] collective bargaining agreements." Refusing to accept an alternate model of "union"—but without claiming that any AFSCME local had ever attempted to strike or bargain—the court asserted that "all of the rights and powers ordinarily inherent in a labor union would exist actually or potentially" in the local, "regardless of the form of its charter and present admissions of appellants."[56]

Similarly, *CIO v. Dallas* discounted the fact that the local union had renounced formal collective bargaining and that its constitution and bylaws barred strikes "or other concerted economic weapons or procedures." The court ruled that the local's "declaration . . . to abandon the usual procedure pursued by labor unions to accomplish their purposes is in irreconcilable conflict with the declared purposes and objects of the unions." The decision cited documents from the national CIO—not the public sector local involved—stating that the CIO was organized to help locals bargain collectively and that such activities "constitute the only effective means possessed by organized labor to accomplish economic security." The court also quoted President Franklin Roosevelt's statement in a letter to NFFE president Luther Steward that collective bargaining "cannot be transplanted into the public service" because of the "very nature and purpose of government" and that strikes in public service could never be allowed.[57]

Even when labor specifically proposed a different, limited, and entirely plausible meaning for "bargaining" in the public sector, judges rejected it, maintaining that the private sector practice defined the term. *Clouse* rebuffed a union's argument that it could engage in some bargaining with a city. The union relied on section 29 of the Missouri constitution, which provided that "employees shall have the right to organize and to bargain collectively through representatives of their own choosing." R. T. Wood, the president of the Missouri Federation of Labor and the man who had originally proposed section 29, presented the court with a model of bargaining in the public sector that seemingly addressed the concerns judges had expressed. Wood stipulated that government workers could not bargain over wages and hours, because such matters were controlled by city officials and by statute. Nonetheless, he contended that collective bargaining was applicable to other matters: "classifications, working conditions of all kinds, night work, day work, and a multiplicity of items aside from wages and hours." Wood urged that "collective bargaining means a good many things"; there were "many types of collective bargaining." When a "representative of the employees of the city sits down at a table and discusses . . . relations between an employee and the city, that is collective bargaining."[58] Such a model of public sector bargaining is common today.

The court, however, refused to consider any alternative to the private sector model. "This is confusing collective bargaining with the rights of petition, peaceable assembly and free speech." Section 29 was "intended to safeguard collective bargaining as that term was usually understood in . . . private industry." Thus the court pronounced a tautology that would continue to haunt public sector workers: since only workers in private industry had established collective bargaining rights, laws establishing collective bargaining rights could apply only to the private sector. James Westbrook correctly labels the reasoning of *Clouse* the "All-or-Nothing Misunderstanding," and concludes that "Mr. Wood had a better grasp of the issues than did the Missouri Supreme Court."[59]

One lone dissent credited the claims of public sector unions that they would behave differently from private sector unions. In *City of Jackson v. McLeod*, Justice Harvey McGehee of the Mississippi Supreme Court would have held that AFSCME membership was not sufficient cause to discharge police officers under a civil service law. Among other things, the "jury was entitled to find . . . that there is a fundamental difference between [AFSCME] and the labor unions in general." McGehee noted that the union's charter forbade strikes and that no AFSCME local had ever struck a police department. Further, the union did not advocate negotiating contracts by collective bargaining. McGehee even quoted a statement from Gompers, issued in 1919 in response to the Boston turmoil, that it was the position of the AFL that police would neither strike nor assume any obligation that conflicted with their duty.[60] Yet beyond this single voice, which itself did not come until 1946, judges well into the 1950s uniformly refused to accept that an organization of workers could be a "union" without striking or bargaining as private sector unions did. In taking this stance, judges not only rejected what unions *said* they would do, but critically they ignored what public sector unions were actually doing.

This judicial construction hurt unions in a second way. Courts held that public sector unions were not covered by state labor relations acts even if the such acts did not explicitly exclude the public sector. Often courts would rely on the fact that the state law mentioned "bargaining," "striking," or even "business" somewhere in its text. Courts reasoned that the law was therefore meant only to cover "real" unions that undertook those activities, and thus that no part of the act could apply to public workers. The specific holding of *Murphy* was that the National Association of Railway Postal Clerks (NARPC), at that time a racially exclusive organization, was not a "labor organization" under a New York civil rights statute. The NARPC was not a "labor organization" because part of this civil rights law listed "collective bargaining" as a task of "labor organizations." So, despite the facts that it had held an AFL charter since 1917, was composed of members who were engaged in a common occupation for a common employer, and represented its members in employment-related matters, the NARPC was not a "labor organization."[61]

Similar logic abounded in decisions that held that state laws applying to "unions" or "labor organizations" or even to "employees" did not cover public sector unions. Often these state laws did not, as the NLRA did, explicitly exclude the public sector. In 1946 *Miami Water Works Local 654 v. City of Miami* held that a statute granting rights for "employees" to organize could apply only to private sector employees. The statute in other places discussed strikes and picketing, and such references "are strange and incongruous terms when attempted to be squared with the governmental process as we know it."[62] *CIO v. Dallas* refused to find that an ordinance forbidding city workers from joining a union violated a state law generally protecting the right to join unions. The legislature could not have had public employees in mind, the court reasoned, because the preamble to the statute referred to "unions affecting . . . practically every business and industrial enterprise."[63] Even when relevant legislative history arguably supported the union's position, judges reached the same result. *King v. Priest* held that a state constitutional provision guaranteeing "that employees shall have the right to organize" did not apply to the public sector, even though language limiting the clause to private employment had been debated and dropped in drafting the provision. The court reached this conclusion in part because the constitution also included a right to bargain, which, the court held, could not apply to public workers.[64]

Courts also constructed "union" to mean an institution that provided countervailing pressure to business. In the public sector, without capitalism and its potential abuses, unions apparently were unnecessary. *Nutter,* holding that a state labor statute was not meant to cover government workers, made this point most explicitly. The "legislature recognized that there has been, and is, oppression of labor in the field of private industry, where there has not been freedom of contract." This situation existed because the incentive of personal gain could drive private employers to seek profits at the expense of their employees. Therefore, private sector workers should be allowed to organize to protect themselves. But, the court reasoned, no evidence existed that this "incentive and its attendant evils are found in public employment." The legislature had "not discerned in public employment the existence of the conflicts between labor and capital that exist in private industry. . . . Altogether different conditions prevail." Government officials did "not have the same incentive to oppress the worker." Public employers echoed this type of objection in their legal arguments. In *Miami Waterworks Local 654,* the city's brief insisted that its officials were not "motivated only by the profit motive," and so "the same compelling necessity for private employees to organize does not exist as to public employees."[65] Such quasi-Marxist analysis is arguably surprising coming from a state appellate court and municipal attorneys.

More broadly, public sector unions did not seem to have a place in the contemporary paradigm of industrial pluralism that justified the NLRA. Industrial pluralism, among other things, assumed that private sector workers and their employers had some opposing interests regarding wages, hours, and working conditions. Pluralists proposed that these interests be resolved as much as possible through private acts of self-governance: equalizing power through unionization and collective bargaining, and then use of private contractual enforcement.[66] It is certainly understandable that the Depression and its attendant labor strife would focus attention on the effects of unrestrained capitalism on labor in the private sector. But government workers too had long sought to unionize. Their efforts came from feelings of oppression in the workplace and from the common desire of workers to organize not only to improve wages but also to seek dignity, an effective voice, and some measure of control over the workplace. Pluralist theorists ignored these activities at least until after World War II. Judges, who accepted these theories for private sector workers, seemed almost willfully ignorant of the public sector, ignoring the evidence of public sector unions organizing and acting on behalf of their members throughout the first half of the twentieth century.

It is likely that if pressed, most state court judges in the first half of the twentieth century would not have insisted that capitalism and only capitalism created the types of labor relations that made unions valuable. But even had judges thought that public employees needed unions to address workplace problems, the judicial construction of "union" solely along private sector lines meant that judges assumed that public sector unions would act to address these problems in exactly the same ways as private sector unions. This construction was especially frightening given the legacy of the Boston strike, and thus its consequences were harsh. In 1920 *McNatt v. Lawther,* upholding a ban on firefighters in Dallas joining the IAFF, referred to the "dire consequences" of the Boston strike. The court suggested that the ban might have been designed "to minimize . . . the probability of some such calamity in the city of Dallas."[67] Such fears were rekindled after the much less dramatic public sector strikes in 1946. Again, these beliefs persisted despite the fact that after 1919 and before the late 1960s, with only a few exceptions in 1946, public sector strikes were rare and insignificant. Nonetheless, courts into the 1960s reflexively read the Boston police strike as a warning against any and all public sector labor rights.[68]

Judges sometimes expressed their concerns quite theatrically. The *Murphy* decision, in a case that did not in any way present a factual or legal issue involving strikes, proclaimed that to "admit as true that government employees have the power to halt or check the functions of government unless their demands are satisfied, is to transfer to them all legislative, executive and judicial power. Nothing would be more ridiculous." Strikes against the government were always unjustified and represented "rebellion against constituted authority." The court quoted Franklin Roosevelt: "A strike of public employees manifests nothing less than an intent on their part to prevent or obstruct the operations of government until their demands are satisfied. Such action, looking toward the paralysis of government by those who have sworn to support it, is unthinkable and intolerable."[69] *City of Los Angeles v. Los Angeles Building and Trades Council,* decided in 1949, also insisted that strikes by government workers would be "rebellion against constituted authority."[70] *City of Cleveland v. Division 268* similarly labeled such actions "rebellion against government." Neither of these cases involved any assertion by a public sector union of the right to strike. Still, the judge in *Division 268* continued: "The right to strike, if accorded to public employees, I say, is one means of destroying government. And if they destroy government, we have anarchy, we have chaos." He added that a ban on such strikes was "merely expressive of the common law."[71] This last assertion was true: a study in 1953 concluded that "in every case that has been reported, the right of public employees to strike is emphatically denied."[72] But such reasoning by courts fundamentally misunderstood the actual nature of public sector unions.

In sum, false constructions of terms such as "union" in the courtroom affected the world of public sector unions outside the courts. But public sector workers continued to contest this construction, acting on their beliefs that they were real unionists. They created labor organizations and represented their members, despite lacking the barest minimum of legal rights. In modern times, many of their alternate understandings of what their rights should be have prevailed in the courts and legislatures. Still, before the 1960s the power of judicial construction was often crippling.

The factors listed above—bias against labor, concerns for state structure, and false constructions of "union"—did not exist in isolation from one another. Decisions made twenty-seven years apart by courts in Texas and California show that judges easily combined these three strands of reasoning into a consistent rule: given the type of organization they perceived unions to be, courts would at minimum not interfere with the decisions of government officials to avoid dealing with them. These two cases, *McNatt v. Lawther* and *Perez v. Board of Police Commissioners,* demonstrate how judges synthesized the three factors into a remarkably constant body of law.

In 1920 the Texas Court of Appeals in *McNatt* upheld a bar on union affiliation by firefighters. First, the court deferred to the local board of commissioners in labor matters. The board should decide what constituted "cause" for removal, and court review of board decisions was limited or nonexistent. Second, demonstrating palpable skepticism toward labor, the court quoted a private sector case: "an employer cannot have undivided fidelity, loyalty, and devotion to his interests from an employee who has given to an association [the] right to control his conduct." Indeed, a "man who is by agreement . . . shackled in his faculties—even his freedom of will—may be well considered less useful or less desirable by some employers." Citing *Coppage,* the court stressed that all employers should be able to decide if union membership "is consistent with the satisfactory performance of the duties of employment." Third, the court's construction of "union"—specifically, the assumption that public sector unions would use all the tactics of private sector unions—bolstered its conclusion. Despite the IAFF's disavowal of strikes, the court explained that the board "may have taken into consideration the increased probability of strikes" if the firefighters affiliated.[73]

Even after the NLRA, World War II, and accompanying shifts in attitudes toward private sector unions, little had changed in public sector case law. In 1947 *Perez* upheld a ban on AFSCME membership by the Los Angeles police department. The union claimed that the ban was unreasonable and arbitrary, and thus exceeded the power of the board of police commissioners to make "necessary and desirable rules and regulations." The union added that the ban violated the federal and state constitutions: among other things, it denied equal protection, free speech, assembly, and petition rights and was impermissible "class legislation."[74]

Perez rejected these claims, refusing to compel government officials to deal with a union, as the court understood the concept. Echoing the biased "disloyalty" charge from older private sector cases, *Perez* approvingly quoted the city's argument that union membership could impair police "independence . . . where controversies exist between employers and employees; . . . a divided responsibility would occur." Next, the court rejected any construction of union not based on the private sector model. It slighted the no-strike clause in AFSCME's constitution, insisting that such rules could be amended, even though it cited no example of an AFSCME police union striking or threatening to strike. Further, because of its misperceptions of labor and workplace realities, the court could not comprehend why government workers wanted or needed unions. "Nothing can be gained by comparing public employment with private employment; there can be no analogy in such a comparison." This analysis made deference to another public body an easy solution. Whether union membership related to competency was for the board of police commissioners to decide. It was "not a judicial question." Reasonable rules must be held valid.[75] Given the court's views on unions, it would be unreasonable to force public officials to deal with them.

Finally, the reply of *Perez* to the union's constitutional claims confirmed how little progress public sector labor had made with judges in the first half of the century. In sweeping and dramatic language, the court indicated that concerns of delegation and democracy could bar *any* involvement by labor in government employment. While the union's argument "sings the praises of the Constitution on the one hand . . . it presages its destruction on the other." Allowing the union to bargain would violate "the power of the people to establish and conduct the government, for it seeks to control governmental processes by indirection. . . . the people have sought no assistance from the labor union." Allowing affiliation "would be a direct violation of the Constitution": public workers served the people, and there could be "neither alienation nor division of this allegiance if constitutional government is to continue." Indeed, failure to prohibit affiliation "would have amounted to a surrender of power, a dereliction of duty, and a relinquishment of supervision and control over public servants."[76]

The logic of cases such as *McNatt* and *Perez* determined the outcome of all public sector labor decisions in this era, not merely those involving particular types of unions. Some opinions claimed to rely on the special nature of police and fire departments, stating that they were in "a class apart." Similarly, nearly thirty years after the Boston strike, *King v. Priest* repeated the concern that AFL police unions would aid private sector strikers. The court took "judicial notice . . . of the fact that members of one union ordinarily refuse to cross the picket line of another union."[77] But cases involving public workers who were not involved in "public safety" always yielded identical results. Judges upheld rules barring all types of public employees, from teachers to janitors, from organizing.[78] Fundamentally, no court until the late 1950s struck down a yellow-dog rule aimed at public workers. Well past World War II, courts uniformly upheld whatever bans on public sector unions local authorities thought to pass. Only in the late 1960s did courts begin to find constitutional infirmities in yellow-dog rules, and even these cases did not suggest that public workers had any rights to bargain, much less to strike.[79]

The next logical question is, why was this area was left to judges for so long? Why did public sector unions not even begin to win some statutory protections in some states until decades after the NLRA had given rights to private sector unions and (as will be shown) other Western democracies had given much greater rights to public sector unions? The absence of beneficial labor statutes was clearly devastating to public sector unions. Yet while statutes often set wages and hours for government employees, and civil service rules sometimes provided rights to individual workers, neither federal nor state statutes gave public sector unions institutional rights. Not only were such unions excluded from the coverage of the NLRA, but state labor relations laws, most of them passed in the decade or so after the NLRA, did little in government employment beyond formally barring public sector unions from striking.

The absence of beneficial statutes can also be explained by the ways in which bias, state structure, and false constructions combined. The long and difficult battles required to pass the NLRA show the power of anti-union groups and ideology generally at the time.[80] But why were public workers not included in the NLRA or in state labor relations laws? Crucially, federalism (the constitutional limits of congressional power over the states) greatly limited opportunities for a national labor statute covering employees of states and local governments. Additionally, institutional rights for unions were often seen as opposed to the "good government" structural reforms of civil service. Also, state governments themselves were highly subdivided, with control over employment matters usually given to local officials. Further, constructions of unions based on the Boston police strike or otherwise assuming that such unions would inevitably act like private sector labor hurt in state legislatures as well as in courts.

Public sector unions did help pass statutes beginning in the mid-nineteenth century, but these were generally limited to wages and hours. The lone statute that granted any institutional rights to public sector unions was the Lloyd-LaFollette Act of 1912, and this was limited to federal employees. Notably, because of the federalist structure of the American state, a labor law covering the federal government did not extend to state and local governments. Practically speaking, Lloyd-LaFollette gave federal sector unions the right to exist, petition Congress, and little else.[81] Unions in state and local government lacked even this minimal form of statutory protection. In the first half of the century, the only federal law that affected the rights of state and local workers as workers was the Hatch Act of 1939, which barred workers from taking "any active part in political campaigns."[82]

Civil service laws sometimes offered some rights to individual workers, but state structure and bias assured that these laws would not protect unions. Civil service rules were designed to protect merit principles: public workers should be hired, fired, promoted, or demoted on the basis of their abilities, not on the basis of favors or punishments meted out by political machine bosses. By 1944 nineteen states and hundreds of cities had adopted civil service systems. Unions fought for these laws and used civil service procedures and hearings to defend their members. Nonetheless, civil service rules did not provide institutional rights for unions. Although proponents and opponents of civil service rules fought over how the state would be structured through its employment practices, neither side had a brief for labor. Unions could pass civil service laws only with the aid of government reformers, but reformers often held the biased view that unions were simply another improper power base that should be kept out of government. Further, with the judicial attitudes described above in full force, civil service provided even less protection than unions had hoped. Even when civil service rules provided that public employers could discharge workers only for "cause," courts allowed local officials to determine that union membership was adequate cause.[83]

Also, federalism strengthened the hands of the machine bosses who opposed civil service. The federal government created a civil service system for its employees with the Pendleton Act of 1883. But, given the diffuse structure of American government, individual states and cities set their own civil service standards. This often allowed the bosses of local political machines to write or administer rules such that they in fact retained significant power. Many states "accepted the merit principle in name only."[84]

Federalism also accounts for the failure of public sector unions to win protections in the burst of national labor and employment laws passed during the New Deal. The failure of government employees to win such rights has seemed to matter more to labor than to historians. The legislative history of the NLRA does not explain the exclusion of the public sector.[85] Neither do histories of labor law or New Deal legislation examine why New Deal initiatives did not protect government workers. Unionists in the 1930s periodically called for a federal statute covering public sector labor relations. In later years too, labor leaders decried the omission. AFL-CIO president George Meany wrote that one of Congress's "most grievous errors" in labor relations was to exclude government workers from the NLRA. "By that action the Congress trampled on the principle of equal justice under law."[86]

But the main reason for the lack of a national public sector statute is fairly obvious: under constitutional doctrines in force at least through the first half of the twentieth century regarding the division of power between the federal and state governments, Congress lacked authority to regulate the labor relations of states and localities. Joseph Padway of the AFL in 1942 admitted that "Congress clearly is without constitutional authority to regulate labor relations between state governments and their subordinate bodies and all of their employees." So, for example, in 1942 the National War Labor Board cited the "sovereign rights of state and local governments" in holding that it did not have jurisdiction over a labor dispute between New York City and the Transit Workers Union, which represented public subway workers.[87] In the 1930s, even the constitutionality of a federal statute governing *private* sector labor relations was questioned. Employers insisted that the NLRA was beyond Congress's commerce clause powers and violated the rights of states under the Tenth Amendment. The NLRA and other federal employment laws survived such attacks,[88] but it is hard to imagine courts in the 1930s and 1940s upholding such laws if they purported to cover employees of state and local governments. Indeed, such concerns remain a live issue: the 1990s saw the Supreme Court return to using federalist and state sovereignty arguments to practically eliminate the rights of employees of state governments to sue under several federal employment laws.[89] Thus, state structure has ensured that no federal law governing the labor relations of state and local governments exists even today.

The significance of the federalist structure of the American state is especially evident in light of the legal and statutory regulation of government employment in other Western democracies. That American public sector labor law developed on such an entirely different track from private sector law is not at all "natural"; it is in fact exceptional. Here, federalism hurt public employees in part because they had no exclusive central government to lobby for rights. Again, although labor was successful in 1912 in passing the Lloyd-LaFollette Act, which ostensibly allowed federal workers to join unions, the legislation applied only to employees of the federal government, and not to any other public employees. In contrast, while governments in Britain and France hardly welcomed public sector unions, those unions won many more rights and won them much earlier than did their counterparts in the United States.

More specifically, one study cites the "long history of public policy in England which has encouraged the spread of unionism and the acceptance of collective bargaining" in the public sector, which "came particularly toward the end of World War I." In England, the Civil Service National Whitely Council, created in 1919, provided for union recognition and collective bargaining. As a result, public sector union membership increased sharply in England from 1920 to 1940. In 1927 Britain barred civil service employees from affiliating with labor organizations that had members in the private sector, but this bar was repealed in 1946. Moreover, beginning in the mid-1920s British law provided for mandatory arbitration of public sector labor disputes; such practices would not even begin to be used in parts of the United States until nearly half a century later. Overall, British laws have not made the sharp distinction between public and private sector labor law that has always existed in America.

Along similar lines, the French government in 1920 opposed state workers' affiliating with the national labor federation, but in 1924 pressure from civil servants forced a reversal of this policy. From 1926 to 1932 the percentage of public workers in the major French labor organizations grew from 30 to 35 percent. The French constitution of 1946 affirmed the right of public workers to join trade unions. French law also has traditionally made no great distinction between public and private sector workers, except for minor differences such as a requirement of giving notice before a strike.[90]

State structure also hurt the ability of public sector unions to pass state labor relations statutes. Federalism did not prevent state labor relations acts from covering government employees, but federalism ensured that statutory law would come from state and local governments, where bias and false constructions played an enormous role. And again, the diffusion of governmental power within individual states combined with judicial deference to give local government bodies dispositive power over labor relations. This gave bias against unions a very specific context. Not surprisingly, local officials were biased against the notion that their own workers needed unions or should have the right to strike or bargain.[91]

But neither state structure nor the bias of local officials is a sufficient explanation for the absence of laws on the state level. Again, the third factor was present: misunderstanding of the nature of public sector unions and exclusive use of the private sector model of what a union could be. Once again the tumultuous but singular Boston police strike played a crucial role in shaping perceptions, helping to create a mass of highly restrictive state and local laws that lasted nearly half a century. As noted in chapter 1, in response to the Boston strike, Congress barred police and firefighters in the District of Columbia from striking or affiliating with unions. Many cities, including Macon, Georgia; Omaha, Nebraska; San Antonio, Texas; and Roanoke, Virginia, soon followed suit, prohibiting various public workers from joining unions. After the Boston strike Massachusetts began enforcing an 1855 law that barred firefighters from joining any organization not approved by government officials. Cities passed similar rules in following decades. In 1932 Philadelphia enacted an ordinance forbidding police to form any group other than a benefit society; in 1942 Dallas passed a rule preventing city employees from forming a labor organization. After AFSCME began organizing police in the early 1940s, many more cities blocked this trend by law or by department order, including Chicago, Detroit, Los Angeles, Saint Louis, and Jackson, Mississippi. It was in this climate that many state labor relations laws, passed to cover groups of employees that the NLRA did not reach, either explicitly excluded or were interpreted to exclude public workers.[92]

After World War II cities and states finally began to pass laws which explicitly covered public sector unions, but these statutes were designed chiefly to provide draconian penalties for government workers who struck. Such laws were partly inspired by the explosion of labor militancy in 1946, which included some strikes by public workers, and they were a product of the era that produced the anti-union Taft-Hartley Act. But again, the laws restricted public sector unions much more significantly than private sector unions; and again, the image of public sector unions in state legislatures was often at odds with the typical practices of public sector unions. Nonetheless, understanding "union" to mean only organizations that struck, cities and states centered their attention almost exclusively on the strike threat. Cities banning public sector strikes by ordinance included Bridgeport, Connecticut; Omaha, Nebraska; and Portland, Maine. States also enacted restrictive laws. In 1946 the Virginia legislature adopted a joint resolution declaring it to be contrary to public policy for any government official to recognize or negotiate with a public sector union. Virginia then enacted a statute mandating discharge for any government worker who struck. New York's Condon-Wadlin Act of 1947, passed after a successful strike by Buffalo public school teachers, banned not only public sector strikes but also any employee participation in setting working conditions. That same year, antistrike laws were passed in Washington, Nebraska, Missouri, Pennsylvania, Michigan, Texas, and Ohio. The Texas law also barred public employers from bargaining with or recognizing unions.[93] While a few of these laws provided minimal rights to exist or to make appeals,[94] public sector unions generally would have to wait until the 1960s and beyond for rights even approaching what private sector unions had won before the NLRA.

From simply reading the laws on the books, one might conclude that before the 1960s public sector unions had barely achieved what private sector unions had over a century earlier in *Commonwealth v. Hunt*. This case held that unions were not illegal conspiracies per se, but it did not permit much actual concerted activity by workers. Similarly, before the 1960s, even where public employees were allowed to join unions, they could not strike or bargain collectively, and their ability to act politically was often limited by law. Robert Hoxie's description of private sector unionism in the progressive era as "in its very essence a lawless thing" seems even more apt for public sector unionism for a majority of the century.[95]

Unionists cited throughout this book argued that NLRA-style statutory protections would have been good for public sector unions; yet a large body of literature argues that the NLRA, or interpretations of it, have been in significant ways harmful to private sector labor.[96] Regrettably, none of these works addresses public sector unions or law. Many of these studies make powerful claims that courts have undermined certain pro-union policies of the act through questionable interpretations. It seems highly unlikely that any of these authors would claim that a legal regime as restrictive as that in government employment would have been desirable or preferable to a regime that granted at least some basic NLRA-style rights. Still, studying the public sector is useful as at least a partial corrective for the most extreme claims that the NLRA, by its very nature and structure, co-opted and muzzled labor militancy and, ultimately, organizational strength. The obvious lesson from the public sector is that the absence of NLRA-style rights artificially repressed the size and strength of unions, and the presence of NLRA-style rights (and even the most modern and generous public sector laws do not provide all the rights the NLRA does, for example, in terms of subjects of bargaining) has greatly aided unions in their ability to organize and act effectively on behalf of their members.

The legal climate in the public sector profoundly affected public sector unions for more than half a century, and by extension influenced all of American labor. The law created a kernel of unions within the labor movement that were interested and skilled in alternative methods of employee representation, including, as will be shown, politics; simultaneously, the law repressed the size of that group until the 1960s. Rules against affiliation kept the number of government workers in the AFL and CIO significantly lower than it otherwise would have been. The absence of a statutory bar on company unions also led to the proliferation of unaffiliated "employee associations" in the public sector long after such groups had largely disappeared from the private. For example, in 1947 the AFT had 50,000 members and the CIO's United Public Workers claimed 12,000 teachers, while the administrator-dominated NEA had 386,000 members. Even when public employee activists forced such organizations to behave more like unions—as was the case with police and fire groups in New York, for example—they were still outside the house of labor.[97]

Yet while the restrictive and surprisingly uniform and static law damaged public sector unions, it did not stop them. Through a variety of strategies, they won real victories for their members. By depriving government employees of the standard weapons of labor, the law drove their unions to engage in political activity and other alternative activities. Also, like private sector unions before the New Deal, public sector unions constantly pushed the limits of their formal legal rights. The law barred collective bargaining in government employment, but public sector unions achieved real gains through informal "agreements" with public officials. The actual experiences of public sector unions representing their members in this era show once again that the "law on the books" does not always determine what happens on the ground.

4

Ground-Floor Politics and the BSEIU in the 1930s

It takes longer to secure what you are after from the politicians than [from] employers of other sources.
PAUL DAVID, BSEIU secretary (1939)

Their only weapon is . . . political pressure.
EDWIN NYDEN, BSEIU Local 140 (1940)

Not all public sector unions faced life-or-death struggles from the moment they organized, nor were all composed of allegedly sensitive employees such as police or teachers. All public sector unions did, however, face similar obstacles. "This type of employee cannot make use of labor's most common weapons—strikes, picketing, etc.," complained Edwin Nyden, leader of a local of public school janitors. This situation remained in effect well past the 1930s, a decade typically portrayed as the central dividing line in American labor history. During the New Deal, worker militance from below combined with more tolerance of private sector unions by the federal government above, producing a larger, stronger, and more active labor movement. Yet this sea-change left the public sector largely untouched. The NLRA excluded government workers, and courts continued to deny any institutional rights to their unions. Strikes and even formal bargaining were, politically and legally, out of the question. So, what did the many small but stable locals of public employees do to represent their members, especially during the ravages of the Great Depression? "Their only weapon is through political pressure," Nyden concluded.[1]

The experiences of the Building Service Employees International Union (BSEIU) illustrate how public sector unions expanded their range of political tactics as widely as they could. In addition to elections, BSEIU locals of government employees across the country used lobbying, public relations, and whatever political influence they had to try to protect individual members, reach informal agreements with employers, increase budgets, win better pay and conditions, and promote civil service laws and related protections. Lacking the rights and the muscle of private sector unions, these locals experienced great difficulties. Indeed, leaders of the BSEIU, which also represented private sector workers, often remarked that it was harder to represent public employees. Today the SEIU (having dropped "Building" from its name) is one of the largest and most powerful unions in the country. John Sweeney led the SEIU before becoming the president of the AFL-CIO. But in the 1930s the BSEIU was a struggling AFL union, trying to represent its members amidst the peculiarities and structures of a wide variety of local political conditions. Sometimes the union was effective. Sometimes it was not.

The BSEIU began in 1912 as a local of private sector janitors in Chicago, led by William Quesse. In 1916 the union organized a local for janitors in the public sector. By 1918 about fifty building service unions existed nationwide. The AFL chartered the BSEIU as an international union in 1920, with Quesse as the first president. Its most powerful locals were in Chicago, but it had a presence throughout the country. In 1926 Paul David became secretary-treasurer of the union. David, who played a key role with public sector locals, was the son of a member of the Knights of Labor, had had a leg amputated as a result of disease, and was a significant figure in the Chicago labor movement as well as the BSEIU. After Quesse died in 1927, Jerry Horan became president. When Horan died in 1937, George Scalise replaced him. William McFetridge, who came from the Chicago public sector janitors' local, became a vice-president of the BSEIU in 1927 and president in 1940, after Scalise was convicted of embezzlement and forgery. Despite some corruption at the top, the BSEIU grew through the 1930s: in 1932 it had more than 10,000 members; by the mid-1930s, more than 40,000; and by 1939, it claimed 70,000 to 75,000 members and more than 200 locals.[2]

From its beginnings, the BSEIU included many women and many blacks, Hispanics, and other ethnic minorities. In 1916 three of the union's founding officers were black. Local 1, the private sector Chicago Flat Janitors' Union, was the founding and largest BSEIU local, and it had a racially integrated membership and leadership. Quesse, David, and other national leaders were also genuinely committed to interracial solidarity. Elizabeth Grady of the Chicago School Janitresses, Local 7, a central figure from the beginning of the union, became a trustee of the International in 1921 and was always a strong advocate for women in the BSEIU. Women don't just work for "pin money," an article in *Public Safety*, the BSEIU's national journal insisted. "So-called 'pin money' is often . . . the only means of holding the family together." Several locals, such as Local 7, were composed entirely of women. Many others, such as Local 3 in Toledo, had a significant female membership, and women served as leaders in a number of the mixed locals. The BSEIU favored equal wages for men and women and sometimes achieved this goal.[3]

The BSEIU organized both public and private sector workers, asserting their common cause but organizing separate locals in deference to reality. The union noted that the actual work of janitors in government buildings was the same as in private establishments. A union leaflet used in Saint Louis in 1925 urged that schools were "a great industry" even though they were "not manufacturing articles of commerce." Thus, school employees, like workers in all industries, could not improve their conditions standing alone, and should organize "to promote their common interest and advance their general well-being individually and collectively." The leaflet also provided an early illustration of the BSEIU's attention to public relations in cases involving government employees: unions would save taxpayer money, the leaflet added, by fighting inefficient and arbitrary management in schools.

Still, the BSEIU explained that its policy was to put public workers in separate locals, because legal restrictions and the different nature of public employers required different tactics. Public workers themselves preferred this division. For example, in Toledo in 1937, the members of Local 13, representing government employees, split from Local 3 (which kept the private sector members) after ninety-six public school workers petitioned the International for a separate charter. They felt that "a separate Local would better enable us to cope with the many problems peculiar to our occupations as employees being paid out of tax monies." BSEIU president Horan agreed to the division because dealing "directly with the City and Board officials" presented different issues from those involved in dealing with owners of private buildings.[4]

From the mid-1920s to 1940 the BSEIU had seventy to seventy-four locals representing public workers, at least a third of the total number in the union. These locals were spread across the country, in Seattle, San Antonio, San Francisco, Toledo, Minneapolis, New York City, West Virginia, throughout Illinois, and in other states. Memberships ranged from a dozen to twenty-five hundred. Most of these employees worked in public schools, but the BSEIU also represented janitors, maintenance workers, and other service workers in public office buildings, libraries, courthouses, hospitals, parks, and universities. As a result, members of the BSEIU were subject to the powers and dispositions of a wide variety of state officials acting as employers, including but not limited to school boards. Local 89 in Chicago represented women working in welfare offices, public libraries, and police stations. Leaders of Local 113 in Minneapolis complained about all the different bodies that employed their members: the board of education, the public library board, the board of public welfare, the council auditorium committee, the ways and means committee, the city council, the city hall building commission, the university board of regents, and the hospital council. "Some of these Boards . . . are very antagonistic toward labor," Local 113 president Owen Cunningham observed. BSEIU locals also had to adjust their methods to fit variations in local state structures, such as whether their employers were elected or appointed. In Chicago alone, the sanitary district commissioners and the Cook County commissioners were elected, while members of the board of education and the park district board were appointed by the mayor.[5]

Although the biggest BSEIU locals represented private sector workers in Chicago and New York City, public sector locals had significant power within the union and sometimes beyond it. William McFetridge, who would become president of the BSEIU in 1940, came out of Local 46, Chicago public school janitors. McFetridge, the nephew of BSEIU founder Quesse, was influential in Illinois politics and labor relations. In 1929 Illinois governor Louis Emmerson appointed him to the Illinois Industrial Commission as a mediator. Later Governor Henry Horner made him a member of the Illinois Relief Commission. While president of Local 46, McFetridge became a vice-president of the Illinois Federation of Labor. Elizabeth Grady of Local 7, dubbed "labor's sweetheart" by the Chicago AFL's paper, was on the legislative committee of the Chicago Federation of Labor.[6]

The union began using politics early in its history. In the 1920s BSEIU members helped work the precincts for Chicago mayor "Big Bill" Thompson's Republican organization. In return, John Jentz writes, Thompson "helped insure that the arbitrators of the union's annual contracts had a sympathetic ear for labor." The BSEIU joined the Cook County Wage Earners' League and, Jentz concludes, generally gave a "strong priority to political action in its program." During the upheavals of the 1930s the BSEIU continued to take advantage of connections with government officials. For example, in New York City in 1934, during a strike by Local 32-B, a private sector local, the union prevailed on Mayor Fiorello LaGuardia to intervene and order an arbitration. Still, in the private sector the union relied primarily on traditional economic pressure to gain its objectives.[7] In the public sector, however, the only viable strategies for improving pay and conditions were in the realm of politics.

Pay and conditions for the public sector members of the BSEIU certainly needed improving, and where the BSEIU was strong in numbers or political influence, it made a difference. Nationally, janitors were the lowest paid of all school employees. In the mid-1920s the median salary for school janitors in cities with a population of at least 100,000 was $1,390 per year. This compared unfavorably with other school support staff, such as attendance officers ($2,020), and administrative clerks ($1,534). As national averages, these disparities continued through the 1930s. In 1932–33, attendance officers averaged $1,971, administrative clerks $1,450, and janitors $1,265; in 1938–39 attendance officers averaged $2,241, administrative clerks $1,628, and janitors $1,429. But in Chicago in 1937, the BSEIU helped janitors and janitresses average $1,800 and $1,500 per year, respectively. David even estimated that the Chicago scales were the "prevailing rates" of unionized janitors. Still, he acknowledged, pay varied in accordance with local conditions, including tax structures. It was "an unfortunate thing that the schools are run out of taxes," David complained. "It is very hard to regulate the same as one would an industrial proposition." Despite the union's gains, David also frequently bemoaned the low salaries of public sector members. "It is hard for one to believe that employees can exist on such small salaries."[8]

The Depression made life much more difficult for public workers and their unions, lowering government revenues and, most importantly for the BSEIU, crippling school budgets. In 1933–34 income in some school districts had fallen 30 to 50 percent. In 1935, 42,000 schools lacked sufficient funds to operate, and nearly 40,000 more operated for less than six months. In 1934 federal aid to state and local governments increased dramatically, to more than $1 billion, but schools received a disappointing share of this money as the portion of state and local government budgets devoted to education plummeted. From 1927 to 1939 state expenditures on schools as a portion of total expenditures dropped from 14.5 percent to 10.9 percent, and municipal expenditures from 26.2 percent to 21.5 percent. In Illinois, with relatively strong AFT and BSEIU locals, the portion of the state government's total net expenditures for elementary and secondary schools decreased from 10.2 percent in 1930 to 9.9 percent in 1938.[9]

These conditions forced school employees to endure layoffs, "payless paydays," or pay in the form of scrip of dubious value. While historians have focused on the plight of teachers in this period, janitors and other workers in the schools suffered considerably as well. For example, poor finances in the Morgantown, West Virginia, schools led to layoffs of many members of Local 42 in 1938. BSEIU members in Minneapolis went without pay, and those in Toledo received scrip. Even in 1940, Local 13 in Toledo called a 12 percent salary cut a "major victory," as the local school board had proposed a reduction of 80 percent. Local 13 also faced school closures. "Cutting wages of school employees has been prevalent all over the country," David observed. Again as late as 1940, Local 40, representing charwomen in the

Cleveland public schools, protested that many of its members had suffered from reduced hours as a result of the "sad financial plight of the Cleveland Board of Education." Local 40's leaders retained some hope based on their successful political action: "We have finally elected a Board of Education in this city who have promised their cooperation."[10]

The Chicago school system was hit very hard because of additional local problems. First, the Depression was especially devastating to the city's entire economy. By October 1932, 750,000 people in the city were unemployed, and only 800,000 had jobs. Second, public finances had been unsound even before the Depression. A real estate assessment in 1927 was so inequitable that the state tax commission ordered a reassessment, which resulted in a suspension of all tax collections until late 1929. Then the Association of Real Estate Taxpayers, composed mostly of large property holders, sued to have the reassessment reversed. The Illinois Supreme Court finally upheld the reassessment in 1932, but in the meantime many businesses carried on an effective tax strike, further depleting public funds. Consequently, in January 1931 the Chicago Board of Education began paying teachers in scrip. A court declared this policy illegal, so in 1932 teachers and other school employees were paid nothing at all. By the end of 1932 the city owed its employees $40 million in back wages. When Edward Kelly became mayor in April 1933, teachers alone were owed $26 million. By the end of 1933 the city had a total debt of more than $100 million, and public services were failing on a widespread basis. Mayor Kelly won approval from the state legislature for the Chicago Board of Education to issue $40 million in school bonds, and he lobbied banks to purchase them. Fourteen thousand teachers marched into the Loop business area, breaking windows and confronting hostile bankers. A compromise was reached, but this left the board of education with a deficit of $9.5 million for the 1933–34 school year. Kelly kept the schools alive through, among other things, a massive loan from the Reconstruction Finance Corporation. This allowed workers to receive some back wages. Still, the school budget was cut severely, and school employees faced payless paydays throughout the decade.[11]

The human consequences were devastating. In 1934 a member of Local 46 in Chicago explained that for "for years, the members of this union were months behind in their pay," and that wages were often in "tax warrants," which merchants discounted at 15 to 20 percent. The average public school janitor was "besieged daily by bill collectors for money he earned but never received, with his wife and children half clothed and half starved." McFetridge and Grady told the BSEIU convention in 1935 that in the previous four years their members had been behind in pay up to eleven months, with paydays as far apart as three or four months. The union had made public demands that workers be given full pay until the system's resources were exhausted, but such calls went unheeded. In 1936 leaders of Local 46 wrote an editorial castigating the Chicago Board of Education's "no pay" policy for "raising havoc with the home life of employees . . . a number of whom have been ejected from their homes for non-payment of rent." They implored the board to provide relief, arguing that "pay days for workers are as important as interest due on bonds. . . . In fact wages are the first consideration."[12]

Wages and layoffs were not the only issues facing the BSEIU in Chicago and elsewhere. Hours could be either too scarce or overwhelming. In 1934 Mary Sudkamp, the president of BSEIU Local 19, representing public school bath attendants, admonished the Chicago Board of Education that "we are now employed on a half-time, $50.00 a month basis." In 1937 members of the local won the right to work a three-quarters-time schedule for $75 a month. Local leaders remained unsatisfied, as even the full-time salary of $110 per month "would scarcely provide for the bare necessities of living." In 1933, when the board transferred work from bath attendants to janitresses, the competition for work led to ill will between union sisters. Local 19 told the board that janitresses "are of a different class—not having had the advantages that the Bath Attendants have." Bath attendants, not janitresses, "are the type of women who are fitted to come in contact with the children and handle them properly." In contrast, in the early 1930s janitors in Local 31 in Columbus, Ohio, complained that they were required to work sixty-hour weeks. Notably, while the FLSA brought overtime rates to some private sector employees in the late 1930s, long hours in the public sector brought no premium pay. In the winter of 1940 members of Local 147, grounds workers at Western Illinois State Teachers College in Macomb, worked fourteen to eighteen hours a day for significant periods and received no overtime pay. Wages for members of Local 147 ranged from $65 to $115 per month.[13]

Further, the work of janitors was hard and fraught with indignities. Even when unionized or covered by civil service rules, janitors were often arbitrarily fired, transferred, or demoted without regard to ability or seniority, sometimes in retaliation for union activities. Their duties were extensive. In Chicago, janitors and janitresses in the schools did all the sweeping, mopping, dusting, and cleaning; they mowed and watered the grass, did grounds work, shoveled snow, and performed "other janitor work." Members of Local 69, high school matrons in Chicago, had to monitor hallways, administer a lost and found, clean and supervise washrooms, launder uniforms, mend students' torn clothes, care for sick and injured students, and inspect students' hair for signs of disease. Janitors and janitresses also had to know how to operate the physical plant. In Chicago they ran 920 steam boilers in the 400 school buildings. In addition to their official duties, janitors and janitresses were often pressured to clean the private homes of principals, teachers, and even members of the PTA.

As the loquacious W. K. Jones of Local 84 in San Antonio put it, the "Little Red School House . . . has disappeared," replaced by "modern buildings, equipped with up to date steam heating." A "school custodian . . . must be up as early as 4 A.M. to properly heat, dust and ventilate his building for the opening of school, and stay on the job after classes are dismissed long enough to clean up and lock up for the night." Janitors also had to get along with faculty, children, and parents. Yet the pay was "frightful." In San Antonio, janitors received seventy-five dollars per month and worked a minimum of nine hours a day; janitresses worked eight hours a day for fifty dollars per month. Beyond regular hours, extracurricular functions or elections could stretch a workday from six in the morning to midnight. This extra work was not compensated, and Jones noted that janitors could not even eat the food furnished at various events. Even by 1940, Local 84's janitor members might work twelve-to-eighteen-hour days, with only fifteen minutes for lunch and no overtime. Chronic problems included working after hours for no pay and performing onerous duties, all to earn seventy-five to eighty-five dollars per month.[14]

In the face of such conditions, David argued that unionization was necessary, often using the Chicago locals as an example of solidarity. In 1928 the BSEIU organized all 1,200 public school janitors in Local 46 and all 400 janitresses in Local 7. In 1934 Local 46 began to accept janitors working in other public buildings, raising its membership to 1,600. BSEIU boasted that membership in both locals was 100 percent of eligible workers. This loyalty stemmed in part from the organizing talent and personal generosity of Grady and McFetridge, who helped members with a variety of needs. "Some historian in days to come . . . will find time to write . . . of the heroic efforts of Miss Grady," an article in *Public Safety* enthused. With little money of her own, she "found means to feed and clothe the members of her union, keep a roof over their heads, bury their dead and comfort their sick."

Grady and McFetridge combined similar acts with public relations and internal organizing. After studies in the mid-1930s revealed that Chicago schools spent a greater percentage of funds on maintenance than the national average, McFetridge wrote editorials and spoke before groups such as the Women's City Club to rebut charges that janitors were overpaid. In addition, Chicago BSEIU locals sponsored bowling leagues and shoveled snow for free; they also helped found WCFL, Chicago's labor radio station, and the Illinois Federation Corporation Labor Mortgage Company, which financed homes for workers. The Chicago locals also sponsored talks on new cleaning techniques, promoting what one janitor called a sense of "professionalization." In 1936 Local 46 began to offer death benefits to families of members, a practice that other BSEIU locals adopted.

The Chicago locals also helped their members on the job. The BSEIU won civil service protections in the late 1920s. In 1937 David could boast that "they have the best working conditions and wages of any school janitors throughout the country." Life often was worse for unorganized members of the trade. Nonunion janitors at State Teachers College in Bemidji, Minnesota, told BSEIU leaders that they worked sixty-to-seventy-hour weeks with no overtime and received pay well below the average for BSEIU members.[15]

Still, representing members in the public sector required imagination and perseverance. Lacking rights to strike or bargain, BSEIU locals across the country turned to various political strategies. Their activities included conventional means such as campaigning for sympathetic politicians and lobbying for new or improved laws. At least as frequently, however, locals used informal channels and political connections: cajoling friendly government officials, soliciting public support, and meeting with administrators to work out unwritten, unofficial "agreements." Given the severe legal restrictions and financial conditions in the 1930s, the BSEIU had a difficult row to hoe, and its overall record reflects this. But in a good number of cases, BSEIU locals were able to achieve real victories.

Though sometimes limited by rules restricting political acts by government workers, BSEIU public sector locals were often involved in local elections that determined the officials who would employ their members. The composition of local boards was crucial, as the prospects or even existence of locals depended on the attitudes of board members. In a familiar scenario, in 1930 three members of the Minneapolis School Board tried to replace BSEIU Local 113 with a hand-picked company union. In response, Local 26 happily publicized a quote from the building commissioner of the Saint Louis schools stating that the Saint Louis School Board would not oppose janitors organizing a BSEIU local.[16]

For these reasons, nationwide, the BSEIU strove to put in place friendly officials—both elected and appointed. Local 84 routinely backed candidates for the county commission and school board in San Antonio. The Chicago locals were also very active politically. In 1936 and 1939 Local 46 sponsored huge political rallies for Franklin Roosevelt that were also used to support the election of Mayor Kelly (who appointed officials who employed BSEIU members) and of other local candidates running for positions that employed BSEIU members (for example, sanitary district commissioners). Judges were also elected, and they had considerable influence in running the courthouses in which BSEIU members worked. The BSEIU backed candidates for these and other positions.[17]

Where the BSEIU was strong, this strategy could work. When two union-ists were elected to the school board in Minot, North Dakota, David was elated. Perhaps confirming fears of union opponents, he expressed hope that in "coming elections, Brother members like yourself may be elected . . . so that the trade union movement will have full control of said School Board." Yet even in private correspondence, David explained that such con-trol was desirable because "the trade unionist is in a position to know the wants of the employees of the School Boards and also the wants of the chil-dren and their families." David often argued that school boards were the servants of all people, including janitors. Politicians did listen. In 1931 R. E. Woodmansee, a member of the Springfield School Board seeking reelection, came to a meeting of Local 15 citing his pro-labor record and promising to support the janitors. In Chicago in 1933 Mayor Kelly pleased the BSEIU by appointing a member of the Typographers Union, Charles Fry, to the Chi-cago Board of Education. In 1938 Kelly appointed an officer of the Steam-fitters Union to the board, and in 1939 he appointed a member of the CIO's Amalgamated Clothing Workers. The BSEIU also helped elect an influential political ally in Oscar Nelson, a Chicago alderman and later local judge who was also a former BSEIU national officer, BSEIU lawyer, and vice-pres-ident of the Chicago Federation of Labor (CFL).

Sympathetic officials did make a difference. In Cheyenne, Wyoming, in the late 1930s the chair of the school board was a member of the Typogra-phers Union. Through his efforts, the board reached an "agreement" ex-pressed in a letter regarding working conditions for janitors. In Saint Louis a secretary of the Steamfitters Union on the board of education helped the BSEIU organize school janitors. In a vain attempt to institutionalize this type of assistance, in 1940 the BSEIU supported a call by the Indiana Feder-ation of Labor for a law that would guarantee labor representation on all school boards.[18]

More typically, the BSEIU had to rely on less direct political means. It lacked the numbers to elect majorities of union supporters to school boards, especially when the attention of the broader labor movement in the turbu-lent 1930s was often diverted to other matters. Candidates whom the BSEIU supported often lost.[19] Overall, the BSEIU relied more on political connections than on elections, using a combination of persuasion and indi-rect pressure.

To this end, public sector locals could offer something that had no anal-ogy in the private sector: joining with their employers to work for increased budgets. Supporting an organizing drive in the Chicago parks in 1929, David reminded the president of the West Chicago Park Board that the BSEIU was "always willing to support all public improvements . . . with our membership of over fifty thousand on the west side." The number was an exaggeration, but the Chicago locals did have real clout. Throughout the 1930s the BSEIU helped the Chicago Board of Education in lobbying for tax levies for the schools, increased authorizations from the state legislature, and federal funds. Other BSEIU locals took the same tack. In 1936 Local 113 in Minneapolis helped pass a law that increased school revenues. "At all times our local unions assist the School Board trying to get better tax adjustments," David noted. Locals supported bond issues and had "other ways of assisting a School Board . . . too numerous to mention." This tactic could produce contradictions, as when Local 50 in Saint Louis campaigned for higher school taxes but against the current commissioner of schools. Also, BSEIU locals published studies of school budgets that, not surprisingly, stressed that cutting pay should be the last resort. Local 3 in Toledo published an analysis quoting a school board member that "we should first diligently curtail expenses in all other respects."[20]

More generally, the BSEIU tried to forge connections with influential politicians. Its greatest success was with Mayor Kelly in Chicago, with BSEIU locals both giving and receiving support. Kelly became mayor in 1933 after his predecessor, Anton Cermak, who had helped create Chicago's famous Democratic machine, was assassinated. Initially backed by both business and the increasingly conservative CFL, Kelly had a rough first year with labor. But he improved his ties with unions, including the BSEIU, over the decade. At the same time, although public school employees had won civil service protections in the late 1920s, the unionized janitors were, Julia Wrigley writes, "staunch supporters of the machine," pounding the pavement in search of voters on election day and distributing campaign materials in the buildings where they worked. Wrigley argues that through these connections, janitors were able to maintain higher rates of employment and pay than they could otherwise have achieved. "Because the janitors served a political purpose," she states, "the Chicago school district employed proportionally more maintenance workers than did other districts." Wrigley even criticizes their comparatively high salaries for raising operating and maintenance costs of the Chicago schools. McFetridge and leaders of the CFL regularly countered similar criticisms by contemporaries.[21]

In any case, the BSEIU and many Chicago public officials had good relations. In the late 1930s the janitors' locals in Chicago sponsored a rally for Kelly attended by 30,000 people. "To be worthy of labor is to be worthy of mankind," the mayor declared. "My door . . . always will be open to the friends of labor." The Chicago locals also hosted huge annual picnics, with attendance reaching 20,000, inviting influential officials, including members of the Cook County Board of Commissioners and local judges. Local 7 invited members of the Chicago Board of Education to speak at its holiday parties.[22]

These connections paid off in various ways. In 1935, when the Chicago superintendent of parks stated that he would seek a police order to keep union organizers away from park employees, David wrote to Mayor Kelly. Very soon thereafter, the organizers were allowed to proceed with their work. Later that year McFetridge reported that he had won a favorable agreement with the city regarding the wages of park employees. Kelly also appointed the president of the Chicago Federation of Musicians to the park board that would oversee the newly unified city park system. By late 1935 Local 145, Park Employees, announced that it was making good progress, adding 100 new members in October alone and "dealing collectively" with management.[23]

Political connections even helped workers who had been converted from public to quasi-private status. In 1932 BSEIU leaders used their influence to help settle a strike by members of Local 80, representing cooks and attendants at the Cook County Psychopathic Hospital. Before 1923 these workers had been covered by civil service rules. Then the Cook County commissioners contracted control of the hospital to a private employer, the Cook County Hospital School of Nursing. In April 1932 the hospital fired over one-third of its staff (forty people), provoking a strike. After a series of communications from David, Horan, and Grady, the Cook County commissioners agreed to arbitrate the matter, even though there was no contract or rule providing for such a procedure. An arbitration board ordered the members of Local 80 to be reinstated and also directed the local and the employer to negotiate an agreement on wages and working conditions that would include an arbitration clause. Politics was also central in ensuring that the order was enforced. When Frank Shaw, the president of the private contractor, told Cook County commissioner Glenn Plumb that the arbitration was not legally valid, Plumb quickly replied that it was valid and ordered a report on its implementation. Shaw and Laura Logan, the dean of the nursing school, resigned. Three years later, Local 80 would gloat that the hospital had been dealing fairly with the union ever since.[24]

Many of the union's activities on behalf of public sector workers consisted of informal lobbying of public officials in their role as employers. The bath attendants were able to increase their hours from half-time to three-quarters-time after David asked the Chicago Board of Education to increase their hours to full-time. In the late 1930s leaders of Local 119, University of Illinois employees, made demands in letters to the director of the physical plant of the university and members of the university board of trustees. In response, they received a raise from fifty-six cents to seventy cents an hour.[25] Sometimes when the officials directly employing BSEIU members were unresponsive, the union had better luck with higher-level politicians. David received a noncommittal reply from the president of the Des Moines

School Board after complaining, on behalf of Local 103, that the board wanted a company union. David then forwarded the correspondence to Iowa's commissioner of education, who told David that he supported organized labor and was willing to help. The company union never materialized.[26]

But in the absence of legal rights and power, such appeals often failed. When Local 11 in Berwyn, Illinois, protested deep pay cuts to E. W. Martin, the superintendent of schools, Martin replied that the "Board of Education has nothing to arbitrate in this matter, nothing to compromise." In 1937 Local 140 in Portland, Oregon, had to fight a long battle against the local school board after the board dismissed or demoted all the officers of the local. In Memphis in the spring of 1936 Mayor Watkins Overton barred all city employees from union membership; although the mayor did not control school employees, the Memphis School Board followed his lead, forbidding teachers to join the AFT and janitors to join the BSEIU. "School Custodians Hit by Union Ban—Drop Membership or Lose Job, Board Rules," announced the *Memphis Commercial Appeal*. The lone dissent on the board came from a union member. Mayor Overton said that he "heartily approved" of the board's action; there should be "no labor unions of those serving the city." David and the Tennessee Federation of Labor prevailed on the national AFL and the U.S. Department of Labor to send representatives to Memphis to make appeals, but to no avail. The teachers dropped their AFT charter; BSEIU Local 56, which had about thirty members, was destroyed.[27]

Of course private sector unions faced hostile employers as well, but in the 1930s they, unlike government workers, won legal rights. The BSEIU did what little it could with the new labor laws for its public employee members. Like other public sector unions, the BSEIU argued that while the New Deal laws formally excluded government employees, they evinced a general policy in favor of unionization that should be applied to the public sector. BSEIU Local 74 in New York City proclaimed that the NLRA "encourages you to affiliate with a labor union whether or not you are in Civil Service." Some private sector unions adopted this rhetoric. In 1933 the Springfield, Illinois, Federation of Labor passed a resolution accusing the Springfield School Board of discharging nineteen members of BSEIU Local 15 because of their union activities, and stating that this action was "not in keeping with the [National Recovery Act] code, which the citizens and taxpayers of this district are subscribing to." Also, BSEIU leaders wrote the heads of agencies such as the WPA, and Harry Hopkins, Roosevelt's point man on public jobs projects, in an attempt to ensure that such work would not undercut government employees. BSEIU leaders also often asserted that the state should be the "model employer," or at least not lag behind private business. Owen Cunningham of Local 113 began a pamphlet for the University of Minnesota Board of Regents by quoting Governor Elmer Benson: "The state itself is the largest single employer and should set an example for paying living wages." Cunningham added that improved wages, conditions, and collective bargaining were "necessary steps being taken by industrial leaders" and it was "unthinkable that an enlightened institution . . . such as the University of Minnesota should lag behind in these respects."[28]

The BSEIU did periodically call for labor laws to cover public employees. In 1933 the CFL endorsed a Code of Fair Standards for Public Schools that specified maximum hours and provided the right to organize. In 1934 David suggested that Local 21 in LaCrosse, Wisconsin, lobby for an eight-hour day using the same rationales that motivated the hours rules in the National Recovery Act and ultimately the FLSA: a fifty-hour week "makes a long work day," and shorter hours would spread employment. In 1937, as the FLSA was moving toward passage, Local 143 in Cleveland promoted a bill that would have set the standard workweek for public hospital employees at forty-eight hours. In 1940 McFetridge told Local 119 at the University of Illinois that he would lobby the state legislature for overtime rules. That same year, Local 50 in Saint Louis called for state labor laws to cover government workers.[29]

But lobbying for such laws typically failed, and public workers increasingly resented their lack of legal rights. In San Antonio in 1938 W. K. Jones bemoaned the fact that members of Local 84 were not protected by "any law that protects other classes of employees." That same year, leaders of Local 173 in Pittsburgh condemned their school board for using "strong pressure" to coerce members to leave the local and join a company union. "Some were threatened, some were promised a promotion." This would have been an unfair labor practice under the NLRA, and a private sector union might have gone on strike. But as school employees, "we cannot use certain methods that are available to other locals." In 1940 the secretary of Local 140 in Portland, Oregon, conceded that "the problem of organizing and retaining in membership public employees is much different from that of private employment," because government workers could not strike or picket, and the law would not permit a closed shop. E. W. Eubanks, head of Local 119 at the University of Illinois, asked David the central question: "May organized state employees really accomplish whatsoever the union program permits?"[30]

The absence of legal rights could lead to a sense of futility and bitterness. In 1940 McFetridge sent a standard set of organizing materials to Local 17, public park employees in Milwaukee. The secretary of Local 17 responded that "our Local believes such [materials] should be displayed wherever possible." But because "we as Civil Service Employees could not post them in

School, Parks, or other buildings under the jurisdiction of our Local Governmental Units," the materials were "of no use to our members." Eubanks of Local 119 and other BSEIU officials were disappointed that unions could not compel public employers to recognize a closed shop. In 1940 Eubanks opined that without a closed shop, public workers could not effectively organize. "If the state will not recognize the priority of labor then unionism for civil service employees is futile." Similarly, Local 50 leader T. J. Dwyer wrote David in 1938 that although a majority of janitors in Saint Louis had joined the local, the few holdouts had created a free-rider problem: janitors who did not pay dues would receive benefits that the union had won. In a moment of frustration in 1937, Joe Lynch, an officer of Local 66 in San Francisco, even told David that there was no reason for a public employee to belong to a union. "Their salaries are fixed by Charter. . . . The only reason that some belong is that they are labor conscious."[31]

David's sharp rejoinder showed his commitment to public sector organizing. Public workers throughout the country in the BSEIU had made "great progress," through their own efforts and through working with other AFL unions, he insisted, especially "when the Budget time comes." Referring to Chicago, David added, "I personally have handled one of these Locals dealing with Budgets for the past 18 years and if it had not been for the members of my Local being in the Trade Union Movement, they would not have received ½ of what they have today." David was adamant that labor helped public employees. "I really know the workings of the Civil Service Locals. . . . Where there is no Local, you do not find any politician being so willing to grant the employees of the city increases." He encouraged Local 66 to organize "all city employees . . . whatever occupations. . . . Everybody all over the country is clamoring for organization. . . . Do not forget that your wages are judged by the lowest one on any payroll."[32]

Still, David himself experienced considerable frustration during times when the union had no political leverage, and he often lamented that public sector unions were worse off than private sector unions. In 1939 he cautioned leaders of Local 147, at Western Illinois State Teachers' College in Macomb, that public workers "cannot make the progress as if you were working for industrial or Real Estate Boards. . . . It takes longer to secure what you are after from the politicians than [from] employers of other sources." The next year he had to tell Local 147 that little could be done for its members because a new, unfriendly administration was in power. Their situation was "very difficult to handle" because they were "dealing with politicians." Leaders of the BSEIU had tried a number of approaches: pushing for civil service coverage, introducing bills in the legislature, and meeting with the president of the state civil service commission. Nothing had worked. Similarly, in 1939 David wrote Local 119 at the University of Illinois that "it is not so easy to deal with politicians as it is with an industrial firm." Politicians offered "plenty of talk . . . when it comes to better wages and conditions for those employed by the State," but then "claim that they don't have the money." David told Local 119 that it was "a very unfortunate thing that dealing with a State, the employees have to go through so much red tape to secure any benefit, which is very discouraging to the members." Indeed, "No one knows better than I do after 18 long years of dealing with officials of cities, counties and States . . . that it is hard to maintain an organization and you can not blame the members for becoming discouraged." David tried to end on an upbeat note: "Our International is in this fight and we are going to assist you wherever we can."[33]

In the absence of formal legal rights, this assistance took several forms. First, BSEIU locals, like other public sector unions, often achieved "informal" agreements with employers. These agreements were typically unwritten, unofficial, or not formally bilateral, and yet employers would honor them. For example, BSEIU International vice-president William Cooper explained that his local in Milwaukee did "not have a signed agreement with the Board of Education . . . [but] we are recognized as the bargaining agency for the employees in all matters pertaining to wages, hours and working conditions." In Milwaukee, as in most jurisdictions, it was illegal "to have a signed agreement with the Board of Education or any subdivision of our government." Yet the union had "never found it necessary to have a signed agreement. We have made our working conditions and wage increases by dealing with the elected bodies, supporting the favorable members and bodies at election time and doing our best to defeat those who oppose us."[34]

Employers did abide by informal agreements, and such arrangements genuinely helped BSEIU members. David regularly instructed locals that school boards rarely signed contracts (typically only where labor had a majority on the school board). More frequently, agreements about pay scales and conditions "are verbal and the School Board lives up to the agreement." The strategy was to "give the School Board the agreement with your demands"; the board could then "agree to recognize your Union and pay your demands without any signatures." The same was true for other public employers. "All State and County Hospitals are under verbal agreements," said David, because "in various States, Public Officials cannot sign a contract with the labor movement." Still, hospitals "do agree to live up to the provisions" in verbal contracts. Pursuant to one such agreement, BSEIU members in a county hospital in Chicago earned from $125 to $180 per month, worked an eight-hour day, and had two weeks of paid vacation and fifteen days of paid sick leave. These terms were superior to "the old conditions of a 12 hour day and some $50 to $55 per month." Notably, "every year the union has been able to increase their wages and reduce their hours." David even advised the leaders of Local 51, in the Cheyenne, Wyoming, schools, that they could try to seek an informal agreement providing for the closed shop. "If you appoint a committee from your union, and have a conference with some of your School Board members . . . you can work out a system," albeit not a signed agreement, "that they must all belong to the union."[35] Local 55, representing school employees in Cedar Rapids, Iowa, obtained a "Working Agreement" in 1938 that granted two weeks of paid vacation, ten days of sick leave, and improvements in promotions, pay, and seniority. Local 84 in San Antonio entered into an agreement providing for year-round work with fifteen days of paid vacation and higher wages. University of Illinois employees achieved an agreement that featured a raise to sixty cents per hour for a forty-eight-hour week, with premium rates for overtime and holidays. Local 63 in Minneapolis reduced the hours of work. Local 60, Cook County employees, won raises, standardized pay rates, seniority rights, and improved sick leave and vacations.[36]

The agreement that made the union most proud was the one that covered Locals 7 and 46, the janitors and janitresses in the Chicago schools. This agreement was in the form of unilateral rules from the employer, but it clearly reflected union input. Because of the BSEIU's political clout and complete organization of the workforce, the board of education—excepting in some of the most difficult periods of the Depression, as described earlier—complied with what was in fact a quite generous pact with the union. Achieved in 1928, the agreement's original terms provided for two to three weeks of vacation, a grievance system, and civil service rules for hiring, leave, and seniority. In 1928 pay was $140 per month for janitors and $125 for janitresses. The workweek was forty-four hours, with overtime rates for additional time. In 1938 janitors received $150 per month and janitresses $125. By that time the union had also won an eight-hour day, fifteen days of sick leave, a closed shop, and a pension fund. Given the financial travails of the Chicago schools, this was an amazing accomplishment.[37]

Related techniques were used elsewhere, providing good illustrations of how informal agreements were achieved and how public sector labor relations often functioned. In April 1939 the leaders of Local 51 in Cheyenne sent a draft contract to David. The draft had a number of ambitious provisions, including higher salaries, increased leave, arbitration, a closed shop, strict seniority rules, two weeks' notice for most discharges, and a bar on working more than fifty-two hours or all seven days in a week. David first noted that the school superintendent had "questioned the constitutionality of signing a contract." To get around this common legal obstacle, he noted that most public sector BSEIU locals "just agree to a verbal contract." Local 51 should "agree with your School Board on the contract and leave them a copy and you keep a copy." In Chicago "we have no contracts signed with either City or Board of Education, but we agree verbally and leave a copy of the contract" with the employer. Using this tactic, the BSEIU had been "very successful throughout the country. . . . You can do likewise." Significantly, David added that "you will not have any trouble even if the contract is not signed," in part because "you have two labor men on your Board." David was right. That fall Local 51 sent a revised agreement to school officials, who recommended its endorsement. The chair of the school board, a member of the Typographers Union, helped convince the board to abide by the agreement.[38]

Similarly, in 1935 Local 15 in Springfield, Illinois, sent David a draft written contract that called for various rights and improvements. David again replied that "most of our agreements are verbal." The local should meet with the local central labor council to draft an agreement ("make it as simple as you possibly can") and then "present it to the School Board." Local 124, school janitors in Welch, West Virginia, won pay increases and dues check-off after giving to the school board a contract that began: "We the janitors in McDowell County Schools do hereby present this Contract . . . with all due respect." Local 183 in La Salle and Peru, Illinois, actually preferred a verbal agreement. After winning a 10 percent raise for janitors in 1939, Local 183 leader J. E. Flannery crowed that he had "partially whipped" into shape "the biggest school board in our Tri-Cities . . . made up of executives of the Chamber of Commerce and also manufacturers." The board had actually offered to sign a written contract, but Flannery felt that the members preferred an oral "mutual agreement," because they feared a legal challenge to the board's authority to execute a formal, written contract.[39]

In this and other strategies, the BSEIU was conscious of the unique political and institutional constraints of public employment. In 1938 David advised Local 151 in Milwaukee to "take it easy and establish the Wage Scale gradually" because "School Boards have only so much money." If the local could get increases every year, it would ultimately attain a good wage scale. But "dealing with a School Board is different than a Commercial House; . . . there has been a great loss in taxes in the past few years." David also frequently stressed the importance of public relations in the political milieu in which government workers existed. The La Salle–Peru local was successful "because they have the public with them, and that is a big point with a Public Employee, to have the Public support them."[40]

Indeed, the BSEIU's political strategies often depended heavily on public opinion. Thus, BSEIU leaders equated unionism and union goals with the public good. David told Local 151 to be a "benefit to the Community. . . . Being Public Employees, you must have the Public's support." To the Des

Moines School Board, David urged that paying a living wage would be a "great help to the Community." The constitution and bylaws of Local 74 in New York City stated that the purposes of the union included bettering the conditions of school children. Local 123 in Hammond, Indiana, issued a statement proclaiming that "in our hands lies the health, which means life to every child in school." It added more ominously that if poor pay and conditions continued, "we will let our responsibilities leak from our minds and find ourselves looking forward only to meeting the paymaster," and concluded that it would be "a sacrilegious, un-American, and criminal act for anyone to neglect the protection of child life and property." Local 19 in Chicago cautioned that abolishing forty-nine bath attendant positions hurt not just the employees, but also the health of children. "Family welfare" was "endangered jointly with the industrial welfare of the dismissed public servants." The job cuts prevented attention to the "needs of the numerous children who we are now unable to care for during the shortened day." Such care was necessary "to maintain healthful and sanitary conditions for both children and school." Some unionists spoke of the advantages of democratic accountability in government services. The CFL demanded that workers in the Cook County Psychopathic Hospital be returned to civil service status, because it was detrimental to the public to give the powers of a county board "to a private Agency over which no public control is exercised."[41]

W. K. Jones of Local 84 in San Antonio was always conscious of public relations. One of his letters to the *San Antonio Dispatch* concluded that "the schools belong to the children, who deserve the best of everything." Schools were "the foundation upon which the future of America is built." Therefore, Jones reasoned, those entrusted with these institutions should receive pensions, sick leave, vacations, regular hours, and evening pay. The local sought to work for the good of the children and parents, he continued. Even when advocating for a closed shop, Jones reassured the community that his local would "always be subordinate to courtesy and efficient service" and merely wanted to serve the schools in the best way possible. David in a letter to the San Antonio School Board added that unions meant "better service not only to the School Board, but also to the school children who are the first consideration in any one's mind." The BSEIU "at all times insists" that its members "give the best service to the school children."[42]

Despite its best efforts at wooing politicians and the public, however, the BSEIU often found itself frustrated by a central bane of public sector unions: political patronage. "Politics prevails in all these public jobs," Elizabeth Grady observed. Patronage "has hindered us to a great extent" in the city sanitarium, the president of Local 50 in Saint Louis confessed. "Attendants are given their jobs through the various Aldermen and Committeemen" who insisted on obedience to "ward organizations before Union-ism." David frequently denounced patronage systems.[43]

For example, Local 84 in San Antonio was relatively powerful, yet it still suffered from problems stemming from patronage. In the late 1930s Local 84 had staged a successful campaign to win improvements in pay, hours, and leave for its members at the county courthouse. The local had gathered thousands of signatures on petitions, and local leader W. K. Jones had writ-ten numerous letters to local newspapers to build public support. Also, Jones boasted of the local's electoral strength. The courthouse commission-ers "all come up for election next year, and if we unchain the wardogs on them, the result will be pitiful." In sum, Local 84 had "used the pressure system" on the commissioners "until they just about went haywire" and granted many of the local's demands. But Local 84 lost out when, in late 1940, the county sheriff successfully claimed jurisdiction over courthouse employees, then fired five BSEIU members and replaced them with his friends. Jones complained bitterly about being under the thumb of politi-cians. Courthouse employees were "about par with the subjects of Hitler and Mussolini."[44]

David sympathized. Such dismissals "happen wherever there are politi-cians involved." The "best politician" was "a dead one." David could only suggest that Jones try to make the union's enemies look bad in the eyes of the public and show that the union "has tried to up-lift the down-trodden." David had summed up the problem for many public employees in earlier correspondence with Jones: "If one party is in power they want their friends taken care of in the city jobs, and if the other party gets in power, they want their friends taken care of. In that kind of situation the union is always in the middle and cannot move."[45]

Partly because of such problems, another major goal for BSEIU locals was gaining coverage under or strengthening civil service laws, which typi-cally provided at least some minimal merit protections. In Chicago until 1928 school engineers hired janitors as independent contractors, under what was called the "indirect system." Under pressure from the BSEIU, the system was changed to the "direct" method, whereby the board of educa-tion directly hired janitors as civil service employees. The BSEIU then orga-nized all the janitors and janitresses in the Chicago schools. Despite contin-uing machine politics in Chicago, janitors benefited from civil service: a member of Local 46 wrote that because of civil service coverage, "we are no longer compelled to pay tribute to some politician to hold our jobs." In 1938 Local 74 in New York City, representing 2,500 employees in schools and public libraries, lobbied successfully for some of its members to be placed in the civil service system without having to take an examination. Then in 1939 Local 74 helped push through amendments to civil service rules that improved sick leave, pensions, and job security. Local 66 in San Francisco, which by 1936 had almost 500 members working in public buildings, won revised civil service regulations that improved pay, hours, and leave. Local 140 in Portland gained civil service coverage for its members in the late 1930s. The BSEIU also assisted its members by explaining relevant civil service rules and regulations. Local 46 in Chicago distributed a pamphlet describing civil service examinations, eligible lists, the requirement of cause for discharge, and the related hearing rights. The pamphlet also guided members through the separate laws governing pensions and workers' compensation for public employees.[46]

Across the country the BSEIU fought for civil service coverage and promised its members that it would maintain "close scrutiny" on all such legislation. Nonetheless, many of the union's efforts to gain inclusion failed. Local 21 in LaCrosse, Wisconsin, tried unsuccessfully to revise civil service rules to include school employees in 1937. Even in Illinois, where the BSEIU was strongest, the union could not convince the state legislature to extend the state civil service law to cover employees of schools in smaller cities. In 1939 Local 15 in Springfield and the BSEIU International unsuccessfully backed a bill that would have put service employees of school districts in cities with populations between 50,000 and 500,000 under civil service rules.

Further, civil service laws often delivered much less than they seemed to promise. For example, a 1935 study of the civil service focusing on Chicago and Cook County found that "Spoils Politics has ham-strung the merit system." Key flaws included "numerous unjustifiable exemptions" of positions from the system, political control of civil service commissioners, a hearing procedure that offered "no guarantee against unjustifiable removance, and use of "temporary appointments" for political purposes. Notably, civil service laws excluded employees of Chicago's powerful sanitary district and municipal courts, as well as many Cook County workers. Indeed, in Cook County "temporary" hires, who were outside civil service coverage, constituted more than 70 percent of all workers. Also, while applicable laws provided that employees could be removed only for cause, the only review outside the employing agency was that of the Civil Service Commission, and it could reverse a decision only if it found political, racial, or religious discrimination.[47]

The BSEIU adapted its strategies regarding civil service to local circumstances. Locals in New York City and Milwaukee used litigation in opposite but equally effective ways to address the exclusion of their members. In both cities the schools used the "indirect system," paying a chief custodian or engineer a lump sum to employ janitors. The janitor was then considered an employee of the engineer or an independent contractor. Local 74 in New

York agreed that its members in the schools were private employees under this system, and these employees then successfully asserted their rights as private sector workers to organize and bargain with their employers, the engineers (who themselves were members of Operating Engineers Local 891). Conversely, Local 17 in Milwaukee fought for civil service protections. The local school board considered the approximately 100 members of Local 17 to be independent contractors, excluded from both the NLRA and civil service. In 1938 Local 17 brought suit over this issue. The union convinced both the Milwaukee Circuit Court and the Wisconsin Supreme Court that the school board was the employer of the janitors, because of the extensive control that the board exercised over the janitors' work. As school employees, the members of Local 17 were covered by civil service protections.[48]

Where civil service rules were in place, the BSEIU took advantage of whatever hearing procedures the rules contained to represent the union members, using the hearings as surrogates for the grievance arbitrations that were becoming more common in the private sector. McFetridge defended members of Local 11 in Cicero in two hearings. One involved a boiler-room operator whom the North Berwyn School Board fired in 1934 for drinking and sleeping on the job. The union objected that the man had been given no prior warnings or chance to defend himself before being fired. The employer argued that drunkenness justified immediate discharge. McFetridge declared that the local's purpose was to ensure that even someone so accused be granted a hearing. The employer agreed to notify the union in advance in future cases. The second case involved a layoff. Local 11 argued that the work should have been divided among the existing staff, and the employer stated that it would give all laid-off workers priority in rehiring.[49]

Thus, the BSEIU used a wide variety of political and related strategies and interacted with public officials on many levels. In the late 1930s Local 138, representing school janitors and other municipal employees in La Salle and Peru, made presentations at school board meetings, supported candidates in elections for the school board and superintendent of schools, drafted and lobbied for a pension law for school janitors, urged the mayor of La Salle to settle a dispute over hiring union janitors, and helped to elect a "friendly Sheriff" in whose office some members of Local 138 worked. In Minneapolis in the mid-1930s, Local 113 successfully championed a new superintendent of buildings who was more favorable to the union, helped get "five new liberal Regents" appointed to the University of Minnesota Board of Regents, brought a suit that produced a millage increase for the schools, won increased pay for its members, defeated a plan by the taxpayers' association to cut salaries, and settled various grievances. As a result of these victories, membership in the local grew from 1,000 to 1,400.[50]

But all of these tactics were often not enough, especially in the face of the budget crises of the 1930s. Jones claimed that Local 84 had "a crack team" that could "hold the balance of power in a close political contest." Perhaps because of this, James Hollers, president of the San Antonio School Board, declared that he had "always been sympathetic" to labor and found Local 84 to be "very reasonable." Yet when David and Jones tried to discuss wages, Hollers and other board members demurred, citing a lack of funds. David tried to be diplomatic. "There is no one in the country that realizes what a School Board member is up against any more than I do." Surely, David continued, board members "would like to have all employees telling the people of San Antonio how fair your School Board has been." The answer was still no. Board member Leo Brewer replied, "I am thoroughly in sympathy with all that you have to say. I realize that the employees doing janitorial service in the schools are not well paid. However . . . our Board does not have authority to increase taxes."[51]

Locals of the BSEIU were often helpless in the face of such responses. In 1936 Local 42 in Morgantown, West Virginia, sent a committee with "papers carefully compiled" proposing modest raises, overtime pay, improved leave, safer equipment, and work for the full year to a meeting of the Morgantown School Board. Local president L. W. Lynch asked David to write to the board, anticipating the "old excuse for not paying decent wages . . . they would like to pay us more" but "they just did not have it." Typically, David advised Lynch that the local "must have the support of the Public." David then wrote to the board and the school supervisor, arguing that the local's requests were "absolutely fair" and that the current scale was "barely giving them an existence." In response, he was told that the school system had lost $83,000 in revenue in the past year and that it was cutting teachers' salaries while merely not increasing those of janitors. Lynch remained unsatisfied, complaining that the union was always "handed the same old answer, of no money. . . . We are sick and tired of being the goat."[52]

The union's defeats sometimes tested the patience of their members with the constraints of the public sector. Of course, during the Depression money problems were an issue in the private sector too, and private sector employers often frustrated their unions by refusing to bargain or to acknowledge their rights under the NLRA. But private sector employees could strike, and this tactic was anathema to the BSEIU public sector locals. This rejection of the strike weapon was consistent with the position of both the AFL and the CIO, even in the militant 1930s. Strikes by government workers were illegal, unpopular, and usually unsuccessful. While private sector locals in the BSEIU used strikes effectively, the BSEIU feared that a strike by any of its public sector locals would be a public relations disaster that would undo all they had tried to accomplish for school and other government employees everywhere. Thus, for example, the constitution of Local 74 in New York City not only barred strikes but also barred members from even advocating strikes by public workers.[53]

The BSEIU's policy did not stop government employers from raising the specter of strikes to combat unionization of school janitors. The Centralia, Illinois, school board was sufficiently alarmed by BSEIU organizing that it wrote to AFL president William Green "to inquire if there is any way to avoid this and thus protect our schools from any sympathetic strike that might occur." Schools were unlike private corporations: "no profit is sought, no additional expenses can be shifted to buyers. . . . Every penny possible is needed . . . to provide educational facilities for the children." Did the AFL "endorse labor organizations where the compensation comes from money furnished by tax payers"? Green answered that the BSEIU had jurisdiction over public school janitors and that the AFL included many public sector unions and other unions who had members in government employment. But, he added, it "is clearly understood" that public employees "shall not become involved in strikes."[54]

Some public sector locals did suggest strikes, but the national leadership vetoed the idea, again demonstrating how constrained public sector unions were in these "turbulent years" of labor militancy. L. W. Lynch of Local 42 in Morgantown wrote to BSEIU president Horan in 1936, promising that if the local struck, "we can tie this County up in a knot." Horan rejected the idea. In 1938 David told leaders of Local 50 in Saint Louis not to strike a hospital, out of concern for public relations. In October 1940 David directed Local 184 in Aurora, Illinois, not to strike without the approval of the BSEIU International, and the strike never occurred.[55]

David took a hard line when public school employees in Local 113 in Minneapolis passed a strike resolution in 1937. Wages had been cut dramatically, the employees said, and the school board was both ignoring sources of revenue and refusing to work with the union. Local leader Owen Cunningham wrote David confidentially, arguing that, given the state of the law, "it would be suicidal to call a strike." In reply, David stressed that the BSEIU public school locals in Chicago had never struck, even after receiving no pay for over a year. Rather, they "worked in harmony with the School Board in trying to secure money for their wages." McFetridge had endured hard times but come away with a strong local; he had refused to take "radical action" and had emerged "victorious." Such an approach should be used in Minneapolis, in part because of the law prohibiting strikes in the public sector.

Further, David was, as always, mindful of public opinion and politics. "It is very delicate when you tie up the School children from going to school, the Public is bound to be rebellious against your Local." It would be "far better to get out pamphlets or have Public Meetings notifying the Public that the Board has the power of getting in money, but does not exercise this power." Then the local should cooperate with the board and work for increased funding. A strike would alienate the public and "jeopardize the standing" of public employees. Perhaps recalling the Boston strike, David added, "if you receive one defeat no matter what city it comes from, you will practically be licked all over the country."[56]

David stopped the move toward a strike. He instructed Local 113 that the BSEIU International could not consider approving a strike unless the local took a specific strike vote. The situation was one "that has never before confronted our International." David also warned that "it is easy to call a strike and very hard to settle one," especially in the public sector. "Every effort must be made to settle this dispute before a strike is called and after a strike vote is taken you must forward the results to our International office to get the sanction before a strike is called." David left no doubt where he stood: the actions of Local 113 were threatening to destroy both it and other BSEIU public sector locals. "There is too much at stake, not only for Minneapolis, but our entire membership of Civil Service Employees." David sent a national vice-president of the union to the city to settle the matter, and the strike never materialized. A few months later, in February 1938, when members of Local 113 in Minneapolis hospitals threatened to strike, pressure came from even higher in the labor movement. The mayor of Minneapolis called Green to object, Green told BSEIU president Scalise that these employees should not strike, and Scalise then wrote Cunningham that "under no circumstances are you to call a strike in Hospitals without the sanction of the International Union."[57]

This policy against strikes could leave locals with comparatively few options, as the school janitors in Minneapolis discovered again two years later. By this time Local 63 had split from Local 113, with Local 63 representing only school employees. In March 1939 Local 63, undeterred by past actions of the BSEIU International, told David that it had taken a strike vote that had carried 285–72, and that it was calling for an impartial arbitration board to hear the local's wage demands. David's pointed reply again emphasized public relations. Because "the Public is vitally interested in the schools . . . every effort must be made before a strike is called for a satisfactory adjustment." David acknowledged the feelings of the workers, but added, "I also realize what a strike would mean for the people of your city and the interest the Public has . . . which must always be taken into consideration before any drastic action is taken." David urged the Local to make every effort to get a peaceful settlement, "so that you will have the Public on your side." The controversy ended with a whimper that emphasized the legal and practical limitations of the era. The school board refused to arbitrate, pursuant to an opinion from the city attorney that arbitration would constitute an impermissible delegation of the board's powers. The city did agree to study the school budget in light of the local's concerns, and the local, given little choice, accepted this resolution.[58]

In very rare cases, BSEIU public sector locals did strike, but again the union turned to politics for settlements. Local 39, Cook County school employees, was able to make the Sterling J. Morton School in Cicero arbitrate the discharge of four union activists fired for "inefficiency" in November 1936. After the firings the employer refused to meet with the local, so its twenty-seven members struck for nearly three weeks in January 1937. The strikers wanted the school board to recognize the union, use hearings in discipline cases, and give the union a formal role in budget preparations. The local central labor union supported the strikers. The matter grew increasingly contentious: delivery of coal to the school ceased when union drivers refused to drive through picket lines, and a group of students hung the school superintendent in effigy. McFetridge tried to negotiate a settlement, as did local businessmen, politicians, and clergy, but they were rebuffed. Always conscious of public opinion, the BSEIU was happy to see the headline "Mediation . . . Refused by Board as It Remains Obstinate" in a local paper. Also, the local tried to be reassuring. "We will protect at all hazards the health and well being of each pupil," it proclaimed. "We will see that the School property is protected. Our position is now as always to discuss this situation and settle it amicably."

McFetridge and David finally persuaded Peter Angsten, chairman of the Illinois Industrial Commission, to intervene. David stressed that the BSEIU wished to settle the matter so that "education may be continued without possible injury or harm to anyone." Angsten helped work out a settlement in late January, after a week of negotiations. The agreement provided for a public hearing for the men discharged and for similar procedures in future cases. David and Horan declared that this outcome was a victory for the principle of public hearings in government employment, and again argued that this helped protect the schools and children. The union continued this battle in the political arena. In 1939 labor helped elect two new, more friendly members to the school board. "It has been a long struggle," the *Chicago Federation News* announced, but the "final result is worth the effort expended."[59]

But strikes could also be disasters, as Local 151 in Ottawa, Illinois, discovered. In late June 1937 the Ottawa School Board refused to deal in any way with Local 151 and barred BSEIU regional representative James Flannery of Local 138 from school board meetings. On June 30 Michael Kelly Jr., president of Local 151, asked David to sanction a strike. David said that he would send a national union vice-president to the city to negotiate. Tensions mounted as the school board hired nonunion janitors. By the end of 1937, BSEIU members had walked out twice in an attempt to gain, among other things, a closed shop. The board asserted that, as a public body, it was "without power to compel employees to affiliate" with Local 151. Going much further, however, the board refused to deal with the union in any way. It would not meet with Flannery because he came from outside the school district, and "the Board is not engaged in any controversy with any organization." The local central labor council and Local 151 then refused to meet with the board without Flannery.

Crucially, the Ottawa School Board won the battle for public opinion. Newspapers claimed that labor had ordered a strike "to force unionization of the institution's five janitors." When the labor council insisted that other unions would refuse to work with nonunion labor, the president of the school board announced that because five janitors would not join the BSEIU, the school cafeteria would have to close, since labor was holding up the delivery of food, and sports and physical education would be discontinued because the dispute had disrupted deliveries of coal necessary to heat water. Labor responded by placing the school system on the "unfair" list, but the strike was a complete defeat, and Local 151 was destroyed.[60]

Public sector locals in the BSEIU, therefore, were left mostly with various political strategies. Without the rights that private sector labor enjoyed, these unions continued to exist, represent their members, and even grow. The methods BSEIU locals employed—especially those resulting in informal "agreements" with public employers—were fairly standard for all public sector unions in this period and beyond. For example, public employees in Wisconsin in 1934 had no bargaining rights. Nonetheless, Arnold Zander, the future president of AFSCME, drafted a proposed contract for the state auto licensing division that set minimum wages, seniority rights, and rights for union stewards and also required employer consultations with the union regarding discipline. No contract was ever signed, but the employer did bargain until an agreement was reached that satisfied all parties. In 1938 AFSCME's executive board boasted that some of its locals had "negotiat[ed] excellent agreements with city officials and governing boards." The *Chicago Federation News* in 1939 could realistically state that Mayor Kelly and the Chicago Board of Education had recognized the powerful AFT local as the "bargaining agency" for teachers in Chicago.[61]

Indeed, through the 1930s all types of public sector unions sought working arrangements that were either unwritten or written and officially unilateral, but forged with union input. Written agreements were set out in memos, letters, or executive statements or incorporated into the employing agency's regulations or civil service rules. Whatever their form, these pacts could be effective. Operating Engineers Local 142 stated in 1934 that "negotiations" between it and the Chicago Board of Education had produced an agreement that the board had "lived up to." The New York Emergency Relief Bureau in 1935 negotiated a grievance procedure with its unionized employees. The first draft was signed by both sides, but after city officials questioned the legality of a bilateral agreement, it was changed to a unilateral announcement without and alteration in content. Such practices existed in federal employment as well, notably in the Tennessee Valley Authority (written agreements that were unilateral in form but were the product of negotiation) and the U.S. Post Office (negotiated oral agreements).[62] These patterns of informal bargaining would increase in scope in the 1940s and 1950s, creating a reality on the ground that was a prerequisite to gaining formal bargaining rights.

While the public sector workers in the BSEIU took part in few dramatic or sensational events, their story shows how labor relations in the government actually functioned on a daily basis. Legal and institutional restrictions channeled the energies of these locals into many forms of fairly quiet political action. In some ways, the mixed results they achieved could be seen as merely a muted counterpoint to the heady victories of private sector labor in this era. In other ways, the willingness of the members of public sector unions such as the BSEIU to continue the struggle despite the limitations on their activities is a tribute to the desire of workers generally to improve their lives through organization. Their efforts are no less admirable because of the restrictions circumstances forced upon them. "Citizens . . . seldom if ever give a thought to the humbler public service employee," a Chicago school janitor and BSEIU member wrote in 1934. But "when the history of this trying period is truthfully written, the careful historian will give honorable mention to the 'forgotten men' of our school janitorial force."[63]

5

The New York City TWU in the Early 1940s

Are organized workers to be unorganized merely because they work
for the government?
PHILIP MURRAY, CIO president (1941)

"It is against the law" is merely another way of saying to workers:
take what you can get and shut up.
Transport Workers Union, CIO, *Transport Bulletin* (1940)

On February 9, 1943, more than 20,000 people crammed into Madison
Square Garden at a rally to support the powerful, leftist Transport Workers
Union, CIO (TWU). Zero Mostel and others provided entertainment. The
event was impressive but not unprecedented. For four years the TWU had
mobilized its members, other unions, and sympathizers in a determined and
creative political and public relations campaign. The goals of the campaign,
however, were more prosaic: the TWU simply wanted the same collective
bargaining, union security, and related rights that it had enjoyed in the late
1930s. It had lost these rights for one reason only. In 1940 the city of New
York took control of two major subway lines that previously had been privately owned. In a stroke, this move converted 26,000 private sector workers covered by the NLRA into public employees excluded from state and national labor statutes, and thus deprived them of union rights that they had
once enjoyed.

The ensuing battle demonstrated how a large, militant CIO union dealt
with the restrictions placed on public sector unions. In some ways, the
TWU was quite different from the BSEIU, the Seattle AFT, and the Boston
police. TWU Local 100 was an established union representing the majority
of the approximately 32,000 employees of the New York City Transit System.[1] Nor did the TWU face a bar on affiliation with labor, although the
employer, the New York City Board of Transportation, wanted little to do

with unions. But the city did impose on the TWU the legal disabilities of public sector labor, most significantly refusing to bargain collectively or to enforce union security, and the TWU was forced into a lengthy battle in legal and political arenas to try to regain these rights. Politically, it did not rely on elections, as the Seattle AFT had, or on back-room deals in the style of the BSEIU. Rather, it used high-visibility coalitions, publicity, and mass demonstrations. This strategy, in conjunction with the desire for labor peace during the war, and evolving attitudes toward public sector unions in some circles, brought real successes. At the same time, the TWU was constantly forced into a debate on the law that it could not win. Indeed, the CIO as a whole, despite its more radical tactics in the private sector, wound up adopting the same approach for public sector unions that the AFL did. Yet while Local 100 never secured the formal institutional rights it had in the 1930s, it won considerable maneuvering room within legal restrictions, emerging as one of the strongest locals of municipal workers in the country.

The Congress of Industrial Organizations was expelled from the AFL in 1937. The CIO had organized along industrial, rather than craft, lines, and it espoused a more left-wing, inclusive, and combative vision of labor. In 1937 the CIO created two public sector unions to challenge two relatively new public sector unions in the AFL. First, the CIO formed the United Federal Workers (UFW) from rebel factions of AFGE. (AFGE had replaced NFFE as the AFL's generic federal sector union in the early 1930s.) Second, the CIO chartered the State, County, and Municipal Workers of America (SCMWA) to compete with AFSCME, which the AFL had chartered in 1936.[2] While the SCMWA and the UFW did not fit the image of the famous CIO unions in the mining, steel, and auto industries, the CIO supported them generously with money and staff time. These two CIO affiliates followed the trend of all public sector labor through World War II: federal sector unions remained fairly static, but unions of state and local government workers flourished. The SCMWA claimed 25,000 members in 1937 and 48,000 in 1946. In 1946 the SCMWA merged with the UFW (which was struggling with Communist influences and anticommunist attacks) and dissident AFT locals to form the United Public Workers of America (UPWA). The UPWA in the late 1940s claimed more than 100,000 members, but the CIO would expel it in 1949 for ties to the Communist party.[3]

The CIO unions had strong leftist credentials and a membership that, according to Robert Zieger, was "impatient with the hat-in-hand approach" of AFL public sector unions. Nonetheless, the CIO unions quickly found themselves facing the same problems and using many of the same strategies as their AFL counterparts. The UFW and the SCMWA generally barred strikes and picketing. John L. Lewis, president of the CIO, explained that the chief methods of public sector unionism should be "legislation and education." As to bargaining, the SCMWA used stronger rhetoric earlier than AFSCME, but AFSCME probably engaged in just as much actual bargaining in the same periods.[4]

As a result, the CIO often sounded much like the AFL on public sector matters. From 1938 to 1940 CIO conventions called for the expansion of civil service coverage advocating the "merit system" over the "spoils system." It made some references to collective bargaining, but a report from the UFW contained an approach identical with that of the AFL's BSEIU. The report explained that various types of "agreements" and "signed statements . . . serve the place of the contract that is used by an industrial union." The UFW also repeated the AFL platitude that government should be the "model employer." In 1939 Abraham Flaxer, head of the SCMWA, again championed "merit" and taking public employees "out of the political clubhouse." The 1940 CIO convention again backed the right to organize, but also supported expanding civil service rules. The UFW's program called for collective bargaining for certain federal agencies, but also for legislation to improve wages and conditions. By 1942 Flaxer, the most radical of the public sector leaders in the CIO, took positions identical with those taken at the time by AFSCME and the AFL. He called for collective bargaining rights for public employees, noting that "government workers join unions for the same reasons and with the same objectives that other workers join unions."[5]

Indeed, the SCMWA's platform in 1939 could have been adopted by the most conservative AFL public sector union. "An outstanding feature of the SCMWA program is the furtherance of civil service status and the merit system, which places it squarely in alliance with the good government forces everywhere." The union's other goals were the same as those of the AFL: just-cause dismissal, grievance machinery, fair civil service exams, and improved wage and hour rules. Notably, the SCMWA wanted statutes to establish all these rights. Achieving this objective required political action, and here the CIO union tried to distinguish its approach. The SCMWA advocated "vigorous participation in politics," not "behind-the-scenes ballplaying." Government workers in the CIO did engage in dynamic public demonstrations to support their goals. The SCMWA local in Detroit won pay increases of more than 34 percent for city workers after using radio addresses, mass meetings, leaflets, public hearings, and press advertisements.[6] Such tactics would reach their pinnacle with the TWU fight in New York.

City ownership of the New York subways was being debated even as the TWU was forming. Through the early 1930s the IRT and BMT lines were privately owned, and the ISS line was a public enterprise. This state of affairs was inefficient and unprofitable, and the private lines were going bankrupt. Beginning in the mid-1930s plans for "unification" under city ownership were proposed. By 1939 the city was prepared to buy the IRT and BMT for $326 million. Meanwhile, the TWU had arisen as an alternative to weak company unions, an ineffective AFL local, and the unaffiliated Civil Service Forum (CSF). With significant help from the Communist party and Irish republican groups, the TWU was born in 1934. Founding members who would be longtime leaders included Mike Quill, Douglas Mac-Mahon, John Santo, and Austin Hogan. Quill was the most powerful. A Catholic, a veteran of the Irish civil war, and probably a Communist party member, he was a successful politician as well as unionist, repeatedly winning election to the New York Board of Alderman. Quill remained influential for decades; in 1964 he directed a TWU strike from a jail cell.[7]

The TWU became dominant on the major private sector transit lines, using aggressive tactics such as the sitdown strike. In December 1935 it had 900 members, mostly on the IRT. By 1937 it had signed contracts with the BMT and IRT that covered 30,000 workers. The agreements brought better pay, hours, and benefits and established the closed shop. In 1937 the TWU joined the CIO (previously, the TWU had been part of the International Association of Machinists, AFL) and became an International union. Local 100 in New York was the largest local. Also in 1937, Quill, now the international president, was elected as an alderman representing the Bronx. Up to the date of unification, the TWU continued to win improvements for its members. The 1939 contracts increased wages and benefits and strengthened the grievance machinery. The union expanded, sponsoring recreational activities, a credit union, a medical plan, and an education program. Unification, however, changed everything. Joshua Freeman, the leading historian of the TWU, explains that when the city took over the IRT and the BMT in June 1940, the "TWU was forced to become a pioneer in public sector unionism." This involved new and unfamiliar "legal, political, and economic problems."[8]

As early as 1935 the TWU had worried about the limited tactics available to public employees. While the union supported a bill to provide civil service coverage for IRT and BMT workers if public ownership became a reality, the TWU newspaper, the *Transport Bulletin,* added that "bills in themselves will not do the trick. They do not provide for higher wages. They do not stop lay-offs. Bills do not stamp out petty tyranny." Mere lobbying for laws, the paper sniffed, was the province of the rival CSF. At a rally later that year, Local 100 leader Austin Hogan argued that the "best of legislation has been riddled full of holes by the powerful banking and industrial interests" and that workers should rely on building the union. The TWU was also concerned about patronage, warning in 1935 that unification would mean loss of jobs and that politicians would award those that remained to their constituents. That same year, Local 100 sponsored a meeting that drew more than 1,000 people to hear the consequences of public ownership debated by labor leaders, politicians, representatives from the Communist party, and others.[9]

Before unification, the TWU cut its teeth on public sector issues in battles over the publicly owned ISS line. In 1936 the union unsuccessfully backed a bill that would have given collective bargaining rights to ISS workers. The employment of those workers therefore continued to be controlled by civil service rules and the New York City Board of Transportation. Ominously, the board early on demonstrated its hostility to the TWU. Two of the board's three members, John Delaney and Francis Sullivan, had ties to the AFL, and while the TWU was in the AFL, the board of transportation had allowed a representation election on the ISS. The TWU scored an impressive victory, but the board refused to bargain. The TWU held a large protest, threatened to strike, and asked Mayor Fiorello LaGuardia for help, but this produced no results. The union then helped pass seven bills in the state senate, four of which would have established collective bargaining for ISS employees and protected IRT and BMT workers in case of unification. But Mayor LaGuardia did not support the bills, and they were not enacted. In May 1937, shortly after joining the CIO, the TWU requested another election, and the board of transportation refused.[10]

The board's attitude was especially problematic because it had considerable independence and broad authority. Members served six-year terms, were appointed by the mayor, and could be removed only for cause. The board alone set the wages, hours, and working conditions of transit workers, except that appointments and promotions were subject to civil service rules and the mayor approved maximum and minimum pay rates. In the mid-1930s the board of aldermen tried to set some wages for ISS line workers, the board of transportation refused to comply, and a court upheld the latter's authority in this matter.[11]

The legal and political issues that would be central after unification began to play out in miniature in the ISS dispute. The TWU petitioned the state labor relations board for certification, the board of transportation refused even to send a representative to the state agency. Delaney, chair of the board of transportation, correctly noted that the state labor relations law excluded public employees. LaGuardia arranged a meeting between the TWU and Delaney, which produced nothing. The TWU tried the "proprietary function" argument, asserting that the city was running the ISS as a business, but in January 1938 the labor relations board ruled that the statutory language was clear: it had no jurisdiction over the public sector.[12] The TWU then asked LaGuardia to compel the board of transportation to recognize the union, but the mayor refused. In 1938 the TWU backed the

Schwartzwald-Crews bill, which would have given the labor relations board jurisdiction over the board of transportation. In this era of AFL rivalry, George Meany, then head of the state AFL, called Schwartzwald-Crews "unconstitutional." The bill did not pass.[13]

Meany's constitutional argument may have been, as the TWU sneered, the type of thing an employer would say, but it was not trivial. The New York state constitution provided that appointments and promotions in the civil service should "as far as practicable" be made through competitive examinations. This provision was arguably contrary to closed-shop provisions, which required union membership as a condition of being hired. Courts had construed this constitutional mandate strictly, striking down a law granting preferences in civil service promotions to war veterans and holding that the legislature could not constitutionally authorize hiring state police officers without competitive examinations. The TWU studied both decisions.[14]

With no meaningful institutional rights, the TWU faction on the ISS crumbled. Freeman states that most ISS workers "saw no point in belonging to a union which could neither bargain nor sign contracts," especially with civil service protections in place. The TWU was also leery of striking against a public employer. Unification now threatened to bring these problems to the IRT and BMT, where the bulk of the TWU's members lay.[15]

A commission had been appointed to promote unification as early as 1921, and in 1935 Austin Hogan predicted that "unification . . . in the near future is a certainty." The TWU never opposed unification in principle. Rather, it focused on winning favorable terms. From 1935 to 1939 the TWU unsuccessfully supported bills that would have provided, in case of city ownership, automatic civil service status, job retention rights, no loss of seniority, and collective bargaining rights for members of Local 100. As these efforts were failing, the November 1938 general election authorized a financing mechanism for city purchase of the private lines. That same month the TWU sponsored a resolution that the first national CIO convention passed, asking the city to assume existing union contracts and to accept collective bargaining after unification.[16]

The TWU continued to insist that civil service rules were insufficient. Workers also needed "union recognition. . . . The right of association is inalienable whether we work for a private employer or for a public employer." Much as other unions that called for bargaining rights had argued, the TWU noted that civil service rules did not address a variety of issues, from lighting to pensions and promotions. In 1939 the union released a report on civil service rules that stressed the many hurdles to obtaining jobs and the weak protections for those who held them. Applicants had to provide extensive personal information, take unfair physical, written, and oral tests, and subject themselves to investigations, the TWU claimed. Seniority meant little. The civil service grievance system was ineffective, and those who used it incurred the "disfavor" of supervisors, especially "if the employee displays aggressiveness and perseverance." Thus, "Anyone believing that civil service has overwhelming advantages is mistaken." It offered "no seniority . . . no security . . . no collective bargaining . . . no guarantee against discrimination and injustices." In sum, "when a person becomes a civil service employee, he not only gives his mind and body to the boss, he gives his soul as well."[17]

In early 1939 the TWU fought its first major political battle over unification, and once again the union encountered problematic distinctions made for government employment. Republican state senator Arthur Wicks submitted a bill that would have required all subway workers after unification to be appointed pursuant to civil service rules. The effect would have been to require employees of the IRT and BMT to reapply for the jobs they held at the time of unification; even if they were hired, they would lose seniority and pension rights. Also, civil service regulations allowed only citizens as workers, and this restriction could have cost thousands of TWU members their jobs. Further, the Wicks bill authorized the city to "dispense with any unnecessary positions" in its transit system. Supporting the bill were Meany and the state AFL, three major New York City newspapers, the state chamber of commerce, the New York Merchants' Association, and the CSF. Wicks demonstrated how "good government" rhetoric could be turned against unions in the public sector, particularly on the closed-shop issue. He stated that he was simply "for the merit system" and "opposed to any group, political or otherwise, controlling employment on all public enterprises." Less diplomatically, he also referred to the union as "a racket." In the same vein, George Harvey, president of the borough of Queens, wrote Herbert Lehman, the Democratic governor of New York, that the TWU was "only endeavoring to retain a highly lucrative racket."[18]

The TWU began an intensive political campaign against the Wicks bill. In January John L. Lewis asked to meet with LaGuardia to discuss it; Lewis also wrote an open letter proclaiming that the CIO "stands shoulder to shoulder" with the TWU. An impressively diverse list of allies joined the fray. By mid-February some 400 local unions (including 40 from the AFL) were opposing the bill, along with 200 church, fraternal, and civic groups, including the Knights of Columbus, United Italian Association, Deutscher-Arbeiter Klub, American Legion, Veterans of Foreign Wars, Jewish War Veterans, and League of Women Shoppers. The TWU sent a petition to LaGuardia with 50,000 signatures. On February 16 Wicks produced a modified bill, allowing waiver of civil service examinations for current IRT and BMT employees and providing that "necessary" workers would be retained.

Unsatisfied, the TWU demanded job guarantees, no citizenship requirement, and bargaining rights, and the state CIO formed a committee to fight
the bill. Hogan called the bill an "aberrant, insidious attack" on the rights
of labor. In early April, under pressure from the TWU, LaGuardia announced that he opposed the bill.[19]

Despite these efforts, a modified form of the bill became law. The state
legislature passed a revised version that did not mention bargaining, although it did make noncitizen workers eligible for employment if they declared that they would become citizens. In May the TWU lobbied Governor
Lehman to veto it. Making its position as politically attractive as possible,
the union claimed that collective bargaining would prevent strikes, which,
the union noted, had been too frequent in the days before the TWU. Bargaining was "the democratic way to secure peace between labor and management." Thousands of TWU members attended rallies and a parade down
Broadway on May 16 in support of the union's position. By May 23 the
TWU had helped send over 15,000 telegrams to Lehman, placed newspaper
ads, and distributed flyers urging a veto. Again, the TWU prevailed on the
mayor, and LaGuardia told Lehman that he should veto the bill. But at least
in part because LaGuardia would not promise more job protection than the
Wicks bill provided, Lehman signed the bill into law.[20]

With plans for unification becoming more concrete, the TWU's failure to
win statutory rights heightened its anxiety about the status of its existing
contracts for BMT and IRT workers. In June 1939 the city signed a contract
to buy the BMT for $175 million; two months later it agreed to purchase
the IRT for $151 million. The TWU's contracts with the BMT and IRT
were set to expire on June 30, 1941. The union argued that these contracts
should remain in force after unification and be applied to workers on the
ISS line, and that workers on the unified lines should be given collective bargaining rights.

Harry Sacher, attorney for the TWU, critiqued the city's purchase agreements, emphasizing the lack of institutional rights for labor and the need
for the city to assume the collective bargaining contracts. Sacher noted disapprovingly that although the agreements provided that the city would assume many existing contracts (for example, for construction, equipment,
and maintenance), there was "not a word" about labor contracts. The
TWU insisted it would maintain its contracts. But in an apparent concession
to public sector rules, the union now advocated not the closed shop but the
union shop: requiring all employees to join the local after being hired.
Sacher also criticized the purchase agreements for adopting by reference the
Wicks bill provision that allowed the city to "dispense with unnecessary positions." Sacher urged the authorities to "give consideration to workers as
they do to the fellows who own the bonds and the stocks." Frustrated with

the legal regime in the public sector, he concluded: "I can't understand why, in the year 1939, labor still has to come around raising the roof off in order to get rights that they have already had." The city should "do at least as much by labor as [by] private industry."[21]

As unification neared, the restrictions on public sector unions became an increasingly pressing issue. LaGuardia announced that the city would take over the IRT and BMT on May 1, 1940. The TWU unsuccessfully tried to amend the Wicks law to provide for collective bargaining. Quill asked to meet with LaGuardia to discuss whether the city would assume existing contracts and bargain in the future, but the mayor did not respond until the TWU threatened to strike. LaGuardia's communications with Quill indicated that the legal climate was about to change significantly. Employment practices would have to conform to civil service laws, the mayor observed, and since civil service rules set out the exclusive qualifications for employment, the union shop was illegal. As to bargaining, LaGuardia specified that workers could "confer" with managers through representatives or individually, as part of the "right of petition," but no group would have any special role. LaGuardia also stressed that the right "to strike against the government is not and cannot be recognized." After adding that aliens would be barred from jobs and that he could make no assurances regarding layoffs, LaGuardia's conclusion that discontent "will be eliminated" when employees became covered by civil service could not have been reassuring.[22]

The union was furious with LaGuardia and frustrated with its new legal status. Quill asserted that the mayor was intent on "destroying" the TWU by imposing "a union-busting, company-union plan." Workers must have the right to bargain collectively, not merely to "petition" and "confer"; the same principles should apply to the government as to private industry. "We asked you for bread and you gave us a stone. Thus do you turn against labor—you who have always pretended to be a staunch friend of labor." Hogan complained that LaGuardia was defying "the fundamental rights of labor." An open letter from the union to the mayor protested that it was "almost incredible that you, who have been a leader in labor's uphill struggle for recognition of the right to bargain collectively," would take this stance. Revealingly, the letter added a technical argument from public sector labor law: the subways were a business, so the "proprietary function" distinction applied. Also, implicitly acknowledging the new context, the union claimed that the right to strike was "academic," because strikes could be avoided by collective bargaining.[23]

LaGuardia, a cosponsor of the Norris-LaGuardia Act of 1932, had indeed been an ally of labor. Yet he sharply distinguished the public sector, arguing that since government employees were protected by civil service rules, they should not be allowed to bargain, strike, or use the closed shop.

In fact, LaGuardia was precisely the type of antimachine politician who preferred civil service to union rights in the public sector. He was elected mayor in 1933, running against Tammany Hall. He insisted that good government came from the "merit system" of civil service, and did not want unions interfering with his authority. When city sanitation workers formed an SCMWA local in 1939, LaGuardia and the New York City sanitation commissioner, unconstrained by any legal requirement to recognize a union with majority support, ignored it and instead dealt with a weak AFSCME group (much to the consternation of Quill, who had helped organize the SCMWA local).[24] Beyond ideology, LaGuardia may simply have been less sympathetic to unions of "his" workers. "For many years, Mr. LaGuardia's boast has been that he is labor's friend," the TWU needled, "but that was before he was a great employer of labor." This label was accurate. Even before unification, the city of New York had over 100,000 employees.[25] Once again, state structure had placed the power to make the rules of public employment in the hands of the employers.

Still, the TWU held some political chips with LaGuardia, although the relationships were complex. The CIO had a large presence in the city and was a mainstay of the American Labor party (ALP). The ALP gave LaGuardia over one-third of his votes in his campaigns for second and third terms in 1937 and 1941. This constituency was crucial, as LaGuardia's 130,000-vote victory in 1941 was the smallest margin in a New York mayoral race since 1905. Quill was one of the ALP's eight vice-chairmen. Demonstrating the interlocking alliances, Quill ran for the board of aldermen in 1937, backed by the ALP and LaGuardia. At the same time, however, national politics played a role in the mayor's stance toward the TWU. Thomas Kessner's biography of LaGuardia explains that the mayor was interested in national office and was trying to appease Roosevelt by opposing the closed shop in public employment. For example, LaGuardia wrote the president in March 1940 assuring him that he took this position.[26]

Tensions increased in the spring of 1940, and although the parties forged a temporary resolution, it did not address the fundamental legal issues. The TWU used both private and public sector tactics, threatening to strike and also organizing an "Emergency Conference Committee" composed of sympathetic union, civic, religious, and consumer group leaders. On March 13, after more political pressure, LaGuardia announced that workers eligible for civil service would not lose their jobs as a result of unification. After meeting with TWU leaders on March 18 and 27, the mayor agreed to continue the IRT and BMT contracts, again with a major legal loophole. The city would assume contract terms "not inconsistent with constitutional or statutory provisions," with "any issues arising from said contracts to be made subject to judicial review." While these caveats were hardly trivial, the

New York Times headline declared that "LaGuardia Yields," the *CIO News* claimed "complete victory in its life and death struggle" for the union shop, and Quill added that "every line of the contracts will remain intact." But then the board of transportation declared that it should be the initial arbiter of what was legal, and it promptly rejected any dealing with the TWU. The union was outraged. Delaney wanted to "usurp the function of Courts to dictate the law himself. . . . He says, 'I am the Law.'" Local 100 threatened to strike. John L. Lewis intervened, appealing to LaGuardia's pride by professing "amazement . . . that Delaney was sufficiently powerful to reverse the mayor's decision." After meeting with Lewis, LaGuardia said that any board of transportation rulings on the contracts "will be held in abeyance pending a final judicial decision, and the provision of the contract affected will be performed in the meantime." On April 3 the board seemingly acquiesced while leaving some ambiguities. Delaney explained that the board would assume "every provision of the contracts . . . not inconsistent with the laws." The union again claimed victory. Its contracts would be "in force under unification," and the board of transportation could not accept only "such terms as it saw fit."[27]

Wary of the dangers of public sector strikes, the TWU, increasingly and resentfully, was forced to debate public sector labor law. The union was skeptical of the legal system. History had shown that employers would "run to subservient courts . . . or prevail upon friendly legislators to pass unfair laws with which to shackle labor." The objection that "'It is against the law' is merely another way of saying to workers: take what you can get and shut up." Philip Murray, who would become president of the CIO in November 1940, told LaGuardia that a "half-century's experience with the courts has demonstrated that they are inherently incapable of providing either a lasting or a satisfactory solution" to "the complex labor relations problems which modern industrial society has created. We cannot, therefore, transfer to the courts the responsibility which is ours." Yet the TWU could not escape the law, and thus was forced to make legal arguments. It cited a 1940 resolution of the New York chapter of the National Lawyers' Guild which concluded that, under the "proprietary function" doctrine, the TWU should have collective bargaining rights. It also quoted Sterling Spero, then a professor at New York University, advocating full bargaining. "It is very dangerous for any public body to insist, as it expands its authority, that the employees should lose their rights." Anticipating his seminal study of public sector unions, Spero contended that public and private sector workers faced many of the same problems and should have similar rights.[28]

With important contract provisions and the future of bargaining in legal limbo, the city acquired the BMT on June 1 and the IRT on June 12, 1940. The city adopted a plan of operation for these lines that provided that the board of transportation would determine wages and have broad powers in setting policy, subject to certain civil service rules and the Wicks Act. Over 26,000 private sector workers instantly became public employees.[29]

The TWU, now mostly a public sector union, had to learn to do what it could for its members in the absence of traditional union rights. It established a civil service department and regularly published explanations of the convoluted civil service regulations. Union leaders met with the board of transportation and LaGuardia to discuss issues ranging from day-to-day grievances to standardizing wages (at the time of unification, the IRT and BMT had over 1,600 pay rates). They lobbied the New York City Civil Service Commission, persuading it to make examination questions more job related. Union officials represented members in administrative hearings, preventing the removal of a number of workers. The TWU saved the jobs of 476 workers by helping them gain citizenship to satisfy the Wicks Act, and the union successfully backed a state law that granted reinstatement to workers who had lost their jobs because they were not citizens but who subsequently became naturalized. It helped defeat other bills sponsored by Wicks designed to limit even further the rights of unions in the subway system. Local 100 also used discrete picketing and small job actions.[30]

Clearly, however, the absence of its former institutional rights hurt Local 100. Union security, which the board of transportation refused to enforce, was especially contentious. The local now spoke only of the union shop (city officials made a point of continuing to refer to the closed shop). Unification had caused a sharp decline in membership, as many IRT and BMT workers believed that the TWU was no longer as necessary or as likely to be effective. An opportunity for a test case came in July 1940, when a few IRT workers who had quit the union asked the New York Supreme Court for a declaratory judgment as to whether the board of transportation could legally assume the union security provisions in the contracts. But neither the union nor management was willing to push the case to resolution, so the court dismissed it. The TWU, worried about a hostile court ruling, did not expel the men; the board of transportation was willing to wait for the contracts to expire. In the meantime, more and more members stopped paying dues. The TWU may have lost half its membership or more on the IRT and BMT lines in 1941.[31]

Local 100 continued to fight for the union shop, insisting that the board of transportation could legally require it in the public sector. It published a "Memorandum of Grievances" berating the board for its failure to honor various contractual provisions and arguing that the board's refusal to grant a union security clause "jeopardizes safe and uninterrupted transportation service." No court had ruled that the existing union security clause was illegal, so the board was bound by it. Elements in the TWU instigated work stoppages that involved hundreds of workers and, in one case in August 1940, 1,000 workers. But the TWU was about to discover that in the public sector context, many of its old tactics were now illegal.[32]

The TWU picketed the homes of workers who did not pay dues, holding around one hundred such demonstrations in late 1940 and early 1941. By March 1941 sixty-six homes had been picketed, some more than once, by up to several hundred people apiece. This strategy, however, led to the case of *Hogan v. Petrucci,* which enjoined against such picketing. *Hogan* repeatedly relied on the public sector setting. "Obviously, the reason for plaintiffs disassociating themselves from the Union is that they no longer required its intercession or protection," Justice Louis Valente began, somewhat gratuitously, "for as Civil Service employees they have obtained a security of position and other satisfactory related benefits, which make union membership unnecessary." More substantively, the state law limiting injunctions in labor cases (ironically, what was called a "little Norris-LaGuardia Act") could not be used in the public sector, even though this law did not specifically exclude government employees. The court reasoned that the state labor relations act excluded public workers, and that it and the anti-injunction law should be read together (in *pari materia*) even though the statutes had been passed during different sessions of the legislature. Therefore, the anti-injunction law also excluded public workers. Additionally, to avoid an injunction, both the means and the goals of picketing had to be legal, and in the civil service context the goal of a union shop was illegal. Civil service employees could be removed only for causes specified by law, and lack of union membership was not such a cause. The court failed to compare court decisions holding that public employers had the discretion to make union *membership* cause for discharge. In sum, the picketing had "an unlawful purpose and involves a malicious intent to annoy and intimidate."[33]

In March 1941 the TWU received another legal blow to its ability to use private sector tactics. Frustrations over various issues had caused work stoppages, notably a walkout involving about 3,500 men on March 10. After twelve days the strike was settled in favor of the union. The state legislature then passed the Wicks Anti-Sabotage and Anti-Violence Bill, aimed at preventing the TWU from using such job actions. Leaving equipment unattended or shutting off power, among other things, would now be felonies. Philip Murray, Quill, Sacher, and other CIO representatives testified against the measure, but the law was enacted.[34]

Negotiations then took center stage, as the existing labor contracts were set to expire in June. The unresolved legal issues concerning collective bargaining rights and the union shop dominated. On April 7 LaGuardia told the board of transportation that civil service rules did not permit discharge for failure to pay dues. He asked the board to rule on the union's requests for discipline against employees who were refusing to pay dues and then hold the matter in abeyance and submit it to a court. As for bargaining, "wages, working conditions, pension rights, vacations, sick leave, are all matters provided by law and . . . cannot in any way be provided by a separate and private agreement." Although "any group of employees" could present its views to the board, "separate agreements" could not be made with any organization. Also, strikes by city workers were illegal, and strikers would be fired.[35]

Instead of holding the union security cases in abeyance, the board of transportation announced that it would not enforce the clause. In an open letter to employees dated April 9, the board asserted that "almost everybody would soon understand that the Civil Service Law protects all civil service employees," who could not be punished for refusing to pay dues. The board added that "attempts to intimidate employees" had forced it to adopt a resolution specifically stating that union security was illegal in the public sector. Also on April 9, pursuant to the board's direction, the city's corporation counsel filed suit for a declaratory judgment that the board of transportation could not bargain collectively with the TWU. The city made the standard argument that bargaining was inextricably linked to strikes: "To hold that . . . collective bargaining applies to government is to hold of necessity that public employees have a right to strike against the government and thus to deny its very sovereignty." Murray said that this "court attack" was an attempt to "upset contracts already held." He wrote LaGuardia that civil service and bargaining were compatible. Further, giving all power to the board of transportation had no more "legal and moral justification" than putting workers at the mercy of the old private owners. The TWU again used the "proprietary function" argument. Running a transit system was not "the performance of government function" but rather was "a business enterprise." Thus, private sector rules should apply.[36]

The TWU pressed the "proprietary function" distinction frequently, albeit without success. Union leaders often noted that both Detroit and Seattle had entered into formal contracts with unions in public transit. But both of these situations involved legislative action permitting bargaining. Washington state had a law specifically authorizing public utilities to bargain with unions, and the Detroit city charter authorized its transit board to contract with a union "as fully and completely as if said board represented a private owner."[37] There was no analogous law in New York.

In addition to legal arguments, the TWU fully embraced the central tool of public sector unions, political action. For the TWU, first and foremost, this meant publicity designed to influence public opinion. The union distributed 500,000 copies of Murray's letter to LaGuardia to the public. Local 100 chastised U.S. secretary of labor Frances Perkins for her remark in April 1941 that the board of transportation could not bargain in the usual sense because in "public employment, nobody makes a profit" and because the transit workers had "access to political expression." Hogan replied in an open letter that the board was trying to make a profit; also, because the board was neither an elected body nor directly under any elected officials, transit workers did not have a political option. Hogan added that public employers such as the Tennessee Valley Authority bargained collectively in some ways. Echoing AFL leaders during World War I, he added that public sector bargaining should be permitted because "more and more the government is assuming a proprietary position and taking over the functions of private business."[38]

The TWU used a wide range of tactics in what the CIO called "one of the greatest local public education campaigns in labor history." From April to June 1941 it distributed millions of copies of five separate leaflets. TWU speakers gave regular radio addresses, and the union sponsored rallies, meetings, and protests outside board of transportation headquarters. On May 14 Quill wrote other CIO leaders to solicit support. "The Mayor claims that civil service gives them all the protection they need. This, of course, is not true." There was "no inconsistency between civil service and collective bargaining. Civil service does not protect the transit workers' hours, wages, or working conditions." The *Transport Bulletin* depicted the board in an unflattering light. It had "reneged, chiseled, and violated nearly all the provisions in the contracts," creating a "dictatorship of three political appointees."[39]

On May 21 the campaign peaked with a rally that overflowed the 18,000-seat capacity of Madison Square Garden, causing many to gather outside to listen to the public address system. The Almanac Singers performed, and the parade to the rally featured, among others, three pipe bands and the TWU's Ladies Auxiliary. The rally, which the *Transport Bulletin* labeled "the most enthusiastic gathering in the history of labor in New York," stressed both the need for and the legality of collective bargaining in public employment. "Government in business should deal fairly with organized labor" and "collective bargaining is the American way," placards proclaimed. "Are organized workers to be unorganized merely because they work for the government?" Murray asked. The "great moral issue" of collective bargaining affected the entire nation because it concerned "the right to be free," he thundered to the crowd. "Collective bargaining . . . means bread, butter, carpets on the floor, pictures on the wall, music in the home, culture, and education." Civil service status was no substitute for the right to bargain, Murray insisted. Civil service rules should not set wages, hours and working conditions, nor be used to enforce an open shop. He promised that the full power of the CIO would back bargaining rights. The United

Mine Workers and the United Auto Workers sent messages of support. The *CIO News* headline repeated that the TWU fight was "Important for All Labor."[40]

The TWU emphasized its most politically sympathetic points, compromising some for the public sector context. Its "Notes for Speakers" for the rally specified that the main issue was bargaining, not the right to strike or the closed shop. Civil service rules should exist to combat the spoils system, but they should not replace labor negotiations. The transit system was a business enterprise. The board of transportation, not the law, set wages, hours, and working conditions, and the board had consistently violated the contracts it had agreed to accept. The board had undercut conditions, discriminated against blacks and women, and refused to hear grievances.[41]

Legal issues took the forefront at the rally. Murray made the "proprietary function" argument and added that the national CIO had hired two attorneys to work on the TWU case. He tweaked LaGuardia, stating that the Wicks Act "destroys the efficacy of the Norris-LaGuardia Act" and created "another injunctive measure." The union's distaste for the law was in evidence, but it was at least matched by the perceived need for legal precedent. One speaker said that "no city ordinance, no judge's decree can take CIO unionism from the men and women." But Joseph Curran, a vice-president of the CIO and a close ally of Quill's, quoted at length from an 1824 U.S. Supreme Court decision on the "proprietary function" doctrine. Local 100 leader John Santo cited a provision in the New York constitution that provided that "employees" had the right to organize and bargain. Santo also quoted the preamble to the NLRA, which stated that the rights to organize and bargain helped prevent industrial strife. This policy, he urged, should be applied equally to public workers.[42]

Also, beginning in 1940 the CIO's advocacy on behalf of all government workers had become more assertive. The New York state CIO in March resolved that the state labor relations act should be amended to cover public employees. In September the UFW convention resolved that the "problems of the 1,000,000 U.S. government workers are those of workers everywhere. . . . Like workers everywhere," they needed grievances adjusted, conditions improved, and rights recognized. In November 1940 Santo told an approving CIO convention that all public employers must "live up to the same laws of collective bargaining that Congress saw fit to pass for private industries."[43]

The TWU case helped inspire the CIO on this issue, but there was another motivation. Just as the expansion of government activities during World War I had caused Gompers and the AFL to pay more attention to public employees, CIO leaders found that the New Deal and war preparations had created more government work. City, state, and federal governments "are extending control over industry," said Santo. As Freeman notes, Murray was interested in the TWU case partly because he saw it as a precedent for the legal rights of public workers, and those rights were important, since Murray felt that "slowly and inexorably the government is assuming many of the functions which have been those of private industry." Citing New Deal and war programs, Murray concluded that "a definitive labor policy must be established for such agencies." Indeed, the total number of government employees in the United States had increased from less than 3.5 million in 1935 to over 4.2 million in 1940, and to over 4.6 million in 1941; by 1943 this figure would exceed 6 million.[44]

By late 1941 the CIO was pushing for the rights of public sector unions even more aggressively. In September the *CIO News* declared that the "fiction" that cities could not bargain with unions should be "laid to rest in the wastebasket of antiquated ideas." A month later the SCMWA announced that "every effort must be made as soon as feasible" to put government workers under the NLRA and state labor acts. In November the CIO convention passed a resolution in favor of collective bargaining for all public employees. Their number was increasing, they "face the same conditions as other workers," and civil service rules (while necessary to end the spoils system) were no substitute for collective bargaining. If cities relied on the exclusion of public workers from labor laws, delegate Allan Haywood warned, "the CIO will challenge that . . . and demand that even government give to the workers . . . the same rights we have in industry." The CIO should provide "every support possible" to force public employers to bargain. Murray declared that the TWU case was a test of the legal rights of all government workers. While public and private sector employees had similar problems, public employees had not made equivalent gains. Civil service "in no way meets the basic problems" of these workers. Murray even asserted that public workers needed unions more than private sector workers did. The CIO continued to support collective bargaining rights for public employees in subsequent years, although, like the AFL, it also backed laws and regulations that set and improved wages and hours.[45]

The TWU continued to link public and private sector workers. In June 1941 it argued that public utilities should follow "labor practices as enunciated by the state and federal labor relations acts." The *Transport Bulletin* observed that "the mere fact of government employment was not a bulwark against the rising cost of living." Labor needed collective bargaining in private industry, the article continued, and "it needs it just as urgently" in public employment. "The title . . . to a factory makes little difference to the man working in it. He still wants and needs a voice in his own conditions." In 1942 the *Transport Bulletin* maintained that "government workers who are unorganized can be and are exploited as cruelly as unorganized workers in private industry." Quill, in his 1943 election platform, called for "genuine collective bargaining . . . in all city departments" in accordance with the principles of private sector law.[46]

This stance meant that TWU and CIO leaders would be drawn deeper into polemics about the law. In April 1941 Murray attacked LaGuardia for relying on civil service statutes and distinguished proprietary functions from pure government functions such as police and fire services. "I know of no law" prohibiting the board of transportation from contracting with labor as it did with steel, coal, and other corporate suppliers, Murray added. Making the same points, the *CIO News* even praised the contract between the AFL's transit union and Seattle. In May the TWU publicized a report by the American Civil Liberties Union (ACLU) concluding that public workers should have the right to bargain because (as unions had frequently argued) the law did not set not all conditions of government employment. Employing officials "frequently have large discretion within budget figures, and entire discretion on questions of promotions, assignments, seniority, etc." Since it was "fully demonstrated by past experience that government workers may be subjected to unreasonable treatment," such workers should have the right to bargain on matters not fixed by law. While civil service rules precluded the closed shop, the rights to organize and bargain involved "issues of civil liberty." The city's position toward the TWU was "wholly untenable." The ACLU even endorsed the right to strike for all public employees except police and firefighters. In November Murray denounced a report from the National Institute of Municipal Law Officers stating that cities could not legally enter into contracts with unions. Later that month the CIO's Joseph Curran asked LaGuardia to issue an executive order permitting collective bargaining for city employees.[47]

The TWU was then forced into a court battle, as the city filed a motion to determine its obligations under the labor contracts. In response, the union used a variety of arguments. Making the "proprietary function" point, the TWU cited a New York Court of Appeals case holding that the subway "was built by and belongs to the city as a proprietor, not as a sovereign." Also, the board of transportation had stated in another case that it was engaged in a "proprietary, not a governmental function." Thus, the union concluded, proprietary operations such as transit systems "do not involve in any respect . . . sovereign rights," as issues of wages, hours and working conditions were "identical in character with those arising under private ownership." Further, the union shop would not violate civil service rules. The board's Rule 16B, which allowed workers to be discharged for "failing or refusing to pay their just debts," could apply to payment of union dues, given that the board had wide discretion in setting employment policy (the law governing the board authorized it "to exercise all requisite and necessary authority to manage and direct" the transit system). The fact that a union shop was more harmonious, efficient, and safe was sufficient justification. Requiring union dues was as valid as requiring workers to pay for their uniforms. Nor were the union shop, arbitration, or bargaining improper delegations of the board's powers. The board, not the union, would remove the employee for not paying dues. It was within the board's discretion to use arbitration and to bargain, since these mechanisms helped ensure labor peace. Further, only collective bargaining could assure safe, efficient, and continuous operation of the subways, and the public policy of New York and the nation favored bargaining.[48]

The union won an initial procedural victory, but there was no final ruling in the case. In late May 1941 the state supreme court heard arguments. The New York City Civil Liberties Union filed an *amicus* brief supporting the union on the bargaining issue. On June 7 Justice Lloyd Church denied the city's motion for judgment on the pleadings, holding that issues must be developed at trial. The contracts covered a wide variety of topics, many "in minute detail." To determine which provisions were valid, a trial was necessary to explore "the actual facts and circumstances of the operation of the transit systems." It could not be held "as a matter of law irrespective of the facts" that the board of transportation "has no power or authority to enter into any kind of contract with its employees." The case was continued, and a trial date was set for September. The TWU promised that Harry Sacher would "prepare the legal case from all angles." But the case would never be decided. The court date was moved to December 15, 1941, at which point the parties agreed to postpone the case indefinitely, partly because of the exigencies of the war, and probably also because both sides feared a conclusive loss.[49]

Meanwhile the contracts neared expiration, and relations worsened. "I know the difference between a real labor leader and a dues collector," La-Guardia sniped, and he refused the union's requests to meet in May 1941. On June 19 he declared that employee groups could give their views on wages and hours to the board of transportation, but that the board would make the final decisions. By this time the board had already finished its own unilateral wage-and-hour plan. Both sides planned for a strike. At a meeting on June 25, after Sacher proposed raises, board member Sullivan replied, "You are not invited to negotiate a contract and . . . we will not sign a contract." When Quill asked if the board would bargain an agreement, Delaney retorted, "A signed contract? No." The TWU walked out. Quill threatened that "we will not work one hour in the month of July without a signed contract," and he publicized a vote authorizing a strike on June 30. Quill was concerned about public support and the law, however, and he did not actually want a strike.[50]

Instead the TWU made political appeals. Locally, twenty-five African-American leaders sent a telegram to Delaney calling for collective bargaining. The TWU had a policy favoring equal treatment for black workers, and these leaders insisted that collective bargaining "would go a long way toward correcting and eliminating" discrimination. Signers of the telegram included Adam Clayton Powell, Paul Robeson, eight unionists (two from the BSEIU), four religious leaders, and two representatives from the Young Women's Christian Association. On the federal level, on June 25 the TWU sought intervention from the National Defense Mediation Board (NDMB). Chairman William Davis indicated that the NDMB would take the case if Frances Perkins certified it. President Roosevelt told Perkins that the NDMB had no jurisdiction over municipal employees. Nonetheless, Perkins, Murray, LaGuardia, and secretary of the interior Harold Ickes, after a series of meetings and telegrams, worked out an ostensible resolution.[51]

This "agreement" consisted of an exchange of telegrams between La-Guardia and Murray that missed each other entirely on fundamental points. On June 27, 1941, LaGuardia wrote that the TWU could not strike; civil service laws barred the closed shop; union officials could "meet and confer" with the board of transportation; the city would create a grievance board for subway workers; and it would continue the status quo under the assumed contracts "pending a judicial determination . . . clarifying the situation." LaGuardia concluded that this "message and/or acceptance thereto" would constitute a "memorandum of understanding." Murray replied that the parties could come to an understanding before a court resolved the union shop and bargaining issues. The union would, therefore, not strike as long as this "agreement" was in effect. But the parties had hardly agreed. Murray then specified that "there are certain clarifications and modifications which I am sure you will find acceptable." First, he incorrectly assumed that the grievance board that LaGuardia mentioned would have full power to decide grievances. Second, Murray stated, somewhat implausibly, that LaGuardia must have meant the words "meet and confer" to mean full collective bargaining, unless and until a court held differently. He concluded that if LaGuardia found anything in his telegram "unclear or with which you are not in agreement, I shall be glad to meet with you at the earliest possible moment."[52]

The TWU portrayed this exchange as a major victory regarding rights that were obviously still highly contested. At the end of 1942 the union claimed that since LaGuardia had not repudiated anything in Murray's reply, "We must assume that the reply accurately expressed their understanding." More realistically, a neutral body studying the matter later concluded that the telegrams from Murray and LaGuardia "do not indicate any definite agreement reached. . . . They are capable of conflicting interpretations, and we find them inconclusive on any of the matters" at issue. Still, on June 29 the union voted not to strike and proclaimed victory. The city had agreed that the "union contract is valid unless the highest court says it is not," the *Transport Bulletin* reported. Clearly overstating the result, the *Bulletin* asserted that the union had "for the second time won the right to be recognized . . . and to bargain collectively." More truthfully, the union attributed the success it had achieved to public relations. It was "the most remarkable and extensive campaign ever carried out by any union on a similar issue." The Madison Square Garden rally was the "greatest labor meeting in the history of New York City."[53]

The gaping holes in the "agreement" were partly disguised by the effect of World War II on national labor policy and the CIO. First, the war, at least initially, increased employment and pay for many workers. In August 1941 the board of transportation granted significant raises and other improvements. Second, the conflict made harmonious labor relations a greater priority. After Germany invaded the Soviet Union in June 1941, the CIO increasingly made production for the war effort a central goal. After the attack on Pearl Harbor in December 1941, the CIO adopted a no-strike pledge. The CIO's position reflected both the influence of the Communist party (and the "popular front" alliance) and the patriotism of CIO members. The TWU continued to demand better conditions, but now in the context of winning the war. In mid-1941 it argued that to "make industrial employees into government employees with the purpose of abrogating their right to bargain collectively would be a blow against national defense. For whatever hurts labor hurts the nation."[54]

While the CIO's no-strike pledge was contentious in the private sector, it helped Local 100 by taking the most controversial issue for any public sector union off the table. Before this, the TWU had walked a fine line, asserting that its members had a right to strike and simultaneously downplaying the possibility of such an action. For example, a single page of the *Transport Bulletin* denounced an attempt to bar transit strikes by statute, but also stated that "all talk of an 'inevitable' strike" came from LaGuardia, who could avoid such an action simply by meeting with the union. During the war the union played up the no-strike policy to curry public sympathy. The policy, the union explained reassuringly, helped it reach peaceful accommodations with the city. LaGuardia's alleged concern about strikes was a "smoke screen." Since Pearl Harbor there "has not been a single threat of strike made in this entire dispute. . . . Bitter as the employees are against the Mayor, they are Americans first." Also, the war pressured both sides to resolve their differences and reminded them of common goals. LaGuardia,

Quill, Joseph Curran, and other key players regularly appeared side by side at "Win the War" rallies.[55] From the perspective of a public sector union, almost any genuine accommodation from management was a step forward.

The unresolved issues of the union's institutional rights would, however, not go away, and tensions grew in late 1941 and early 1942. The board of transportation remained intransigent. Although the TWU had, in Freeman's term, "most favored union" status, its legal position had weakened it in numbers and in its relations with management. In late 1941 the union issued a report calling for "genuine collective bargaining," again making extensive legal arguments. The transit system was a business, not a sovereign function. Further, even the "government, as sovereign," could bargain, as some federal agencies and cities had already done. Bargaining was especially appropriate for the TWU, because the board of transportation, not the legislature, fixed wages, hours, and working conditions. Civil service coverage was no substitute for the right to bargain.[56]

Local 100 was also disappointed in the grievance board that LaGuardia had promised, and the problems with the that body underscored the difficulty of adopting effective procedures in the public sector. The three members of the grievance board were sworn in on January 10, 1942, and their political background was encouraging. Member Andrew Armstrong was a former ALP alderman and labor leader, and member Nathan Frankel had been LaGuardia's labor secretary (W. Francis Fitzgerald was the third member). But although the board facilitated some improvements, the system had a fatal flaw. The board only had the power to recommend solutions to the board of transportation, and the board of transportation was largely unreceptive. Despite Murray's recommendation that the grievance board should have the authority to make binding decisions, the transportation board had created the body and specifically limited its power. Again, the ability of the direct employer of labor to determine legal rules and processes was fatal to union rights. Thus, although the TWU granted that the grievance board had "capable and conscientious members," the union complained that the board of transportation largely ignored it. This situation only hurt workers, because the grievance board issued recommendations only if it felt an employee's grievance was justified. By the end of 1942 the grievance board had made 252 such recommendations, and the board of transportation had acted on only 30 percent of them. "Never has labor grievance machinery worked less satisfactorily," the TWU grumbled.[57]

In June 1942 the TWU began one more extended political and legal campaign to try to regain at least some of its former rights. In addition to the union's problems with disputes over its institutional status, inflation had now eroded earlier wage gains, and the board of transportation was long overdue in releasing work rules. The board itself admitted that many pay rates were low: 40 percent of the over 32,000 workers earned thirty-one dollars a week or less, after deductions. On June 29 the union unveiled a "Four-Point Victory Program." This included a wage hike to 15 percent above the levels of January 1, 1941; a maintenance of membership requirement (union members could not withdraw until a current contract expired); revised work rules in line with union recommendations; and a joint labor-management committee that would engage in some form of bargaining. Pitching labor's demands in the context of the war, the *CIO News* called these requests a part of the "national victory program." From July to September LaGuardia and Delaney met with the TWU. They made little progress. Delaney agreed to consider some issues of working conditions, but nothing else. Murray tried unsuccessfully to intercede. After October 20, 1942, the transportation board refused to meet with union representatives, despite repeated union requests.[58]

The TWU now tried a new legal strategy, one unique to the wartime climate. On November 9, 1942, it appealed to the National War Labor Board (NWLB), the successor to the NDMB. Over the summer the NWLB had created a framework for national labor policy in the private sector through its "Little Steel" decision. The TWU would have been happy to live under the terms of this decision. "Little Steel" permitted maintenance of membership and made contracts binding until the end of the war. In exchange, the NWLB exerted control over wages and essentially barred strikes. The TWU's petition to the NWLB stated that the city's failure to grant raises and maintenance of membership in accordance with "Little Steel" had demoralized and disrupted the transit workforce and created a dispute "which might interrupt work which contributes to the effective prosecution of the war." Soon after this petition was filed, LaGuardia announced a wage increase of 1.4 cents per hour; the union told the NWLB that this was only one-fifth of what the "Little Steel" formula would have produced and was thus "an incitement to rebellion." Meanwhile, city officials insisted that the NWLB had no jurisdiction over municipal employees.[59]

The TWU mixed politics with this legal tactic, arguing that the need for labor peace in wartime mandated NWLB intervention. "Dividing workers may be a luxury in which management can indulge in time of peace," union leaders wrote LaGuardia, but "when our nation is engaged in a war for its very survival it is nothing short of criminal." The TWU publicized a resolution by the National Lawyers Guild stating that the NWLB had authority in any labor dispute that "might interrupt work which contributes" to the war effort. The *Transport Bulletin* declared that "Justice for Workers in Transit System Is Urgent War Need" and that the "security of the U.S. demands a just settlement." It also quoted Newark mayor Vincent Murphy, who insisted that it was "a waste of time to argue legalities in times like these. It is an undermining of our nation's war effort." The services of city workers were as vital as those rendered by private industry, he continued. Public officials should not question the power of the NWLB but rather assist it, to help win the war.[60]

The CIO took an active interest in the TWU case, which the NWLB combined with cases involving an SCMWA local in Newark, New Jersey, and an AFSCME local in Omaha, Nebraska. Abraham Flaxer, president of the SCMWA, urged that "total war must include the 3,500,000 state, county and municipal workers throughout the country." The CIO convention in November 1942 called on the NWLB to take jurisdiction, with Quill and Murray warning that all labor disputes could threaten the war effort, and that those involving public employees should not be excluded. After all, they noted, the government could be soon be operating shipyards and steel mills.[61]

In the TWU's brief, Sacher argued that distinguishing the public sector and excluding it from the NWLB's jurisdiction undermined the vital purpose of the NWLB. While the executive order creating the NWLB did not mention public employees, it charged the agency with "adjusting and settling labor disputes which might interrupt work which contributes to the effective prosecution of the war." The "Little Steel" case had asserted broad jurisdiction for the NWLB, holding that in "wartime there is no basis for questioning the power of the President to order what amounts to compulsory arbitration for the settlement of any labor dispute . . . which threatens the war effort." Sacher quoted NWLB member Wayne Morse, who had said that "the possible effect of a given labor dispute upon the war effort is the only criterion to be consulted in determining" whether the NWLB should take jurisdiction. He also quoted NWLB vice-chairman George Taylor that in "time of war, the nation cannot be complacent about unresolved shop grievances which might seriously interfere with the maximum production of war goods." Such concerns were acute in the case of Local 100, Sacher continued. Hundreds of thousands of New York City residents had jobs directly relating to the war effort, and they relied on the subways. "We need not elaborate on the effects which an interruption of work . . . would have on the war effort." The TWU would not strike, but poor labor relations would hinder service. "War work is necessarily interrupted when morale, efficiency and production are lowered by a dispute."[62]

Anticipating the traditional legal objections to institutional rights for public sector unions, the brief also quoted "Little Steel" for the proposition that the president's war powers are "governed by the laws of national preservation rather than by the rules of the common law. . . . They are not subject to examination through the magnifying glass of strict legalistic doctrine or technical legal rules applicable to peace-time situations." The "very life of our nation depends" on the proper exercise of the war power. The "only premise on which jurisdiction can be declined is that we can afford the suicidal luxury of going down to national defeat and destruction if only a local governmental agency is shown to be a party to the dispute." Sacher also repeated the "proprietary function" argument.[63]

On December 9, 1942, the NWLB held a hearing in the TWU case. La-Guardia and Delaney, maintaining that the NWLB had no authority, did not send a representative, prompting a stern rebuke from the NWLB. One biographer attributes the mayor's behavior to his "erratic emotional state" caused by Roosevelt's failure to appoint him to national office. In any event, LaGuardia did try to affect the outcome. He and seventy-eight other mayors issued a statement denying that the NWLB could intervene in cases involving city workers, and LaGuardia wrote separately to both NWLB chairman William Davis and Roosevelt to convey this view. Typically, Delaney went further, announcing that the TWU's appeal ended any obligations the city had under the contracts and freed the board of transportation to act "in accordance with its own judgment."[64]

On December 23 the NWLB refused to take jurisdiction. Its decision, however, gave the TWU some political ammunition and a hope of regaining some of its bygone rights. The opinion, written by public member Wayne Morse, rejected the union's position on the grounds of state sovereignty.[65] "Well established doctrines . . . pertaining to the sovereign rights of state and local governments clearly exclude" public workers from federal authority. "There is no doctrine more firmly established in American jurisprudence than the one that state governments and their subdivisions within the sphere of their own jurisdiction are sovereign." The NWLB noted that the federal government had not attempted to regulate the wages or hours of employees of state and local governments. Also, the War Labor Board during World War I had held that it could not compel jurisdiction over cities.[66]

But the decision gave the TWU some material to work with. The NWLB explained that it *could* take jurisdiction over public workers in certain circumstances, and it called for greater rights for public sector unions. During wars, the NWLB cautioned, local governments could not "follow any course of action they care to" in labor relations "irrespective of the effects . . . upon the prosecution of the war. Sovereignty is not a 'suicidal doctrine.'" In some situations, the federal government could use its war powers in these matters. As the TWU had argued, "labor controversies between local governments and their employees can be as disruptive to the war effort as disputes in private industry." In such cases, insisting that sovereignty barred NWLB jurisdiction would be "a strained interpretation of the Constitution so unrealistic as to be repudiated by all patriotic citizens." Ironically, the NWLB agreed that a transit strike could hurt the war effort, but approvingly observed that the TWU was not likely to strike. In the companion SCMWA dispute, the NWLB added that it was "unthinkable" that the NWLB "would endanger the war effort by failing to concern itself with the problems of municipal employees." The NWLB even offered to render advisory opinions in public sector disputes if both parties requested it.[67] In fact, in the SCMWA case the NWLB actually made formal recommendations that strikers be rehired, that the city of Newark recognize the local, and that the parties negotiate a procedure to settle their differences. If they could not, they should return to the NWLB.[68]

Further, the decision showed a real evolution in attitudes toward public sector unions. The NWLB quoted the part of Roosevelt's letter to NFFE president Steward stating that public employee organizing was "natural." The NWLB added that government workers could "participate in limited forms of collective bargaining." There was "nothing illegal in . . . formal discussions by officials of government with representatives of their organized employees relative to wages and to conditions of employment." The decision pointedly remarked that "very serious labor problems confronting the country" existed because some public employers had adopted "uncooperative and antagonistic attitudes" toward unions. Good labor relations were essential, as government was the largest employer in the country. Echoing union leaders, the NWLB described increasing government involvement in formerly private sector economic activity. Government was "in business in a 'big way.' " It was troubling that, despite this expansion and the success of private sector labor, there were "such low standards in public employment." Many problems were caused by the refusal of public employers "to even discuss" issues with unions and their "very uncompromising and unenlightened attitude" toward labor relations. The NWLB encouraged public officials to use their discretionary power within applicable legal limits, as unionists had long said they could. Few if any laws barred meetings with union representatives "for the purpose of hearing complaints, discussing possible adjustments in working conditions . . . and working out fair and impartial machinery for the review of grievances." It was "this type of collective bargaining . . . which is so sorely needed today." In sum, "within the limits of their legal powers," public employers should provide effective grievance machinery, opportunity for communication, and bargaining to the limits of discretionary authority.[69]

The NWLB also gave the TWU specific ammunition regarding its employer. The opinion chided LaGuardia for not sending a representative. His explanations "fell far short of justifying the city's failure to . . . cooperate." The TWU had made a prima facie case that the city had not provided "a proper employee relationship policy." Delaney's "antagonistic attitude" toward the union was shown by his claim that the NWLB appeal had released the city from any obligations to the TWU. "Such provocative statements . . . certainly are not conducive to harmonious relations." The union was not without fault. Yet the NWLB seemed to give its view of the matter in quoting a report by Bishop Francis McConnell, which blamed the board of transportation for having "never accepted the spirit of free negotiation with its employees." Instead, the board had sought "the advantage of every technicality of the law." The bishop—and, in a very real sense, the NWLB— concluded that instead of relying on "legalistic questions . . . the local authorities must learn to deal with their employees by some system of negotiations analogous to collective bargaining in private industry."[70]

The TWU thus could make fairly good public relations use of a case that it lost. A *Transport Bulletin* headline gibed, "Absence of NYC Officials at War Board Hearing Shows Contempt for FDR, Employees." There "could be no better proof of the City's contemptuous attitude toward the transit employees." The paper quoted comments from Wayne Morse and William Davis outside the decision calling the refusal to appear "a bad slip" that "does not contribute that type of cooperation that is so essential to domestic morale and to the winning of the war." The union also emphasized the positive commentary in the decision about public sector unions. Douglas MacMahon, now president of Local 100, told union members that the decision had held that "government agencies should be guided by the same principles . . . as in private industry." While the *CIO News* criticized parts of the decision, it also stated that the NWLB had asked cities to "meet with unions" and even claimed that the decision meant that city and state governments had a "solemn duty to engage in collective bargaining."[71]

Meanwhile the TWU had been exploring other options. Strong sentiments for a strike emerged. The legal and historical context of public sector labor relations, however, weighed heavily against such a move. In December Murray told Quill that the CIO would release Local 100 from the no-strike pledge, "since there was no court to go to." A week later the union threatened to strike, but the leadership backed down. Notably, John Santo said he believed LaGuardia wanted to be another Calvin Coolidge—this over twenty years after the Boston strike.[72]

Instead, the union continued to pursue politics through public relations. As part of this campaign, the CIO had in November 1942 formed a "Citizens Transit Committee" to study the matter. Headed by Professor Arthur MacMahon of Columbia University, this committee tilted to the left, with members including Mary Van Kleek, Louis Boudin, Lillian Hellman, Adam Clayton Powell, and Freda Kirchwey, along with an additional six ministers and seven professors. Not surprisingly, the committee stated early on that the subways were "an integral part of the war effort." The committee held public hearings and invited testimony from both sides. The board of transportation did not participate.[73]

The committee's report, published in early January 1943, did not agree with the TWU on every point. But, like the NWLB, the committee showed an increased tolerance for public sector unions, advocating maximum maneuverability for unions within legal limits. Instead of full collective bargaining, the report recommended "collaborative labor relationships." Adopting the NWLB and traditional union arguments, the report accepted the crucial point that public officials had the discretion to negotiate over certain issues. It was "pretty close to disingenuous" for the city to say that it could not bargain because civil service law set out a "complete scheme of public employment." Even "very complete schemes" for civil service "leave many interstitial and surrounding aspects of employment to be arranged in the course of administration." In this case, the board of transportation had "sweeping discretion over salaries and wages." The report approvingly cited bargaining by certain public utilities and federal agencies and stated that bargaining could exist without strikes. Similarly, although a closed shop was not permissible, "overt recognition" of the union "as an instrument of consultation" would help resolve the issue. The report quoted the NWLB decision, mostly for its blame of "unenlightened" public employers and encouragement of a "type of collective bargaining, falling within the sphere of the discretionary powers of government officials." It denounced the board of transportation for ignoring the grievance board and rebuked Delaney for his assertion that the transportation board "cannot share its responsibilities" with the TWU. "The harm that may spread from an obstinate handling of the labor aspects of municipal operation, especially in New York, is literally incalculable." Going considerably further than contemporary courts, the committee concluded that public sector labor disputes "should be brought within the field of mediation and arbitration."[74]

The union kept up the pressure, holding public hearings to promote its cause. As always the law was central, and more than ever Sacher shaped his arguments to fit the public sector context. Before a large gathering on November 28, 1942, Sacher again insisted that the board of transportation could enforce a maintenance of membership under its power to discharge an employee who did not pay "just debts." Further, the board could bargain as the NWLB and the Citizens Transit Committee had suggested, using official discretion within legal limits. No law prevented the transportation board "from saying that we considered, discussed and conferred with the TWU and were persuaded" that certain pay rates were fair. "That is not a surrender of sovereign power. It is a matter of doing the just thing." Quill added public relations points, stressing the no-strike pledge and the common problems of public and private sector workers.[75]

The union made another concession to the public sector context as tensions mounted again near the end of 1942. It began to call for binding arbitration—an aspiration of many public sector unions—to settle wage and other disputes. It held a huge membership meeting that voted unanimously for arbitration. It also distributed leaflets, publicized an editorial from the journal *PM* supporting arbitration, and bought print advertisements and radio time. Hundreds of AFL and CIO unions contributed money to the cause. The TWU sent the press a report from the grievance board that was very critical of the board of transportation. Still, in mid-January pay disputes caused several short work stoppages, one involving 1,100 men. On February 9, 1943, 20,000 people attended another TWU rally in Madison Square Garden. Zero Mostel performed while sympathetic community leaders, including Lionel Barrow of the National Association for the Advancement of Colored People, looked on from the podium. A resolution favoring arbitration of wages was passed.

With fundamental problems still unresolved, LaGuardia and the union agreed that an impartial panel should analyze the situation. On January 11, 1943, LaGuardia announced the formation of a committee headed by Fordham Law School dean Ignatius Wilkinson to examine labor relations in the transit system.[76]

The TWU and the mainstream press sparred over the extent to which union goals could be adapted for the public sector. The *New York Times,* while praising the TWU's no-strike pledge, editorialized that the city could not bargain over wages "with the freedom of a private employer" and "cannot legally contract" for the closed shop. The TWU "cannot offer its members in city service the same protection it offers under private ownership." The only alternative proposed by the paper was wage equalization. The *CIO News* stressed that pay was low and that only bargaining could remedy this problem. It argued that over half of the 32,000 workers in the transit system did not earn enough to maintain their health. After deductions, 40 percent of the subway workers earned $1,478 per year, and 20 percent earned $1,750. This, according to the calculations of the city's own officials, was "starvation level." The *CIO News* maintained that the Wilkinson Committee should establish collective bargaining in the transit system.[77]

The Wilkinson Committee was crucial to the union. At the committee's hearings, the TWU asked for a raise of 15 percent, the replacement of Delaney, maintenance of membership, advisory arbitration, and labor-management committees. On April 28, 1943, the committee issued its report, which inevitably focused on the law. Indeed, the report began that the committee's role was to make recommendations "to which no legal objection can be raised."[78] Like the NWLB and the Citizens Transit Committee, the Wilkinson Committee concluded that the board of transportation could and should be more flexible within legal limits. The report is a classic statement of both the legal constraints on public sector unions and the activities possible within those limits. It was also further confirmation that these unions had gained a measure of legitimacy.

The Wilkinson report noted the oddity of the changed legal status of the workers and counseled compromise. The employees were "accustomed to . . . collective bargaining . . . and ultimately . . . the right to strike." It was "hard for them to understand and adjust themselves to the difficulties which the law . . . set up against continuance of such methods." Workers had moved from a system of union contracts to civil service, in which the law governed their rights and duties. Both sides must adapt. "Management must learn that the inflexibility of law inherent in Civil Service" did not prevent consultations with labor. The union must learn that "limitations of statute law . . . necessarily mean that increases of wages and improvement of working conditions must come by a different process than in private industry."[79]

The Wilkinson report then rejected the union's position on several issues. The union shop and traditional bargaining were illegal. Under applicable law, the board of transportation could discipline workers only for dereliction of duty, incompetency, or misconduct, and failure to pay dues did not rise to this level. The report ignored the union's argument that the board could discharge employees for not paying just debts; nor did it discuss whether precedent giving public officials wide discretion in determining what constituted "misconduct" could allow them to include failure to pay dues. The report also rejected some of the union's suggestions about bargaining. Traditional bargaining would not work, the report reasoned, because the union could not strike at impasse, and because binding arbitration would constitute an illegal delegation of the authority of the board of transportation or Civil Service Commission. Therefore, "it is idle to talk of collective bargaining with Civil Service employees as such bargaining exists" in private industry. Delegation also barred any real improvement to the grievance board. The report acknowledged that the board of transportation had been "almost wholly uncooperative" with the grievance board and "had no concept" of its "potential usefulness." Still, the report concluded that the transportation board could not legally delegate its authority to make final decisions to the grievance board. Thus, the report recommended that the latter be replaced and that the deputy commissioner in charge of the department of labor relations (a position to be created) make final decisions on grievances. It is unlikely that the TWU felt that replacing the sympathetic grievance board with an officer of the employer would constitute a victory.[80]

Significantly, though, the Wilkinson report recommended measures short of bargaining both to resolve the immediate issues over wages and for the long term. As to the pending dispute, the report essentially adopted the TWU's suggestion of advisory arbitration. The board of transportation should hold "reasonable conferences" with Local 100 and try to reach agreement. If this measure failed, a three-person board should be appointed to give advice that "while without actual legal effect would . . . command public confidence." There was "no legal objection to and a great practical benefit to be gained" from such a process. The report also criticized the transportation board's refusal to involve the union in the past. "A great deal of the discontent" had arisen from the board's having made wage and other adjustments without even notifying the union. As to the future, again, bargaining and arbitration as used in the private sector were "legally impossible." But this fact "necessitates an attempt to provide some permanent alternative means within the limits of the law." Specifically, the report recommended that the board hold yearly "conferences on the question of wages and hours" (the newly created position of deputy commissioner would be responsible for these events). There should also be "a provision for an independent advisory investigation and report in the event of disagreement."[81] Thus union input and public scrutiny would be institutionalized, albeit without even advisory arbitration.

The TWU put a positive spin on the Wilkinson report, stressing the quasi-bargaining procedures recommended. This "historic victory" was a "milestone in the struggle of all American labor for greater industrial and political democracy." The report would result in "collective bargaining machinery," raises, better conditions, upward reclassifications of jobs, and, the union claimed, advisory arbitration. The *CIO News* claimed that the report "calls for genuine collective bargaining." Again, more accurately, the TWU credited its success to its publicity campaign, which, it had recently boasted, was "the greatest of its kind in labor history."[82]

Most of the recommendations in the Wilkinson report were adopted, and this was in fact a major achievement. Freeman contends that it was a significant victory, institutionalizing union representation on all important matters. The key was how the union made the process work. The *New York Times* reported that the labor consultations were "substantially similar to collective bargaining." Many of the union's proposals were accepted, yielding an agreement that, effective July 1, 1943, raised every pay rate to at least 15 percent more than it had been on September 1, 1941. This increase exceeded what the "Little Steel" formula allowed private sector workers. A labor relations department was established, and other improvements were made. With these successes, the TWU began to recoup its membership losses. In August 1943 it began pushing for the "voluntary closed shop," and soon had 100 percent of the workers in a number of IRT sections. As of 1948 Local 100 had 35,000 members.[83]

On the other hand, the union was forced to accept a highly diluted form of the rights it had previously held. One historian writes that unification was "a disaster for the union," and that by the end of World War II "the union enjoyed only an informal tradition of consultation." The TWU did remain sensitive about its rights, especially in repeatedly using the term "collective bargaining" to describe what it was doing. For example, a single paragraph from a *Transport Bulletin* article stated that the agreement in 1943 "was reached through the process of collective bargaining," and that this "genuine collective bargaining . . . demonstrates the complete feasibility of applying collective bargaining procedures to government employment."[84]

Fundamentally, the TWU had achieved about as much as public sector unions would get for nearly two decades to come. The strike wave of 1946 brought more restrictive laws, and state bargaining laws would not begin to be implemented until the 1960s. The TWU did use a number of unusual factors to help it win what it did: a size, strength, and tradition of militancy developed in the private sector; the wartime context; and the political culture of New York City.

But also, the TWU took advantage of an evolving approach toward all public sector unions. This approach, promoted by liberals and labor relations specialists, accepted many of the legal limits that courts imposed in this era. Yet it also gave unions of government workers both theoretical legitimacy and practical suggestions as to how to work within the law. In part, this view reflected the greater toleration that unions in general had won during the New Deal and earlier. In part, it reflected the reality that many public sector unions had found ways to force themselves to the table in some manner. In part, it reflected the dimming of fears related to the Boston strike and "class domination" of government. For example, in 1946 the National Civil Service League issued a report that largely matched the sentiments expressed by the NWLB and the Wilkinson Committee. The report urged public employers to enter into agreements with groups that represented the majority of workers. While public employers had ultimate authority in employment matters, they should listen to and try to accommodate unions. The report also denounced yellow-dog requirements. They should not be used unless "the danger of partisanship or impaired public service is real." A "general indiscriminate attempt" use of such contracts "is out of step with the times."[85]

These trends helped public sector unions throughout the country in the

1940s. In 1941 AFSCME and the state and local branches of the UPWA had a combined total of 94,000 members in 491 locals; in 1946 they had 126,604 members in 1,462 locals. A 1947 survey revealed that public sector unions affiliated with the AFL or CIO were in 46 percent of 674 cities polled. The *Municipal Yearbook* for 1946 listed 97 cities that had written agreements of some form with unions. The methods and results of such bargaining still took unconventional forms. G. J. Richardson, a national officer of the IAFF, explained in 1946 that a "city ordinance is just as effective as any agreement, and probably has more legal status." Still, more than 200 cities with populations over 10,000 reported that they met with representatives of labor to discuss wages, hours, and working conditions. And workers continued to join public sector unions. In 1947 approximately 600,000 of the nearly 5.9 million government workers in the United States were in employee organizations. About 60 percent of these million workers were affiliated with organized labor: over 500,000 in the AFL and just under 100,000 in the CIO. The rate of union density in the public sector would hold steady at a bit over 10 percent until the 1960s. And government employees were a large portion of the American workforce. In 1947 about one-tenth of the workforce was in the public sector.[86]

The constraints of the interwar period, however, continued. The *Municipal Yearbook* for 1946 listed sixty-six cities that refused to meet with unions and eleven that forbade their workers to belong to unions. In the mid-1940s thirty-eight cities banned police locals before they could get off the ground, and others forced existing police locals to sever their affiliation with labor. The Boston strike continued to be a factor. In 1945, after AFSCME chartered a police local in Saint Louis, Governor Philip Donnelly warned that "history reveals the dangers inherent in the organizing of police officers into unions." Further, the bargaining that public sector unions could do was much less extensive and secure than analogous activity in the private sector. An agreement between the UPWA and the city of Yonkers, New York, in 1946 provided that the city recognize the union "as a collective bargaining agent . . . without prejudice to the right of other employees . . . to bargain on their own behalf either individually or collectively." In 1955 George Meany would complain that it was "impossible to bargain collectively with the government."[87]

As the reality on the ground became even more at odds with legal rules, public sector unions would insist, with increasing force, that the strict limitations on their institutional rights were both unfair and unrealistic. In the 1950s some of these unions began to develop enough political strength to do something about it.

6

Wisconsin's Public Sector Labor Laws of 1959 and 1962

The sea of public controversy over the right of the public employee to belong to a labor union has been lapping against the dike of adverse legislative and legal opinion. . . . The dike was breached in Wisconsin.
Wisconsin City and County Employee Union News (1962)

Is there another star for organized labor to hitch its wagon to?
Christian Science Monitor (1961)

For private sector labor, the 1950s featured both unequaled successes and ominous portents. Union density climbed to nearly 35 percent, a peak from which it has declined ever since. But the image—and sometimes the reality—of unions as increasingly bureaucratic and occasionally mob-influenced grew, leading to the Landrum-Griffin Act of 1959. The CIO's expulsion of Communist-led unions in 1949–50 also left a mixed legacy. Yet the same year that Landrum-Griffin was enacted, Wisconsin passed the first state law granting organizational and proto-bargaining rights to public workers.[1]

This victory was not the end of the old regime in public sector labor relations. Nor was it the beginning of a conclusive end, considering that even today, at the beginning of the twenty-first century, around twenty states still do not grant collective bargaining rights to government employees generally. But it was the end of the beginning for public sector unions, and the start of an American labor movement increasingly composed of public workers.

For public sector labor, the 1950s was a decade of heightened contradictions. The legal regime had become brittle, as popular opinion and actual practices increasingly tolerated unions of government workers. Wisconsin's 1959 law, strengthened in 1962, was the first crack in the legal structure. Fittingly, it was passed only after a decade-long political struggle by a public sector union, in this case AFSCME. AFSCME encountered the full range of obstacles to public sector unions: fear of police strikes, which had helped defeat earlier bills; concerns about state structure, notably objections to state agencies' regulating the labor relations of local governments; and political power, as changes in the governor's mansion and legislature ultimately proved critical. The growth of the labor movement and the increased numbers of public employees helped considerably, as did the related rejuvenation of the Wisconsin Democratic party. Increased experience with stable labor relations in the private sector probably also played a role. Excluding police from the law and compromising on the power of state agencies over local governments were necessary concessions. But it was the continuing fight for legitimacy by public workers themselves that made the first laws possible. AFSCME's success paved the way for future state laws. The issues debated in Wisconsin over the proper extent of union rights in the public sector have continued in that state and the rest of the country to the present day.

In the late 1940s and into the 1950s, public sector unions (outside courtrooms) were winning increased acceptance. The growth of government and civil service had created more professionalized public sector management, reflected in publications such as *Public Personnel Review*.[2] Discussions of the role of unions had become more realistic. One essay in the 1946 book *Elements of Public Administration* argued that while collective bargaining would have to take "different forms" in government employment, there was "considerable room for constructive participation of unions in grievance procedures and work relations generally." Another essayist decried the old "authoritarian attitude" of government managers who simply invoked sovereignty; fortunately "the rank and file have pushed forward the boundaries of recognition." A third author pointed out that the sheer number of union members made them "an important facet of personnel administration." This article also challenged the notion that unions could not be allowed in government for fear of loss of public services, noting that private sector workers in utilities, transportation, and food industries could strike. In addition, it argued that the government had some authority to bargain, and it rejected the idea that unionized public workers would be biased in labor disputes.[3]

Academics increasingly stressed the similarities between private and public sector workers. Morton Godine wrote in 1951 that public employees "are essentially wage earners" who had the same economic interests and desire for a voice in their working conditions as did employees in private industry. Rollin Posey agreed in 1956 that "the essence of unionism in the public service—as in private employment—is the endeavor to improve wages, hours, and working conditions." Harry Rains, a professor of industrial relations at Hofstra University, argued that public workers were "entitled to rights similar to those enjoyed by the rest of the working population." Godine quoted Franklin Roosevelt's observation that the desire of public employees for reasonable pay, hours, and working conditions "is basically no different from that of employees in private industry." Godine added that civil service and related laws were insufficient to ensure adequate pay and conditions. Nor did job security balance the ledger, as even civil service coverage did not "confer a particularly secure status." Rains agreed that public employees did not have superior job security and, countering another traditional argument of union opponents, added that "the absence of profit motive in government agencies is compensated by constant pressures for governmental economy." Irving Bernstein, then associate director of the University of California Institute of Industrial Relations, explained in 1959 that public sector unions were "going through the same struggle for the right to organize and bargain collectively as unions in private industry were going through in the early '30s."[4]

Arguments dating from the Boston police strike were encountering the reality that public sector unions rarely struck, and that their affiliation with the labor movement had not created divided loyalties. "The power of a strike lies at the root of all suspicion of public unions," the *Providence Evening Bulletin* editorialized in 1957, but it added that in exchange for a bar on strikes, public sector unions should have binding mediation and arbitration to settle bargaining impasses. Godine explained that "the fear that unity with trade unions in private industry will lead to sympathetic strikes . . . has not been supported by experience."[5]

The fact that strikes in the private sector decreased significantly in number and size in the 1950s probably also helped to undercut fears of public sector strikes. Grievance arbitration, increasingly handled by experts, was replacing job actions as the primary vehicle to resolve day-to-day disputes at the workplace as labor contracts grew increasingly detailed and played a larger role. More generally, the 1950s featured more stable, routinized, and professionalized labor relations. It was increasingly difficult to link the concept of unions with disruptive radicalism. The theory and practice of industrial pluralism seemed viable, and it was now largely accepted by politicians and courts, at least with regard to the private sector. Melvyn Dubofsky captures the sense of contemporaries: "This form of industrial relations would guarantee economic stability . . . [and] protect the rights of individual workers through institutionalized, nondisruptive collective action." Even strikes, Dubofsky concludes, lost their "association with militancy, unruliness, and violence."[6]

Thus began explorations of how labor law could be adjusted to fit the public sector. Rights to organize and to do *some* bargaining were increasingly seen as reasonable, but descriptions of how far to extend such rights—especially, what to do if bargaining reached an impasse—remained unclear. Godine echoed union arguments that civil service and other laws left room for bargaining, since they did not "exhaustively define the conditions of public employment." Thus, "collective negotiation . . . becomes feasible," and indeed bargaining in some form was "inevitable." When quoting Franklin Roosevelt's letter to Steward, Godine added the following emphasis: "collective bargaining *as usually understood,* cannot be transplanted into the public service." This, said Godine, meant only that private sector practices could not be adopted indiscriminately. While the state was sovereign, bargaining was not *ipso facto* an improper delegation of authority, and while strikes should be barred, grievance machinery should be created. Banning strikes alone was a "barren approach to a critical problem." Still, his solution was rather vague. Godine called for "a measure of employee participation" less than full collective bargaining: "some system of collective consultation which would recognize the right of public employees to share in the determination of their conditions of employment."[7] Debates over the extent of bargaining rights and specifically what to do when bargaining reached impasse would be central not just in Wisconsin but in the development of all modern public sector labor law in America.

Mainstream organizations showed similar evolving attitudes. In the 1950s the National Civil Service League came out in favor of the right of government employees to organize. In 1959 the ACLU issued a statement arguing that public workers should have the right to organize, negotiate conditions of employment, and, except in essential services, strike. In 1955 the American Bar Association's Section on Labor Relations Law declared that public employees should have the right to organize, and that statutory bars on organizing, negotiating, and even striking were "not satisfactory approaches." Again, the precise solution was unclear. The ABA concluded that wherever "practicable," rights in the private sector should be extended to the public sector, "modified to meet the unique needs of the public service."[8]

Even some public employers were becoming more amenable. A 1950 study of public administrators noted "an increased sense of responsibility on the part of unions." The International City Managers Association (ICMA), observing that the "emergence of municipal employee organizations" would "have to be dealt with," labeled AFSCME a "responsible" organization. Employers were more tolerant of organizing than of bargaining or arbitration. Still, a 1958 report by the ICMA listed "guidelines for constructive negotiation" with unions and even contained one contributor's call for state laws that would allow recognition and written bargaining agreements. This was in part, as AFSCME national president Arnold Zander suggested, simply a result of the persistence of organized public workers. "Unions are here to stay on the municipal level," the ICMA explained, "and it would be practical to recognize the fact."[9]

No doubt the relative maturity of the private sector labor movement, with its increased size yet decreasing strike rate, helped reassure some public employers. Further, these more accepting attitudes were consistent not only with industrial pluralism, which reached its pinnacle of success in the 1950s, but with a broader political pluralism that also peaked in the 1950s. The theory of group pluralism generally stressed that democracy functioned best when government facilitated resolutions of the interests of competing groups, including unions.[10]

The overall strength of the labor movement undoubtedly also played a role. Union membership had risen from about 3.6 million in 1929 to about 18 million in 1954. Moreover, by the later 1950s public sector unions were a growing part of the labor movement. In 1956 there were 915,000 members of public sector unions; by 1964 there were 1,453,000. This trend increased the proportion of public employees in the labor movement from 5.1 to 8.1 percent.[11] Also, the AFL-CIO leadership had become more supportive. In 1948 the AFL's national convention urged state federations to press for state laws granting public workers "the same legal rights and privileges (that is, coverage by state labor relations acts . . .) now enjoyed by other workers in organized labor." AFSCME's national journal, the *Public Employee*, claimed that the "national AFL-CIO is taking an active interest" in public sector rights: "never before has the word gone down from the top to every state." In 1959 the AFL-CIO Executive Council called for rights to organize and bargain in the public sector, and the AFL-CIO convention resolved to intensify efforts to pass laws guaranteeing those rights.[12]

Most important, public sector unions were growing, despite legal restrictions. The overall expansion of public employment contributed to the growth. From 1947 to 1956 the number of government workers nationally grew from 5.4 million to almost 7.3 million. By 1962 the 8.8 million public employees accounted for approximately one-eighth of the nation's labor force. Notably, this growth took place almost entirely in state and local government: from 3,560,000 workers in 1946 to 6,380,000 in 1962. This increased scale caused legislatures to give administrators more authority to deal with public workers, which in turn made prospects for collective bargaining seem more realistic.[13]

The boom in state and local government employment greatly benefitted AFSCME, the "Union of the Future," according to an article in *Business*

Week. "Industrial unions seem to be at the end of a line . . . as more and more plants are automated," the article explained, and employment for craft unions "is growing only slowly. In public employment, however, there is an expanding reservoir of workers." AFSCME would, the article accurately predicted, eventually rival the Teamsters in size and influence. Similarly, the *Christian Science Monitor* asked, "Is there another star for organized labor to hitch its wagon to?" There "lies outside industry an entire untapped pool of potential union membership—local and state government employees." The "union that now holds the inside track in this virgin territory" was AFSCME.[14]

The law lagged behind these trends considerably. By the mid-1950s the biggest court victory for public sector unions remained a 1951 holding by the Connecticut Supreme Court in *Norwalk Teachers' Association v. Bd. of Education* that in the absence of a formal bar, organizing by government workers in Connecticut was legal. *Norwalk* did not allow any negotiations without the employer's permission, rejected most forms of arbitration, did not allow strikes, and stated that an employer could always choose to bar even organizing. But *Norwalk* did hold that in the absence of such a bar, public workers had a right to organize and that some voluntary, limited bargaining would not necessarily violate antidelegation rules. In 1958 the Arkansas Supreme Court became the first court to strike down a ban on organizing in the public sector. Ironically, *Potts v. Hay* held that the ban violated the "right-to-work" clause in the state constitution, which provided that employment could not be based on union membership or the lack thereof.[15] *Norwalk* and *Potts* were the public sector equivalent of the minimalistic rights to organize, and do little else, that private sector workers had won in *Commonwealth v. Hunt* over a century earlier.

Nonetheless, the practice of negotiating at least informal agreements was on the rise. In 1946 AFSCME claimed that it had 40 bilateral agreements with public employers and had helped formulate fifty ordinances or similar labor policies. In 1957 AFSCME declared that it had "agreements" for 445 local unions or councils (out of over 1,500 locals). The increasing disparity between the law on the books and actual practice focused attention on how, if at all, such contracts could be formed and enforced in light of sovereignty or delegation concerns. The National Civil Service League explained that a city could join a union "not in a binding joint contract, but in a memorandum, freely accepted," which the employer would administer. The ABA argued that negotiated agreements could bind governments pursuant only to an unequivocal grant of power to the public employer. In 1956 a local in New Haven, Connecticut, became the first AFSCME union to use the American Arbitration Association to resolve a contractual grievance.[16] But whether arbitration of grievances or bargaining impasses could or should generally be allowed remained controversial.

Further, opponents of public sector union rights were numerous and influential. The strongly anti-union National Institute of Municipal Law Officers and its general counsel Charles Rhyne argued through the 1950s that without specific legislative authorization public employers could not bargain at all, and that such authorization should not be granted. Private sector business interests tended to agree. Indeed, in 1959 bills designed to limit the rights of public sector unions were introduced in Georgia, North Carolina, Texas, Tennessee, and Arkansas. The North Carolina bill became law, barring all public employees from organizing and forbidding contracts or even "understandings"—written or oral—between government employers and unions.[17]

Commentators noted the increasing discrepancy between law and reality. Edward Cling argued that the "great deal of informal collective bargaining" in the public sector meant that "the legalistic approach," that collective bargaining contracts inevitably were improper delegations of legislative power, "must be reviewed from a practical standpoint." Posey wrote that the risk of strikes in the public sector came from refusing to recognize unions, not from bargaining. Fundamentally, public workers had created a reality on the ground that made their call for bargaining rights seem both realistic and inevitable.[18] This trend made it possible for AFSCME in Wisconsin to wage its lengthy and ultimately successful campaign.

AFSCME was chartered in 1936. It had grown out of the Wisconsin State Administrative Employees Association, which was established in 1932. The organization affiliated with AFGE in 1935–36, but soon left.[19] Its subsequent growth was stunning. In 1936 it had 5,355 members. By 1941 it claimed 42,000; in 1946, it claimed 78,164.[20] This figure rose to over 100,000 in 1954, over 120,000 in 1956, and to 185,000 by 1958. In 1959, with around 200,000 members, AFSCME was the twentieth-largest of the AFL-CIO's 125 unions; by 1961, with 210,000 members, it was eighteenth. Contrary to the image of public employees as "white-collar," in 1959 about 70 percent of AFSCME's membership were blue-collar workers.[21]

During the late 1950s and early 1960s the upper echelons of AFSCME were engaged in a struggle between the supporters of longtime president Arnold Zander and the more militant Jerry Wurf, who would replace Zander as president in 1964.[22] But the roiling waters atop the organization had no discernible impact on the campaigns in Wisconsin.

By the 1950s AFSCME national had begun to press more seriously for bargaining rights. In 1936 AFSCME's convention called for such rights; at the 1948 AFL national convention Zander insisted that bargaining was not "synonymous with strikes." But by about 1954, Kramer argues, AFSCME was putting more emphasis on bargaining. Governments had "failed to practice what they have compelled private industry to do." In 1957 Zander wrote that AFSCME had "begun to seek true collective bargaining, with contracts wherever and whenever possible." This was "a shift in emphasis," from stressing civil service and "some form of bargaining" to a "clearly defined policy of gaining formal recognition and establishing . . . collective bargaining." In 1959 Zander insisted that "collective bargaining has emerged . . . as both the most effective operating tool this union possesses and the right we must struggle hardest to win."[23]

This program required changes in the law. After the AFL-CIO merger in 1955, AFSCME passed a resolution asking the entire labor movement to help pass statutes granting organizing and bargaining rights, and at its 1958 convention it announced a major push for such laws. The union had experienced limited success at the local level. In 1955 Philadelphia adopted a civil service regulation authorizing agreements with AFSCME Council 33 as the collective bargaining agent for wages, hours, and working conditions, subject to applicable laws. In 1958 AFSCME Council 37, then led by Wurf, helped convince New York City mayor Robert Wagner Jr. to sign Executive Order 49, which gave municipal workers organizing and bargaining rights.[24] But AFSCME wanted state laws, insisting that recognition and bargaining rights were "the central need of the union." AFSCME made international comparisons, noting that in seven of Canada's ten provinces there was "no distinction" between private sector and municipal workers; public employees had the right to organize, bargain, and even strike. The "issue of legal sovereignty . . . does not seem to have become a factor." Also, in England the "problem" of public sector bargaining and organizing "simply does not exist. . . . There are no special laws" for public employees. "They are governed by the same laws . . . as everyone else." Arbitration had been the norm since 1919; strikes were allowed, but arbitration worked so well that strikes were "few and far between."[25]

Fittingly, AFSCME's first success in passing a state law would be in the state in which the organization was born. In 1938 there were around 6,000 members of AFSCME in Wisconsin; there were 12,000 by 1960. By the late 1950s AFSCME alone had organized 7 to 8 percent of Wisconsin's public workforce. In 1957 there were about 140,000 public employees in the state, a majority of whom worked for local governments. AFSCME members were fairly equally divided between the local government workers in the Wisconsin Council of County and Municipal Employees (WCCME), which became AFSCME Council 40, and AFSCME's State Employees Council, which became Council 24. The county and municipal employees in the WCCME were the force behind the public sector labor laws. In 1951 the WCCME claimed seventy-nine locals, and by 1958 it had ninety-seven, spread among nearly all the major cities and most of the counties in Wisconsin. In 1946 the WCCME had 700 members; in 1956, 4,500; and by

1960, 6,000. This rise outpaced the growth of government employment in Wisconsin. Many WCCME members worked on highway construction projects, as Wisconsin undertook massive highway construction and road improvement programs in the 1950s.[26]

The WCCME was always active in politics and related forms of bargaining. Reclaiming a political tradition for labor, the WCCME's paper, the *Wisconsin City and County Employee Union News,* quoted Gompers: "There is not an action which the unions take, whether it be an increase of wages, [or] an hour more leisure . . . without it being at the same time a political act." The WCCME engaged in informal bargaining well before any law authorized it; for example, it claimed that "negotiations" with the Kenosha County Highway Board in 1948 had yielded, among other things, a workweek reduced to forty hours. As early as 1949, WCCME locals met to discuss "bargaining techniques . . . and the nature of requests to be made to county boards." Some agreements were written and signed by both parties. Through the 1950s the WCCME claimed significant successes from such processes; in 1950 Local 655, Jefferson County Highway Employees, had a signed agreement covering union dues, a guaranteed workweek, vacations, and arbitration. In 1956 the *Union News* declared that "negotiations with management are carried on so smoothly that it is almost like regular business meetings." Tellingly, however, the WCCME also referred to its practices as "petitioning." Certainly "bargaining" had a different meaning than it had in the private sector. For example, one local appointed a seven-member "bargaining committee" that successfully lobbied the Kenosha County Highway Board for a pay increase.[27]

The WCCME's influence grew, and forms of bargaining spread. In the mid-1950s the state's seventy-one county highway departments employed around 6,000 workers. Of these seventy-one, forty-seven had unions, thirty-one recognized their union as some form of bargaining agent, and eighteen had contracts or written agreements with unions. In 1955, out of forty-nine towns with populations of over 5,000 responding to a poll, thirty-four stated that at least some of their employees were organized. Most of these (outside fire departments) were in AFSCME. Fifteen towns reported that they did some bargaining, and twenty-eight of the remaining thirty-four reported "informal" union participation in wage determinations. Ten towns had entered into a written agreement with their employees. Highlighting an old issue that still had life in some quarters, four towns stated that they denied police the right to affiliate with the AFL or CIO.[28]

AFSCME was not satisfied with its limited successes. In 1956 the *Union News* complained that wages and hours in the public sector were worse than in private employment. WCCME executive director Robert Oberbeck claimed that the majority of AFSCME members made less than $1.40 an hour, while the average wage for production workers in the state was $2.02. He also claimed that sixty-seven of the seventy-one county highway departments required forty-five-to-sixty-hour weeks, while the average in private industry was less than forty-two hours. Moreover, sixty county highway departments paid no premium for overtime. Such discrepancies were common nationally. Workers in the same jobs in the same cities (for example, stenographers, nurses, and draftsmen) made significantly less in the public sector than in the private. Also, Oberbeck argued that in Wisconsin some local government employers discriminated against union supporters.[29]

Further, significant pockets of popular and legal opposition remained. In 1943 Milwaukee garbage workers not affiliated with labor had struck for several days, alarming segments of the public. The *Milwaukee Journal* called for a law formally outlawing public sector strikes, and it remained skeptical of labor in government employment through the 1950s. In 1953, after AFSCME organized a union of Milwaukee County deputy sheriffs, the local civil service commission banned the union, citing fears of divided loyalties. AFSCME took this issue to court and lost. In 1956 Milwaukee's city attorney opined that collective bargaining would constitute an improper delegation of legislative power. AFSCME turned out between 400 and 500 members to a hearing on the matter to no avail.[30] AFSCME knew it needed a state law.

Wisconsin had been a pioneer in employment legislation. It was the first state to enact a workers' compensation law in 1911, and it helped lead the way on unemployment compensation, industrial safety, and child labor. "Wisconsin ranks among the leading states in the extent and quality of its labor laws," one author concluded in 1958. This status reflected a concentration of progressive movements in the state: most famously, the Republican party's progressive wing, led by governors Robert LaFollette Sr. and Philip LaFollette; the strong and politically active state AFL and CIO, with their significant socialist influences; and the close relationship of the University of Wisconsin to state government. The university was home to key industrial pluralists such as John Commons and William Leiserson, who were central to New Deal policy. The American Association for Labor Legislation was organized in Madison in 1907 and later had its headquarters in Commons's office in the State Historical Library.[31]

The Wisconsin Labor Relations Act of 1937, modeled on the NLRA, was the first state labor statute. It applied only to private employers. The law was administered by a three-member board (with members representing employers, labor, and the public) called the Wisconsin Employment Relations Board (WERB). By the mid-1950s the WERB was handling 400 to 500 cases a year: unfair labor practices (ULPs), representation cases, mediations, and arbitrations. The Wisconsin Industrial Commission, which administered workers' compensation and other employment laws, had authority to mediate and arbitrate private sector labor disputes. But it had never had authority in the public sector. No state body or statute regulated unions in government employment. In 1923 the Wisconsin Assembly debated but did not pass a bill that would have made it illegal for any public worker to belong to a union.[32]

After 1939 Wisconsin's progressive tradition flagged considerably. While ranking around tenth in the nation in industrialization, Wisconsin also had a strong agricultural industry that pushed for restrictive labor laws. Indeed, Cling argues that the state took a "conservative view" of labor legislation after the New Deal. The Progressive party fell apart after the pivotal elections of 1938, in which LaFollette lost the governor's seat and many other progressives were swept out of office. This election led to traditional Republican control of practically all arms of state government until 1958. Republicans held the governorship from 1939 to 1959, along with the offices of lieutenant governor, secretary of state, state treasurer, and attorney general (except from 1948 to 1951, when Democrat Thomas Fairchild was attorney general). And Republicans controlled both houses of the state assembly in this era.[33]

The rights of public sector unions would be a central battleground for a recovering Democratic party and the dominant Republicans in the 1950s. After the demise of the Progressive party, liberal groups ultimately reorganized within the Democratic party. Labor was the most important of these constituencies, and labor and the Democrats increasingly looked to each other for support, a situation that helped AFSCME. In contrast, the Republican leadership from the late 1930s through the 1950s was dominated by industrialists such as Thomas Coleman, president of the Madison-Kipp Corporation, and Governor Walter Kohler. The party was hardly friendly to labor or public workers. Wisconsin historian William Thompson observed that from 1947 to 1957 it was "painful for many Republicans" to realize that public employment was increasing and that public employees would not work at "servant's wages. . . . Anathema to such Republicans was the possibility that these public employees would form unions."[34]

The legal rights of public workers had been a contentious issue. In 1938 Wisconsin attorney general Orlando Loomis opined that "we know of no rule of law that would prohibit governmental employees from . . . organizing." Many municipal officials accepted that public employees could unionize in the absence of a local bar. For example, the city attorney of Milwaukee declared organizing lawful. But in 1940 Republican attorney general John Martin opined that in the absence of specific statutory authority, public employers could not enter into collective bargaining agreements. AFSCME unsuccessfully argued that a 1945 law giving counties the power to contract for employee services authorized bargaining. In 1947, as a wave of statutes passed across the country barring public sector strikes, the Wisconsin Chamber of Commerce sponsored a bill that provided for discharge, fines, and imprisonment of strikers. It did not pass, although a bill restricting strikes against public utilities did. This statute also provided collective bargaining rights for public utility workers, but the U.S. Supreme Court struck down the law, ruling that it was preempted by the NLRA. Also in 1947, the legislature rejected a bill that would have given government workers the right to organize and limited bargaining rights. In 1949 AFSCME was on the defensive. While claiming credit for defeating the strike bill, it added that it would be "in large measure a success" simply to keep "any anti-public employee legislation from passing."[35]

AFSCME extemporized by making some use of the WERB, even though the private sector law did not actually cover the public sector. The WERB would conduct representation elections when both a government employer and a union requested it to do so, even though such elections were not legally binding. Also, if both sides requested, the WERB would assign mediators or fact-finders to help governments and unions resolve differences. For example, in the summer of 1950 the WERB held a representation election for city employees in Mensasha, which AFSCME Local 1035 won, and in 1949 the Two Rivers City Employees Local requested WERB intervention in a wage dispute between the city and the union. But even these limited procedures required atypically agreeable employers. In 1956 Council 48 requested a formal collective bargaining contract with Milwaukee, noting that 2,700 of the city's employees were union members. AFSCME national president Zander came to Milwaukee to lobby for the cause. But the city merely referred the matter to its attorney for advice, and there it died.[36] AFSCME realized it needed a state law that would provide substantive rights and that would bind even anti-union employers.

Like other public sector unions, AFSCME in Wisconsin had always lobbied for various laws affecting its members.[37] The struggle for institutional rights for public sector labor started in earnest in 1951 with a bill introduced by the WCCME, and it would continue for decades. The initial attempt in 1951 foundered on rocks frustratingly familiar to public sector activists, notably the fear of police strikes.

Central to these battles was attorney John Lawton. Born in 1917, Lawton graduated from the University of Wisconsin Law School in 1942 and served as an assistant district attorney for Dane County, Wisconsin, from 1942 to 1946. While in that job, he became president of AFSCME Local 720 (Dane County Employees). Lawton was the WCCME's executive secretary-treasurer from 1944 through the 1950s. He also acted as the WCCME's legislative representative in Madison and provided legal counsel to it and other public sector unions in Wisconsin from the late 1940s into the 1970s. While in private practice, Lawton was briefly a partner of future governor Gaylord Nelson, the man who would ultimately sign Wisconsin's first public sector statute into law. In the late 1940s Lawton began calling for a state law granting public workers the rights to organize and to bargain.[38]

In early 1951 Lawton drafted Bill 462-S for the WCCME.[39] The bill covered "municipal" employees, defined as employees of any city, town, village, county, school board, or other subdivision of the state. It provided a clear right to organize (giving employees the right to "form and join labor organizations of their own choice") but was more ambiguous regarding bargaining. The bill stated that its purpose was to promote "collective considerations" and to "encourage mutual understandings" concerning wages, hours, and working conditions. "Collective considerations" were defined as "the study . . . of terms or conditions of employment in a mutually genuine effort to reach an agreement." There was a limited recourse in case of impasse: If collective considerations failed to produce an agreement, then either party could petition the WERB for a conciliator. The bill did not propose formal collective bargaining along private sector lines, probably because of the opinion of Vernon Thomson, the Republican attorney general and future governor, which cast doubt on the validity of collective bargaining contracts in the public sector. Still, the *Union News* enthused that the bill would grant the right to "bargain." The bill also made it an unfair labor practice for an employer to interfere with the rights that the bill provided.[40]

The pitched legislative battle that followed featured the usual types of partisans and the predictable issue of police strikes, but it also foreshadowed new, practical issues involving the precise scope of union rights and the power of state labor agencies over local governments. Organized public employers, the Wisconsin County Boards Association and the League of Wisconsin Municipalities, opposed the bill, as did private sector business interests such as the state chamber of commerce and the Wisconsin Manufacturers Association. Opponents successfully sponsored an amendment that dropped the concept of "collective considerations" and added language stating that the bill did not confer a right to strike. The WCCME tried unsuccessfully to amend the bill to clarify that the WERB had the power to investigate complaints of violations of the law and to issue findings of fact and recommendations. The senate then passed the bill. In the assembly, AFSCME defeated an amendment that would have eliminated police and fire personnel from coverage. Another amendment added state employees to the bill's coverage.[41]

Even though the bill stated that it did not grant a right to strike, opponents stressed that issue and related fears. The *Wisconsin State Journal* raised the classic specter of the police strike, agreeing with A. J. Thelen, the executive secretary of the County Boards Association, that the bill should explicitly bar strikes and exclude law enforcement. Lawton gave the traditional responses that there had never been a strike of police or firefighters in Wisconsin and that the rules of the relevant unions barred such actions, but this fear would ultimately prove fatal to the bill. And some opponents went further. Assemblyman Robert Travis (R–Platteville), sponsor of the amendment that would have excluded public safety employees, complained that "we in Wisconsin do not want to be one of the states that says a labor form of government is the best form of government, and that is just what this bill does."[42]

The WCCME made standard union replies but also tried to move the conversation forward by making specific, realistic compromises. Echoing labor's position in Seattle decades earlier, the WCCME noted that "lawyers, doctors, businessmen and farmers" all belonged to organizations. The right to organize was "a basic right of citizenship." Focusing on the bill at hand, the WCCME added that it "does not require that the employer must give anything to his employees—it simply says they must talk to them about their problems." Further, the WERB could conciliate but it could not force the parties to agree. Appealing to modern sentiments that at least tolerated public sector unions, Lawton focused on specific instances of discrimination against workers for union activity. Still, labor was trapped in older concerns. Lawton felt it necessary to argue that by "no stretch of the imagination" could the bill be interpreted to permit strikes. As to public safety workers, he repeatedly stated that most firefighters and some police in the state were already organized; that AFSCME required the constitutions of its police locals to bar strikes; and that no AFSCME police local had ever struck or even been accused of actually acting in a manner biased toward labor.[43]

The final version of the bill retained the right to organize, but the proto-bargaining and enforcement rights were weakened even further. The original concepts of "collective considerations" and "mutual understandings" were replaced with the even less specific idea of promoting better relations between the parties. Conciliation by the WERB was now possible only if both parties, as opposed to either party, requested it. The WERB could investigate alleged violations of the law and issue findings of fact and recommendations, but the recommendations were not binding, and there were no sanctions for ignoring them. AFSCME did succeed in keeping coverage of police and fire services, and while the bill stated that it did not confer a right to strike, it did not specify penalties for striking. The bill thus amended passed and was sent to the desk of Governor Walter Kohler Jr.[44]

Walter Kohler was the governor of Wisconsin from 1951 to 1957. "Born to wealth and power," in Thompson's words, Kohler was the son of leading businessman Walter Kohler Sr. (who served a term as governor during the 1920s). Generally considered a moderate Republican whose accomplishments included constructing the Wisconsin highway system, the younger Kohler had strong connections to business. He had past ties to his family's concern, the Kohler Company, and later became the president of the Vollrath Company, a manufacturer of steel equipment. Kohler was not especially sympathetic to labor; for example, he praised the Taft-Hartley Act as a "protection" for workers. Further, in 1951 Kohler had broken from tradition in his appointments to the WERB by replacing the labor representative with a second public representative.[45]

AFSCME and its members lobbied Kohler to sign the bill, appealing to notions of rights now well established in the private sector. Hundreds of workers signed petitions stating that "public employees should have the same right to organize and negotiate . . . as our fellow workers in private industry." Local 1436, Jackson County Highway Employees, wrote Kohler that although "the county boards, the League of Wisconsin Municipalities, the State Chamber of Commerce and the Wisconsin Association of Manufacturers are urging you to veto this bill, we believe this is directly against the rights and privileges of the American way of life." There should be "better understanding . . . through collective bargaining." Local 407, City of LaCrosse Employees, wrote that the bill would provide "a fair means" to discuss problems. Individual workers echoed Lawton's emphasis on antiunion discrimination. Highway employee Clayton Randorf explained that his co-workers had been "pushed around" for union activities. AFSCME president Zander wrote and telegraphed Kohler and even came to Madison to meet with him to promote the bill. Other smaller public sector unions, such as the Wisconsin County Police and Police Radio Operators Association, wrote Kohler in favor of the bill. The Wisconsin Paid Firemen's Association argued that the bill "is a natural for Wisconsin, which has long led the way" in progressive legislation.[46]

While a few public officials endorsed the bill, most argued against it on the basis of the old fears of strikes and police organizing. Henry Ahrens, mayor of LaCrosse, wrote Kohler that the bill was "fair for labor and municipality alike." But more typically, Oliver Grootemaat, president of the village of Whitefish Bay, objected that the "mere elimination of one phrase could grant municipal employees the right to strike" and that permitting police to organize "might place them in the anomalous position of being called upon to police a strike called by a brother union." Similarly echoing the old "divided loyalty" charge, the mayor of Wausau, Herbert Giese, argued that it was "very bad public policy" to permit police to organize, because in a strike the labor movement would pressure police to favor the striking union. The League of Municipalities added that allowing police to organize was contrary to the "semi-military" nature of police duties and that "a democratic system . . . depends upon the unbiased and impartial enforcement of laws." The league explicitly cited Coolidge and the Boston police strike as support. Another opponent claimed that allowing Milwaukee police to join the labor movement would be the same as "unionization of the army." The league added another argument that would be central in future debates: the state should not legislate in this area, but rather local officials should deal with such matters (and have the power to ban unions). Indeed, the league argued, the bill would probably violate home-rule provisions of state laws. Also, the league and others raised delegation concerns about anything approaching bargaining. But the police issue was central. A memo to Attorney General Thomson stated that the main practical effect of the bill would be to allow police to organize, and added that "there is a strong sentiment in many sections of the country against" police unions, and "many localities have prohibited" them.[47]

Kohler vetoed the bill, objecting to the affiliation of police with labor and specifically citing the need for police to maintain order in labor disputes. Public employers were pleased. "It disturbed me considerably to know that our state Legislature would even consider such a proposal," wrote A. P. Kuranz, water utility manager for the city of Waukesha. "Constant vigilance is the only way to protect ourselves against the insidious pressure groups." The *Union News* put the best spin it could on this defeat, stressing Kohler's remark that "for the overwhelming majority of state and local employees, the present laws and customs embrace the privilege of belonging to labor unions." Kohler's objection was only to unionizing "employees in the uniformed services."[48]

But while concerns about police, strikes, and the proper extent and enforceability of bargaining rights remained, law and reality were becoming more and more out of sync. The WCCME continued to grow, its locals continued to engage in limited negotiations, and the WERB sometimes helped to settle disputes. Meanwhile, prospects seemed dim for a new law in 1953. In 1952 Kohler had been reelected with 63 percent of the vote, the largest margin of victory to that date in Wisconsin history; further, the *Union News* described the 1953 legislature as being "generally unfavorable . . . toward public employees and toward labor generally."[49]

Nonetheless, on February 11, 1953, the WCCME introduced Bills 209-S and 210-S. Bill 209-S would have allowed local government employers to agree to union shops if two-thirds of the employees affected voted in favor. This bill died in committee. The more realistic Bill 210-S would have provided that contracts between local governments and unions with durations of up to one year would be enforceable. "The biggest problem in public employment," Lawton had concluded in a report to the WERB, was "the lack of machinery for effective negotiations."[50]

Once again the WCCME and other unions, including private sector bodies such as the Wisconsin AFL's Federated Trades Council, squared off against the League of Municipalities, the County Boards Association, the Wisconsin Manufacturers Association, and the state chamber of commerce. But this time the delegation issue would prove fatal. In response to a request by the senate, Attorney General Thomson opined that the bill was probably unconstitutional on nondelegation grounds because it would allow contracts that would restrict the discretion of legislative bodies regarding governmental functions. Compensation of public workers "has been considered a legislative function" that "may not be surrendered or delegated," especially not to private parties. Previous attorney general opinions had stated that public employers could negotiate conditions of employment but could not enter into binding agreements. Case law indicated that at least some common provisions of labor contracts were invalid in the public sector. "It is conceivable that some aspects of public employment might be dealt with by contract," Thomson concluded, "but such questions as wages and hours of employment—and probably most other working conditions normally dealt with in collective bargaining agreements—involve the exercise of legislative functions." Shortly after the senate received this opinion, the bill was indefinitely postponed on a vote of seventeen to fifteen. Most of the votes to kill the bill came from Republicans.[51]

Undeterred, the WCCME directed Lawton to reintroduce the 1951 bill at the 1955 legislative session, and simultaneously the WCCME focused on political action. In December 1954 the WCCME held a legislative conference that attracted 150 delegates from various unions to discuss strategies. The WCCME tried to craft a compromise with the League of Municipalities, but the process broke down over whether a law should cover police, impasse resolution (AFSCME wanted alternative mechanisms in exchange for a strike ban), and the league's insistence that a state law would violate home rule. Still, the league took this matter seriously, cautioning local officials that to "avoid state interference in this essentially local matter" they must prove both willing and able "to handle their labor problems at home."[52] In the end the 1955 round of the battle produced at best a draw in the form of a promise to study the issue.

The WCCME had Bill 89-S introduced on January 27, 1955. Like the 1951 bill, Bill 89-S granted the right to organize and to engage in "collective considerations" with employers, made employer interference with such rights unfair labor practices, and provided for WERB conciliation. Proponents of the bill at the hearings included a greater range of private as well as public sector unionists from the CIO and the AFL. Again, the League of

Municipalities, the County Boards Association, and the Wisconsin Chamber of Commerce led the opposition. Three key amendments were adopted to address the concerns of opponents. First, the WCCME reluctantly agreed to exclude law enforcement. Second, the concept of "collective considerations" was replaced with the phrase "better relations with unions through conferences and negotiations." Third, a clause was added stating that the law did not grant a right to strike.[53]

Union opponents focused on the most contentious issues and insisted that "home rule" principles should give individual public employers the discretion to ban unions. The WCCME again tried to appeal to evolving attitudes, stressing that anti-union discrimination was wrong and that the bill would "interfere" with home rule only to the extent that local governments were engaged in such discrimination. Nor did the bill create a right to strike. In contrast, the chamber of commerce pushed the "divided loyalty" point, again demonstrating why business interests worried about public sector labor. The chamber argued that government, which was responsible for regulating business and labor, was already pressured by private sector unions, and that such pressures should not come from within the government as well. Taking a slightly more modern view, the *Milwaukee Journal* focused its opposition not on the right to organize but rather on the concept of negotiations. Public workers already had sufficient influence, the paper objected; in Milwaukee, they "sit in on discussions of wages, working conditions and other problems" and "often keep elected officials jumping through hoops." Further, any bargaining would be incompatible with civil service rules.[54]

The senate rejected Bill 89-S on June 24, 1955, although the WCCME salvaged a face-saving agreement providing for a study. Joint Resolution 81-S stated that in view of the controversies over the rights of public workers to organize, whether the state should provide machinery for mediating or arbitrating disputes, and the related constitutional and policy questions, the Legislative Council should investigate and make a report to the 1957 legislature. The League of Municipalities and chamber of commerce opposed even this, but it passed anyway.[55]

The WCCME bemoaned the power of its "two toughest opponents": the broadly anti-union chamber, and the league, which was fighting "against granting some meager rights to its own employees." Further, labor as a whole was increasingly dissatisfied with Governor Kohler (who had been narrowly reelected in 1954) and his fellow Republicans. The president of the Wisconsin Federation of Labor declared that the 1955 session featured "the worst legislature since Wisconsin was incorporated as a state." Still, AFSCME optimistically noted that the advisory committee of the WERB had approved of Bill 89-S, and its opinion "should have some weight with the Legislative Council."[56]

Both sides jockeyed over the study in words and political mobilization. In September 1955 the WCCME held a statewide meeting that focused on building political activity at the local level. Rhetorically, the *Union News* stressed that allowing discrimination against public sector unionists was out of step with the times. Government workers "were the only major group of employees in the state of Wisconsin that has not been granted collective bargaining rights." The chamber of commerce again replied with claims of divided loyalty: public sector organizing "constitutes a threat to maintaining governmental functions available to all our people. . . . Loyalty of a public employee must be to all the people and should never be simply to a labor official or organization." The chamber also warned that labor's political power would only increase with the AFL-CIO merger. Still, Lawton optimistically predicted that a law granting recognition and bargaining rights was a goal "now in sight."[57]

The debate turned much nastier, however, after a group of public employees participated in something similar to secondary activity in support of a private sector strike. This action prompted opponents to call for a ban on all public sector unions. In July 1955, during a strike by private sector workers at the Kohler Company, some municipal employees at the Milwaukee docks represented by AFSCME temporarily refused to unload some goods destined for Kohler. Although the workers later agreed to unload the cargo, the owners of the ship filed secondary boycott charges. The NLRB then dismissed the charges on the grounds that the NLRA did not apply to the public sector. In reaction to this incident, on August 6, 1956, the chamber of commerce called on the Legislative Council to recommend laws that would bar public workers from forming AFL-CIO affiliated unions. Ironically, the chamber argued that the *exclusion* of public employees from the NLRA left the public unprotected from "big union-affiliated governmental labor organizations." Chamber representative Joseph Fagan used this event to bolster his argument that public employees "should owe their loyalty to all the people and not simply the big merged AFL-CIO."[58]

The *Union News* was outraged. The chamber was "attempting to get revenge" and trying "to cripple public employee unions." The secondary action was an "isolated case" and was no excuse for denying public workers the right to organize. Lawton predicted that the chamber's proposal would be "soundly rebuffed" by the 1957 legislature. Needling, he noted that AFSCME would never propose legislation denying businessmen the right to form their own organizations. The *Public Employee* added that Fagan's name "sounds like that of a Dickens villain." Still, labor took the threat seriously and marshaled considerable forces against it. George Haberman, president of the Wisconsin Federation of Labor, wrote a public letter insisting that "the labor movement feels very strongly that public employees should be given the legal right to organize and bargain collectively," and the Wisconsin federation passed a resolution pledging to "exert constant efforts" to enact laws to rectify the "discriminatory, unfair, and un-American" legal status of public workers. Charles Schultz, president of the state CIO, also publicly pledged "wholehearted support." The *Union News* called on members and supporters to oppose the chamber's plan. AFSCME national officers, including President Zander, promised to help fight the chamber's "vicious attack." Showing some confidence in its political power, the WCCME sent a questionnaire to all 195 candidates running for state office in Wisconsin's November election asking whether public workers should have the right to organize: 78 of the 79 respondents answered "yes."[59]

Opponents displayed equal confidence. The chamber issued a memo on November 20, 1956, the day the Legislative Committee released its report, asking for a statewide referendum during the April 1957 elections on the right to organize. "We are convinced that the Wisconsin people will overwhelmingly support a prohibition of AFL-CIO affiliated labor unions in Wisconsin government." The memo emphasized "THE IMPORTANT DIFFERENCES BETWEEN PUBLIC AND PRIVATE EMPLOYMENT." Again revealing the concerns of private employers, Fagan added that the AFL-CIO merger would mean that labor would be "nearly a third party," which "could mean the end of our capitalistic system." The League of Municipalities took a more moderate and more successful tack, again stressing that the unionization of municipal workers was a local concern and not a matter for state legislation. Robert Sundby, the league's legal counsel, also told the Legislative Council that municipal labor relations were generally good. Therefore, no law granting rights to unions was needed.[60]

The Legislative Council's report of November 20, 1956, reflected contemporary attitudes that increasingly tolerated the existence of public sector unions but had not yet worked out what rights they should have. The council determined that prohibiting all public employees from joining unions would be "unreasonable and extreme"; that "agreements" with these unions were legal but "contracts" were not; that the union shop, exclusive bargaining, compulsory arbitration, strikes, and pickets could not be permitted in public employment; and that "no serious state-wide problem" existed in local government labor relations. The council noted that in Wisconsin, government employees (except, in some cases, police) were usually allowed to form unions. Adopting the league's position, the council concluded that because the "home rule principle" had produced "generally satisfactory labor relations . . . state dictation of a labor policy would be unwise." Assemblyman Isaac Coggs of Milwaukee authored a minority position that recommended a law such as AFSCME had advocated.

That AFSCME avoided a ban on organizing was a product of evolving attitudes, reality on the ground, and, as the *Union News* noted, the WCCME's growing strength. But AFSCME did not win bargaining or even organizing rights, and again it remained unclear what types of bargaining or other activities were permissible. Still, the *Union News* promised that AFSCME would "continue to press for legislation" and that "political action at the local level will ultimately give us success!" Lawton emphasized that "the only remedy . . . is a political one."[61]

In 1957 the WCCME tried compromising from the start by excluding law enforcement. Otherwise, Bill 235-S repeated the same themes. It provided public employees the right to organize and to be represented by unions "in conferences and negotiations" with employers regarding "wages, hours, and conditions of employment." The WERB could appoint conciliators and then fact-finders to help resolve disputes. Again, Lawton appealed to contemporary sensibilities. The bill was necessary because "a substantial minority" of employers, "particularly in county government," were opposing unionization through "threats of discharge, demotion, and other forms of discrimination." Again, the main opposition came from the League of Municipalities, the County Boards Association, and the chamber of commerce.[62]

The bill was killed in committee by a highly partisan vote. A crucial motion to release the bill to the senate floor failed by seventeen votes to fifteen, with all seventeen "nays" coming from Republicans (ten of the fifteen "ayes" came from Democrats). The WCCME now turned its full attention to electoral politics. "If we ever needed proof that political organization and political action are absolutely necessary," WCCME executive director Oberbeck fumed, this "Chamber of Commerce dominated legislature" provided it. The *Union News* listed the votes of senators on the bill, advising its readers: "Study it carefully! Find out who is friend and who is foe. Clip it out and carry it in your billfold. When you see your state senator, pull out the roll call to see how he voted."[63]

Crucially, the WCCME—unlike the unions featured in previous chapters—was finally in a position both to help cause political change at the state level and to take advantage of it. "Public employees are steadily growing in influence," the *Union News* noted. "With each succeeding legislative session we are listened to with a more attentive ear." Similarly, in late 1957 the *Waukesha Freeman* observed that the "public employees of Wisconsin are beginning to flex their political muscles" and were "being organized more effectively each year." The "public employee lobby can be a formidable one." AFSCME increasingly focused on elections. In October 1958 Oberbeck decried anti-union firings in a county highway department and insisted that the legislation was the only solution. With the next month's elections obviously in mind, he recalled the veto of the 1951 bill by "your present governor" and later bills blocked by "influential opponents in the legislature." He advised AFSCME supporters to ask their representatives about organizing and collective bargaining rights. If a representative was opposed, "don't vote for him." The *Union News* regularly urged similar political action. "With this kind of activity at the local level," it concluded prophetically, "we will succeed in the 1959 session of the legislature." Sensing broader political trends, national president Zander predicted that "1959 looks like a time of breakthrough on the legislative front for AFSCME, a time when we will secure those rights which have never been spelled out in . . . public service."[64]

In Wisconsin the key change came with the elections of 1958. For the first time in decades, Wisconsin elected a Democratic governor, Gaylord Nelson, and a Democratic state assembly. Nelson, a former state senator, defeated Kohler's successor, Vernon Thomson, to become only the second Democrat elected governor of the state in the century. Nelson was much more friendly toward unions than his predecessors had been. He had worked in Lawton's law firm (he and Lawton were law school classmates) and served as a field representative for the WCCME. The *Public Employee* enthused that Nelson had "compiled an outstanding record as a legislator." For example, in contrast to Kohler, Nelson had opposed "right to work" laws. Further, 1958 marked the first year since 1932 that Democrats had won a majority in the state assembly. Indeed, between 1947 and 1957 the Republicans had failed to win a two-thirds majority in both houses of the state legislature only once (in 1955, when they held "only" 64 of the 100 seats in the assembly). Now Democrats had a 55-to-45 advantage in the assembly. Democrats also won back the offices of lieutenant governor, attorney general, and state treasurer. They even gained three state senate seats, although Republicans retained a majority there, twenty to thirteen.[65]

Sudden as the shift was, the forces driving it had long been in motion, and labor was a central factor. Republicans had been increasingly divided over issues ranging from legislative reapportionment (along "one man, one vote" lines) to anticommunism, and by internal factions. As governor, Thomson had never had good relations with Republican legislators, and in the 1958 elections he was saddled with Republican support of the unpopular ideas of creating a sales tax and making Wisconsin a "right to work" state, along with a recession in which 90,000 Wisconsinites had lost their jobs. Meanwhile, by the mid-1950s the Democrats had become revitalized, with the help of former Progressive Republicans, including Nelson and future Democratic attorney general John Reynolds, and labor. The Democrats were increasingly successful at fusing their prolabor ideals with a sizable portion of Wisconsin's farm vote. The 1954 election produced the largest

gains for the Democrats since the end of the war. In 1957 E. William Proxmire, who had narrowly lost the governor's races in 1954 and 1956, won
the special election for senator to replace Joe McCarthy after his death.
Proxmire was Wisconsin's first Democratic senator since 1939. The Democratic party had regained respectability.[66]

Unions provided crucial money and manpower for these Democratic victories. In the mid-1950s labor contributed from 25 to 33 percent of the
money received by the state party, union political action committees made
additional independent expenditures, and labor provided the mass of volun-
teers in voter-registration drives and phone banks. "The triumph of the
Democratic party in the late 1950s would have been difficult, perhaps impossible, without these various contributions of the unions," Thompson explains. Indeed, after Proxmire received over half of his funds from unions in
1954, Republicans pushed through the Catlin Act in 1955, which barred
unions from contributing to political parties or candidates. But unions simply shifted money into "educational" activities, and labor stepped up voter
mobilization. Further, in 1958 direct labor contributions to the Democrats
were 21.7 percent of all such funds. The "law was not going to be enforced," Thompson concludes, and indeed in 1959 the legislature repealed
the Catlin Act.[67]

Labor also helped turn the growth in the cities and the decline in the farm
population into a political advantage through reapportionment. Wisconsin
was one of only two states at the time that gave equal weight to urban and
rural districts. Thus in 1950, while Wisconsin's urban areas held 55 percent
of the population, a working majority in both state legislative houses still
represented rural areas. Larger farm interests were often suspicious of
unions, and urban Republicans tended to be less antilabor. Powerful Republican assemblyman Alfred Ludvigsen, representing the rural northern
half of Waukesha County, explained that he had "watched the big cities.
Their representation has been under the control of organized labor . . . both
Republicans and Democrats elected in the big cities vote for labor bills."
Tensions around legislative reapportionment heightened in the 1950s as
urban areas grew by nearly 26 percent while the rural population grew by
only 1 percent. Finally, after various battles, a reapportionment plan was
adopted based on population, becoming effective with the election of the
1955 legislature.[68]

Meanwhile the WCCME continued to try to devise an acceptable public
sector statute, learning from past defeats. In late 1958 it held a legislative
conference that called for statutory bargaining rights for all local government workers except law enforcement. The WERB could engage in mediation, conciliation, fact-finding, arbitration, or other services, but only if
both parties consented. The WCCME stressed the reasonableness of its pro-

posal. It would be unfair to ban strikes without some alternative for settling negotiating disputes. Basic organizing and bargaining rights did not usurp the government's sovereignty, Oberbeck insisted, and "sovereign" power should be accountable "to the people it represents." Lawton noted that the WERB had already successfully conducted elections and offered nonbinding mediation and arbitration in the public sector, and thus it could safely be given such powers in a statute.[69]

Democratic victories did not ensure enactment of AFSCME's agenda. Even those generally sympathetic to public sector unions were unsure of the scope of formal rights that should be granted, and powerful forces still opposed any such rights. Thus AFSCME's Bill 309-A, introduced on February 26, 1959, contained compromises designed to help it pass. To counter objections of improper delegation and improper state control over local governments, the bill specified that the WERB would have the power to conduct representation elections, mediation, and voluntary arbitrations only if both parties agreed. The bill again excluded public safety personnel. Beyond that, it again provided for the right to organize and the right of unions to engage in "conferences and negotiations" regarding "wages, hours, and conditions of employment." It was later amended to add employee unfair labor practices. A modified version of the bill became law, but only after a lengthy struggle.[70]

AFSCME took advantage of new attitudes by characterizing traditional objections as outdated. After the *Milwaukee Sentinel* complained that collective bargaining would "mark the end of unprivileged, non-partisan government," Zander replied that "like those who once opposed child-labor laws and social security, the men of little minds today are fighting a rearguard action." State senator Kirby Hendee (R–Milwaukee) introduced Bill 47-S, which would have mandated harsh penalties for strikers, and the *Union News* turned this into an argument for AFSCME's bill. Any such law that did not provide alternative dispute resolution mechanisms "is not fair. A union must have a way of getting its grievances and requests acted upon." AFSCME again made the moderate argument that the bill was needed because "a substantial minority" continued to discriminate against union supporters.[71]

The hearings on the bills were hotly contested, with unusually large numbers registering both in favor and in opposition.[72] It was soon clear that the WCCME's bill was more viable: over 150 people registered in favor of it, and around 45 registered against it; whereas only 9 registered in favor of Hendee's bill and 85 against it. Hendee maintained that public workers should have no right to bargain. Lawton argued that the issues were whether public employers could fire an employee for joining a union and whether public employees could have dispute-resolution machinery. He cited numerous allegations of discrimination. J. F. Freidrich, representing the Milwaukee Federated Trades Council, testified that a right to organize would be meaningless as long as public officials could fire an employee for exercising that right. The Wisconsin AFL-CIO strongly supported the WCCME's bill.[73]

The WCCME was willing to make further compromises. The WERB's advisory committee was initially evenly split on the bill, with the six labor representatives favoring it and the six employer representatives in opposition. But WERB chair Laurence Gooding reported that a majority would support the bill if clauses were added providing union ULPs and stating that employees had the right to refrain from union activities. Foreshadowing a key issue for the future, Gooding noted that he had concluded that nothing in the bill actually required the public employer to bargain with the union, but this point was apparently overlooked by both sides at the time. Picking up on the first suggestion, the WCCME agreed to an amendment that added union ULPs and the right not to join unions.[74]

AFSCME focused its rhetoric on the politically palatable right of association while pushing political action on the ground. The League of Municipalities and the County Boards Association had organized; how could they maintain that it was "unconstitutional, morally wrong, and bad . . . to have a public employee belong to a union?" In senate testimony, Lawton again cited anti-union discrimination and the need for machinery for settling disputes. Oberbeck urged political action, sensing victory. "Now is the time for every union member . . . to buttonhole their assemblyman and senator and tell him that you want favorable action on bill 309-A." If a local legislator opposed it, "We can contact the legislator . . . and attempt to overcome his objection." Pointing out that legislators were usually home on weekends, Oberbeck suggested that members "get your legislative committee or your whole local together and make a trip over to your legislator's home" to discuss the bill. Indeed, a history of Wisconsin labor states that "legislators at home on weekends were deluged with visits by the local public employees" supporting the bill. Oberbeck also recommended a letter-writing campaign. The WCCME was "standing on the threshold of a new era," and this legislative "Bill of Rights" was its "top goal."[75]

The League of Municipalities countered with its own moderate and previously successful arguments. The league claimed that it did not oppose unionization per se; rather, state powers over local governments were both bad policy and unconstitutional. Sundby wrote assembly members that "state control" represented "unwarranted interference with municipal employee labor relations." The WERB should not handle municipal employee relations. The "prospect of an elected municipal official being called by subpoena to justify the exercise of his legislative discretion before a state agency" in a ULP hearing was "completely repugnant." While mediation and arbitration were voluntary under the bill, the league correctly predicted that unions would later try to make such procedures mandatory. The league also cited former attorney general Thomson's opinion regarding the 1953 bill that "there was grave doubt of the constitutionality" of collective bargaining. Further, the mediation and arbitration provisions were also unconstitutional delegations, because while engaging in the process was voluntary, the results would be binding, and Thomson had disapproved of restricting the "free exercise of discretion" of public officials in labor matters. Sundby insisted that "the legislature may not provide for delegation of legislative functions," including pay and working conditions. Anticipating the defense that the bill did not provide for full, traditional bargaining, the league publicized a *Milwaukee Journal* editorial arguing that unions would "use it as a wedge" for further bargaining rights, "which the courts have consistently held to be beyond the authority" of local governments. Various local public employers echoed these complaints. For example, the counsel for the city of Racine wrote Nelson that he had "very serious doubt as to the constitutionality" of the bill on nondelegation grounds. Further, the bill was "one step closer to recognition of the right of public employees to strike."[76]

The bill passed, albeit after further concessions. The original bill carried by a vote of sixty-seven to twenty-three in the assembly, with all dissenting votes cast by Republicans. On July 23 the senate adopted a Republican amendment deleting the provisions authorizing the WERB to aid in elections, bargaining impasses, and arbitration of grievances. However, the senate rejected an amendment by Hendee that would have provided for harsh penalties for strikers. With the powers of the WERB reduced, the delegation concerns were apparently sufficiently diluted. The amended bill passed by twenty-three to ten in the senate and then passed the assembly on a voice vote. Both sides lobbied Governor Nelson, but he had already indicated that he would sign the bill into law, and he did so on September 22. Attorney General Reynolds later told AFSCME that this law had been won through labor's organization and efforts, but obviously the friendly administration was crucial, as were compromises on the police issue and the powers of the WERB.[77]

AFSCME was jubilant. Employees of local governments (excluding police) for the first time anywhere had a statewide statutory right to organize and to be represented by unions in "conferences and negotiations" over wages, hours, and working conditions. "Passage of the bill caps a long fight" by the WCCME "to win for city and county workers the same rights enjoyed by workers in private employment." The law opened an "enlightened era." The national AFSCME proclaimed that the WCCME had won a "collective bargaining bill" that forbade public employers from interfering with the right to organize. Speaking for private sector unions as well, the *Madison Union Labor News* cheered that "public employees of Wisconsin have finally gained the right to join a union . . . without interference from their employers." But mindful of the significant compromises on impasse and enforcement procedures, the WCCME began looking ahead. While the bill was certainly "a start in the right direction," the "legislative wheels in Wisconsin have been grinding for the last 13 years" on these issues. "Whether the Legislature has ground fine enough may arouse considerable debate."[78]

The 1959 law was a historical landmark that facilitated improved labor relations, but, reflecting contemporary ambivalence, it was still woefully unclear on the extent of union rights. At first bargaining seemed to be a success. In January 1960 the *Union News* claimed that negotiations "under the requirements of the bill have produced the expected gratifying results." Many public employers "have indicated that they want to comply with the law to the letter," and this acquiescence had promoted bargaining even where none had existed before. The law truly had ushered in "a new era." The *Public Employee* reported that a survey had "disclosed considerable gains through negotiations completed by 94 locals" in Wisconsin, with gains or new rights in areas including wages, benefits, hours, leave, seniority rights, grievance procedures, maintenance of membership, and dues check-off.[79]

Still, these negotiations were far removed from bargaining in the traditional private sector sense, and public sector unions in Wisconsin still relied in substantial measure on the goodwill of the local public employer. For example, the mayor of Madison, Ivan Nestingen, explained how bargaining worked in that city. Union proposals were referred to a city bargaining committee, which then negotiated with the union. A council of five aldermen made final decisions after considering the results of bargaining. While the city negotiated over pay, benefits, leave, medical insurance, and dues check-off, it refused to negotiate about specific grievances, promotions, or what it termed "employment practices." Bargaining resulted in an "agreement," but not a written contract, because Madison's city attorney had indicated that written labor contracts were still illegal under current law. Nestingen did support using WERB conciliation to resolve bargaining impasses. It was "a reasonable solution to a difficult problem," and it would help prevent strikes.[80]

Given these limits and ambiguities, it is not surprising that Oberbeck was soon complaining that "some very obvious problems have ripened for solution. For example, the law is not clear as to what the collective bargaining relationship should be." Lawton called for amendments to clarify procedures on bargaining and recognition. Oberbeck suggested that formal, written contracts should be the norm, demurring that any "question of legality" of such contracts "is a purely academic one." The "practical solution" was to put the relationship "on a formal and written basis." The *Union News* urged locals to insist on written agreements, either signed by both sides or mutually negotiated and then enacted by the public body. Far from a legal problem, this was merely a "written record of what has been agreed to," analogous to a bank record. Also, the law left open issues of how the law would be enforced or administered. Although provisions regarding the WERB had been removed, the WERB would still sometimes intervene. For example, in 1960 the WERB successfully mediated a dispute over wages and hours between the Green County Highway Committee and AFSCME Local 226. WERB member Arvid Anderson called for amendments to clarify the WERB's authority in the public sector. The law "should be undergirded with enforcement procedures either in a circuit court, or before this agency, and not left in a nebulous fashion."[81]

At the same time, some felt the law had already gone too far, and they now looked to the 1960 governor's race. In the fall of 1960 Nelson's opponent, Philip Kuehn, issued a position paper that opposed all public sector bargaining, called for punitive measures for public sector strikers (as in the old Hendee bill), and opposed extending organizing rights to police and fire employees. Adopting older visions of labor relations, Kuehn insisted that there could be no right to bargain with the government because there was no right to strike against the government. He even added that public workers beyond police and firefighters could be denied the right to organize "in other situations" that risked "divided loyalty."

AFSCME was outraged: "wealthy . . . men like Kuehn" wanted to make "the working man . . . a second class citizen." Lawton, Nelson, and Attorney General Reynolds excoriated Kuehn. Lawton stressed new understandings born in the public sector. The term "negotiations" in the 1959 law, he said, meant a type of bargaining, and bargaining could exist without strikes. For example, arbitration could be used to resolve impasses, as the ABA had suggested. Lawton vowed that AFSCME would propose amendments in 1961 that would strengthen bargaining through provisions for mediation, conciliation, and fact-finding by the WERB. Nelson and Reynolds also argued that the WERB should be more involved in the public sector, and that the legislature should clarify that the WERB could normally be used in elections or ULP cases. Rejecting increasingly outmoded fears that organizing or even bargaining necessarily meant strikes, Nelson added that the 1959 law did not provide a right to strike, and if Kuehn wanted "jail sentences, I disagree."[82]

In a sense, both Kuehn and AFSCME were wrestling with the same fundamental and unresolved problem. Kuehn argued that with no right to strike, "collective bargaining is robbed of its mutuality." AFSCME was also frustrated with a law that authorized "negotiations" but provided no method to resolve impasses. But it was AFSCME that properly claimed confidence in its political power as the November elections neared. Asserting that public sector labor rights would be one of the hottest issues in the election, the *Union News* concluded with regard to Kuehn that it was "a poor sailor indeed who does not knoweth which way the wind bloweth." AFSCME labeled Kuehn's program a key example of why public workers should be politically active: if Kuehn were elected and the Republicans retained their senate majority, it would mean "second-class citizenship." Wisconsin had 25,000 organized government workers, the *Union News* claimed, and "every public employee in the state must be at the polls" to vote "for candidates who are in favor of an enlightened labor policy for public employees." Governor Nelson, the *Union News* noted, was a "friend of the public employee.[83]

Nelson won a second term as governor in 1960, and Reynolds won a second term as attorney general. But Republicans Warren Knowles and Dena Smith recaptured the lieutenant governorship and the office of state treasurer. Further, the Republicans retook the state assembly (fifty-five to forty-five) and kept a twenty-to-thirteen majority in the senate.[84] The stage was set for a battle over amendments to clarify the law, specifically over state powers in the area of bargaining impasses.

On March 2, 1961, the WCCME introduced Bill 336-A, the point of which was to grant the WERB formal authority to enforce union rights, especially in bargaining. The original version of Bill 336-A provided that the WERB could function as a mediator or an arbitrator in bargaining. Again, in an attempt to blunt criticisms based on nondelegation and home-rule concerns, the bill specified that participation in arbitration would be voluntary, but WERB decisions in such voluntary proceedings would be binding. Also, if negotiations reached an impasse, or if one side refused to bargain in good faith, either party could ask the WERB to name a fact-finder who would make recommendations. The bill provided that these procedures would also apply to public safety personnel, including police. Also, either side could petition the WERB to conduct a representation election. Finally, the bill explicitly authorized written contracts.[85] Opponents again contested even this level of state involvement, resulting in another set of compromises that was, nonetheless, another historic victory for labor.

Governor Nelson and leading Democrats supported the bill. Deputy Attorney General Nathan Heffernan explained that the absence of procedures to implement the rights in the 1959 law had created confusion. But the fights over the bill were intense. The assembly finally passed the bill by a vote of sixty-four to fifteen in July, after adopting an amendment that expressly prohibited strikes. Attempting to avoid further amendments in the senate, Lawton argued that the bill was already modest: employers were not required to sign contracts or to engage in arbitration, and recommendations by fact-finders would be only advisory. But the senate then added amendments providing that arbitrations would also be only advisory, and that fact-finding would be allowed only when *both* parties agreed to it. The bill was then put off until the November session of the legislature. The *Union News* complained that opponents had carried on their "most intensive" campaign ever, using "a good deal of false and misleading propaganda." Thelen, of the County Boards Association, had led a "continued and monotonous fight against change."[86]

Neither side was entirely satisfied with the amended bill. Lawton still wanted fact-finding if *either* party requested it; he noted that under the 1959 law or even before, fact-finding could occur if both sides were willing. Further, private industry had to abide by arbitration awards (in the context of grievances); governments should at least be able to agree to be bound. Meanwhile, opponents felt that the bill violated principles of home rule and sovereignty. The league again complained that it transferred power to the WERB over "ALL" issues of local government employment, again raised the specter of the WERB subpoenaing municipal officials, and again cited Thomson's 1953 attorney general's opinion to argue that the new bill was unconstitutional. Thelen insisted that even voluntary, nonbinding arbitration was of questionable constitutionality and would cause "chaos and discord." The Dane County Board of Supervisors and the Wisconsin Municipal Alliance echoed that the bill would give the WERB too much power, and a number of school boards objected. But opponents had no clear answers. The *Milwaukee Journal* unhelpfully suggested that the bill "ought to be killed," because "squaring government sovereignty with the realities of employee-employer relations poses problems." The *Wisconsin State Journal* decried AFSCME's political power, adding that "public and private employment are not the same and cannot be made so." The duties of public officials "cannot be delegated or shrugged off to some other body." The Milwaukee Government Service League objected that binding contracts violated the sovereign right of governments "to change their minds without restriction."[87]

As to the erosion of local authority, AFSCME responded that nothing in the bill prevented public employers from making final decisions in bargaining. The bill did not require employers to submit to arbitration, and, as amended, the employer was not bound by arbitration decisions. Local government already had to comply with state procedures in such matters as budgets, taxes, and street design, so the limited requirements of the labor bill were clearly constitutional.

More broadly, labor was succeeding by making specific, practical proposals. The *Union News* published excerpts from a *Wisconsin Law Review*
article written by Arvid Anderson that attempted to clarify how labor law
should work in the public sector. Public sector unions would continue to
grow, Anderson explained, and absent adequate grievance and bargaining
procedures, public sector labor disputes would increase. He compared developments in the public sector with those in the private sector around the
time the NLRA was passed. Anderson suggested principles for state laws,
mostly along the lines of what AFSCME was advocating. Relevant to the
current debate, Anderson wrote that public sector unions should act as exclusive bargaining agents with the right to form written, binding contracts.
Both unions and public employers should be required to bargain in good
faith concerning wages, hours, and working conditions, excluding subjects
exclusively covered by external law, such as civil service rules. Strikes
should be barred, and the parties should instead use mediation and voluntary arbitrations, as well as advisory fact-finding.[88]

As in 1955, opponents attempted to derail the bill with a study, but by
now AFSCME was too strong. The County Boards Association introduced
Joint Resolution 94-S, which called for a study. The WCCME did not object (although the *Union News* said it did not "expect any value out of such
a study"), and the resolution passed both houses of the legislature. Crucially, however, the WCCME made sure that this study would not be in lieu
of the WCCME's bill.

AFSCME'S political power was drawing notice. The WCCME "may well
become any day now the most potent of the lobbying forces in the state
capitol," wrote John Wyngaard, a correspondent for several Wisconsin
newspapers, in an article titled "Public Employee Union Has Gained Real
Political Power." As to the WCCME's bill, the union "has won a resound-
ing, even an embarrassingly decisive victory" in the assembly. "A dozen
years ago, the county boards could have knocked down such a rival power
with scarcely a serious effort." But public sector unions had "grown rapidly
and now represent a considerable voting power; they are well led; and they
promise to grow even more powerful." Notably, "it was Republican leadership in the Assembly . . . which gave Mr. Lawton his triumph. The rarity of
Republican favoritism for the union side of a political argument is a certificate to his persuasive talents." No doubt it was also the political clout of
public and private sector labor, the increased experience with public sector
labor (which made it more difficult to link such unions with strikes, bias, or
other old-fashioned nightmarish scenarios), and the fact that the amended
bill made most WERB involvement both voluntary on the part of the employer and nonbinding. In any case, Wyngaard's words were encouraging as
the legislature prepared to reconvene on November 1. The October 1961

Public Employee called the Wisconsin bill one of the most "enlightened labor legislation bills" ever and predicted a "bitter, showdown fight."[89]

Again, both sides were forced to compromise. Thelen made a last-ditch effort to postpone what increasingly appeared to be the inevitable, asking that the bill be deferred until the 1963 legislative session. He cited editorials from relatively minor newspapers: the *Marinette Eagle Star* (a "dangerous bill") and the *Appleton Post Crescent* ("exhaustive study" still required). But even the league acknowledged that the "pressures which have been brought to bear" to pass the bill "are well known." Still, opponents were able to attach amendments that gave public employers more discretion and the WERB less power, again apparently sufficient for sovereignty and delegation concerns. The final bill eliminated the arbitration provisions entirely, stated that a contract would be binding only if it contained express language to that effect, and provided that the WERB would not initiate fact-finding if the employer had established adequate fact-finding procedures.

Thus, the final bill provided for WERB mediation only if both parties requested it, but allowed for WERB-conducted representation elections or fact-finding at the request of either party. The fact-finder had the power to call hearings, issue subpoenas, and make nonbinding recommendations. Indicating how much the winds had shifted, the provision allowing public safety personnel to use the fact-finding procedures was retained, apparently with little controversy. The bill also required contracts to be in writing, "in the form of an ordinance, resolution, or agreement." Strikes were "expressly prohibited," but no penalties were specified. On January 10, 1962, the legislature approved Bill 336-A, and Governor Nelson signed it on January 31.[90]

This law represented "the culmination of nearly 15 years' work" by AFSCME, beginning with the defeat of the 1947 bill designed to punish strikers, Lawton proclaimed. The amendments were "meaningless." While the WERB could act as a mediator in bargaining and ULP cases only if both parties agreed, effective mediation was really possible only if both parties agreed anyway. Further, either party could initiate fact-finding after a bargaining impasse or ask the WERB to conduct a representation election. Local fact-finding boards would have to meet state standards, and no local employing official could be on a board. The WERB was not authorized to do arbitrations, but Lawton optimistically noted that employers could still agree to arbitrations conducted by other neutrals, such as the American Arbitration Association. "We gained our basic objectives," he insisted. Indeed, he called the new law "the Magna Carta for public employees" and said it meant as much as the NLRA did in private industry. For years opponents had been "crying that public employees should not have the right to strike," the *Union News* exulted, but "they gave no alternative." The new law provided "a way to settle labor disputes successfully . . . mediation and fact finding." The *Public Employee* claimed that the law provided "many of the collective bargaining rights now afforded workers in private industry." Fundamentally, the creation of actual procedures for public sector bargaining was a milestone. A later study concluded that this law "converted a statement of policy [the 1959 law] into a functional process for true collective bargaining."[91]

Politically, AFSCME had arrived. Standing next to Governor Nelson at the signing ceremony were AFSCME national vice-president Steven Clark, WCCME vice-president Harmon Skown, and WCCME president Herb Einerson. Other public officials curried AFSCME's favor. At AFSCME's state convention, Attorney General Reynolds hailed the law as a "giant step forward" born of the WCCME's "tireless" campaign. "In the century-long struggle to protect the rights of workers to bargain collectively with their employers, our public employees have been ignored. These new laws put Wisconsin in a leadership position in the nation." Reynolds was running for governor in the 1962 elections against Kuehn and would win, with AFSCME's support. A month before the election, Reynolds stated that the "objective of the law is to provide collective bargaining rights for municipal employees similar to that provided to employees in private industry. With this objective I agree."[92]

AFSCME linked the Wisconsin law with an important victory at the national level. On January 17, 1962, President John F. Kennedy signed Federal Executive Order 10988, which gave limited bargaining rights to federal workers.[93] "The sea of public controversy over the right of the public employee to belong to a labor union has been lapping against the dike of adverse legislative and legal opinion in Wisconsin and throughout the United States," the *Union News* proclaimed. "The dike was breached in Wisconsin. . . . Recently, President Kennedy . . . breached the dike again. . . . The public employee movement is here to stay and thus must be dealt with realistically." AFSCME predicted that Kennedy's order would undercut arguments against bargaining by state and local government employers.[94]

The WCCME quickly took advantage of various aspects of the new law, especially the WERB's enforcement powers. On July 27, 1962, the WERB told the Green Lake County Highway Commission to reinstate a fired employee on the grounds that the local highway commissioner had engaged in anti-union discrimination during organizing; Local 514 then successfully organized Green Lake workers. The first fact-finder's report involving AFSCME was issued on June 1, 1963, and the WCCME happily announced that it recommended a seven-cent-per-hour raise for Local 678, DePere City Employees, which had requested the fact-finding. The WERB handled its new responsibilities and caseload well. On the ground, bargaining was also improving. Oberbeck bragged that while in 1959 about 60 percent of WCCME's locals had signed contracts, by fall 1964 almost all had. Other public sector unions in Wisconsin, such as the AFT, also took advantage of the new law.[95]

AFSCME also encountered the limits of the law, and fights over the scope of rights would continue for decades. For example, the WCCME was greatly annoyed when DePere City and some other employers simply rejected the fact-finders' recommendations. The *Union News* called for binding arbitration or fact-finding. Beginning in 1962, AFSCME repeatedly introduced bills that would have allowed a union shop if two-thirds of the bargaining unit had voted for it. Such a bill passed both houses in 1965 but was vetoed by the new Republican governor, Warren Knowles. On the positive side for AFSCME, in 1965 the law was expanded to extend limited bargaining rights to state employees. In 1966, however, the WCCME suffered a setback when the WERB held, in a case involving the city of New Berlin and AFSCME Local 647, that the Wisconsin law did not actually impose a duty to bargain in good faith.[96]

But by this time the battle had spread across the country. By 1966, sixteen states had enacted laws extending at least some organizing and bargaining rights to at least some public employees.[97] Struggles over statutory language and its interpretations continued in other states and in Wisconsin. In 1967 the WCCME won a key decision on grievance arbitration and, more broadly, on the delegation issue, when the Wisconsin Supreme Court held that a public employer's contractual agreement to submit grievances to binding arbitration was enforceable and was not an unlawful delegation of the city's legislative power. In 1971 the WCCME won legislative amendments providing for the agency shop and for binding arbitration impasse procedures for firefighters and most police, and requiring that both sides bargain in good faith. In 1977 Wisconsin enacted a law (again backed by AFSCME) that provided for binding impasse arbitration for other local government employees and authorized a very limited right to strike, finally giving a relatively definite answer to the question that both sides had struggled with for so long.[98]

The Wisconsin laws of 1959 and 1962 were both an opening salvo and a historic watershed in Wisconsin and the nation.[99] In 1966 Arvid Anderson wrote that the "fundamental question to be answered by this Wisconsin experiment is whether the principles and practices of collective bargaining, which have been developed and protected by law in private employment . . . can be transferred in whole or in part to public employment. . . . We think the tentative answer is 'yes.' " Indeed, in 1968 Ed Johnson, the executive director of the League of Municipalities, stated that "a pretty good law has been in effect for seven years which might stand some minor touch-ups but certainly is not in need of major surgery." Still, Johnson made a point of adding that the "word 'sovereignty' may be archaic, but I know of no better word to describe the responsibility elected officials have to their constituents. Such responsibility cannot be shared with representatives of public employees."[100] Similar objections, resonating with the history of public sector labor relations, are still made today, as disputes over the proper extent (if any) of public sector bargaining, impasse resolution procedures, and related rights have continued into the twenty-first century. But after the Wisconsin laws and the related laws of the 1960s, public sector labor relations, the American labor movement, and American politics have never been the same.

Conclusion

> Government workers who are unorganized can be and are exploited
> as cruelly as unorganized workers in private industry. Whatever
> progress government workers have made in recent years they have
> made only through labor organization.
>
> TWU, *Transport Bulletin* (1942)

> The organizers of this union have met all the opposition by employ-
> ers that other unions have encountered. In public service we know
> the burning shame of yellow dog contracts, the sting of the black
> list, and the bite of anti-union . . . discrimination.
>
> ARNOLD ZANDER, AFSCME president (1946)

Following in the footsteps of the victory in Wisconsin, in the 1960s government workers and their allies dismantled significant portions of the legal
edifice that had held back public sector labor. With the help of new laws,
these unions exploded in size. In 1955 public sector unions had about
400,000 members; by the 1970s the total was more than 4,000,000. From
1955 to 1991 the AFT increased its membership from 40,000 to 573,000;
AFSCME grew from 99,000 to 1,191,000; the SEIU from 50,000 to
108,000; the IAFF from 72,000 to 151,000; and the IUPA (the AFL-CIO
police union) was founded and grew to 18,000 members.[1]

With the simultaneous decline of private sector unions, government
workers became an increasingly large part of the labor movement. From
1955 to 1991 the total membership of the AFL-CIO rose only from
12,622,000 to 13,933,000. The growth of the public sector thus had both
a quick and a lasting impact. The number of public employees in the organization grew from 915,000 (about 5 percent of total AFL-CIO membership) in 1956 to 1.7 million (about 9 percent) in 1966. By 1993 around 40
percent of union members in the United States were in the public sector. By
the end of the 1990s, although public workers made up less than 16 per-

cent of American workers, they constituted more than 43 percent of all workers represented by unions in America. Also by the end of the 1990s, almost 43 percent of government employees were represented by unions. Fulfilling the prediction of *Business Week* in the 1950s, by 1997 AFSCME's 1.3 million members made it the second-largest union in the AFL-CIO, after the Teamsters. That same year, the AFT claimed 1 million members.

This boom—and the new state public sector bargaining laws that were inextricably linked to it—had a variety of causes, some of which are described in other studies. The increased size of public employment probably played a role, although levels of employment were not growing much relative to the economy as a whole. The number of public employees nearly doubled in the 1960s and 1970s (with most of the growth in state and local government employment), bringing the total to more than 16 million in 1980. Still, in 1960 public workers constituted 15.4 percent of nonagricultural employees, and by 1991 this figure was still less than 17 percent. Other factors were crucial to the boom as well. Along with the growth of government and changes in the law, Richard Kearney also cites the continuing experience with stability in private sector relations and the climate of social change of the 1960s and 1970s. Further, legal developments beyond state labor laws helped. As chapter 3 shows, in the 1960s courts finally agreed with labor that the right to form a union in government employment was protected by the U.S. Constitution. Also, in 1964 the U.S. Supreme Court instituted on a national scale a key policy that had helped the WCCME in Wisconsin: *Reynolds v. Sims* ordered legislative reapportionment in all fifty state legislatures on the principle of one person one vote. This decision ended the ability of rural, anti-union interests to dominate state governments disproportionately.[2]

These events created what was in many ways a new era in public sector labor history, and they are therefore beyond the scope of this book. But it is important to understand that the successes of the 1960s and later decades were built on a foundation laid by previous decades of determined struggle, and they were the result of continuing activism on the part of unions, often along the same lines as the events recounted here. Fundamentally, it was the agency of workers themselves, matched with new political and social circumstances, that made the legal and organizational successes possible. Paul Johnston writes that the modern public sector labor statutes were "more the effect than the cause of labor movement activity." Of course, there is a chicken-and-egg problem: union activity creates better laws, which in turn allow for more activity. Johnston is certainly right, however, that the new laws did not spring forth spontaneously from the heads of legislative gods or, as some works at least implicitly suggest, mainly in reaction to

Kennedy's executive order. Public workers and their unions continued to use political agitation to win more rights.[3]

In the 1960s some of this activism took a more militant form, with teachers, sanitation workers, and even police engaging in job actions. The point here is not to compare strategies in different decades but rather to stress that the more recent events would not have been possible without the struggles of the past. And the earlier history must not be discounted just because it provides fewer examples of open, militant confrontations. Scholars should beware of valorizing only the events in labor history that were literally bloody, while discounting determined struggles to organize that encountered legal or other less violent forms of repression. Certainly, some incidents involving public employees after the Boston strike were not lacking in traditional drama. In Rochester, New York, during an AFSCME strike in 1946, the *New York Times* reported that the police "swept down . . . in a way which had not been seen in private industry since the passage of the National Labor Relations Act."[4] But the daily denial of rights in the public sector well into the 1960s and the daily struggles by workers and unions in response—on the job, in union halls, in courts and agencies, and in communities—were more important.

Also, while the 1960s signaled, in significant respects, the beginning of a new era, the overall history of public sector unions is not entirely dichotomous. The earlier history of these unions is linked to and continues into the modern era in a surprising number of fundamental ways. Further, the early era of public sector unions sheds important light on the history of private sector unions and on American politics.

First, the period before the 1960s created the central institutions and determined much of the basic character of the public sector labor movement. The major players of today—the AFT, AFGE, AFSCME, NEA, IAFF, SEIU, and others—have been in place for a long time. As early as 1950 the International City Managers Association noted that unionization in municipal government had "already passed the preliminary stage and [was] beginning to assume sizable proportions." Of course these unions have grown considerably, but significant changes in the size of private sector unions in the modern era have not caused historians to view private sector labor history as entirely discontinuous. Consider that the rise in the rate of unionization in the public sector since the early 1960s, from around 10 percent to around 40 percent, has been an almost perfect reverse image of the decline in the private sector, from almost 35 percent to around 10 percent, since the mid-1950s. Instead of treating this decline in private sector union density as a complete break from the past, many historians look to the 1930s and 1940s to help explain it.[5]

Second, looking at the law reveals an obvious way in which the history of public sector unions is not dichotomous. Although many states have now passed public sector labor relations statutes, many others have retained restrictive rules that are quite similar to those before the 1960s. Although union *organizing* is now uniformly legal, with regard to bargaining and other institutional rights public sector unions have engaged in an ongoing, state-by-state struggle that continues today. In 2002 the AFSCME convention resolved that public sector labor laws in America were still a "patchwork quilt of conflicting, confusing, and often inadequate legislation." Indeed, it has been estimated that there are currently more than 110 separate state statutes governing public sector labor relations, augmented by numerous local ordinances, executive orders, and other legal authority. And these rules vary widely. Currently, by one calculation, twenty-nine states and the District of Columbia allow bargaining for all major groups of public employees; about thirteen more allow only one to four types of public employees to bargain (most commonly teachers or firefighters); and eight states do not allow any public employees to bargain. Thus, over twenty states do not allow many or in some cases any public employees to bargain. Further, only twelve states allow any public workers the right to strike (and even in those states, only under fairly limited circumstances), and a number of states that do not allow strikes also do not require binding arbitration to settle bargaining impasses. Some states still ban not only bargaining and striking but also any kind of official recognition. For example, the Commonwealth of Virginia forbids public employers to recognize or deal with public sector unions in practically any form. Just as in the earlier era, unions in such jurisdictions find ways to represent their members through administrative hearings, political appeals, use of other employment laws, and whatever other means are available.[6]

Also, the tools that help explain court decisions before the 1960s are often directly relevant to understanding cases in the modern era. In 1977 the Virginia Supreme Court held that a school board could not bargain with a public sector union even though it wanted to do so, essentially because of delegation concerns. This decision, like others from states that lack protective public sector labor laws, melds concerns about state structure and concepts of unions in government in much the same fashion as judicial opinions written fifty years earlier. In 1993 the U.S. Supreme Court seemed to repeat a mistake that courts had made throughout the twentieth century in public sector cases. The Court was interpreting the term "representative" in a provision of the FLSA that applied to public workers. Under this provision representatives had certain rights to enter into agreements regarding the use of compensatory time in lieu of premium pay for overtime. The case arose in Texas, another state that does not allow public employers even to "recognize" a union unless a local jurisdiction has voted to do so. The Court held that "representative" could not mean a union that lacked the formal right to bargain. It came to this conclusion even though the statute was silent on the matter and the applicable federal regulation indicated that a union could be a "representative" even if it could not bargain.[7] This ruling was equivalent to those of courts in the first half of the century that construed "union" to signify exclusively the private sector model.

In addition, the basic strategies and goals of public sector unions and their members continued from earlier times. By the 1960s their long fight to win institutional rights was bearing fruit. But the fight continued (and continues today) in the efforts to pass statutes in states without them and, in states that have statutes, over issues such as subjects of bargaining and methods of impasse resolution. Even where public sector unions have some bargaining rights, they still use politics and a variety of nontraditional forms of representation, taking advantage of employment laws and constitutional protections.

Thus, even though public sector unions are larger today, and even though many have significantly more institutional rights that permit them to employ a broader range of tactics, the goals, strategies, and obstacles of earlier decades often remain the same. Moreover, the history of public sector unions is relevant not only to those unions themselves but also to an understanding of the past and present of the entire American labor movement, and to an understanding of American politics.

Most broadly, including public sector unions in labor history as a whole means reconceptualizing the periodization of institutional labor history. In the traditional view, 1935 to 1945 was the watershed, with a small, embattled core of unions before the New Deal and a stable, mostly successful labor relations regime after World War II. This view has already been partially challenged by the decline of labor in the private sector. The postwar order, Melvyn Dubofsky's "almost perfect machine," clearly broke down some time ago.[8] Now, however, historians must acknowledge that the rise of public sector unions has been as meaningful to American labor as, for instance, the creation of the CIO. The significance of the 1960s and beyond comes as much from the workers who entered the labor movement as from those who left it. At the same time, the claims that can still rightly be made about the importance of the early NLRA era must be tempered by the knowledge that this era left untapped an enormous reservoir of potential union members in the public sector.

Including the public sector does more than alter the temporal contours of American labor history. It also helps explain the reasons for the gains and declines. Specifically, knowledge of the history of public sector labor improves historians' capacity to evaluate claims about the effects of law and other factors—notably employers—on the development of unions. This history shows that law can be crucial. Simultaneously, it argues against certain theories that scholars have proposed as to how the NLRA harmed private sector labor.

Some aspects of the NLRA, and some interpretations of it, have undoubtedly hurt the union movement. Joel Rogers, Paul Weiler, and others have made a convincing case about the deficiencies of the law from the perspective of private sector labor. They cite, among other things, weak enforcement procedures fraught with delays, the separation of card showing and union elections, related delays in representation elections, the lack of a realistic duty to bargain or any requirement to come to an agreement, inadequate protections for recognitional strikes, allowing the "permanent replacement" of strikers, and bans on secondary activity and other restrictions on union economic power. The damage done to labor in the private sector seems clear.[9]

Other critics have gone further, suggesting not so much that the NLRA needs strengthening in specific areas, but rather that the entire project has been significantly misguided or even harmful. These studies attribute the enervation of labor in the postwar period to core concepts of the NLRA that previously had been viewed as positive or at least necessary. Christopher Tomlins has argued that the involvement of the government itself in issues such as unit determinations sapped the ability of labor to act as an independent force, ultimately causing unions to "lie down like good dogs." Katherine Stone takes an equally dim view of the industrial pluralism at the heart of the NLRA, decrying the use of arbitration, as opposed to courts, to resolve the grievances of union members. Karl Klare criticizes arbitration on similar grounds. He adds that the duty of fair representation doctrine that courts created should have been broadened, making it easier for individual workers to sue their unions.[10]

These are important ideas, and the debates they sparked should continue.[11] But the experience of the public sector has much to add to the discussion, and it has yet to be included. Were the WCCME and other public sector unions deluded in battling so hard and so long for NLRA-style rights and in demanding that arbitrators resolve their grievances? How can we reconcile these critiques of the NLRA with the great growth of unions in the public sector under laws that are modeled upon the NLRA but give workers *fewer* rights? Modern state public sector labor laws closely track the NLRA on such matters as grievance arbitration, unit determinations, and the duty of fair representation, but they typically leave fewer topics open to negotiation and most commonly deny workers the right to strike. Yet these laws have accompanied a growth in the size and vitality of public sector unions that is unmatched in American labor history. It seems hard to maintain, therefore, that analogous provisions in the NLRA were a significant cause of the decline of private sector labor.[12]

Thus, factors beyond the law must have been central to the fall of private sector unions. The history of public sector unions helps identify one of the most important of these factors: the role of private sector *employers*. It supports the arguments of Joel Rogers and others that the decline in the private sector can be explained only by understanding the significance of the aggressive anti-union stance of private sector employers in recent decades.[13] More generally, this history supports the arguments made by Sanford Jacoby, Patricia Sexton, and others that what is unique about private sector labor relations in the United States is the extreme hostility of employers. From the use of spies and private armies from the nineteenth century through the New Deal (and sometimes beyond), which produced the most violent labor history in the Western world, to the routine expenditure of millions of dollars today on "consultants" to defeat organizing drives or destroy existing unions, the tactics that American employers have used to fight unions—extremely aggressive and often marginally legal at best—have been truly exceptional among industrialized democracies. One telling modern statistic is the ratio of the number of workers illegally disciplined by employers for union activity to the number of workers who vote for unions in elections, a ratio that has dropped steadily and dramatically.[14]

Both the early and the modern eras of public sector unions bolster the argument that the attitudes and actions of employers are crucial. As this book shows, before the 1960s hostile government employers were often devastating to unions, while cooperative employers could permit effective union action even in the absence of formal rights. In the modern era, Harry Wellington and Ralph Winter have shown that public employers typically offer less resistance to unions than do private sector employers. While government employers can and do oppose the unionization of their employees, there is no doubt that public sector unions use politics and public relations to inhibit their employers from attacking labor as aggressively as private businesses have. Democratically accountable government officials cannot engage as easily in the ethically and legally questionable tactics that have been too common in the private sector for much of American history. Also, civil service protections prevent mass firings of union supporters, another tactic too familiar in the private sector. Thus, as Nelson Lichtenstein notes, the "relatively neutral" management in government employment contributed to the relative success of public sector unions. In sum, understanding the significant role that employers play helps explain why public sector unions experienced their great expansion under laws that were, at best, still more restrictive than the NLRA.[15]

Additionally, this book supports a broad claim about the historical importance of the political activities of public sector unions: before the 1960s the law artificially repressed the size of these unions. The twofold effect of this repression was to restrict the potential size and strength of the labor movement as a whole and to promote the voluntarism of labor. This history, arguably, is part of the answer to the venerable Sombart question. In other words, what would have happened if the most political unions had been larger and more influential in the labor movement's formative years, or when labor was larger and more influential within society as a whole?

Addressing this question requires a specific appraisal of the politics in which public sector unions engaged. Also, some initial disclaimers are necessary. Historians have already established that the AFL was never so voluntarist that it did not participate in some campaigns in some places.[16] It was, rather, the manner of the participation of AFL unions that defined their voluntarism: nonpartisan, defensive, and often isolated from other groups. Further, leaders of public sector unions were no more active in calling for explicitly socialistic goals, such as a labor party or government ownership of the means of production, than their private sector counterparts. Nor were public sector unions consistently partisan. As in Seattle, some of the most important races for these unions were literally nonpartisan. Also, given the continuing prevalence of patronage, public sector unions could not invariably ally themselves with one party. And even though Democrats were typically more favorable to unions than were Republicans, reformist Democrats could champion civil service to the exclusion of institutional union rights. In addition, the Hatch Act and analogous state and local laws often barred direct partisan activities by public workers.

On the other hand, in line with the aspirations of many of those who formed labor, socialist, and social-democratic parties in Europe, public sector unions in the United States used democratic, political processes to determine wages, hours, and other conditions of employment, notably through statute and government regulation. While public sector unions often would have preferred to use forms of collective bargaining to resolve these issues, use of politics was inevitable simply because the members of these unions were employees of politicians. Evidencing this reality, these unions remain highly active politically today, even where they can bargain. Further, public sector unions have often acted in a decidedly politically progressive manner both externally and within the AFL-CIO.[17] Thus public sector unions, often relatively liberal, became especially adept at lobbying, elections, and other political strategies, and comfortable with some government regulation of terms and conditions of employment.

What if these experiences had been shared by a broader portion of the AFL in earlier times? Until 1932 the AFL was so voluntarist that it opposed unemployment compensation and other protective laws.[18] A stronger faction of public sector unions, more at ease with (for instance) laws regulating wages and hours or broader insurance matters, could have caused a different outcome on many key issues of public policy.

Furthermore, a labor movement more influenced by public sector unions would almost certainly have reached out earlier and more often to other groups and movements in society. The voluntarism of the AFL was conservative in part because of its insulation from other social movements. Its private sector unions relied first and foremost on their own economic muscle. Public sector unions could not follow this strategy. Indeed, Paul Johnston's observation about modern public sector unions was even more true of these unions in the past: they often had to frame their demands as being in the public interest, and thus had to seek broad political coalitions rather than simply asserting power in the labor market.[19] Every union surveyed in this book tried to follow this strategy. This was the opposite course to the one taken by the dominant private sector unions in the AFL in at least the first three decades of the twentieth century.

Other factors indicate that stronger public sector unions could have made a major difference in labor and American politics as a whole. Public sector unions had an even greater stake in electing prolabor candidates at all levels than private sector labor did. Had public sector unions been stronger before the 1960s, they would presumably have elected more prolabor officials, making the state, at least at some levels, more sympathetic to all unions. Notably, this shift would have happened when the private sector component of organized labor was much stronger. One need not credit the fears of "class control" of the state articulated by employers to think that stronger public sector unions might have blunted some of the most anti-union acts of government. It is certainly plausible that AFL-affiliated police officers would have been less likely to attack strikers. It is equally plausible that a larger contingent of labor-affiliated teachers would have provided a more positive portrayal of the labor movement to more students.

Of course, historians must also ask whether public sector unions could have been larger in the first half of the twentieth century. This book argues that they could have been. If the Boston police strike had not occurred, the legal and political environment for public sector unions would not have been as hostile, and public sector organizing might well have expanded much earlier. Admittedly, it is hard to imagine that courts would have upheld a national labor relations law applicable to public workers. Also, the legal doctrines of state sovereignty, as well as the highly subdivided American state, would still have been obstacles, and subjects of bargaining, impasse-resolution mechanisms, strikes, and other sticking points in modern public sector law could still have been controversial. However, it is not hard to believe that, but for the Boston strike, some states would have passed labor relations laws in the late 1930s or 1940s that provided at least some institutional rights for public sector unions, along the lines of laws and practices in England, France, and Canada. It is also plausible that some courts could have accepted much earlier than they did union arguments that yellow-dog contracts in public employment were unconstitutional, thus saving many actual and potential local unions from destruction. Also, if public sector unions had been a somewhat larger presence, judges might have constructed "union" (as used generically in statutes) to include workers in the public sector.

Of course, all counterfactual history is necessarily speculative. It is, at the end of the day, too much to claim that had public sector unions been larger earlier, America would have had a labor party on the European model.[20] Still, the relevant history was sufficiently contingent to indicate that labor in America could have been more political, more willing to determine employment rules through governmental processes, and more eager to form alliances with other social movements. It could have been much stronger much earlier. It might be hard to guess precisely which political and other mechanisms unions would have used to exercise this strength. It is easier to imagine the substantive content of the impact on the workplace and society.

At minimum, historians should ponder the implications of the unsynchronized development of American private and public sector unions. Private sector unions were large and powerful in the decades when public sector unions were comparatively small and weak, and vice versa. It is well worth considering what might have happened if both of these segments of the organized American working class had been able to reach their potential at the same time.

Finally, however, the significance of public sector unions before the 1960s is not primarily a matter of what they might have done. It lies mainly in what they and their members actually did. They fought for the same goals as other workers, and for the same reasons. Throughout this period their experiences contradicted the notion that government employees were somehow privileged. They were often poorly paid. During the Depression many worked for no pay. For decades after the Depression they were not covered by wage and hour rules or other employment laws applicable to the private sector, and their hours were often much longer than the forty-hour standard that became common for private employees. Their jobs could be quite dangerous, notably (but not exclusively) in the cases of police and firefighters. Their very employment could be subject to shifting political winds or local budgets. And the organization of public sector work often mimicked the most oppressive forms in the private sector: around World War I, government employees and their unions battled "scientific management"; in 1941 the TWU described labor relations in the New York City Sanitation Department as a "feudal system of tyranny."[21]

Many public workers responded by attempting to organize for better wages, hours, and conditions, more control of the workplace, and rights for their unions. On one level, their story can be seen as an instructive example of how the "agency" of a determined but marginalized group can counterbalance the very real constraints used against them. One should not exaggerate the power of public sector unions in this period or underestimate the effectiveness of those constraints. Lacking the right to bargain, strike, or even exist, those unions that could not find a way to exert some political power were either destroyed or reduced, almost literally, to "collective begging," the derisive term some would later use to describe this era.[22]

On the other hand, one must not simply read the laws and rules governing public sector labor relations in the early era, combine them with preexisting stereotypes of what unions or "workers" are, and conclude that these unions were impotent or trivial. They had real successes in achieving goals through political strategies and means other than formal bargaining. These victories genuinely helped their members at the time. They also formed a foundation for the stunning rise of public sector unions in the past forty years. In word and deed, they insisted, against decades of court decisions to the contrary, that they had a fundamental right to organize and to represent their members, and they ultimately prevailed both practically and legally. Like unionists in the private sector and others who have sought greater social or economic rights, members of public sector unions fought to make history but did not control the circumstances under which they battled. With the law and the structure and attitude of the state so firmly against them, it is remarkable that they accomplished as much as they did.

Notes

Introduction

1. *Congressional Record,* 66th Cong., 1st sess., 1919, 58: 5141; *Perez v. Board of Police Commissioners of the City of Los Angeles,* 78 Cal.App.2d 638, 647 (1947) (epigraphs). Nelson Lichtenstein, *State of the Union: A Century of American Labor* (Princeton: Princeton University Press, 2002), 185. In 1953 union density was 35.7 percent in the private sector and 11.6 percent in the public. By 1996 the rate in the private sector had dropped to 10.2 percent while the public sector rate had risen to 37.7 percent, and it has remained near 40 percent since; Sharon Margalioth, "The Significance of Worker Attitudes: Individualism as a Cause for Labor's Decline," *Hofstra Labor and Employment Law Journal* 16: 160 (1998); Stephen Befort, "Labor and Employment Law at the Millennium: A Historical Review and Critical Assessment," *Boston College Law Review* 43 (2002): 361–62.

2. Robert Shaffer, "Where Are the Organized Public Employees? The Absence of Public Employee Unionism from U.S. History Textbooks, and Why It Matters," *Labor History* 43 (2002): 315–334. Shaffer notes, among other things, that from 1990 to 2000 the journal *Labor History* published only two articles concerning public sector unions; ibid., 331, citing Joseph Slater, "Public Workers: Labor and the Boston Police Strike of 1919," *Labor History* 38 (1997): 7–27.

3. John Commons, *Labor and Administration* (New York: Macmillan, 1913), 106, 115. See Selig Perlman, *A Theory of the Labor Movement* (New York: Macmillan, 1928); Philip Taft, *The AFL in the Time of Gompers* (New York: Harper and Bros., 1957); Irving Bernstein, *The Turbulent Years: A History of the American Worker, 1933–1941* (Boston: Houghton Mifflin, 1969).

4. Sterling Spero, *Government as Employer* (New York: Remsen Press, 1948), 71, 76; Leo Troy, *The New Unionism in the New Society: Public Sector Unions in the Redistributive State* (Fairfax, Va.: George Mason University Press, 1994), 4; Bureau of Labor Statistics (BLS) data provided by the AFL-CIO Public Employee Department (in possession of the author); U.S. Bureau of the Census, *Historical Statistics of the United States from Colonial Times to 1970* (Washington, D.C.: Government Printing Office, 1975), part 1: 137, 178.

5. See, e.g., David Brody, *Steelworkers in America: The Nonunion Era* (Cambridge:

Harvard University Press, 1960). In 1930 the rate of unionization in the nonagricultural private sector was 11.6 percent; in 1934 it was 11.9 percent. BLS data provided by the AFL-CIO Public Employee Department.

6. See, e.g., Lichtenstein; Robert Zieger, *The CIO, 1935–1955* (Chapel Hill: University of North Carolina Press, 1995); Foster Dulles and Melvyn Dubofsky, *Labor in America: A History,* 4th ed. (Arlington, Ill.: Harlan Davidson, 1984).

7. See, e.g., Melvyn Dubofsky, *We Shall Be All: A History of the IWW* (Chicago: Quadrangle Books, 1969); Peter Cole, "Shaping Up and Shipping Out: The Philadelphia Waterfront during and after the IWW Years, 1913–1940" (Ph.D. diss., Georgetown University, 1997); Leon Fink, *Workingmen's Democracy: The Knights of Labor and American Politics* (Urbana: University of Illinois Press, 1983).

8. See, e.g., David Montgomery, *The Fall of the House of Labor: The Workplace, the State, and American Labor Activism, 1865–1925* (New York: Cambridge University Press, 1987); Harry Braverman, *Labor and Monopoly Capital* (New York: Monthly Review Press, 1974).

9. For overviews, see Alice Kessler-Harris, "Treating the Male as 'Other': Redefining the Parameters of Labor History," *Labor History* 34 (1993): 190–204; Eric Arnesen, "Up from Exclusion: Black and White Workers, Race, and the State of Labor History," *Reviews in American History* 26 (1998): 146–74; Howard Kimmeldorf, "Bringing Unions Back In (or Why We Need a New Old Labor History)," with comments by Michael Kazin, Alice Kessler-Harris, David Montgomery, Bruce Nelson, and Daniel Nelson, and a response by Kimmeldorf, *Labor History* 32 (1991): 91–129. A notable exception is Marjorie Murphy, *Blackboard Unions: The AFT and the NEA, 1900–1980* (Ithaca: Cornell University Press, 1990), which applies gender analysis to organized teachers.

10. See Paul Johnston, *Success While Others Fail: Social Movement Unionism and the Public Workplace* (Ithaca: Cornell University Press, 1994), 218.

11. Michael Zweig, *The Working Class Majority: America's Best Kept Secret* (Ithaca: Cornell University Press, 2002), 3. Zweig does not analyze the class status of public employees. E. P. Thompson, *The Poverty of Theory and Other Essays* (New York: Monthly Review Press, 1978), 106–7.

12. Michael Kazin, "Struggling with Class Struggle: Marxism and the Search for a Synthesis of U.S. Labor History," *Labor History* 28 (1987): 497–514; Joseph Slater, "The Rise of Master-Servant and the Fall of Master Narrative: A Review of *Labor Law in America,*" *Berkeley Journal of Employment and Labor Law* 15 (1994): 143–44.

13. See, e.g., Joan Scott, "On Language, Gender, and Working Class History," *International Labor and Working Class History* 31 (1987): 1–13. For a criticism of this method, see Bryan Palmer, *Descent into Discourse: The Reification of Language and the Writing of Social History* (Philadelphia: Temple University Press, 1990). David Montgomery also decries the "disciples of Derrida and Foucault [who] would have us believe, contrary to Marx, that it is the social consciousness of people that determines their social being"; Kimmeldorf, comment by Montgomery, 129.

14. Marion Crain, "Between Feminism and Unionism: Working Class Women, Sex Equality, and Labor Speech," *Georgetown Law Journal* (1994): 1943, critiquing labor's acceptance of women, seemingly excludes public sector labor. She states that "even though the percentage of women who are represented by unions relative to men has increased" from 18.3 percent in 1960 to 37 percent in 1992, "the increase appears to be attributable largely to women's disproportionate entry into public sector jobs." Lichtenstein, 181; see chapter 6 for figures on AFSCME's composition.

15. For an overview, see Daniel Ernst, "Law and American Political Development, 1877–1938," *Reviews in American History* 26 (1998): 205–19. Theda Skocpol, a founder of this "new institutionalism," has discussed the NLRA, but neither she nor her critics discuss unions of government workers. Theda Skocpol and Kenneth Finegold, "Explaining New

Deal Labor Policy," with response by Michael Goldfield, *American Political Science Review* 84 (1990): 1297–1315. See also William Forbath, *Law and the Shaping of the American Labor Movement* (Cambridge: Harvard University Press, 1991); Richard Oestreicher, "Urban Working-Class Political Behavior and Theories of American Electoral Politics, 1870–1940," *Journal of American History* 74 (1988): 1257–86. Exceptions include P. Johnston, 9, 215–16 ("public workers are, through their movements and their unions, state-builders"; thus "we need a theory of the state . . . that includes the world of public work and the social movements of those who toil there"); Steven Skowronek, *Building a New American State: The Expansion of National Administrative Capacities, 1877–1920* (New York: Cambridge University Press, 1982) (discussing the federal sector union NFFE); Edna Johnston, "Rendering a Permanent Service: Organized Labor and Federal Workers in the United States, 1900–32" (forthcoming Ph.D. diss., University of Virginia).

16. Melvyn Dubofsky, *The State and Labor in Modern America* (Chapel Hill: University of North Carolina Press, 1994), 197–231; Mark Maier, *City Unions: Managing Discontent in New York City* (New Brunswick, N.J.: Rutgers University Press, 1987), 9; Lichtenstein, 181–85; Ira Katznelson, "The 'Bourgeois' Dimension: A Provocation about Institutions, Politics, and the Future of Labor History," *International Labor and Working Class History* 46 (1994): 7–32.

17. See, e.g., Forbath; Dubofsky, *State and Labor;* Victoria Hattam, *Labor Visions and State Power: The Origins of Business Unionism in the United States* (Princeton: Princeton University Press, 1993); Karen Orren, *Belated Feudalism: Labor, the Law, and Liberal Development in the United States* (New York: Cambridge University Press, 1991); Christopher Tomlins, *The State and the Unions: Labor Relations, Law, and the Organized Labor Movement in America, 1880–1960* (New York: Cambridge University Press, 1985); Christopher Tomlins and Andrew King, eds., *Labor Law in America: Historical and Critical Essays* (Baltimore: Johns Hopkins University Press, 1992); Karl Klare, "Labor Law as Ideology: Toward a New Historiography of Collective Bargaining Law," *Industrial Relations Law Journal* 4 (1981): 450–82; Katherine Stone, "The Post-War Paradigm in American Labor Law," *Yale Law Journal* 90 (1981): 1509–80.

18. Even today, around twenty states do not allow most or even any public sector unions to bargain, and only twelve allow public workers to strike. See Conclusion; Michael Leibig and Wendy Kahn, *Public Employee Organizing and the Law* (Washington, D.C.: BNA Books, 1987); Krista Schneider, *Public Employees Bargain for Excellence: A Compendium of State Public Sector Labor Relations Laws* (Washington, D.C.: AFL-CIO Public Employee Department, 1993).

19. See, e.g., Felix Frankfurter and Nathan Greene, *The Labor Injunction* (New York: Macmillan, 1930), chap. 3; Louis Brandeis, "The Living Law," *Illinois Law Review* 10 (1916): 463–71.

20. See, e.g., Willard Hurst, *Law and the Conditions of Freedom in the Nineteenth Century United States* (Madison: University of Wisconsin Press, 1956); Lawrence Friedman, *American Law in the Twentieth Century* (New Haven: Yale University Press, 2002).

21. See Robert Gordon, "Critical Legal Histories," *Stanford Law Review* 36 (1984): 57–125; Slater, "The Rise of Master-Servant."

22. Morton Horwitz, *The Transformation of American Law, 1780–1860* (Cambridge: Harvard University Press, 1977), xiii; idem, *The Transformation of American Law, 1870–1960: The Crisis of Legal Orthodoxy* (Oxford: Oxford University Press, 1992), vii–viii; Tomlins and King, 13.

23. For teachers, see Steven Cole, *The Unionization of Teachers: A Case Study of the UFT* (New York: Praeger, 1969); William Eaton, *The American Federation of Teachers, 1916–1961* (Carbondale: Southern Illinois University Press, 1975); Murphy; Wayne Urban, *Why Teachers Organized* (Detroit: Wayne State University Press, 1982). For police, see William Bopp, *The Police Rebellion: A Quest for Blue Power* (Springfield, Ill.: Charles Thomas, 1971); John

Burpo, *The Police Labor Movement: Problems and Perspectives* (Springfield, Ill.: Charles Thomas, 1971); Allen Gammage and Stanley Sachs, *Police Unions* (Springfield, Ill.: Charles Thomas, 1972). For AFSCME, see Richard Billings and John Greenya, *Power to the Public Worker* (Washington, D.C.: Robert Luce, 1974); Joseph Goulden, *Jerry Wurf: Labor's Last Angry Man* (New York: Atheneum, 1982); Leo Kramer, *Labor's Paradox: The American Federation of State, County, and Municipal Employees, AFL-CIO* (New York: Wiley, 1962). For postal unions, see John Walsh, *Labor Struggle in the Post Office: From Selective Lobbying to Collective Bargaining* (Armonk, N.Y.: M. E. Sharpe, 1992). Exceptions include P. Johnston, who uses state theory in a study of fairly recent events; and Murphy.

24. Two good collections were recently published: Richard Kearney and David Carnevale, eds., *Labor Relations in the Public Sector,* 3d ed. (New York: Marcel Dekker, 2001); and Joyce Najita and James Stern, eds., *Collective Bargaining in the Public Sector: The Experience of Eight States* (Armonk, N.Y.: M. E. Sharpe, 2001). The works by Schneider and by Leibig and Kahn are still valuable but can be hard to find. For older but still useful works in this vein, see, e.g., Winston Crouch, *Organized Civil Servants* (Berkeley: University of California Press, 1978); Richard Freeman and Casey Ichniowski, *When Public Sector Workers Unionize* (Chicago: University of Chicago Press, 1988); David Lewin et al., eds., *Public Sector Labor Relations: Analysis and Readings* (Lexington, Mass.: Lexington Books, 1988); Jack Stieber, *Public Employee Unionism: Structure, Growth, Policy* (Washington, D.C.: Brookings Institution, 1973); Harry Wellington and Ralph Winter Jr., *The Unions and the Cities* (Washington, D.C.: Brookings Institution, 1971); and generally, the *Journal of Collective Negotiations in the Public Sector.*

25. Lichtenstein, 181; *Government Employee Relations Report* 40, Feb. 6, 2002, 122. Determining the precise numbers of public employees in this era is difficult, and estimates vary somewhat. The Census Bureau compiled some figures for some public workers in certain years, but left large gaps. For example, it stopped calculating the density of public sector unionization in 1934 and did not resume for decades. The figures on police are from U.S. Bureau of the Census, "State and Local Government Quarterly Employment Survey" (Oct. 22, 1940), 1. The other figures are derived from Solomon Fabricant and Robert Lipsey, *The Trend of Government Activity in the United States since 1900* (New York: National Bureau of Economic Research, 1952), 29. Other numbers in this book come from sources that are not always precisely consistent in methodology or results, but every effort has been made to ensure as much accuracy as possible.

26. Kimmeldorf.

27. Dubofsky, *State and Labor,* xi; Brian Kelly, *Race, Class, and Power in the Alabama Coalfields, 1908–21* (Urbana: University of Illinois Press, 2001), 9. As to employers, two fine discussions with different perspectives are Daniel Ernst, *Lawyers against Labor: From Individual Rights to Corporate Liberalism* (Urbana: University of Illinois Press, 1995); and Patricia Sexton, *The War on Labor and the Left: Understanding America's Unique Conservatism* (Boulder: Westview Press, 1991). Still, these and other major works on management study only the private sector. See, e.g., Sanford Jacoby, ed., *Masters to Managers: Historical and Comparative Perspectives on American Employers* (New York: Columbia University Press, 1991). Treatments of public sector employers focus on recent times, e.g., Miller Berkeley and William Canak, "There Should Be No Blanket Guarantee: Employer Opposition to Public Employee Unions," *Journal of Collective Negotiations in the Public Sector* 24 (1995): 17–36.

28. Peter Novick, *That Noble Dream: Objectivity and the American Historical Profession* (Cambridge: Cambridge University Press, 1988), 469–92.

29. E. P. Thompson, *The Making of the English Working Class* (New York: Vintage, 1966).

30. Despite the not-unrelated declines of traditional socialist ideology among both European political parties and academics, the Sombart question rightly remains alive. See Oestre-

icher, 1257 (calls for the "exorcism" of this question are "misguided"); Rick Halperin and Jonathan Morris, eds., *American Exceptionalism? U.S. Working Class Formation in an International Context* (New York: St. Martin's Press, 1997).

Chapter 1. The Boston Police Strike of 1919

1. Jack Tager, *Boston Riots: Three Centuries of Social Violence* (Boston: Northeastern University Press, 2001), 143–44, 160–66.

2. Montgomery, 6. But this work does not discuss the Boston strike; nor does Taft. Dulles and Dubofsky mention it in passing; Dubofsky, *State and Labor,* in an entire chapter on 1917–1920, refers to the strike with only four words: "even police walked out," 77. Exceptions that study this event as part of labor history are Philip Foner, *History of the Labor Movement in the United States,* vol. 8: *Postwar Struggles, 1918–20* (New York: International Publishers, 1987), 88–101; and Zachary Schrag, "Nineteen-Nineteen: The Boston Police Strike in the Context of American Labor" (A.B. honors thesis, Harvard University, 1992).

3. For a brief take on the "contradictory" class status of police, see Ron Bean, "Police Unrest, Unionization, and the 1919 Strike in Liverpool," *Journal of Contemporary History* 15 (1980): 652.

4. Francis Russell, *A City in Terror: The 1919 Boston Police Strike* (New York: Viking, 1975); Thomas Reppetto, *The Blue Parade* (New York: Free Press, 1978), 107–17; Jonathan White, "A Triumph of Bureaucracy: The Boston Police Strike and the Ideological Origins of the American Police Structure" (Ph.D. diss., Michigan State University, 1982); Frederick Koss, "The Boston Police Strike of 1919" (Ph.D. diss., Boston University, 1966).

5. Robert Repas, "Collective Bargaining Problems in Federal Employment," in *Collective Bargaining in the Public Service,* ed. Daniel Kruger and Charles Schmidt (New York: Random House, 1969), 24–26; Murray Nesbitt, *Labor Relations in the Federal Government Service* (Washington, D.C.: BNA Books, 1976), 6, 26, 35, 90. See generally Spero.

6. Spero, 78–81; Nesbitt, 22–23.

7. Spero, 378–81; Hugh O'Neil, "The Growth of Municipal Employee Unions," in *Unionization of Municipal Employees,* ed. Robert Connery and William Farr (New York: Academy of Political Science, 1971), 2; Crouch, 14–15.

8. O'Neil, 1, 2, quoting Commons, 111; Maier, 12, quoting Commons, 115.

9. *American Federationist,* Jan. 1918, 56; Spero, 17, 129, 474; Eaton, 6–10; The American Federation of Labor and the Unions: National and International Union Records from the Samuel Gompers Era (Sanford, N.C.: Microfilming Corporation of America, 1981) (hereafter AFL Records), reel 5; *American Federationist,* Sept. 1919, 815; M. Brady McKusko, *Carriers in a Common Cause: A History of Letter Carriers and the NALC* (Washington, D.C.: NALC, 1986); David Ziskind, *One Thousand Strikes of Government Employees* (New York: Columbia University Press, 1940), 53; Philip Kienast, "Police and Firefighter Employee Organizations" (Ph.D. diss., Michigan State University, 1972), 279. NFFE left the AFL in 1931.

10. In 1900, 15,000 government employees were in unions, out of 1,094,000 total, about 1.4 percent; in 1905 there were 24,000 out of 1,335,000, about 1.8 percent; in 1910, 58,000 out of 1,630,000, about 3.6 percent; in 1915, 90,000 out of 1,861,000, about 4.8 percent; and in 1921, 172,000 out of 2,397,000, about 7.2 percent; U.S. Bureau of the Census, *Historical Statistics,* 137, 178. Beard quoted in Edward Cling, "Industrial Labor Relations Policies and Practices in Municipal Government, Milwaukee, Wisconsin" (Ph.D. diss., Northwestern University, 1957), 176. For a description of the improving legal status of private sector labor in the early twentieth century before the NLRA, see Ernst, *Lawyers against Labor.*

11. *American Federationist*, Jan. 1918, 55–57; Feb. 1919, 132; Aug. 1919, 735–37 (supporting pensions and bans on Taylorist management for federal employees); Sept. 1919, 812–18 (quotes from union leaders), 845–56 (overtime for public employees, raises for postal workers, and reduced hours for firefighters); *Proceedings of the Thirty-eighth Annual Convention of the American Federation of Labor* (Washington, D.C.: Law Reporter Printing, 1918), 114, 317 (teachers' pensions), 163, 212 (hours for firefighters), 178–79, 238–39 (rights of public sector unions), 115–16, 211, 331 (minimum wage for government workers).

12. The assertion in Murphy, 108–9, that Gompers's attention to public sector unions in 1919 was essentially entirely caused by his attempts to head off a labor party is unconvincing. It misses the breadth and depth of the interest that the AFL and government workers had in each other at all levels, fails to address the considerable activity in the public sector in the preceding years, and ignores broader trends in the government and in the economy.

13. Lloyd-LaFollette Act, 37 Stat. 555 (1912); U.S. Bureau of the Census, *Historical Statistics*, 137, 178.

14. *American Federationist*, Jan. 1918, 55–57; Robert Murray, *Red Scare: A Study in National Hysteria, 1919–1920* (Minneapolis: University of Minnesota Press, 1955), 5; Frank Grubbs, *Samuel Gompers and the Great War: Protecting Labor's Standards* (Wake Forest, N.C.: Meridional Press, 1982); Dubofksy, *State and Labor*, 61–81; Spero, 98–100. The WLB also issued a number of decisions declining to take jurisdiction in public sector cases; Spero, 406–7; see chapter 5.

15. *Proceedings of the Seventeenth Annual Convention of the American Federation of Labor* (Washington, D.C.: AFL, 1897), 43; American Federation of Labor, *American Federation of Labor: History, Encyclopedia, Reference Book* (Washington, D.C., 1919), 27; Samuel Gompers, *Seventy Years of Life and Labor: An Autobiography*, 2d ed. (New York: E. P. Dutton, 1967), 96, 122–23; *Proceedings of the Thirty-seventh Annual Convention of the American Federation of Labor* (Washington, D.C.: Law Reporter Printing, 1917), 394; AFL Records, reels 5, 6.

16. *Proceedings of the Thirty-ninth Annual Convention of the American Federation of Labor* (Washington, D.C.: Law Reporter Printing, 1919), 302; Spero, 256–57. Morrison's letter of Aug. 1, 1919, listed police as one of seven types of workers on which organizers should focus; AFL Records, reel 5.

17. The rationale for allowing police unions was not discussed further in convention or EC records, Gompers's official correspondence, or the *American Federationist*. AFL Records, reels 5, 6, 15, 16.

18. "Address by Samuel Gompers before Commissioners of the District of Columbia Regarding Organization of Policemen, Sept. 4, 1919," AFL Records, reel 114, 3–5 (for a longer version, see AFL Records, reel 125). Gompers cited locals in Los Angeles; Pueblo, Colo.; Washington, D.C.; Miami and Key West, Fla.; Macon, Ga.; Peoria and East St. Louis, Ill.; Evansville and Terre Haute, Ind.; Cumberland, Md.; Boston; St. Paul, Minn.; Meridian and Hattiesburg, Miss.; St. Joseph and Moberly, Mo.; Jersey City, N.J.; Janesville and Warren, Ohio; Tulsa and Oklahoma City; Portland, Ore.; Knoxville and Chattanooga, Tenn.; Fort Worth, Tex.; Norfolk, Portsmouth, and Richmond, Va.; Wheeling, Clarksburg, and Huntington, W.V.; and Superior, Wis. By mid-September 1919, there were also locals in Belleville, Ill.; Topeka, Kans.; Lynn, Mass.; and Vicksburg, Mo. *Boston Labor World* (hereafter *Labor World*), Sept. 27, 1919, 7.

19. AFL Records, reel 125, 660, 670, 672–73. President Roosevelt's order of Jan. 31, 1902, was an extension of Postmaster Wilson's 1895 edict. The gag order forbade all federal workers, on pain of dismissal, from seeking legislation in their behalf, "individually or through associations," except through their employers. The Lloyd-LaFollette Act of 1912 reversed this order; Spero, 17, 122. Gompers was correct that the restrictions on police affiliation were new, but of course the AFL did not charter police unions before the war.

20. AFL Records, reel 114, 10–14 and A–C; reel 125, 652, 656, 659–62, 667–74; *American Federationist,* Jan. 1918, 56; Ziskind, 33–39.

21. AFL Records, reel 114, 2; reel 125, 664–66, 675.

22. Ibid., reel 5; Montgomery, 271; *New York Call,* July 13, 1919, 2; July 29, 1919, 4; editorial, Sept. 4, 1919.

23. Crouch, 160–62; AFL Records, reel 6; *Labor World,* Aug. 9, 1919, 2; editorial, Aug. 16, 1919; Sept. 6, 1919, 2; Sept. 20, 1919, 1, 2. The Detroit dispute involved a lodge of the Fraternal Order of Police, which was not part of the AFL but in this case had a fairly aggressive union mentality; *Labor World,* Aug. 23, 1919, 6.

24. *AFL Proceedings* (1918), 302; Ziskind, 53–54, 63–64, 195, 242; Spero, 10, 231–32; Russell, 76–77.

25. AFL Records, reel 6 (advice to police); reel 29, *City Policemen's Union No. 16718 v. Commissioners of the District of Columbia,* Equity No. 37142 (D.C., Sept. 4, 1919); *Labor World,* Sept. 6, 1919, 2; 41 Stat. 364 (1919); 41 Stat. 398 (1920).

26. Kienast, 30; *Labor World,* Aug. 9, 1919, 1–2, 5; editorial, Aug. 16, 1919, 6; Aug. 23, 1919, 1–2, 7; editorial, Sept. 13, 1919.

27. Gammage and Sachs, 34; Kienast, 30; Ziskind, 23–32, 92–94; *Boston Evening Transcript,* Aug. 9, 1919, 5 (phone workers); *Labor World,* Aug. 23, 1919, 1; Sept. 13, 1919, 1; Kearney, 221.

28. *The Boston Police Strike: Two Reports* (New York: Arno Press, 1971) (hereafter *Two Reports*), 8; *Labor World,* Sept. 13, 1919, 10–11. Governor Coolidge appointed Curtis after O'Meara died in December 1918.

29. Koss, 3–6; *Labor World,* editorial, Sept. 13, 1919, 2; Spero, 250. In fact a police station had been condemned six years earlier, but nothing was done about it; Ziskind, 39.

30. *Labor World,* Sept. 6, 1919, 1; Sept. 13, 1919, 2.

31. *Labor World,* Sept. 13, 1919, 10–11. Order 110 created Rule 35, Section 19, which provided: "No member of the Police Force shall join or belong to any organization, club or body composed of present, or present and past members of the force, which is affiliated with or a part of any organization, club, or body outside the department," excepting specified veterans' groups. Boston Police Department General Order 110, Aug. 11, 1919, reprinted in *Two Reports,* 10–11.

32. Russell, 91–92, 98; Ziskind, 43–44; Koss, 73–77; *Labor World,* Aug. 30, 1919, 1; Spero, 260; *Two Reports,* 5–6, 10–11; Boston Police Department circulars, "The Police Department Has Always Opposed Any Scheme of Divided Authority over the Boston Police Force" [Sept. 1919] and "Should a Police Union Be Affiliated with the American Federation of Labor, the Real Issue" [Sept. 1919], Calvin Coolidge Collection, box 19, Massachusetts State House Library.

33. Tager, 160–66; Koss, 160–205; Russell, 121–89; Ziskind, 44–48; Spero, 278; James McGinley, *Labor Relations in the New York Rapid Transit Systems, 1904–1944* (New York: King's Crown Press, 1949), 348. For replies to the BCLU's charges, see the circulars "Governor Coolidge's Actions" [Sept. 1919] and "Police Commissioner Curtis's Activities Complete Answer to His Critics" [Sept. 1919], Coolidge Collection.

34. *Labor World,* editorial, Aug. 9, 1919, 1–2; Aug. 16, 1919, 1; Aug. 23, 1919, 1–2, 7; editorial, Sept. 20, 1919, 1, 2; Sept. 27, 1919, 7.

35. Communications to Edwin U. Curtis regarding the Boston Police Strike, 1919, From Organizations, vols. 1–2, and From Individuals, vols. 1–2, Special Collections, Boston Public Library (hereafter Curtis Letters), e.g., from Curtis and Co. Manufacturing, Sept. 18, 1919, and *Buffalo Courier,* Sept. 14, 1919; Coolidge Speech to the Middlesex Club, Massachusetts, Oct. 27, 1919, Coolidge Collection; *Two Reports,* 8, 10, 11; *Labor World,* editorial, Sept. 20, 1919; editorial, Sept. 6, 1919.

36. *Labor World,* editorial, Sept. 13, 1919; Sept. 20, 1919, 7; Oct. 4, 1919, 7.

37. *Coppage v. Kansas,* 236 U.S. 1 (1915); Russell, 101–12, 183–84; *Labor World,* Sept.

6, 1919, 1. Vahey also argued that the ban on AFL affiliation was not "needful" and that it violated rights to personal liberty; *Labor World,* Aug. 30, 1919, 1; Koss, 85–92. The technical difference between "employees" and "officers" that Devlin emphasized was not well defined. Even when courts used this dubious distinction, the category into which police fell depended on the jurisdiction; Ziskind, 12.

38. Russell, 81; *Labor World,* editorial, Aug. 23, 1919; *Two Reports,* 10, 11; White, 113.

39. *Two Reports,* app., 37–38; Koss, 82; Curtis Letters, from, e.g., Employers' Association of Eastern Massachusetts, Aug. 16, 1919; Employers' Association of Worcester County, Aug. 21, 1919; Boston Fruit and Produce Exchange, Aug. 27, 1919; Haverhill Chamber of Commerce, Aug. 28, 1919; Massachusetts Real Estate Exchange, Aug. 29, 1919; Fitchburg Steam Engine Co., Sept. 10, 1919; E. B. Badger and Sons, Sept. 13, 1919; Carter's Ink. Co. (New York), Sept. 13, 1919; Boston Bar Association, Sept. 17, 1919 (noting its earlier stand); Employers' Association of Berkshire County, Sept. 18, 1919; Curtis and Co. Manufacturing, Sept. 18, 1919; and Exchange Club of Indianapolis, Oct. 6, 1919. For concerns about the potential behavior of unionized police in the District of Columbia during strikes, see the remarks of Senator Charles Thomas, *Congressional Record,* 66th Cong., 1st sess., 1919, 58: 4, 890.

40. Koss, 114–15, 156; Russell, 108–12; Ziskind, 12, 43, 49. The commission, led by James Storrow, recommended that a special panel consider the demands of the officers after they left the AFL. The Boston Chamber of Commerce and most Boston newspapers endorsed this plan, but Curtis rejected it before the Police Union could formally reply to it. See *Two Reports* for the commission's final report and app., 8, for Storrow's concerns about affiliation.

41. White, 113; *Labor World,* editorial, Sept. 27, 1919; *New York Call,* editorial, Aug. 8, 1919; Sept. 3, 1919, 3; Sept. 11, 1919, 7 (cartoon).

42. Tager, 151; Murray, 9; Montgomery, 6; Russell, 74; Spero, 273; Ziskind, 12, 188; Koss, 45; *Labor World,* Aug. 23, 1919, 5, 7; editorial, Sept. 20, 1919. Curtis letters, e.g., from New Hampshire Manufacturing Association, Aug. 22, 1919; Spencer Wire Co., Sept. 12, 1919 (Seattle strike); MacGregor Investment Co., Sept. 12, 1919 ("Soviet rule"); N. D. Cass Co., Sept. 12, 1919; George Leonard Shoes, Sept. 13, 1919 ("Bolshevik tendencies of organized labor"); *New York Sun,* Sept. 13, 1919; *Newport Daily News,* Sept. 29, 1919. Schrag describes the Boston strike in the context of other general strikes. Bean shows that affiliation with labor was also a key point in the English police strikes.

43. *Labor World,* Aug. 9, 1919, 1; Aug. 16, 1919, 1; editorial, Aug. 23, 1–2; Aug. 30, 1919, 2; Sept. 20, 1919, 2.

44. Ibid., editorial, Aug. 9, 1919, 2; editorial, Aug. 23, 1919.

45. Ibid., editorial, Sept. 6, 1919; editorial, Sept. 13, 1919; Sept. 20, 1919, 2; Sept. 27, 1919, 7. Legal objections could have been raised to the arbitration proposal. See chap. 3.

46. Koss, 223, 226; *Labor World,* Sept. 13, 1919, 1; Sept. 20, 1919, 1; Aug. 23, 1919, 1; Ziskind, 12, 48; Russell, 90–91.

47. *Labor World,* Sept. 20, 1919, 2.

48. Ibid., Sept. 27, 1919, 1; Oct. 11, 1919, 1–2; Ziskind, 12, 49; Koss, 340 (blaming labor). Russell, 193–97, argues that Gompers's secretary, Guy Oyster, pressured the BCLU not to engage in a general strike. Other labor newspapers, such as the *Buffalo Labor Journal,* supported the BCLU's decision; *Labor World,* Oct. 11, 1919, 2.

49. Ziskind, 12, 46–49; Russell, 190–91; Koss, 239–40; *Labor World,* Sept. 13, 1919, 1–2; editorial, Sept. 20, 1919; editorial, Sept. 27, 1919, 1, 2; Oct. 4, 1919, 1; Oct. 11, 1919, 1, 2, 7; Oct. 18, 1919, 2; Oct. 25, 1919, 1; Henry Long, "The Boston Police Strike" (n.d.), Coolidge Collection.

50. *Labor World,* Oct. 4, 1919, 7; Nov. 8, 1919, 7; *American Federationist,* Feb. 1920, 134–36.

51. Koss, 303; *Labor World,* editorial, Sept. 20, 1919; editorial, Sept. 27, 1919, 1, 2; Oct.

4, 1919, 1; Nov. 8, 1919, 1; Russell, 211; Henry Wyman, "Opinion of Sept. 11, 1919," in *Official Opinions of the Attorneys General of the Commonwealth of Massachusetts*, vol. 5: *1917–1920* (Boston: Wright and Potter, 1922), 399–400.

52. Curtis Letters, from Cameron Appliance Co., Sept. 15, 1919; from Dorchester American Legion, Post 216, Oct. 6, 1919; Ziskind, 50; Russell, 203–4; AFL Records, reel 30. Neither order by the court explained the basis of its holding. *McInnes v. Police Commissioner of the City of Boston*, No. 16836, Law (Suffolk County, Mass. 1919), Mandamus Petition (case file, Court Archives, Suffolk County, Mass.); Answer and Return of Defendant, ibid.; Order for Judgment, Nov. 7, 1919, ibid.; Exceptions, ibid.; Judgment, Dec. 16, 1919, ibid.

53. *Labor World*, Sept. 20, 1919, 1; Nov. 8, 1919, 1; Ziskind, 50; Spero, 281; William McNulty, "Boston Killed Police Union, but Then Came Corruption," Building Service Employees International Union, *Public Safety*, Sept. 1930, 19.

54. AFL Records, reel 30.

55. Coolidge maintained that the event was a "desertion of duty," not a strike. White, 181; Ziskind, 50, 234, 241–42; Russell, 203–11; Spero, 29–30, 283; *Labor World*, Oct. 18, 1919, 1; editorial, Nov. 8, 1919; *Proceedings of the Fortieth Annual Convention of the American Federation of Labor* (Washington, D.C.: Law Reporter Printing, 1920), 272.

56. *AFL Proceedings* (1920), 272; *AFL-CIO News*, Feb. 22, 1969. Some police locals affiliated with AFL unions such as AFSCME beginning in 1939. The International Union of Police Associations, AFL-CIO, formed in 1979, still exists today.

57. *American Federationist*, Feb. 1920, 182; Ziskind, 65, 204–07; Kienast, 35–37; *Labor World*, Oct. 4, 1919; Nov. 8, 1919, 1; Spero, 9, 231, 288.

58. In 1923, 180,000 of 2,524,000 public workers were in unions; in 1925, 193,000 of 2,765,000; in 1927, 212,000 of 2,945,000; in 1929, 247,000 of 3,065,000; and in 1930, 264,000 of 3,148,000. U.S. Bureau of the Census, *Historical Statistics*, 137, 178.

59. Spero, 209; Leibig and Kahn, 22.

60. Coolidge, speech to the Middlesex Club, Oct. 27, 1919, Coolidge Collection; Edwin Curtis to Henry Long, Apr. 13, 1920, ibid.

61. International Association of Chiefs of Police Bulletin, *Police Unions* (Washington, D.C., 1958), 4; "Cal Coolidge and the Boston Police Strike," *Wall Street Journal*, editorial, Aug. 13, 1981; *National Labor Digest*, Oct. 1919, 16; Cling, 57; Ray Wachs, "How to Organize to Deal with Employee Groups," in *Papers on Bargaining Relationships and Practices* (Madison: League of Wisconsin Municipalities; Wisconsin Association of School Boards, 1968), 17; Goulden, 27. Coolidge's phrase was cited sixty years later in *City of New Orleans v. Police Ass'n of Louisiana*, 369 So.2d 188, 189 (La. Ct. App.), cert. denied, 376 So.2d 1269 (La. 1979). The *Call* responded to Wilson with a cartoon capitalist labeled "Grab-it-all" telling a policeman: "Your strike is a crime against civilization and I'm the civilization"; *New York Call*, Sept. 14, 1919, magazine section, 12.

62. Russell, 90; *New York Call*, editorial, Oct. 2, 1919.

63. Kienast, 35–37; Spero, 408. See chapter 3.

Chapter 2. Yellow-Dog Contracts and the Seattle Teachers, 1928–1931

1. Dubofsky, *State and Labor*, 83–102; Irving Bernstein, *The Lean Years: A History of the American Worker, 1920–1933* (Baltimore: Penguin, 1966); Dana Frank, *Purchasing Power: Consumer Organizing, Gender, and the Seattle Labor Movement, 1919–1929* (New York: Cambridge University Press, 1994). Some of the material in this chapter originally appeared in Joseph Slater, "Petting the Infamous Yellow Dog: The Seattle High School Teachers Union and the State, 1928–31," *Seattle University Law Review* 23 (2000): 485–501.

2. *Seattle High School Teachers, Chap. 200 v. Sharples*, 159 Wash. 424, 293, P. 994 (1930); *Seattle Post-Intelligencer*, May 12, 1928, 3.

3. King County (Wash.) *State Labor News* (hereafter *Labor News*), July 6, 1928, 1. For the private sector, see Daniel Ernst, "The Yellow Dog Contract and Liberal Reform, 1917–32," *Labor History* 30 (1989): 251–74. For the legal rules on yellow-dog contracts in the public and private sectors, see chapter 3.

4. *American Teacher,* May 1946, 6–7; June 1927, 22; Julia Wrigley, *Class Politics and Public Schools: Chicago, 1900–50* (New Brunswick, N.J.: Rutgers University Press, 1982), 126–46; Murphy, 97–108; Urban, 149–50; Spero, 315; *Chicago Federation News,* Sept. 21, 1935, 12.

5. Murphy, 117–21; *American Federationist,* Nov. 1927, 303; *Proceedings of the Forty-eighth Annual Convention of the American Federation of Labor* (Washington, D.C.: Law Reporter Printing, 1928), 265; *Labor News,* Nov. 25, 1927, 1. The board employed 489 high school teachers. *Sharples,* Affidavit of Directors of Seattle School District No. 1, 1, Washington State Archives, Central Branch, Ellensburg (hereafter WSA).

6. *American Teacher,* Apr. 1928, 18; *Post-Intelligencer,* Nov. 24, 1927, 1; *Labor News,* Aug. 29, 1930, 7; *Sharples,* Brief of Respondents, 43, WSA.

7. The other officers were Leah Griffin, recording secretary; Belle McKenzie, corresponding secretary; and George Smith, treasurer. *American Teacher,* Apr. 1928,19; American Federation of Teachers Collection, Walter Reuther Archives, Wayne State University (hereafter AFT Archives), AFT Series XII, box 11, Local 200 folder (hereafter Local 200 folder); Murphy, 71. About 300 of the nearly 500 high school teachers at this time were women. Seattle School District, *Record No. 24, Fiscal Year 1927–1928,* Seattle Public School Archives and Records Management Center (SPSARMC) (hereafter Board Minutes, 1927–28), 365–69. The bar on married women was not altered until October 1942; *American Teacher,* Nov. 1942, 29.

8. *Post-Intelligencer,* Nov. 24, 1927, 1; *Labor News,* Nov. 25, 1927, 1; *American Teacher,* Sept. 1928, 23; Board Minutes, 1927–28, 160–61.

9. *Seattle Star,* Dec. 9 and 12, 1927, AFT Archives, Local 200 folder.

10. See, e.g., *Labor News,* Dec. 2, 1927, 2 (praising Local 200); Apr. 13, 1928, 4 (quoting Walter Lippmann that "teachers will be slaves if they act like slaves"); July 13, 1928, 2 (collective bargaining for city workers); *American Teacher,* Jan. 1928, 21, 28, 30.

11. *Labor News,* Jan. 20, 1928, 1, 2; Jan. 27, 1928, 2; *Post-Intelligencer,* Nov. 24, 1927, 4; Bruce Nelson, *Good Schools: The Seattle Public School System, 1901–30* (Seattle: University of Washington Press, 1988); NEA, "Research Bulletin," Mar. 1927, 75 (U.S. Department of Labor library, Washington, D.C.); Board Minutes, 1927–28, 223, 232, 241. From 1920 to 1930, enrollment in Seattle high schools ballooned from under 10,000 to nearly 17,000; Joseph Hazard, *Pioneer Teachers of Washington* (Seattle: Seattle Retired Teachers Association, 1955), 207.

12. *Post-Intelligencer,* Feb. 18, 1928, 1–2; Feb. 19, 1928, 4; *Labor News,* Feb. 24, 1928, 1; Mar. 3, 1928, 1; Mar. 10, 1928, 1; Board Minutes, 1927–28, 284, 289.

13. Morrow to Hanson, Mar. 3, 1928, AFT Archives, AFT State Federation Collection, box 14 (hereafter SFC), folder 3; *American Teacher,* Apr. 1928, 18–22, 30; *Labor News,* Apr. 27, 1928, 8.

14. *American Teacher,* Apr. 1928, 20–21; *Labor News,* Apr. 27, 1928, 8; *Post-Intelligencer,* Apr. 23, 1928, 1.

15. *Labor News,* Mar. 9, 1928, 2; Mar. 2, 1928, 2, 4; Feb. 10, 1928, 1; Feb. 17, 1928, 1; *Post-Intelligencer,* Feb. 4, 1928, 2. In the early 1920s Shorrock had succeeded in joining the school board elections with other municipal elections. Ironically, his goal was to ensure a turnout sufficiently large that labor or socialists could not elect a member. Nelson, 145.

16. Sharples received 39,915 votes to 38,230 for Shorett. *Post-Intelligencer,* Mar. 16, 11; Mar. 14, 1928, 1; Mar. 17, 1928, 3; May 6, 1928, 1; AFL *Proceedings* (1928), 265;

Seattle School District No. 1, 1963, *Annual Report for the Year Ending June 30, 1963*, 33–34.

17. Miliken to Hanson, Mar. 20, 1928, SFC, folder 3; *Sharples*, 159 Wash. at 425.

18. *Post-Intelligencer*, Apr. 29, 1928, 1; Apr. 28, 1928, 1; *Labor News*, May 4, 1928, 2; Board Minutes, 1927–28, 318, 344.

19. *Sharples*, Complaint, 1, WSA; *Sharples*, 159 Wash. at 425; *Post-Intelligencer*, May 4, 1928, 12.

20. *Post-Intelligencer*, May 5, 1928, 1–2; *Labor News*, May 11, 1928, 1; Seattle School Board Resolution, May 4, 1928, quoted in *Sharples*, Brief of Appellants, 5–8, WSA; Board Minutes, 1927–28, 363–64.

21. *Sharples*, Brief of Appellants, 5–9; *Sharples*, 159 Wash. at 426, 427; *Post-Intelligencer*, May 5, 1928, 1–2; *Labor News*, May 11, 1928, 1.

22. *Post-Intelligencer*, May 6, 1928, 1–2; *Labor News*, May 11, 1928, 1; *Sharples*, Restraining Order and Order to Show Cause, WSA; *Seattle Times*, May 6, 1928, 1.

23. *Post-Intelligencer*, May 6, 1928, 1–2; May 7, 1928, 7; May 8, 1928, 1; May 11, 1928, 1; *Seattle Times*, May 6, 1928, 1, 3; May 8, 1928, 3; May 15, 4; *Labor News*, May 11, 1928, 1; *Sharples*, Order Continuing TRO, WSA.

24. Frank, 1, 184, 202, 244.

25. *Seattle Times*, May 5, 1928, 1, 3; May 9, 1928, 10; May 10, 1928, 5; *Post-Intelligencer*, May 8, 1928, 1; May 12, 1928, 3; *Labor News*, May 11, 1928, 1.

26. Telegrams, SFC, folder 5; AFT, "Seattle," [1928], SFC, folder 17, 1–3, 6; Baker to Hanson, ibid.; Hanson to M. E. Morgan, May 12, 1928, SFC, folder 3; *American Teacher*, Sept. 1926, 1; June 1928, 3–6.

27. AFT, "Seattle," 5; *Labor News*, May 18, 1928, 1; "Press Statement by Florence Hanson," May 14, 1928, SFC, folder 3; press release, May 11, 1928, ibid. National opinion was turning against yellow-dog contracts in the late 1920s; Ernst, "Yellow Dog Contract."

28. *Labor News*, May 18, 1928, 1; AFT, "Seattle," 3; telegrams, SFC, folder 5; Henry Linville to Hanson, May 9, 1928, SFC, folder 3; *Post-Intelligencer*, May 13, 1928, 12; "Copies of Telegrams Sent to Seattle Board of Education," Local 200 folder. The Chicago locals were the Chicago Federation of Women High School Teachers, Chicago Federation of Men Teachers, and Chicago Elementary Teachers.

29. *Post-Intelligencer*, May 13, 1928, 12; *Labor News*, May 18, 1928, 1; May 25, 1928, 1; Aug. 10, 1928, 2.

30. AFT, "Seattle," 4–6; "Copies of Telegrams Sent to Seattle Board of Education"; *Seattle Times*, May 14, 1928, 16.

31. *Post-Intelligencer*, May 11, 1928, 1; May 12, 1928, 3; *Seattle Times*, May 6, 1928, 3.

32. Ironically, a few months earlier the chamber had written Local 200 to suggest that the AFT hold its convention in Seattle. *Post-Intelligencer*, May 16, 1928, 1; May 12, 1928, 3; *Seattle Times*, May 16, 1928, 3; Trial Transcript, SFC, folders 14–15, 47, 54; *Labor News*, May 18, 1928, 1; Hazard, 327.

33. *American Teacher*, Sept. 1928, 23, 26.

34. Jay Brigham, "Public Power and Progressivism in the 1920s" (Ph.D. diss., University of California, Riverside, 1992); *Labor News*, May 3, 1929, 2; *Post-Intelligencer*, Apr. 14, 1928, 7; June 2, 1928, 3; June 7, 1920, 13; June 30, 1928, 4; *American Teacher*, Sept. 1928, 7; June 1928, 3; *Labor News*, June 22, 1928, 4; Aug. 3, 1928, 3; AFT, "Seattle," 1, 7; "Press Statement by Florence Hanson," May 14, 1928, SFC, folder 17; Hanson to FTC, May 14, 1928, SFC, folder 3; *Annual Convention of the AFL* (1928), 266; Hanson to Linville, May 17, 1928, SFC, folder 3; Ralph Johnson to Hanson, May 27, 1928, SFC, folder 4; Henry Linville, radio address, June 20, 1928 (Linville Address) 1, 4, SFC, folder 17.

35. *Post-Intelligencer*, May 8, 1928, 1; Mar. 16, 1928, 1, 2; *Seattle Times*, May 17, 1928, 5; May 20, 1928, 1, 10; May 15, 1928, 4; *Sharples*, Brief of Appellants, 17–18.

36. Trial Transcript, State Supreme Court Case No. 21346, 160–65, WSA; *Post-Intelligencer,* May 17, 1928, 1; *Labor News,* May 18, 2.

37. *Seattle Times,* May 16, 1928, 3; Trial Transcript, 101–2, 105–7, 111–12, 115, 117–18, 121–30, 133–34; *Post-Intelligencer,* May 17, 1928, 1; Trial Transcript, May 16, 67, SFC, folder 15; *Sharples,* Brief of Appellants, 9–10.

38. Quoted in *Sharples,* Brief of Appellants, 4, 12.

39. Trial Transcript, May 15, 1928, 21, 22, 27, SFC, folder 13; *Sharples,* Brief of Appellants, 14–17.

40. *Sharples,* Brief of Appellants, 11; *Post-Intelligencer,* Mar. 16, 1928, 2; Trial Transcript, 10–14, 23, 31, 35, 46, SFC, folders 13–14.

41. *Sharples,* Brief of Appellants, 16; *Post-Intelligencer,* May 17, 1928, 1; Miliken to Hanson, May 20, 1928, SFC, folder 3; *Labor News,* May 18, p. 2.

42. *Seattle High School Teachers Chap. 200 v. Sharples,* Case No. 209483 (Super. Ct., King County, Wash., May 28, 1928), 2–8, WSA, citing *McAuliffe v. Mayor of New Bedford,* 155 Mass. 216 (1892); *Fursman v. City of Chicago,* 278 Ill. 318 (1917); *Frederick v. Owens,* 25 Oh. Cir. Ct. Rpt. 581 (Ct. App. 1915). See chapter 3.

43. *Post-Intelligencer,* May 24, 1928, 17; *Sharples,* Memorandum in Support of Motion to Supersede, 1–4, WSA; *Sharples,* Memorandum in Opposition to Motion for Supersedeas, 1, WSA; *Sharples,* Affidavits of Cole, Sharples, Shorrock, Holmes, Thorgrimson, and Smith, WSA.

44. *Post-Intelligencer,* May 26, 1928, 2; May 25, 1928, 17; May 24, 1928, 1–2; *Seattle Times,* May 26, 1928, 2; Miliken to Hanson, May 26, 1928, SFC, folder 4; Baker to Hanson, May 26, 1928, ibid.

45. *Post-Intelligencer,* May 26, 1928, 2; May 29, 1928, 1.

46. *Sharples,* Order of May 31, 1938, WSA; *Labor News,* June 1, 1928, 1; *Post-Intelligencer,* June 1, 1928, 1, 3; Linville to Hanson, May 25, 1928, SFC, folder 4.

47. Schwartztrauber to Hanson, June 3, 1928, SFC, folder 4; *American Teacher,* Sept. 1928, 31; *Labor News,* June 8, 1928, 1–2; *Post-Intelligencer,* June 6, 1928, 1–2; Miliken to Hanson, June 3, 1928, SFC, folder 3; Morrow to Hanson, June 20, 1928, SFC, folder 4.

48. Selma Borchardt to Mary Baker, [1928], SFC, folder 4; Miliken to Hanson, June 3, 1928, ibid.; Hanson to Morrow, June 7, 1928, ibid.; Hanson to Schwartztrauber, June 4, 1928, SFC, folder 5.

49. *Labor News,* June 8, 1928, 1–2; *Post-Intelligencer,* June 6, 1928, 1–2.

50. *Post-Intelligencer,* June 1, 1928, 31; *Seattle Times,* May 13, 6; May 24, 1928, 5. The *Times* made the doubtful claim that it would have approved the board's action if it had *required* union membership; ibid.

51. *Labor News,* May 25, 1928, 2.

52. Ibid., June 29, 1928, 1; July 13, 1928, 8; Aug. 31, 1928, 1.

53. *American Federationist,* July, 1928, 786; *Labor News,* July 20, 1928, 1; *American Teacher,* Oct. 1928, 4–7.

54. Linville Address, 2, 5–8.

55. *American Teacher,* Sept. 1928, 22, 31; Dec. 1928, 18.

56. Murphy, 90–93; *American Teacher,* Nov. 1928, 15–17; Sept. 1928, 5, 6; May 1946, 6–7. Many Seattle administrators were NEA members; *Post-Intelligencer,* Apr. 19, 1928, 10. In 1930 O. C. Pratt, the Spokane superintendent of schools, became president of the Washington Education Association (WEA); ibid., Dec. 7, 1930, 11; Dec. 31, 1930, 15. The Seattle board had good relations with the WEA; it closed the schools the day of the WEA's convention in October 1929 to permit teachers to attend. Seattle School District, *Record No. 24, Fiscal Year 1927–1928,* SPSARMC, 80.

57. *Labor News,* June 8, 1928, 1–2; *American Teacher,* Sept. 1928, 5.

58. *Labor News,* Sept. 14, 1928, 1; June 29, 1928, 2; July 13, 1928, 3.

59. *Post-Intelligencer,* June 7, 1928, 7.

60. Ibid., June 16, 1928, 1; June 30, 1928, 4; *American Teacher,* Sept. 1928, 31; *Labor News,* June 22, 1928, 4; July 6, 1928, 6; June 29, 1928, 1. Morrow was charged with kissing a student, an allegation he denied; Belle McKenzie to Hanson, Mar. 10, 1929, SFC, folder 6.

61. The judicial race was nonpartisan; *Post-Intelligencer,* Sept. 9, 1928, 16; Sept. 12, 1928, 1, 6; *Labor News,* Sept. 7, 1928, 4; Sept. 14, 1928, 2; William Satterthwaite, "Seattle Local 200," [1928], Local 200 folder; *American Teacher,* Oct. 1928, 30; Nov. 1928, 29; Feb. 1929, 31–32.

62. AFL *Proceedings* (1928), 265–66; *Labor News,* Oct. 26, 1928, 8; Nov. 23, 1928, 3; *American Teacher,* May 1929, 8; Satterthwaite, "Seattle Local 200."

63. *American Teacher,* Apr. 1929, 14, 23; May 1929, 6.

64. Ibid., Apr. 1929, 2; *Labor News,* Apr. 26, 1929, 7.

65. *Post-Intelligencer,* Mar. 4, 1929, 12; Mar. 13, 1929, 1; Mar. 11, 1929, 24; *American Teacher,* Apr. 1929, 1.

66. *Labor News,* Mar. 8, 1929, 1; Sept. 7, 1928, 4; *American Teacher,* Apr. 1929, 1. As to Patterson, the CLC had previously argued that a woman should be on the board; *Labor News,* Jan. 18, 1929, 1.

67. Two other candidates received a total of under 8,000 votes; Seattle School District, *Record No. 25, Fiscal Year 1928–1929,* SPSARMC (hereafter Board Minutes, 1928–29), 221; *Post-Intelligencer,* Mar. 13, 1929, 1; *Labor News,* Mar. 15, 1929, 1, 2.

68. *Post-Intelligencer,* Apr. 20, 1929, 1–2; *American Teacher,* June 1929, 31; Board Minutes, 1928–29, 273.

69. *Post-Intelligencer,* Apr. 20, 1929, 1–2; *Labor News,* Apr. 26, 1929, 2.

70. *Labor News,* Apr. 26, 1929, 2.

71. *American Federationist,* May 1929, 559–61; *Labor News,* Apr. 26, 1929, 2. See, e.g., *Labor News,* June 28, 1929, 8 (New Orleans AFT); Nov. 29, 1929, 3 (Montana teachers); Feb. 21, 1930, 2 (Memphis AFT); Aug. 2, 1929, 2, 4, 7 (IAFF); Aug. 16, 1929 (city workers).

72. *Post-Intelligencer,* Jan. 10, 1930, 1, 12; *American Teacher,* Mar. 1930, 15; *Labor News,* Jan. 17, 2.

73. *American Teacher,* Mar. 1930, 15; *Labor News,* Jan. 17, 1930, 2; *Post-Intelligencer,* Jan. 22, 1930, in Dietrich Schmitz Collection, University of Washington Archives (hereafter Schmitz Collection), box 19, folder 6.

74. *Post-Intelligencer,* Jan. 10, 1930, 12; Mar. 10, 1930, 1; *Labor News,* Mar. 14, 1930, 2; Feb. 28, 1930, 1; John Wallace, Associated Industries of Seattle, to Schmitz, Jan. 23, 1931, Schmitz Collection, box 22, folder 1; "Is Trade Unionism the Issue in the School Board Election?" ibid., folder 2.

75. *Post-Intelligencer,* Feb. 13, 1930, 3; Feb. 20, 1930, 15; Schmitz to Joe Stoddard, *Seattle Star,* Feb. 21, 1930, Schmitz Collection, box 22, folder 1; Schmitz to Cole, Feb. 5, 1930, ibid., box 19, folder 1; Schmitz to J. N. Lyle, ibid.

76. Indeed, when Holmes came to the board, he had replaced another member of the same firm; *Labor News,* Mar. 7, 1930, 1; *Post-Intelligencer,* Mar. 10, 1930, 10, 13; *American Teacher,* Apr. 1930, 12–13.

77. *Post-Intelligencer,* Mar. 9, 1930, 8.

78. Schmitz received 43,430 votes; Bailey, 38,568; Griffiths, 37,300; McDonald 37,258. A fifth candidate trailed far behind; *Post-Intelligencer,* Mar. 13, 1930, 2; Mar. 12, 1930, 3.

79. Ibid., Mar. 13, 1930, 2; *Labor News,* Mar. 14, 1930, 1.

80. *Post-Intelligencer,* Mar. 22, 1930, 1–2; *Labor News,* Mar. 28, 1930, 1; Aug. 15, 1930, 2; Aug. 29, 1930, 7; Nov. 14, 1930, 1. As to other public sector unions, see, e.g., *Labor News,* July 18, 1930, 1 (IAFF).

81. *Sharples,* Case No. 21346, Order of Oct. 14, 1930, WSA; *Sharples,* Brief of Appellants, 2, 5, 19–38.

82. *Sharples,* Brief of Respondents, 5, 6, 8–21, 25, 27, 30, 32, 38–40, 44–50, WSA.

83. *Sharples,* Reply Brief of Appellants, 2–9, 12–16, 18–20, 25–26, WSA.

84. *Post-Intelligencer,* Dec. 3, 1930, 17; *Labor News,* Dec. 12, 1930, 4.

85. Justices Mark Fullerton, Emmett Parker, Warren Tollman, William Millard, John Main, and Adam Beeler joined Mitchell's opinion. Justice Holcomb concurred but did not write separately. Justice Walter Beals dissented.

86. *Sharples,* 159 Wash. at 425–32. The law provided that school boards had the power "to employ for not more than one year, and for sufficient cause to discharge teachers"; ibid., 428. The yellow-dog clause included the promise that the teacher "will not become a member [of the AFT] during the term of this contract"; ibid., 426.

87. Ibid., 433–438.

88. Ibid., 438–41 (Beals, dissenting).

89. Schmitz became the board's vice-president; *Post-Intelligencer,* Jan. 3, 1931, 1; *Seattle Times,* Jan. 3, 1931, 7; *Labor News,* Jan. 9, 1931, 1; Seattle School District, *Record No. 27, Fiscal Year 1930–31,* SPSARMC, 188–89.

90. Satterthwaite to Linville, Jan. 11, 1931, Local 200 folder.

91. *American Teacher,* Feb. 1931, 10. Harlin had worked for the Washington State Federation of Labor and was a member of the Teamsters when elected; ibid., Oct. 1931, 23. After his election, Dore immediately barred all city employees from "communicating with the City Council" without his written consent; *Labor News,* Oct. 14, 1932, 1; *American Teacher,* Jan. 1932, 21; Schmitz remained on the school board through 1961; Seattle Public Schools, *Annual Report for the Year Ending June 30, 1963,* 34–36.

92. *Labor News,* May 22, 1931, 2. See, e.g., ibid., Aug. 28, 1931, 1 (IAFF); July 15, 1932, 2 (opposing the bar on lobbying by city employees); Dec. 30, 1932, 1 ("Boards of Education are mainly composed of wealthy men, former employers"); Aug. 11, 1933, 2 (the "ruling element of society" is attacking the public schools); Andrew Elwick to Hanson, Apr. 30, 1935, Local 200 folder.

93. *Labor News,* May 23, 1931, 1; May 29, 1931, 2; June 5, 1931, 1; Dec. 29, 1933, 2; *American Teacher,* Mar.–Apr. 1937, 12; Nov. 1938, 26; McKenzie to Hanson, SFC, folder 7; Satterthwaite to Worth McClure, June 8, 1932, Schmitz Collection, box 2, folder 12. For the financial woes of schools during the Depression, see chapter 4.

94. "Monthly Report to the Secretary-Treasurer," Local 200 folder; *American Teacher,* Nov.–Dec. 1936, 17; Jan.–Feb. 1937, 27; Sept.–Oct. 1937, 20; Nov.–Dec. 1937, 6.

95. *American Teacher,* May–June 1936, 5–9; May–June 1937, 17; Nov.–Dec. 1937, 14–15; Jan. 1943, 4; Oct. 1944, 35; Dec. 1944, 3; Feb. 1945, 7–8; Oct. 1945, 3; Mar.–Apr. 1938, 7–8; Mar. 1930, 17; May–June 1938, 18–19; *CIO News,* Dec. 21, 1942, 8. The Wisconsin case was *State ex rel. Brister v. Weston,* 241 Wis. 584 (1942).

96. *Chicago Federation News,* May 21, 1938, 12; July 2, 1938, 7; Nov. 18, 1939, 2; Murphy, 120–21, 159.

97. *Labor News,* Apr. 8, 1932, 1; *American Teacher,* Dec. 1931, 8, 10, 16; Cling, 70, 79; see chapter 3. Cases citing *Sharples* as precedent include *City of Los Angeles v. Los Angeles Building and Trades Council,* 94 Cal.App.2d 36 (1949).

Chapter 3. Public Sector Labor Law before Legalized Collective Bargaining

1. See works discussed in Slater, "The Rise of Master-Servant"; and Joseph Slater, "The Court Does *Not* Know 'What a Labor Union Is': How State Structures and Judicial (Mis)Constructions Deformed Public Sector Labor Law," *Oregon Law Review* 79 (2000): 982 n. 6 (the latter article is an earlier version of this chapter).

2. Forbath; Hattam. For a contrary view, see Robin Archer, "Unions, Courts, and Parties: Judicial Repression and Labor Politics in Late Nineteenth Century America," *Politics and Society* 26 (1998): 391–422.

3. See, e.g., James Westbrook, "The Use of the Nondelegation Doctrine in Public Sector Labor Law: Lessons from Cases That Have Perpetuated an Anachronism," *St. Louis University Law Journal* 30 (1986): 331–84.

4. See, e.g., Frankfurter and Greene, chap. 3; Felix Frankfurter, "Hours of Labor and Realism in Constitutional Law," *Harvard Law Review* 29 (1916): 353–73.

5. Slater, "The Rise of Master-Servant," 146, quoting Melvyn Dubofsky that labor law has always related "to shifts in the balance of power between labor and capital"; Robert Gordon, "The Past as Authority and as Social Critic: Stabilizing and Destabilizing Functions of History in Legal Argument," in *The Historic Turn in the Human Sciences,* ed. Terrence McDonald (Ann Arbor: University of Michigan Press, 1996), 348–49.

6. 236 U.S. 1 (1915).

7. 25 Oh. Cir. Ct. Rpt. 581, 593 (Ct. App. 1915), error dismissed, *Owens v. Board of Education,* 95 Oh. 407 (1916).

8. See, e.g., *Sharples,* discussed in chapter 2.

9. 223 S.W. 506, 511 (Tex. Ct. App. 1920).

10. 278 Ill. 318, 319 (1917).

11. 278 Pa. 119, 220 (1923).

12. 198 S.W.2d 143, 146, citing *Sharples; Fursman; Frederick; Hutchinson v. Magee,* 278 Pa. 119 (1923); *Carter v. Thompson,* 164 Va. 312 (1935); *Fraternal Order of Firemen v. Harris,* 306 Mich. 68 (1943), cert. denied, 321 U.S. 784 (1944); *City of Jackson v. McLeod,* 199 Miss. 676 (1946), cert. denied, 328 U.S. 863 (1946); and *Perez v. Board of Police Commissioners,* 78 Cal.App.2d 638 (1947); 198 S.W.2d at 149 (dissent).

13. Gordon, "The Past as Authority," 360. Ernst, *Lawyers against Labor,* argues that labor law decisions are better understood as part of a world view based on the social and economic values of the Victorian era, which emphasized individualism, proprietary capitalism, and a skepticism of emerging interest group pluralism; Charles McCurdy, "The Roots of Liberty of Contract Reconsidered: Major Premises in the Law of Employment, 1867–1937," *Supreme Court Historical Society Yearbook,* 1984, 20–33, stresses the importance of concepts of freedom, especially regarding work, in the context of the history of slavery. Slater, "The Rise of Master-Servant," 168–71, suggests that a theory of class-based ideology helps explain labor and employment cases in this era.

14. Melvyn Urofsky, "State Courts and Protective Legislation During the Progressive Era: A Reevaluation," *Journal of American History* 72 (1985): 63–91, claims that state court decisions on labor and employment law were not as bad as progressives claimed. But for extensive lists of injunction, conspiracy, and other cases decided against unions, see Forbath, 37–58. On the Supreme Court level, workers and unions certainly did not fare well. See *Lochner v. New York,* 198 U.S. 45 (1905) (state law capping hours for bakers violates liberty of contract); *Adair v. United States,* 208 U.S. 161 (1908) and *Coppage* (state laws prohibiting yellow-dog contracts are unconstitutional); *Lowe v. Lawlor,* 298 U.S. 274 (1908) (individual workers as well as unions engaged in a nonviolent product boycott liable under the Sherman Act); *Hammer v. Dagenhart,* 247 U.S. 251 (1918) (Federal Child Labor Act unconstitutional); *Adkins v. Children's Hospital,* 261 U.S. 525 (1923) and *Morehead v. New York ex. rel. Tipaldo,* 298 U.S. 587 (1936) (New York and D.C. minimum wage laws for women unconstitutional).

15. For negative portrayals of labor by judges in this era, see Dianne Avery, "Images of Violence in Labor Jurisprudence: The Regulation of Picketing and Boycotts, 1894–1921," *Buffalo Law Review* 37 (1989): 1–117.

16. 198 S.W.2d 143, 145. Although *Murphy* was reversed on other grounds, judges in other public sector cases continued to quote it approvingly as late as 1966. See, e.g., *Weinstein v. New York City Transit Authority,* 267 N.Y.S.2d 111, 127 (Sup. Ct. 1966).

17. Tomlins, *State and the Unions;* Ernst, *Lawyers against Labor;* Dubofsky, *State and Labor,* chaps. 1–4. Dubofsky, ibid., 162–67, even argues that from the late 1930s to the early 1940s courts were the branch of government most helpful to labor. Strong arguments have been made that the courts did not interpret the NLRA as broadly in favor of union rights as they could or should have. See, e.g., Karl Klare, "Judicial Deradicalization of the Wagner Act and the Origins of Modern Legal Consciousness: 1937–41," *Minnesota Law Review* 62 (1978): 265–339; James Atleson, *Values and Assumptions in American Labor Law* (Amherst: University of Massachusetts Press, 1983). But there is no comparison to the hostility that courts showed toward public sector unions.

18. Compare *Goldfinger v. Feintuch,* 276 N.Y. 281 (1937) (allowing secondary boycott) with *Carpenters & Joiners Union Of America, Local 213 v. Ritter's Café,* 149 S.W.2d 694 (Tex. Civ. App. 1940), aff'd 315 U.S. 722 (1942) (barring peaceful secondary picketing). I am grateful to Allan Hyde and Timothy Sears for advice on this point.

19. 24 So.2d 319, 321 (1946), cert. denied, 328 U.S. 863 (1946).

20. 198 S.W.2d at 144.

21. 180 Misc. 868 at 876; 44 N.Y.S.2d at 607–8.

22. A comprehensive law setting out the relations between courts and agencies, the Administrative Procedure Act, was passed in 1946. See Skowronek; Frank Bates and Oliver Field, *State Government* (New York: Harper and Bros., 1939), 260–75; Kenneth C. Davis, *Administrative Law Treatise,* vol. 1, 2d ed. (San Diego: K. C. Davis, 1978), 14.

23. 116 N.E. 158 at 160.

24. 223 S.W. 506 at 509, 511, 512.

25. 25 Oh. Cir. Ct. Rpt. 581 at 592.

26. 164 Va. 312, 316 (1935).

27. 24 So.2d 319, 320–21 (1946).

28. *Schechter Poultry Corp. v. United States,* 295 U.S. 495 (1935). For a discussion of delegation to private parties in state court cases, see Davis, *Administrative Law Treatise,* 193–98. Some secondary sources refer to the delegation problem as a "sovereignty" issue; Kurt Hanslowe, "The Emerging Law of Labor Relations in Public Sector Employment," in *Labor Relations Law in the Public Sector: Cases and Materials,* ed. Harry Edwards, R. Theodore Clark, and Charles Craver, 4th ed. (Charlottesville, Va.: Michie, 1991), 24. The doctrines are related, as Hanslowe's formulation shows: determining the conditions of government employment is a sovereign power that cannot be "given or taken away"; ibid., 26. Contemporaries used both terms. Arguing that the main point is delegation are Westbrook, 353; and Neil Fox, "PATCO and the Courts: Public Sector Labor Law as Ideology," *University of Illinois Law Review,* 1985, 259.

29. See, e.g., Westbrook, 362 n. 183.

30. 185 Md. 266 at 270 (1945).

31. 74 Cal.App.2d 292 (Ct. App. 1946).

32. 57 Oh. Abs. 173, 174 (C.P. 1949).

33. For modern cases holding that arbitration constitutes an unlawful delegation of public power, see Karen Speiser, "Labor Arbitration in Public Agencies: An Unconstitutional Delegation of Power or the 'Waking of a Sleeping Giant'?" *Journal of Dispute Resolution,* 1993, 340–42.

34. 74 Cal.App.2d at 298; Spero, 342–43. But see *Mugford,* which did allow taxpayer standing to challenge dues check-off for city workers.

35. 356 Mo. 1239, 1251 (1947).

36. 356 Mo. at 1251, 1250.

37. 44 N.Y.S.2d 601 at 608; Charles Rhyne, *Labor Unions and Municipal Employee Law* (Washington, D.C.: National Institute of Municipal Law Offices, 1946), 528–29 (quoting Padway).

38. 44 N.Y.S.2d at 607; 198 S.W.2d at 145.

39. 44 N.Y.S.2d at 607.

40. Nesbitt, 84–85, 89 (1976); Davis, *Administrative Law Treatise,* 193–96 (quote on 196), 204–5; Westbrook, 366; Kenneth C. Davis, *Administrative Law Text,* 3d ed. (St. Paul: West Publishing, 1972), 525–27; idem, *Administrative Law* (St. Paul: West Publishing, 1951), 868–69.

41. Frank Cooper, *State Administrative Law,* vol. 1 (Indianapolis: Bobbs-Merrill, 1965), 84; *State Bd. of Dry Cleaners v. Thrift-D-Lux Cleaners, Inc.,* 40 Cal.2d 436 (1953); Speiser, 345; Rhyne, 530, 540.

42. *Cook v. United States,* 91 U.S. 389, 398 (1875); *Lindsay-Strathmore Irrigation District v. Bekins,* 304 U.S. 27 (1938) (state contracts); *Louisiana v. Pilsbury,* 105 U.S. 278 (1881) (city contracts enforceable despite state act to nullify them).

43. John McBride, Thomas Touhey, and Barbara McBride, *Government Contracts: Law, Administration, Procedure,* vol. 1 (New York: Matthew Bender, 1984), 1.10, 1.20, 1.120, 3.50, 3.60; Rhyne, 536.

44. *McAuliffe v. Mayor of New Bedford,* 155 Mass. 216, 220 (1892).

45. *CIO,* 198 S.W.2d at 146. See, e.g., *Perez* at 649; *King v. Priest,* 357 Mo. at 87; *AFSCME Local 201 v. City of Muskegon,* 369 Mich. 384 (1963) (seventy-one years after *McAuliffe,* bar on unions upheld, no constitutional right to public employment).

46. See *Board of Regents v. Roth,* 408 U.S. 564 (1972) (due process clause can protect property right in government employment); *Pickering v. Board of Education,* 391 U.S. 563 (1968) (First Amendment rights for public workers); and *Keyeshian v. Board of Regents,* 385 U.S. 589 (1967) (public employment cannot be predicated on relinquishing right of association); *Atkins v. City of Charlotte,* 296 F. Supp. 1068, 1077 (W.D.N.C. 1969) (ban on firefighters unionizing violates First Amendment rights).

47. See, e.g., *Perez* at 649 (no property right in government employment); *Sharples;* and other cases cited herein.

48. Around 1940 a few states, including Michigan and Washington, passed laws granting some rights to unions of employees of public utilities; Spero, 349–350; *Amalgamated Ass'n of Street, Electric Railway & Motor Coach Employees v. WERB,* 340 U.S. 383 (1951); see chapter 6.

49. 330 U.S. 258 (1947).

50. *Garcia v. San Antonio Metropolitan Transit Authority,* 469 U.S. 528, 546–47 (1985) (the case that permitted the application of the FLSA to public employees).

51. 74 Cal.App.2d 292 at 302.

52. See Slater, "The Rise of Master-Servant."

53. See chapters 1, 4, and 5 regarding the no-strike policies of public sector unions. For Padway's explanation of the AFL's position on strikes and bargaining, see Rhyne, 528–32.

54. Spero, 38, 219; Murphy, 184; Kramer, 42. Ziskind, *One Thousand Strikes of Government Employees,* has a misleading title. The vast majority of the incidents he catalogues are brief stoppages by workers in the WPA and similar agencies during the New Deal. A leading study concludes that after the Boston strike, "no further important work stoppages took place in municipal government until after World War II"; Sterling Spero and John Capozolla, *The Urban Community and Its Unionized Bureaucracies: Pressure Politics in Local Government Labor Relations* (New York: Dunellen, 1973), 246–47. For the lack of strikes after 1946, see chapter 6.

55. 357 Mo. 68, 82 (1947).

56. 357 Mo. at 83.

57. 198 S.W.2d at 148–49; ibid., 144–45, quoting Aug. 16, 1937, letter from Roosevelt to Steward. Roosevelt's position on this issue was not clear-cut. He supported laws that allowed limited bargaining in certain New Deal agencies, notably the Tennessee Valley Authority. Spero, 346, 438–40; Nesbitt, 99.

58. 356 Mo. 1239 at 1246–47, citing Missouri constitution of 1945, art. 1, sec. 29.

59. 356 Mo. at 1247; Westbrook, 338, 342.

60. 24 So.2d at 327–28.

61. 180 Misc. 868, 871–73.

62. 157 Fla. 445, 450 (1946).

63. 198 S.W.2d 143 at 144, 147 (emphasis omitted).

64. 357 Mo. 68, 86.

65. 74 Cal.App.2d at 296–97; Rhyne, 318–19.

66. See Katherine Stone, "The Legacy of Industrial Pluralism: The Tension between Individual Employment Rights and the New Deal Collective Bargaining System," *University of Chicago Law Review* 59 (1992): 622–44; Ronald Schatz, "From Commons to Dunlop: Rethinking the Field and Theory of Industrial Relations," in *Industrial Democracy in America,* ed. Nelson Lichtenstein and Howell Harris (Cambridge: Cambridge University Press, 1993).

67. 223 S.W. 503 at 506.

68. See, e.g., *Levasseur v. Wheeldon,* 79 S.D. 442 (1962) (on public sector organizing rights but raising no issue regarding strikes and still citing Coolidge on the Boston strike).

69. 44 N.Y.S.2d at 607–8.

70. 94 Cal.App.2d 36 (1949).

71. 57 Oh. Abs. at 176–78.

72. Cited in Spero and Capozzola, 256–57.

73. 223 S.W. at 504–6, citing, e.g., *State v. Kreutzberg,* 114 Wis. 530 (1902).

74. AFSCME organized several police locals in California in the early 1940s. Opposition caused most to disband. The Los Angeles local was formed in 1943 and banned in 1946; 78 Cal.App.2d 638 at 640, 642; Crouch, 162 (1978).

75. 78 Cal.App.2d at 640, 643–47.

76. Ibid. at 650–51.

77. *City of Jackson v. McLeod* (ban on police affiliating); *Fraternal Order of Police v. Lansing Board of Police & Fire Commissioners,* 306 Mich. 68 (1943) (ban on firefighters affiliating); *Carter v. Thompson* (firefighters), 164 Va. 312 at 317; *King,* 357 Mo. at 84.

78. See, e.g., *City of Cleveland v. Division 268* (public transportation); *Mugford* (mostly street cleaners); *Nutter* (public bus drivers); *Miami Water Works* (public utility workers); *Clouse* (city workers); *CIO v. Dallas* (city workers); chapter 2 (AFT); chapter 4 (janitors in public buildings).

79. Compare *Government and Civic Employees Organizing Committee, CIO v. Windsor,* 262 Ala. 285, 78 So.2d 646 (1955) (upholding bar on organizing) with *McLaughlin v. Tilendis,* 398 F.2d 287 (7th Cir. 1967) (ban on AFT in Cook County schools is unconstitutional).

80. See, e.g., Dubofsky, *State and Labor,* chaps. 1, 2, 4, and 5.

81. As noted in chapter 1, the Lloyd-LaFollette Act reversed Theodore Roosevelt's "gag order" of 1902; it also stated that federal workers could be discharged only for cause and that union membership was not cause if the union imposed no duty to strike. While this rule was better than nothing, courts often eviscerated it. Spero, 3, 17, 41–43, 71, 81–91, 383, 430–31; Nesbitt, 23, 91–94; see *Levine v. Farely and Howes* (allowing discharge for union activities).

82. This act, as amended in 1940, applied not only to most federal executive branch employees (and their families) but also to thousands of workers in state and local government offices that received federal funds. Discharge was mandatory for violations. Spero, 45, 47, 49, 58. A CIO union challenged the constitutionality of the Hatch Act, but the Supreme Court upheld it in *United Public Workers v. Mitchell,* 330 U.S. 75 (1946).

83. For more details on the evolution of civil service laws, see Joseph Slater, "Down by Law: Public Sector Unions and the State in America, World War I to World War II" (Ph.D. diss., Georgetown University, 1998), 122–25; Kramer, 27; Daniel Grant and H. C. Nixon, *State and Local Government in America* (Boston: Allyn and Bacon, 1969), 349; Kienast,

41–42. AFSCME was founded in part to fight the gutting of civil service in Wisconsin; Steven Kropp, "Reflections on Law, Economics, and Policy in Public Sector Labor Relations in Canada, The United States, and the United Kingdom," *Law and Policy in International Business* 27 (1996): 844; Spero, 41–43; see, e.g., *Carter v. Thompson.*

84. Even for individual workers, these laws often held out greater promise than they fulfilled. Civil service rules often covered surprisingly few employees of a given jurisdiction, and protections were often minimal. Fabricant and Lipsey, 91 nn. 17, 18; Grant and Nixon, 349 ("in name only"); Kramer, 11, 27–30; Slater, "Down by Law," 125–26.

85. NLRA secs. 2(2)–(3) exclude employees of "the United States . . . or any state or political division thereof." The only comment in the extensive legislative history on this exclusion is Francis Biddle's remark: "I suppose Mr. Connery in drawing the bill thought it wise to exclude Government employees as that is suggesting a debatable question and he did not want to overload the bill." National Labor Relations Board, *Legislative History of the National Labor Relations Act of 1935,* vol. 2 (Washington, D.C.: Government Printing Office, 1949), 2653.

86. See, e.g., Dubofsky, *State and Labor;* Tomlins, *State and the Unions;* Lichtenstein; Irving Bernstein, *A Caring Society: The New Deal, the Worker, and the Great Depression* (Boston: Houghton Mifflin, 1985). As to unionists calling for federal statutory coverage, see chapters 4 and 6; Murphy, 162; George Meany, "Union Leaders and Public Sector Unions— AFL-CIO," in *Public Employee Unions: A Study of the Crisis in Public Sector Labor Relations,* ed. Lawrence Chickering (San Francisco: Institute for Contemporary Studies, 1976), 165.

87. Rhyne, 528; Spero, 407. See chapter 5.

88. *NLRB v. Jones & Laughlin Steel Corp.,* 301 U.S. 1 (1937) (upholding the NLRA); see, e.g., *United States v. Darby,* 312 U.S. 100 (1941) (upholding the FLSA).

89. *Board of Trustees v. Garrett,* 531 U.S. 356 (2001) (states mostly immune from private suits by state employees under the Americans with Disabilities Act because of Eleventh Amendment and general state sovereignty concerns); *Kimel v. Florida Bd. of Regents,* 528 U.S. 62 (2000) (same for the Age Discrimination in Employment Act); *Alden v. Maine,* 527 U.S. 706 (1999) (same for the FLSA). While these cases do not hold that Congress cannot apply federal employment laws to state employees, they do bar state employees from suing for money damages. In theory, the Department of Labor can also enforce these laws against the states. But this still presents enormous obstacles to state employees attempting to vindicate their rights under these laws.

90. Harold Levinson, *Collective Bargaining by British Local Authority Employees* (Ann Arbor: University of Michigan Press, 1971), 5, 7; Spero, 4, 13, 419–20, 479–84; William Keller, ed., *International Labor and Employment Laws,* vol. 1 (Washington, D.C.: BNA Books, 1997), 3-1–3-30, 7-1–7-41; Frederic Myers, *The State and Government Employee Unions in France* (Ann Arbor: University of Michigan Press, 1971), 29. Mandatory arbitration in public employment in the United States was illegal everywhere until the 1960s and is still prohibited in some jurisdictions today. Speiser; Westbrook. See also Kearney, 45 (U.S. public sector labor law "is in stark contrast to other industrialized nations, wherein a single, national collective bargaining law prevails for all public workers").

91. For example, as chapter 5 shows, Mayor Fiorello LaGuardia of New York, generally a friend of labor, took a dim view of city workers in New York organizing.

92. Spero, 16, 29–32, 289–90.

93. Spero, 31–37; Kramer, 159; Theodore Kheel, "Introduction: Background and History," in *Public Employee Unions: A Study of the Crisis in Public Sector Labor Relations,* ed. Lawrence Chickering (San Francisco: Institute for Contemporary Studies, 1976), 2.

94. The 1947 Texas statute allowed some public workers to organize but did not allow public employers to "recognize" unions. The city of Dallas continued to bar organizing by ordinance until 1956, when a court finally held that this rule violated the state law; *Beverly*

v. City of Dallas, 292 S.W.2d 172 (Tex. Civ. App. 1956), writ refused, n.r.e. Michigan in 1947 made its state mediation board available for some public employee disputes. The New Jersey constitution of 1947, art. I, sec. 19, gave some government employees limited rights to organize. The Nebraska statute, while providing for the imprisonment of strikers, allowed limited arbitrations in a Court of Industrial Relations. North Dakota in 1951 gave limited organizing rights to some public workers. Spero, 16, 35–36, 349–50; Kramer, 43, 156–58.

95. *Hunt,* 4 Met. 111 (Mass. 1842); see Christopher Tomlins, *Law, Labor, and Ideology in the Early American Republic* (New York: Cambridge University Press, 1993), 180–219; Robert Hoxie, *Trade Unionism in the United States* (New York: D. Appleton, 1923), 30.

96. See, e.g., Atleson; Tomlins, *State and the Unions;* Stone, "The Post-War Paradigm"; Klare, "Judicial Deradicalization of the Wagner Act"; for an overview, see Slater, "The Rise of Master-Servant."

97. Maier, 20; Spero, 71, 75. The unaffiliated Fraternal Order of Police is still the largest police union. In recent decades, some employee associations have begun to act more like traditional unions, e.g., the NEA (which is still larger than the AFT), and some have joined the AFL-CIO.

Chapter 4. Ground-Floor Politics and the BSEIU in the 1930s

1. Paul David to Kenneth Hodges, July 5, 1939, Microfilm Records of the BSEIU, Walter Reuther Archives, Wayne State University (hereafter MRB), reel 8.10; Edwin Nyden to David, Feb. 3, 1940, MRB reel 9.1; Dubofsky, *State and Labor,* 107–67; Bernstein, *Turbulent Years.*

2. Tom Beadling, Pat Cooper, Grace Palladino, and Peter Pieragostini, *A Need for Valor: The Roots of the Service Employees International Union, 1902–1992* (Washington, D.C.: SEIU, 1992), 6–12, 20–21, 27, 34, 88; John Jentz, "Citizenship, Self-Respect, and Political Power: Chicago's Flat Janitors Trailblaze the Service Employees International Union, 1912–21," *Labor's Heritage* 9 (1997): 4; David to Kenneth Hodges, Mar. 19, 1940, MRB reel 8.6; *Chicago Federation News,* Sept. 22, 1933, 6; May 11, 1935, 1; May 18, 1935, 2; June 29, 1935, 3; Sept. 3, 1938, 29; Sept. 2, 1939, 29; *Public Safety,* Jan. 1, 1930, 11.

3. Beadling et al., 9; *Proceedings of the Eighth General Convention of the Building Service Employees International Union* (Chicago: BSEIU, May 1940), 5; Jentz, "Citizenship, Self-Respect, and Political Power," 7, 14–19; *Public Safety,* Nov. 1, 1929, 17. See Local 84, "New Members List," Sept. 20, 1937 (heavily Hispanic), MRB reel 8.6; Local 3, member list (ca. late 1930s) (about one-third female), ibid.; Local 55, Charter Application, 1938 (Cedar Rapids, Iowa, local begins with women holding three of seven offices), ibid. Male and female members of Local 31 in Columbus, Ohio, earned the same pay in the mid-1930s. D. W. Donley to David, Jan. 21, 1934, MRB reel 8.3. More often, women were paid less and charged lower dues; e.g., Local 50 in Saint Louis in the early 1930s charged two dollars a month for men and one dollar for women, to adjust for pay differences; MRB reel 8.9.

4. Saint Louis leaflet, Feb. 20, 1925, MRB reel 8.1; David to Mollie Anderson, Nov. 17, 1936, MRB reel 8.3; David to E. C. Jasper, Dec. 8, 1937, MRB reel 8.6; Petition, [1936]; David to D. G. Bowles, Feb. 3, and David to John Pemberton, Feb. 25, 1937, ibid.

5. BSEIU, *Building Service Employee,* Mar.–Apr. 1942, 13, MRB reel 8.6; Owen Cunningham, "Report to the Policy Committee of the Minneapolis CLU," Sept. 1, 1938, ibid.; City of Chicago, *Chicago's Report to the People, 1933–46* (Chicago, 1947), 18. The numbers of locals are compiled from MRB reels 8.1–8.11 and 9.1–9.6.

6. *Chicago Federation News,* Sept. 28, 1929, 1, 3; Nov. 18, 1939, 6; Feb. 4, 1939, 2; Feb. 29, 1936, 8.

7. Beadling et al., 13, 22–24, 37; Jentz, "Citizenship, Self-Respect, and Political Power,"

4; idem, "Labor, the Law, and Economics: The Organization of the Chicago Flat Janitors' Union, 1902–1917," *Labor History* 38 (1998): 413–31.

8. NEA, "Research Bulletin," Mar. 1927, 75, 77, 79; NEA, "Research Bulletin," Mar. 1941, 70; Elmer Henry to David, Nov. 28, 1937, MRB reel 8.6; David to Elmer Henry, Nov. 29, 1937, ibid.; David to D. W. Donley, Oct. 10, 1933, MRB reel 8.3; David to Bertie, Sept. 8, 1936, ibid.

9. Murphy, 133–34; U.S. Bureau of the Census, *Historical Statistics,* 1126; Fabricant and Lipsey, 73, 78; NEA, "Research Bulletin," May 1941, 104.

10. Notice from Walfred Smedberg, [1938], MRB reel 8.7; Toledo newspaper article (ca. mid-1930s), MRB reel 8.3; L. W. Lynch to David, July 1, 1938, MRB reel 8.7; Toledo newspaper article (ca. 1940), MRB reel 8.11; David to Joseph Haberstock, Feb. 1, 1940, ibid.; D. G. Bowles to David, Jan. 31, 1940, MRB reel 9.1. For teachers, see Murphy, 133–34; Spero, 320, 445.

11. City of Chicago, *Report to the People,* 1, 147–48, 319–20; Roger Biles, *Big City Boss in Depression and War: Mayor Edward J. Kelly of Chicago* (De Kalb: Northern Illinois University Press, 1984), 22–27; *Chicago Federation News,* Dec. 16, 1933, 3; Sept. 3, 1934, 6, 7; Mar. 6, 1937, 6; Murphy, 133–34, 139–40; Spero, 323–24; Wrigley, 208–10.

12. *Chicago Federation News,* Oct. 20, 1934, 12; *Proceedings of the Seventh Convention of the Building Service Employees' International Union* (Chicago: BSEIU, May 6, 1935), 15, 21; Local 46, "The N.P.F.T. Plan of Chicago School Board a Hardship on School Employees," MRB reel 8.2; *Public Safety,* June 1935, 21; Mar. 1934, 3.

13. Mary Sudkamp to James McCahey, Dec. 17, 1934, MRB reel 8.3; Sudkamp, Margaret Swaim, and Frances Hildruth to McFetridge, Aug. 1, 1933, ibid.; Sudkamp to W. J. Bogan, [1933], ibid.; Swaim, Sudkamp, and Hildruth to Bogan, May 19, 1933, ibid.; Chicago Board of Education, Notice, Sept. 12, 1932, ibid.; Chicago Board of Education, Notice, Feb. 17, 1933, ibid.; Irene Bending to David, May 8, 1937, MRB reel 8.6; D. W. Donley, Questionnaire (ca. 1932–33), MRB reel 8.3; Kenneth Hodges to David, Nov. 19, 1940, MRB reel 9.1; John Arnett to McFetridge, June 27, 1940, ibid.

14. Chicago Board of Education, "Rules, Regulations and Salary Schedules of Firemen, Janitors, Etc." (June 20, 1928), MRB reel 8.3; *Chicago Federation News,* Sept. 2, 1933, 36, MRB reel 8.10; Frieda O'Neil to David (ca. 1939), ibid.; Saint Louis Leaflet, Feb. 20, 1925, MRB reel 8.1; F. C. Brown to George Womrath, May 13, 1936, MRB reel 8.6. Jones to David, Sept. 20, 1937, ibid.; Jones to *San Antonio Dispatch,* [1938], MRB reel 8.8; Jones to *San Antonio Dispatch,* [1940], MRB reel 9.1.

15. BSEIU, *Proceedings of Seventh Convention,* 15, 21; *Chicago Federation News,* Apr. 11, 1936, 13; Oct. 20, 1934, 12; Oct. 27, 1934, 1; Feb. 1930, 7; Sept. 22, 1934, 1; May 29, 1937, 11; June 26, 1937, 1; July 3, 1937, 3; Sept. 6, 1937, 20; Oct. 20, 1934, 12; Apr. 11, 1936, 13; *Public Safety,* Mar. 1935, 4; Aug. 1934, 4–5; Sept. 1931, 5–6; R. W. Clarke to Owen Cunningham (ca. 1937), MRB reel 8.6; David to W. K. Jones, Sept. 9, 1937, ibid.; David to Nygren, Nov. 10, 1939, MRB reel 8.10; Wrigley, 222, 304, n. 124; Jentz, "Citizenship, Self-Respect, and Political Power."

16. Roy Weir to David, Sept. 8, 1938, MRB reel 8.9; pamphlet quoting *Saint Louis Times,* Sept. 25, 1923, MRB reel 8.1; *Public Safety,* Nov. 1936, 6–8.

17. Sections 20–21 of the Illinois Civil Service Statute barred political contributions from civil service employees. San Antonio articles, [1939], MRB reel 8.10; *Chicago Federation News,* Oct. 25, 1930, 6; Oct. 31, 1936, 3, 5, 8; Sept. 2, 1939, 2; Nov. 19, 1938, 10; telegrams from Sam Paul, president, Local 11, Dec. 21, 1931, MRB reel 8.2.

18. E. P. Fitzgerald to David, Oct. 23, 1939, MRB reel 8.11; Saint Louis newspaper article, Dec. 21, 1938, MRB reel 8.9; David to B. J. Franklin and Alvin Green, May 5, 1939, ibid.; David to James Roberson, Apr. 25, 1925, MRB reel 8.3; *Chicago Federation News,* Feb. 11, 1933, 5; Apr. 30, 1938, 9; Aug. 5, 1939, 5; *CIO News,* July 29, 1939, 8; *Public Safety,* Mar. 1931, 20; Apr. 1, 1930, 5; Nov. 1, 1929, 7, 9; July 1936, 8; Indiana Federation

of Labor Biennial Legislative Conference (Dec. 14–15, 1940), MRB reel 9.3. Fry had a mixed record with labor issues; Wrigley, 239–40.

19. For example, a BSEIU member lost in a school board race in Cicero, Illinois, in 1933. *Chicago Federation News,* Apr. 8, 1933, 2.

20. David to John Robertson, July 18, 1929, MRB reel 8.1; Owen Cunningham, "Report to the Minneapolis CLU," Sept. 1, 1938, MRB reel 8.6; telegrams from McFetridge to state representatives, Feb. 15, 1937, supporting a tax levy for the Chicago schools, ibid.; David to Ernest Casner, Feb. 8, 1939, MRB reel 8.9; J. T. Latham to David, 1938, MRB reel 8.7; Local 3, "Analysis of the Toledo Public School System" (Mar. 24, 1933), MRB reel 8.3.

21. Wrigley, 201, 222–24, 235–36.

22. *Chicago Federation News,* Feb. 16, 1935, 8; Mar. 9, 1935, 12; Apr. 1, 1939, 2; Dec. 17, 1938, 7; June 25, 1931, 1, 3; Christopher Ansell and Arthur Burris, "Bosses of the City Unite! Labor Politics and Political Machine Consolidation, 1880–1910," *Studies in American Political Development* 11 (1997): 23; Biles, 63–64; Wrigley, 18, 23, 200, 216, 237–39.

23. David to Edward Kelly (ca. 1935), MRB reel 8.4; *Chicago Federation News,* Jan. 12, 1935, 1, 3; Nov. 2, 1935, 8; Nov. 16, 1935, 1–2.

24. BSEIU, "Facts Brought Out in the Hearing," [1932], MRB reel 8.3; Arbitration Award, June 9, 1932, ibid.; newspaper article (ca. 1932), ibid.; Frank Shaw to Glen Plumb, June 13, 1932, ibid.; Plumb to Shaw, June 15, 1932, ibid.; *Chicago Federation News,* Sept. 3, 1935, 1; *Public Safety,* Jan. 1936, 24; Nov. 1, 1929, 22; May 1932, 7.

25. Lee Pettys to David, Apr. 21, 1939, MRB reel 8.11; Pettys to C. S. Havens, Sept. 30, 1940, MRB reel 9.1; Pettys to McFetridge, Sept. 30, 1940, ibid.; David to Chicago Board of Education, July 15, 1933, MRB reel 8.3.

26. Jason Daugherty to David, [1936], MRB reel 8.3; David to George Peak, Aug. 4, 1936, ibid.; Peak to David, Aug. 6, 1936 ibid.; David to J. M. Studebaker, [1936], ibid.; Studebaker to David, Aug. 17, 1936, ibid.

27. David to E. W. Martin, May 3, 1933, MRB reel 8.3; Martin to Samuel Paul, Apr. 21, 1933, ibid.; *Chicago Federation News,* Apr. 18, 1936, 8; David to Nyden, Aug. 16, 1937, MRB reel 8.4; David to J. M. Gann, Mar. 30, 1936, MRB reel 8.3; David to L. W. Lynch, May 8, 1936, ibid.; R. S. McCann to David, May 22, 1936, ibid.; Gann to David, May 11, 1936, ibid.; *Memphis Commercial Appeal* articles, [1936], ibid.

28. Springfield Federation of Labor, Resolution, Aug. 23, 1933, MRB reel 8.3; Mollie Anderson to David, July 6, 1933, ibid.; BSEIU Local 74, *The Custodial,* Aug. 1937, MRB reel 9.5; BSEIU Resolution, May 14, 1935, MRB reel 8.5; Allen Forsberg, WPA, to David, Jan. 15, 1937, ibid.; David to Harry Hopkins, Dec. 14, 1936, ibid.; W. K. Jones to WPA, Oct. 15, 1938, MRB reel 8.8; Owen Cunningham, "A Wage Increment and Working Condition Request" (Oct. 29, 1937), MRB reel 8.6; Cunningham to Board of Regents, University of Minnesota, Oct. 29, 1937, ibid.; *Public Safety,* Oct. 1, 1929, 9.

29. David to F. O. Walls, Oct. 10, 1934, MRB reel 8.3; McFetridge to Pettys, Dec. 5, 1940, MRB reel 9.1; Minutes of Central Trades and Labor Union Council of Saint Louis, Feb. 25, 1940, ibid.; Fred Stapler to David, Jan. 26, 1937, MRB reel 8.6; newspaper article, [1938], MRB reel 8.8; A. C. Aageberg to representatives and senators, Mar. 19, 1940, MRB reel 9.1.

30. Nyden to David, Feb. 3, 1940, MRB reel 9.1; Local 173 to David, Dec. 27, 1938, MRB reel 8.9; E. W. Eubanks to David, Nov. 1, 1939, MRB reel 8.10; Jones to *San Antonio Dispatch,* [1938], MRB reel 8.8.

31. E. W. Eubanks to David, Feb. 23, 1940, MRB reel 9.1; Dwyer to David, Apr. 12, 1938, MRB reel 8.6; Otto Schneider to McFetridge, Nov. 13, 1940, MRB reel 8.1; Joe Lynch to David, May 4, 1937, MRB reel 8.3.

32. David to Joe Lynch, May 14, 1937, MRB reel 8.3.

33. David to Kenneth Hodges, July 5, 1939, MRB reel 8.10; David to Hodges, Mar. 19, 1940, ibid.; David to Hodges, Nov. 26, 1940, ibid.; David to E. W. Eubanks, Nov. 13, 1939,

ibid.; David to Lee Pettys, Nov. 3, 1939, ibid.; Joseph Benema to McFetridge, Apr. 28, 1939, MRB reel 9.1.

34. William Cooper to P. J. Cunningham, Apr. 12, 1938, MRB reel 9.1.

35. David to Ernest Casner, Feb. 8, 1939, MRB reel 8.9; David to Kenneth Hodges, Jan. 10, 1939, MRB reel 8.6; David to Donald Crater, Jan. 11, 1938, MRB reel 8.10; David to Walfred Smedberg, Mar. 16, 1939, ibid.

36. Local 55, "Working Agreement" (Oct. 1938), MRB reel 8.7; W. K. Jones to David, June 16, 1939, MRB reel 8.10; David to Kenneth Hodges, Jan. 10, 1939, MRB reel 8.6; BSEIU Local 63 *Bulletin,* [1938], MRB reel 8.7; BSEIU, *Building Service Employee,* Mar.–Apr. 1942, 13.

37. Chicago Board of Education, "Rules, Regulations and Salary Schedules of Firemen, Janitors, Etc.," MRB reel 9.9; David to Patrick Cunningham, Apr. 23, 1938, ibid.; Officers of Local 46 to David, Nov. 3, 1937, MRB reel 9.5; David to Patrick Cunningham, Apr. 23, 1938, MRB reel 8.9.

38. Local 51, draft contract, [1939], MRB reel 8.9; David to Jules Fluhrer, May 5, 1939, ibid.; E. P. Fitzgerald to David, Nov. 9, 1939, MRB reel 8.11; Fitzgerald to David, Oct. 23, 1939, ibid.

39. Local 15, draft contract, [1935], MRB reel 8.3; David to Ida Davis, Apr. 22, 1935, ibid.; J. E. Flannery to David, June 28, 1939, MRB reel 8.8; David to Flannery, Oct. 4, 1939, MRB reel 8.10; article, [1939], MRB reel 9.6; *Public Safety,* Jan. 1937, 29–30.

40. David to Frank Schlosser, May 19, 1937, MRB reel 8.6.

41. Ibid.; Irene Bending to David, May 8, 1937, ibid.; David to George Peak, Aug. 4, 1936, MRB reel 8.3; *Chicago Herald,* Oct. 20, 1936, ibid.; Local 123 statement, [1936], ibid.; *Chicago Federation News,* Sept. 24, 1932, 1, 3; Apr. 27, 1935, 1, 6; Local 74, constitution and bylaws (1938), MRB reel 9.5.

42. Jones to David, Apr. 25, 1940, attaching articles, MRB reel 9.1; Jones to *San Antonio Dispatch,* [1938], MRB reel 8.8; Jones to Leo Brewer, Aug. 23, 1938, ibid.; David to Jones, Aug. 26, 1938, ibid.; Jones to James Hollers, Oct. 30, 1939, MRB reel 8.10; David to Hollers, Aug. 31, 1939, ibid.

43. Grady to Scalise, Mar. 4, 1938, MRB reel 9.4; T. J. Dwyer to David, May 18, 1938, MRB reel 8.6; David to Dwyer, May 19, 1938, ibid.

44. Jones to David, Apr. 25, 1940, attaching articles, [1940], MRB reel 9.1; Jones to David, Sept. 28, 1939, MRB reel 8.10; David to Jones, Nov. 28, 1938, MRB reel 8.8; Jones to David, Oct. 25, 1940, MRB reel 9.1.

45. David to Jones, Oct. 30, 1940, MRB reel 9.1; David to Jones, Aug. 3, 1938, MRB reel 8.8.

46. *Chicago Federation News,* Feb. 1, 1930, 7; Jan. 24, 1931, 6; *Public Safety,* Mar. 1931, 14; H. J. Rigby to Scalise, May 15, 1939, MRB reel 9.5; Local 74, flyer (civil service without examination), Dec. 4, 1937, ibid.; Materials re Field-Crews Bill to expand New York Civil Service laws, [1938], ibid.; Local 74, flyer (Local 74 wins civil service bill), [1939], ibid.; Local 66, *Union News,* Oct. 7, 1936, MRB reel 8.6; San Francisco civil service scale (ca. mid-1930s), ibid.; Nyden to David, Feb. 3, 1940, MRB reel 9.1; Local 46, "Civil Service and Pension Information" (1938) MRB reel 8.7.

47. Proposed Bill 79-S, Wisconsin State Senate, Mar. 1937, MRB reel 8.1; Mollie Anderson to David, May 9, 1939, MRB reel 8.9; David to Horace Luce, May 22, 1939, ibid.; Crouch, 131; Joseph Pois, Edward Martin, and Lyman Moore, *The Merit System in Illinois* (Chicago: Joint Committee on the Merit System, 1935), 5, 9, 11, 15, 28–29, 31, 45, 48.

48. *In re New York State Labor Relations Board,* 37 N.Y.S.2d 304 (1942), aff'd, 267 App. Div. 763, 45 N.Y.S.2d 942 (1943), aff'd, 293 N.Y. 671, 56 N.E.2d 263 (1944); *Local 891, Operating Engineers, and Local 74, BSEIU,* New York State Labor Relations Board, case SU-4254 (Nov. 1940), MRB reel 9.1; H. J. Rigby to Scalise, May 15, 1939, MRB reel 9.5.; Alexander Schwartz to Scalise, Feb. 1940, ibid.; Local 74, "School Custodial Employ-

ees Uniform Agreement," MRB reel 9.1; BSEIU, *Building Service Employee,* Apr. 1944, 8; Winfield Schad to David, Dec. 19, 1938; David to Schad, Dec. 21, 1938, MRB reel 8.7; *State ex rel. Cooper v. Baumann,* 286 N.W. 76 (Wis., 1939), MRB reel 8.9.

49. School Board, North Berwyn, Illinois, transcript of hearings (1934), MRB reel 8.3.

50. J. E. Flannery to David, Feb. 23, 1938, MRB reel 9.6; David Planer to David, Dec. 8, 1938, ibid.; David to Bradtke, Aug. 30, 1937, MRB reel 8.6; article, [1937], ibid.; Cunningham, "Report to the Minneapolis CLU," Sept. 1, 1938, ibid.; Cunningham, "Report," Aug. 26, 1937, ibid.

51. Jones to David, Oct. 25, 1940, MRB reel 9.1; James Hollers to Jones, Sept. 5, 1939, MRB reel 8.10; David to San Antonio School Board, Aug. 3, 1938, MRB reel 8.8; Leo Brewer to David, Aug. 10, 1938, ibid.

52. L. W. Lynch to David, July 22, 1936, MRB reel 8.3; Lynch to Jerry Horan, Oct. 23, 1936, ibid.; David to Lynch, Aug. 24, 1936, MRB reel 8.6; David to Charles Ambler and Floyd Cox, Aug. 3, 1936, ibid.; Cox to David, Aug. 20, 1936, ibid.

53. Local 74, constitution (1938), MRB reel 9.5; for the BSEIU in the private sector, see Jentz, "Labor, the Law, and Economics"; Beadling et al. The 1930s did see public sector strikes, but these were mostly short stoppages in public works projects. Indeed, of Ziskind's "thousand strikes," 664 were by WPA workers. Spero, 14; Ziskind, 187. The AFL criticized the WPA strikes, suggesting that "the remedy lies with Congress" instead; AFL Press Release (ca. early 1930s), MRB reel 9.6.

54. Centralia, Illinois, School Board to William Green, Aug. 14, 1934, MRB reel 8.3; Green to Centralia School Board, Aug. 23, 1934, ibid.

55. L. W. Lynch to Horan, Oct. 23, 1936, MRB reel 8.3; David to T. J. Dwyer, May 19, 1938, MRB reel 8.6; Carl Beckner to David, [1940], MRB reel 9.2; David to Beckner, Oct. 9, 1940, ibid.

56. Local 113 Strike Resolution, Oct. 1937, MRB reel 8.6; John Herman to David, Oct. 25, 1937, ibid.; Cunningham to David, Oct. 25, 1937, ibid.; David to Cunningham, Oct. 28, 1937, ibid.; David to Cunningham, Nov. 5, 1937, ibid.

57. David to Herman, Nov. 3, 1937, MRB reel 8.6; David to Herman, [1937], ibid.; Scalise to Cunningham, Feb. 15, 1938, MRB reel 9.5.

58. Local 63, Press Release, Mar. 18, 1939, MRB reel 8.9; I. A. Bremnes to David, Mar. 18, 1939, ibid.; David to Bremnes, [1939], ibid.; Bremnes to David, May 1, 1939, ibid.

59. BSEIU, summary of the case, MRB reel 8.3; Peter Angsten to David, Jan. 19, 1937, MRB reel 8.6; David to Angsten, Jan. 22, 1937, ibid.; David to Sidney Johnson, Jan. 28, 1937, ibid.; *Chicago Federation News,* Apr. 22, 1939, 1, 3; *Public Safety,* Jan. 1937, 6–10.

60. Michael Kelly Jr. to David, June 30, 1937, MRB reel 8.6; David to Kelly, July 1, 1937, ibid.; David to Kelly, July 20, 1937, ibid.; newspaper editorial, [1937], ibid.; David to Flannery, Dec. 23, 1937, ibid.; Flannery to David, Sept. 6, 1938, MRB reel 9.6; David to Flannery, Aug. 31, 1938, ibid.; David to Flannery Aug. 18, 1938, ibid.; newspaper articles, [1937–38], MRB reel 8.8; David to Flannery, Apr. 7, 1939, MRB reel 8.10.

61. Kramer, 10, 33–34, 43–44; *Chicago Federation News,* Sept. 2, 1939, 16.

62. *Chicago Federation News,* Sept. 3, 1934, 7; Spero, 362–63, 368, 416–17; Kramer, 37.

63. *Chicago Federation News,* Oct. 20, 1934, 12.

Chapter 5. The New York City TWU in the Early 1940s

1. Brief of the TWU before the National War Labor Board, Transport Workers Union Collection, Tamiment Library, New York University, box 44, Executive Board, Local 100, Unification (hereafter TWU Collection), Petition before War Labor Board folder (hereafter Brief of TWU), 2, 29.

2. A dispute over a pay classification bill caused NFFE to disaffiliate from the AFL; the AFL then chartered AFGE. In 1936 AFGE surrendered jurisdiction over state, county, and municipal employees to the newly formed AFSCME. Spero, 187–89, 191, 212.

3. Zieger argues that CIO president John L. Lewis actually devoted too much money to the SCMWA and the UFW; Zieger, 95–96, 256, 290; Spero, 198, 201, 329; Kramer, 26; O'Neil, 7–9; *CIO News*, Oct. 19, 1942, 7.

4. Zieger, 80, 82; Nesbitt, 69; Spero, 198, 216–17, 476; Joshua Freeman, *In Transit: The Transport Workers Union in New York City, 1933–1966* (New York: Oxford University Press, 1989), 183.

5. CIO, *Daily Proceedings of the First Constitutional Convention of the Congress of Industrial Organizations* (Pittsburgh, 1938), 231–32, 250–52; CIO, *Daily Proceedings of the Second Constitutional Convention of the Congress of Industrial Organizations* (San Francisco, 1939), 141–42; CIO, *Daily Proceedings of the Third Constitutional Convention of the Congress of Industrial Organizations* (Atlantic City, N.J., 1940), 214, 259; Cling, 24–25.

6. *CIO News*, Sept. 25, 1939, 5; Feb. 10, 1941, 2; Mar. 22, 1943, 3.

7. Maier, 18; Spero, 397; Freeman, 40–51, 55–57, 75. In 1948 Quill helped expel the Communists from the TWU; Freeman, 286.

8. Freeman, 58–109, 113–22, 165.

9. *Transport Bulletin*, Nov. 1, 1935, 1–2; Mar. 1935, 1, 2, 3.

10. Freeman, 166–75.

11. Brief of TWU, 4–6; Wilkinson Committee, "Report of the Mayor's Committee Appointed to Study Labor Relations on the City's Transit System," Apr. 28, 1943, TWU Collection, Wilkinson Committee Report folder (hereafter Wilkinson report), 10.

12. Chap. 443, sec. 715, of the New York State Labor Relations Act provided that the act did not apply to employees "of the State or of any political or civil subdivision or other agency thereof"; *In the Matter of the City of New York, acting by the Board of Transportation of the City of New York and Transport Workers Union of America*, New York State Labor Relations Board Dec. No. 56 (Jan. 22, 1938), reprinted in *Decisions and Orders of the N.Y. State Labor Relations Board* (Albany, 1938), 219–21; Freeman, 179–80.

13. Freeman, 181–82; Notes, [1938], TWU Collection, Transit Bills Introduced folder (1938); *Transport Bulletin*, Apr., 1938, 1.

14. New York State Constitution, art. 5, sec. 9 (this later became art. 5, sec. 6); *Barhelmess v. Cuckor*, 231 N.Y. 435 (1921); *Andresen v. Rice*, 277 N.Y. 271 (1938); cases and notes, TWU Collection, Transit Bills Introduced folder; notes, [1939], TWU Collection, 1939 folder.

15. Freeman, 180–83.

16. Ibid., 185–86, 192–93; text of bills, TWU Collection, 1937 folder and Transit Bills Introduced folder; *Transport Bulletin*, Jan. 1936, 7; ibid., Oct. 15, 1935, 2.

17. *Transport Bulletin*, Oct. 15, 1935, 4; Oct. 1937, 5; J. B. English, "The Transit Worker Getting and Holding a Job in Civil Service," TWU Collection, 1939 folder.

18. Freeman, 186–88; Arthur Wicks to LaGuardia, Apr. 13, 1939, TWU Collection, 1939 folder; CSF leaflet on Wicks Bill, [1939], ibid.; George Harvey to Herbert Lehman, May 19, 1939, ibid.; *Transport Bulletin*, June 1939, 1–2.

19. Freeman, 188–89; TWU leaflet on Wicks Bill, [1939], TWU Collection, 1939 folder; *Kingston Daily Leader*, Apr. 3, 1939, ibid.; John L. Lewis letter, [1939], ibid.; TWU, "Why the Wicks Bill Should Be Vetoed," [1939], ibid.; *Transport Bulletin*, June 1939, 1–2; *CIO News*, Jan. 6, 1939, 1; Feb. 27, 1939, 2; Mar. 13, 1939, 7; May 15, 1939, 7.

20. Wicks Act, New York Laws of 1939, chap. 927; Freeman, 190–91; *Transport Bulletin*, June 1939, 1–2; TWU, "Why the Wicks Bill Should Be Vetoed"; *CIO News*, May 22, 1939, 2.

21. *Transport Bulletin,* July 1939, 3, 11; Freeman, 191–92; Maier, 18.

22. *Transport Bulletin,* Mar. 1940, 1; LaGuardia to Quill, Mar. 2, 1940, TWU Collection, 1940 folder; Freeman, 197–98; Spero, 387.

23. Quill to LaGuardia, Mar. 4, 1940, TWU Collection, 1940 folder; Hogan to TWU members, Mar. 12, 1940, ibid.; TWU, "Open Letter to Mayor Fiorello H. LaGuardia," [1940], ibid.; Freeman, 198; Spero, 387.

24. Thomas Kessner, *Fiorello H. LaGuardia and the Making of Modern New York* (New York: McGraw-Hill, 1989), 237–53; Freeman, 216–18; Kheel, 7; Maier, 23–25; *CIO News,* Mar. 3, 1941, 7; May 19, 1941, 2.

25. TWU Local 100, letter to editor, *New York Times,* Nov. 20, 1942, TWU Collection, Citizens Transit Committee folder; CIO, *Daily Proceedings of the Fifth Constitutional Convention of the Congress of Industrial Organizations* (Boston, 1942), 219. New York City in early 1940 had 107,063 public workers, and this figure excluded those in schools, on work relief, and contractors; U.S. Bureau of the Census, "State and Local Government Quarterly Employment Survey" (Mar. 29, 1940), 3.

26. *CIO News,* July 29, 1940, 2; Martin Shefter, *Political Parties and the State: The American Historical Experience* (Princeton: Princeton University Press, 1994), 201–4; Elliot Lawrence, *Little Flower: The Life and Times of Fiorello LaGuardia* (New York: Morrow, 1983), 238; Freeman, 179; Kessner, 459–61.

27. Freeman, 198–200; Spero, 387–88; *CIO News,* Mar. 18, 1940, 3, 6; *Transport Bulletin,* Apr., 1940, 1, 2; June 1940, 1; Apr. 1940, 1, 3; TWU leaflet, [1940], TWU Collection, 1940 folder; *New York Times,* Apr. 3, 1940, ibid.; Quill statements, Mar. 29 and 31, 1940, ibid.; LaGuardia to Lee Pressman, Apr. 2, 1940, ibid.; Lewis statement, Apr. 2, 1940, ibid.; Brief of TWU, 8–9.

28. *Transport Bulletin,* Apr., 1940, 9; Murray to LaGuardia, Apr. 21, 1941, TWU Collection, 1941 folder; Dubofsky, *State and Labor,* 172.

29. Wilkinson report, 3, 10.

30. *Transport Bulletin,* June 1940, 4; Dec. 1943, 14; Oct. 1941, suppl., 1, 3; Feb. 1942, 1; July 1943, 1; Apr. 1943, 5; Jan. 1941, 12; Local 100, "Inter-Office Communication to All IRT and BMT Organizers," Jan. 3, 1941, TWU Collection, 1940 folder; Brief of TWU, 22; Freeman, 201–3.

31. Freeman, 204–6; *Transport Bulletin,* Jan. 1941, 12.

32. *Transport Bulletin,* Oct. 1941, 7; TWU, "Memorandum on Grievances of the Transport Workers Union of Greater New York against the Board of Transportation of the City of New York," [1940], TWU Collection, 1940 folder; Freeman, 206.

33. 27 N.Y.S.2d 718, 720–23, 725–26, 728 (1941); Freeman, 207.

34. Freeman, 203, 214; *CIO News,* Apr. 14, 1941, 8; Apr. 21, 1941, 2; Maier, 19.

35. Freeman, 214; LaGuardia to Delaney, Apr. 7, TWU Collection, 1941 folder.

36. *Transport Bulletin,* June 1941, 3; Delaney, Frank Sullivan, and George Keegan to All Employees of the New York City Transit System, Apr. 9, 1941, TWU Collection, 1941 folder; Board of Transportation Resolution, Apr. 9, 1941, ibid.; McGinley, 348; *CIO News,* Apr. 14, 1941, 8; Freeman, 214–15.

37. *Transport Bulletin,* June 1941, 8; TWU, "Transit Truths," [1941], TWU Collection, 1941 folder; Spero, 397.

38. Freeman, 216, 218; Hogan to Frances Perkins, Apr. 23, 1941, TWU Collection, 1941 folder; *Transport Bulletin,* May 1941, 8.

39. Freeman, 215; *CIO News,* Apr. 28, 1941, 7; *Transport Bulletin,* June 1941, 3; May 1941, 3; Quill letter, May 14, 1941, TWU Collection, 1941 folder.

40. Freeman, 215; *Transport Bulletin,* June 1941, 3, 4; Murray speech, TWU Collection, Philip Murray Speech folder; *CIO News,* May 26, 1941, 6.

41. "Notes for Speakers, the Transit Situation," [May 1941], TWU Collection, Philip Murray Speech folder.

42. *Transport Bulletin,* June 1941, 8; Murray speech; notes from speeches, [1941], Philip Murray Speech folder.

43. CIO, *Proceedings of First Convention,* 234–35; *CIO News,* Sept. 23, 1940, 6; CIO, *Proceedings of Third Convention,* 290–91.

44. CIO, *Proceedings of Third Convention,* 290–91; Freeman, 216; text of speeches [May 1941], TWU Collection, Philip Murray Speech folder; U.S. Bureau of the Census, *Historical Statistics,* 137.

45. *CIO News,* Sept. 8, 1941, 8; Oct. 6, 1941, 2; Dec. 1, 1941, 2; Feb. 15, 1943, 6; Jan. 18, 1943, 5; CIO, *Daily Proceedings of the Fourth Constitutional Convention of the Congress of Industrial Organizations* (Detroit, 1941), 233–35; CIO, *Report of Philip Murray to the Fourth Constitutional Convention of the Congress of Industrial Organizations* (Detroit, Nov. 17, 1941), 61–62; *Transport Bulletin,* Dec. 1941, 16; CIO, *Proceedings of Fifth Convention,* 93.

46. *Transport Bulletin,* June 1941, 9; July 1941, 3; Aug. 1942, 10; Oct. 1943, 13.

47. ACLU, "Report on the Rights of Workers in Public Agencies," May 23, 1941, TWU Collection, 1941 folder; *CIO News,* Apr. 14, 1941, 8; June 2, 1941, 2; Nov. 30, 1941, 2; CIO, *Report of Philip Murray,* 62–63.

48. Memorandum Submitted by the TWU, *City of New York v. Transport Workers Union of America,* [1941], citing, e.g., *Matter of Railway Commissioners,* 197 N.Y. 81 (Ct. App. 1909), TWU Collection, 1941 folder; Memorandum Submitted by the Corporation Counsel of New York City, [1941], ibid.; TWU Brief in Answer, June 17, 1941, ibid.

49. Brief of TWU, 46, 48; *Transport Bulletin,* June 1941, 3, 4; July 1941, 3; *CIO News,* June 16, 1941, 5; Wilkinson report, 5; Freeman, 242.

50. Freeman, 216–20.

51. Telegram from E. R. Alexander et al. to Delaney, June 27, 1941, TWU Collection, 1941 folder; Freeman, 220–21.

52. Brief of TWU, 10–14; Freeman, 221–22; Spero, 389–91.

53. Brief of TWU, 15; Wilkinson report, 5; *Transport Bulletin,* July 1941, 1, 2–3.

54. Dubofsky, *State and Labor,* 169–95; Zieger, 144–88; *Transport Bulletin,* July 1941, 3. See, e.g., *CIO News,* Nov. 9, 1942, 1 ("'Win the War' Keynote of 5th CIO Convention").

55. Zieger, 150–52, 169–79; *Transport Bulletin,* June 1941, 3; Apr. 1943, 2; Local 100, letter to editor, *New York Times,* Nov. 20, 1942; *CIO News,* Apr. 27, 1942, 3; May 10, 1943, 6.

56. Freeman, 242; *Transport Bulletin,* Oct. 1941, 7.

57. *Transport Bulletin,* Dec. 1941, 16; Feb. 1942, 1; Dec. 1942, 5; Wilkinson report, 5, 7–9; Brief of TWU, 17–21; Spero, 418.

58. Freeman, 242–43; Wilkinson report, 13; Committee of Citizens, "Labor Relations in the New York City Transit System" (Jan. 1943), 7–8, TWU Collection, Citizens Transit Committee folder; Brief of TWU, 26–27; *CIO News,* July 6, 1942, 2.

59. TWU Petition to the NWLB, Nov. 9, 1942, TWU Collection, Petition before War Labor Board folder; Dubofsky, *State and Labor,* 184–86; Brief of TWU, 27.

60. Quill and Douglas MacMahon to LaGuardia, [1942], TWU Collection, 1942 folder; *Transport Bulletin,* Nov. 1942, 5; Dec. 1942, 1, 2, 5.

61. *CIO News,* Dec. 14, 1942, 3; CIO, *Proceedings of Fifth Convention,* 214–17.

62. Brief of TWU, 27, 30–32, 39, 40, 50.

63. Ibid., 33, 34, 39, 41, 42–43.

64. Kessner, 545; Freeman, 243; Wilkinson report, 8.

65. *In re Municipal Government, City of Newark, N.J., and SCMWA Local 277 (CIO); Board of Transportation of the City of New York and TWU (CIO) and TWU Local 100 (CIO); Metropolitan Utilities District, Omaha, Neb., and AFSCME Local 431 (AFL),* Case Nos. 47 and 726, 5 *War Labor Reports* 286 (Dec. 24, 1942). The members of the NWLB were William Davis (chairman), George Taylor, Frank Graham, Wayne Morse, Matthew

Woll, George Meany, Van Bittner, Delmond Garst, Roger Lapham, Cyrus Ching, Harry Derby and Reuben Robertson; ibid.

66. *5 War Labor Reports* (Dec. 24, 1942), 286, 288, 299. Labor's representatives on the NWLB, including old TWU nemesis Meany, concurred. Their only quibble regarded the relevance of a statement in the decision that public workers could not legally strike. Ibid., 299. The employer representatives wrote a concurring opinion adding that if "public authority were to be centralized in the hands of Federal officials, it would be inevitable that the American system of government would be destroyed"; ibid., 299–300.

67. Ibid., 289, 298, 292, 304, 299.

68. Again revealing the importance of the many layers of the American state, in the Newark case the director of the relevant city department had denied that the NWLB had jurisdiction. But Newark's mayor and city commissioners overruled the director, stating that they wanted the NWLB to resolve the matter. Ibid., 304–5. An employer representative dissented from the holding in the Newark case; ibid., 305–10.

69. Ibid., 294–96, 298.

70. Ibid., 296–98.

71. *Transport Bulletin,* Dec. 1942, 1; Douglas MacMahon to members, Jan. 5, 1942, TWU Collection, 1942 folder; *CIO News,* Dec. 21, 1942, 1; Jan. 4, 1943, 5.

72. Freeman, 244.

73. Arthur MacMahon to Delaney, Nov. 20, 1942, TWU Collection, Citizens Transit Committee folder; untitled documents, [1942], ibid.

74. Committee of Citizens, "Labor Relations in the New York City Transit System" (Jan. 1943), 4, 13–25.

75. "Proceedings of Public Hearing," Nov. 28, 1942, TWU Collection, Proceedings of Public Hearings folder.

76. *Transport Bulletin,* Jan.–Feb. 1943, 4; *CIO News,* Feb. 1, 1943, 2; *PM,* editorial, Dec. 17, 1942, TWU Collection, Labor's Transit Committee to Support TWU folder; untitled documents, [1943], ibid.; untitled documents, [1943], TWU Collection, Madison Square Garden Rally folder; Freeman, 244–45. The members of the Wilkinson Committee were Ignatius Wilkinson, George Agger, Joseph Chamberlain, and Howard Colman; Wilkinson report.

77. *New York Times,* editorial, Mar. 2, 1943, TWU Collection, Transit Labor Convention folder; *CIO News,* Feb. 15, 1943, 3; Feb. 22, 1943, 2.

78. Freeman, 245; Wilkinson report, 11–12.

79. Wilkinson report, 14, 11, 19.

80. Ibid., 7–9, 14, 15, 17, 18.

81. Ibid., 12, 14–16; *Transport Bulletin,* May 1943, 4, 5.

82. *Transport Bulletin,* May 1943, 2, 5; Apr. 1943, 2; *CIO News,* May 10, 1943, 8.

83. Freeman, 246, 247, 263; *Transport Bulletin,* Aug. 1943, 3.

84. Maier, 19; *Transport Bulletin,* July 1943, 1, 3, 11; Aug. 1943, 4.

85. Nesbitt, 13–16; Spero, 12.

86. Morton Godine, *The Labor Problem in the Public Service* (Cambridge: Harvard University Press, 1951), 95; Spero, 5, 71, 76, 217–19, 242; Kramer, 45; Spero and Capozzola, 68; Troy, 4, 223.

87. Spero, 219, 289–92, 401, 441; Kramer, 41.

Chapter 6. Wisconsin's Public Sector Labor Laws of 1959 and 1962

1. Dubofksy, *State and Labor,* 208–13; Zieger, 294–371; Lichtenstein, 142–71; Kearney, 60; William Houlihan, "Interest Arbitration and Municipal Employee Bargaining: The Wisconsin Experience," in Najita and Stern, 70.

2. See, e.g., Rollin Posey, "Employee Organizations in the United States Public Service," *Public Personnel Review,* Oct. 1956, 238–45; W. G. Torpey, *Public Personnel Management* (New York: Van Nostrand, 1953); W. E. Mosher, J. D. Kingsley, and O. G. Stahl, *Public Personnel Administration* (New York: Harper, 1950); Fritz Marx, ed., *Elements of Public Administration* (New York: Prentice-Hall, 1946).

3. Harvey Mansfield and Fritz Marx, "Informal Organization," in Marx, 313; Henry Reining Jr., "The Art of Supervision," ibid., 487–88; Milton Mandell, "Personnel Standards," ibid., 574–75.

4. Godine, 14, 11, 25, 36–40, 133; Cling, 738; Posey, 241; Harry Rains, "Collective Bargaining in Public Employment," *Labor Law Journal* 8 (Aug. 1957): 548–50; *Public Employee,* July 1959, 3.

5. *Public Employee,* June 1957, 14; Ziskind, 195; Cling, 161.

6. The number of major work stoppages per million private nonfarm employees dropped throughout the decade, from 115 in 1951 to fewer than 70 in 1959. The percentage of union members involved in strikes dropped from around 17 percent in 1951 to around 8 percent in 1959. J. Bartlett Lambert, "The Right to Strike in American Political Development: Labor, The State, and Social Policy" (Ph.D. diss., University of Wisconsin, 1998), 6, 7, 11. See also Dubofsky, *State and Labor,* 213–14; David Brody, *Workers in Industrial America* (New York: Oxford University Press, 1980), 198–210.

7. Godine, 28, 84 (quoting Roosevelt and adding emphasis), 87–89, 173, 2–3, 29, 9, 42; Cling, 152; *Public Employee,* Sept. 7, 1962, 5, 7.

8. Cling, 87, 283, 743; *Wisconsin City and County Employee Union News* (hereafter *Union News*), Apr., 1959, 2; *Public Employee,* May 1959, 3; American Bar Association Section of Labor Relations Law, "Summary of the Committee on Labor Relations of the Governmental Employees," in *1955 Proceedings* (Chicago: American Bar Center, 1956), 90–91, 89.

9. Mosher, Kingsley, and Stahl, 355; Cling, 195,174; *Public Employee,* Jan. 1961, 4–5; ICMA, "Negotiations with Municipal Employee Organizations," quoted in ibid., Dec. 1958, 18, 19.

10. Reuel Schiller, "From Group Rights to Individual Liberties: Post-War Labor Law, Liberalism, and the Waning of Union Strength," *Berkeley Journal of Employment and Labor Law* 20 (1999): 1–73.

11. U.S. Bureau of the Census, *Historical Statistics,* 176–77. Figures for 1929 are from the Bureau of Labor Statistics. Everett Kasalow, "Recent Developments in Collective Bargaining for Public Employees," in *Collective Bargaining for Public Employees,* ed. Jack Triplett (Eugene: University of Oregon, 1966), 10.

12. *Union News,* Nov.–Dec. 1948, 1, 4–5; *Public Employee,* Feb. 1957, 20; July 1959, 4; Nov. 1959, 4.

13. Kasalow, 10; *Public Employee,* Sept. 7, 1962, 5.

14. *Business Week,* Mar. 21, 1959, quoted in *Public Employee,* May 1959, 8; *Christian Science Monitor,* Dec. 16, 1961, quoted in ibid., Feb. 5, 1962, 5.

15. 138 Conn. 269; 104 Ark. 438.

16. Cling, 130, 123–24, 126, 292; Godine, 244; *Public Employee,* Oct. 1957, 3; Feb. 1957, 13.

17. *Public Employee,* July 1959, 5, 19.

18. Cling, 1–80, 85–86, 90–93, 134, 136, 741, 750.

19. Goulden, 27–31.

20. Godine, 128; Kramer, 1–23.

21. *Public Employee,* Mar. 1958, 12; *Union News,* June 1958, 1; Apr. 1959, 4; *Public Employee,* Nov. 1959, 5; May–June 1961, 3.

22. Compare Kramer (supporting Zander) with Goulden (supporting Wurf).

23. Kramer, 32, 33; *Union News,* Nov.–Dec. 1948, 1, 4–5; Sept.–Oct. 1955, 1; *Public Employee,* Jan. 1957, 3; July 1959, 3; Mar. 1959, 3.

24. Cling, 460, 285–86; *Union News,* June 1958, 1; Goulden, 54.

25. *Public Employee,* Jan. 1957, 11, 17; Apr. 1957, 5.

26. Cling, 350–51; John Lawton to Walter Kohler, [1951], Walter Kohler Archives, State Historical Society of Wisconsin, Madison (hereafter Kohler Archives), box 77, folder 6; Industrial Commission of Wisconsin, "Wisconsin Employment Trends," Feb. 28, 1955, ibid., box 68, folder 3; *Union News,* Apr. 1958, 1; Mar.–Apr. 1956, 2; May 1956, 1; *Madison Union Labor News,* Sept. 1960, 2; Gordon Haferbecker, *Wisconsin Labor Laws* (Madison: University of Wisconsin Press, 1958), 4; William Thompson, *The History of Wisconsin: Continuity and Change, 1940–65,* vol. 6 (Madison: State Historical Society of Wisconsin, 1988), 107, 467–73, 616.

27. *Union News,* Sept.–Oct. 1952, 2; Nov.–Dec. 1948, 4; July–Aug. 1949, 1; Jan.–Feb. 1950, 4; June 1956, 4; Nov.–Dec. 1949, 4; May–June 1950, 4.

28. Cling, 352–55.

29. *Union News,* Aug. 1956, 1; *Public Employee,* Jan. 1957, 16 (wage gaps in other states); Dec. 1957, 16–17 (public sector wages in various states typically 70 to 80 percent that of private sector production workers).

30. Cling, 363–64, 573–75.

31. Haferbecker, vi, 5–6, 9–11, 13, 183; Arvid Anderson, "Wisconsin: A Pioneer in Labor Relations Law," in *State and Social Legislation: A Symposium in Honor of Elizabeth Brandeis Raushenbush* (Madison: Industrial Relations Research Institute, 1966), 60; Cling, 378.

32. Haferbecker, 15, 162–67, 170; Cling, 320–21; Bill 565-A, Wisconsin Assembly Bills, 1923, Wisconsin Legislative Reference Bureau, Madison (hereafter WLRB).

33. Cling, 317, 323; W. Thompson, 401–2, 408–9.

34. W. Thompson, 407, 413–15, 434–39, 456–59, 482, 614.

35. Cling, 326–28, 334–35, 344, citing 27 *Opinions of the Wisconsin Attorney General* (hereafter *OAG*) 245 (Apr. 29, 1938) and 29 *OAG* 82 (Feb. 28, 1940); *Union News,* May–June 1950, 1; Mar.–Apr. 1949, 2; *Amalgamated Ass'n of Street, Electric Railway & Motor Coach Employees v. WERB,* 340 U.S. 383 (1951); Haferbecker, 174–75.

36. Cling, 330–32, 570–76; *Union News,* July–Aug. 1950, 4; June–July, 1949, 4.

37. *Union News,* Nov.–Dec. 1965, 1–2 (listing legislative actions since 1943, on topics including pensions, health insurance, pay, and budgets).

38. Ibid., July 1956, 1, 4; Mar.–Apr. 1950, 1, 4.

39. Ibid., May–June 1951, 1.

40. Bill 462-S, Wisconsin Senate Bills, 1951, WLRB; Memo from B. Lampert to [Vernon] Thomson, June 27, 1951, Kohler Archives, box 77, folder 6; 42 *OAG* 97 (1953); *Union News,* Mar.–Apr. 1951, 3; Cling, 336–37.

41. *Union News,* Mar.–Apr. 1951, 2; Substitute Amendment to No. 1-S. to Bill 462-S, Wisconsin Senate Bills, 1951; Lawton to Kohler, [1951]; *Journal of the Senate Proceedings of the 70th Session of the Wisconsin Legislature* (Madison: Democrat Printing, 1951), 1183. This version of the bill was the only proposed law for over a decade that would have covered state workers. Apparently state employees felt that AFSCME lobbyist Roy Kubista adequately represented them. See A. J. Thelen, "Items Presented to the Hearing," [1951], Kohler Archives, box 77, folder 6; *Public Employee,* Nov. 1957, 12. Lawton once demurred that the WCCME bills did not cover state workers because labor relations in state governments were "entirely different"; e.g., discharge for union activities was not a problem for state employees. Lawton to Committee on Labor and Management Relations, [1951], WLRB, Legislative Drafting Records, 1951 Senate Bills 451–513.

42. *Union News,* Mar.–Apr. 1951, 3; "Arguments on 462-S," [1951], Kohler Archives, box 77, folder 6.

43. *Union News,* Mar.–Apr. 1951, 2, 3; Lawton to Committee on Labor and Management, [1951]; Lawton, "Memorandum re Bill No. 46-S" to Sen. Gordon Bubolz, May 4, 1951, Kohler Archives, box 77, folder 6.

44. Bill 462-S as amended, Kohler Archives, box 77, folder 5; Lawton to Kohler, [1951]; Memo from Lampert to Thomson, June 27, 1951; Amendment 1-S to Substitute Amendment 1-S to Bill 462-S, Wisconsin Senate Bills, 1951; *Senate Proceedings of 70th Session,* 1365, 1399; Cling, 337.

45. W. Thompson, 594, 620; Michael Essin, "Open Letter to Gov. Kohler," Nov. 22, 1952, Kohler Archives, box 68, folder 2; "History of Appointments to Labor Relations Boards in Wisconsin," Gaylord Nelson Archives, State Historical Society of Wisconsin (hereafter Nelson Archives), box 107, folder 2.

46. AFSCME Local 407 to Kohler, July 2, 1951, Kohler Archives, box 77, folder 5; Leo Flaherty (Wisconsin County Police) to Kohler, July 11, 1951, ibid.; Clayton Randorf to Kohler, ibid.; see, e.g., Petition to Kohler by Green Bay employees, Apr. 10, 1951, ibid., folder 6; Zander telegraph to Kohler, July 19, 1951, ibid.; Zander to Kohler, June 22, 1951, ibid.; Bob Madden (Paid Firemen) to Kohler, June 21, 1951, ibid.

47. Henry Ahrens to Kohler, July 3, 1951, Kohler Archives, box 77, folder 5; Oliver Grootemaat to Kohler, July 2, 1951, ibid.; Herbert Giese to Kohler, ibid., folder 6; Frederick MacMillin to Kohler, July 2, 1951, 1, 2, ibid.; Cyrus Philipp to Kohler, June 14, 1951, ibid.; Memo from Lampert to Thomson, June 27, 1951, ibid.

48. *Union News,* May–June 1951, 1; Cling, 338; A. P. Kuranz to Kohler, Aug. 7, 1951, Kohler Archives, box 77, folder 5.

49. *Union News,* May–June 1953, 1. See, e.g., ibid., Nov.–Dec. 1951, 3 ("negotiations" bring gains in Polk, Vernon, and LaCrosse Counties); Nov.–Dec. 1953, 3 (WERB hearing in Antigo City wage dispute).

50. *Journal of the Senate Proceedings of the 71st Session of the Wisconsin Legislature* (Madison: Democrat Printing, 1953), 202; Wisconsin Senate Bills, 1953, WLRB; *Union News,* May–June 1953, 4; Cling, 338–40 (quoting Lawton).

51. Hearing Records, 1953, S.B. 129–271, WLRB. Thomson's report cited *Mugford* and *Cleveland v. Division 268,* discussed in chapter 3; Vernon Thomson to the Senate, May 5, 1953, Legislative Drafting Records, Bill 210-S, WLRB; 42 *OAG* 97 (1953); *Senate Proceedings of 71st Session,* 1079; Cling, 341.

52. *Union News,* Nov.–Dec. 1953, 1; Nov.–Dec. 1954, 1, 2.

53. Bill 89-S, Wisconsin Senate Bills, 1955, WLRB; Substitute Amendment 1 to Bill 89-S, ibid.; "Bill History," 1955 Hearing Records, S.B. 2–142, ibid.; Amendment 2-S to Bill 89-S, ibid.; Cling, 342–43.

54. *Union News,* Jan.–Feb. 1955, 1; Cling, 343–45 (quoting *Milwaukee Journal*).

55. *Journal of the Senate Proceedings of the 72nd Session of the Wisconsin Legislature* (Madison: Democrat Printing, 1955), 1702; *Union News,* May–June 1955, 1, 3.

56. *Union News,* May–June 1955, 1, 2, 3, 4; Haferbecker, 178; W. Thompson, 604, 662–65.

57. *Union News,* July–Aug. 1955, 1, 2; Aug. 1956, 2; Mar.–Apr. 1956, 1; Jan. 1957, 1; Cling, 346–47 and n. 33 (quoting chamber of commerce).

58. *Union News,* Sept. 1956, 1 (quoting news release dated Aug. 6, 1956); Oct. 1956, 4; Cling, 347–48, 711–19. See generally Walter Uphoff, *Kohler on Strike: Thirty Years of Conflict* (Boston: Beacon Press, 1966).

59. *Public Employee,* Jan. 1957, 14; *Union News,* Sept. 1956, 1, 3; Oct. 1956, 1, 2, 3; Nov. 1956, 1, 2, 3–4.

60. *Union News,* Jan. 1957, 1, 3; Cling, 348–49.

61. Governmental Labor Relations Committee Report, Nov. 20, 1956, Nelson Archives, box 22, folder 5; *Union News,* Jan. 1957, 1, 2, 3; Feb. 1957, 1, 2, 4; Cling, 349.

62. *Union News,* May 1957, 2; July 1957, 2; Apr. 1957, 1, 4.

63. Ibid., July 1957, 1, 2.

64. Ibid., Feb. 1958, 4: Oct. 1958, 1; Oct. 1957, 1; *Public Employee,* Jan. 1959, 3. In 1959 AFSCME sponsored bills that would grant some recognition and bargaining rights in

Colorado, Michigan, Minnesota, Illinois, Nebraska, Maryland, Massachusetts, Washington, Oregon, Connecticut, Texas, Wisconsin, Rhode Island, and Utah; *Public Employee,* Jan. 1959, 11, 22; Feb. 1959, 12–13, 18–19; Apr. 1959, 15; May 1959, 12; July 1959, 15.

65. W. Thompson, 676–77, 528, 534; Larry Swoboda and Gail Schneider, "The Impact and Effect of the Municipal Employee Collective Bargaining Law upon Wisconsin's Public Elementary and Secondary Education Environment: Its Historical Context and Political Perspective" (1988), WLRB, 53; *Public Employee,* Dec. 1958, 5; Gaylord Nelson to W. J. Tanking Jr., Sept. 10, 1962, Nelson Archives, box 22, folder 5.

66. W. Thompson, 52, 528–29, 538–53, 560–70, 669, 602–11, 671–73.

67. Ibid., 662–65.

68. Ibid., 641, 661, 177, 644, 226–29, 645–52; Haferbecker, 188.

69. *Union News,* Dec. 1958, 1; Jan. 1959, 1, 2; Madison *Union Labor News,* Dec. 1958, 16.

70. Bill 309-A, Wisconsin Assembly Bills, 1959, WLRB; Substitute Amendment 1-A to Bill 309-A, ibid.; *Union News,* Mar. 1959, 2. The 1959 legislative session was the longest on record at that time; W. Thompson, 677.

71. *Public Employee,* Mar. 1959, 3; *Union News,* Feb. 1959, 1, 2, 4; Apr. 1957, 4.

72. "Bill History," 1961, Hearing Records, AB 319–435, WLRB.

73. *Union News,* Apr. 1959, 1, 2.

74. Gooding to Allen Flannigan, Apr. 6, 1959, 1959 Drafting Records, chaps. 505–9, WLRB; *Union News,* May 1959, 1, 3.

75. *Union News,* Apr. 1959, 4; May 1959, 1, 4; *Public Employee,* June 1959, 11; Robert Ozanne, *The Labor Movement in Wisconsin* (Madison: State Historical Society of Wisconsin, 1984), 75.

76. Sundby to Members of the Assembly, May 20, 1959, Nelson Archives, box 8, folder 21; League of Municipalities to Wisconsin Legislature, July 2, 1959, ibid.; Sundby to Wisconsin Senate, July 17, 1959, ibid.; James Wimmer to Nelson, Sept. 11, 1959, attaching *Milwaukee Journal,* July 29, 1959, ibid. For local opponents, see Harry Curry (Bayfield County Highway Commission) to Nelson, May 26, 1959; Don LeBlanc (Rusk County Board of Supervisors) to Nelson, July 14, 1959; Resolution, Washburn County Board of Supervisors; Recommendation of (Dane) County Board on Certain Bills, Oct. 25, 1961; Nelson to Isabel McPike (City of Spooner School Board), Dec. 4, 1961; Ted Holthusen (Wisconsin Association of School Boards) to Nelson, Jan. 17, 1962; Donald Smith (Pierce County Board of Supervisors) to Nelson, Oct. 25, 1961; Edward Krenzke (Racine) to Nelson, July 29, 1959; all in ibid.

77. Amendment 1-S to Bill 309-A and Substitute Amendment 1–2 to Bill 309-A, Wisconsin Senate Bills, 1959, WLRB; *Index to the Journals of the 74th Session of the Wisconsin Legislature* (Madison: Democrat Printing, 1989), 694. The law was codified as chap. 509 of the laws of 1959, subchap. IV of chap. 111 of the Wisconsin statutes; its effective date was Oct. 3, 1959. *Union News,* July 1959, 1; Sept. 1959, 1; May 1960, 1; Lawton to James Wimmer, Sept. 9, 1959, Nelson Archives, box 8, folder 21; Ed Johnson to Wimmer, Sept. 15, 1959, ibid.

78. Madison *Union Labor News,* Aug. 1959, 5; *Public Employee,* July, 1959, 20; *Union News,* July 1959, 2, 4.

79. *Union News,* Jan. 1960, 1, 4; *Public Employee,* June 1960, 21; Apr. 1960, 21–22.

80. *Union News,* Jan. 1961, 1, 3, 4.

81. Ibid., July 1960, 1, 3; Sept. 1960, 1, 3; Mar. 1960, 1; Arvid Anderson to N. S. Heffernan, Nelson Archives, box 107, folder 2, 1–3.

82. *Union News,* Sept. 1960, 1–3, 4.

83. Ibid., 3, 4; Nov. 1960, 1, 4.

84. W. Thompson, 697; Swoboda and Schneider, 61.

85. Bill 336-A, Wisconsin Assembly Bills, 1961, WLRB; *Union News,* Mar. 1961, 1–2.

86. *Union News,* May 1961, 1–2; June–July 1961, 1; Sept. 1961, 1, 4; *Journal of Proceedings of the 75th Session of the Wisconsin Legislature* (Madison: Democrat Printing, 1961), 1623, 1703; Amendment 3-A to Bill 336-A, Wisconsin Assembly Bills, 1961; Amendment 1-A to Bill 336-A, ibid.; Substitute Amendment 1-S to Bill 336-A, ibid.; Lawton to Members of the Assembly, July 5, 1961, Legislative Drafting Records, chap. 663, 1961, WLRB.

87. *Union News,* Sept. 1961, 1; Lawton to the Assembly, "Analysis of Amendment No. 1-A," [1961], Legislative Drafting Records, chap. 663, 1961; Thelen to the Senate, July 21, 1961, ibid. (attaching articles from the *Milwaukee Journal,* July 15, 1961, and the *Wisconsin State Journal,* July 14, 1961); Thelen to the Assembly, July 6, 1961, ibid.; Ed Johnson (League of Municipalities) to the Senate, [1961], ibid.; Dane County Legislative Committee to the Senate, July 12, 1961, ibid.; Lawrence Waldorf (Wisconsin Municipal Alliance) to the Senate, July 26, 1961, ibid.; J. A. Lawrence (Milwaukee County School Board) to Sen. Jerris Leonard, Nov. 15, 1961, ibid.; E. J. Zeidler (Whitefish Bay Schools) to Colleagues, Nov. 14, 1961, ibid.; H. M. Ihling (Government Service League) to Bruce Thomas, Jan. 18, 1962, Nelson Archives, box 8, folder 21.

88. *Union News,* Sept. 1961, 2; Nov. 1961, 2.

89. Ibid., Sept. 1961, 2, 3; *Public Employee,* Oct. 1961, 2.

90. The law was codified as chap. 663 of the laws of 1961, amending subchap. IV of chapter 111; the effective date was Feb. 6, 1962. Thelen to the Senate, Jan. 8, 1962, Legislative Drafting Records, chap. 663, 1961; Johnson to the Senate, Jan. 8, 1962, ibid.; *Journal of the Proceedings of the 75th Session of the Wisconsin Legislature,* 2578; *Union News,* Jan. 1962, 2; Mar. 1962, 1.

91. *Union News,* Jan. 1962, 1–2, 4; May 1962, 1; *Public Employee,* Feb. 5, 1962, 1; Robert Krause, "The Short, Troubled History of Wisconsin's New Labor Law," *Public Administration Review* 25 (1965): 302–07, 303.

92. *Union News,* Mar. 1962, 1; May 1962, 2; Oct. 1962, 1.

93. The executive order granted exclusive bargaining rights (over very limited topics) to a union chosen by a majority of employees in a bargaining unit; gave formal recognition to a union representing 10 percent of employees (entitling the union to consultation rights); and gave informal recognition to a union representing any employees (allowing it to express its views on policies affecting its members); *Public Employee,* Apr. 6, 1962, 4; Sept. 7, 1962, 7.

94. *Union News,* Mar. 1962, 4; Krause, 302; *Public Employee,* May–June 1961, 2.

95. *Union News,* Aug. 1962, 1, 2, 4; Sept.–Oct. 1964, 1; Goulden, 120; Ozanne, 76–77.

96. *Union News,* Nov.–Dec. 1963, 4; Jan. 1963, 1, 4; Nov.–Dec. 1965, 1, citing Bill 389-A; Swoboda and Schneider, 57; *Union News,* Mar.–Apr., 1966, 3; Anderson, 62; Houlihan, 72.

97. Allen Weisenfeld, "Collective Bargaining by Public Employees in the U.S.," in *Collective Bargaining in the Public Service,* ed. Gerald Somers (Milwaukee: Industrial Relations Research Association, 1966), 5, listing Alaska, California, Connecticut, Delaware, Florida, Maine, Massachusetts, Michigan, Minnesota, Missouri, New Hampshire, Oregon, Rhode Island, Washington, Wisconsin, and Wyoming.

98. *Local 1226, Rhinelander City Employees, AFSCME v. City of Rhinelander,* 35 Wisc.2d 209 (1967); *Union News,* Nov.–Dec. 1971, 1; Swoboda and Schneider, 69; chap. 178, laws of 1977 (S. B. 15); Jane Henkel, "Wisconsin Legislative Council Report No. 3: Legislation Relating to Municipal Collective Bargaining," Apr. 6, 1981, State Historical Society, 3; *Union News,* Nov. 1976, 1; Houlihan, 73. For political reasons, Milwaukee police have been covered under different rules. The circumstances under which strikes are legal are apparently so rare that this option has never been used. Houlihan, 71, 84.

99. Lichtenstein, 182–83, cites only Mayor Wagner's executive order and Kennedy's executive order, then asserts that after the latter, "many Northern and Western states would

soon follow the federal government." That version of events is somewhat parochial. The Wisconsin law was more influential, certainly as a model for other states.

100. Anderson, 62; Ed Johnson, "Emerging Problems in Labor Relations in Wisconsin Cities and Villages," in *Papers on Bargaining Relationships and Practices* (Madison: League of Wisconsin Municipalities, 1968), 4, 6.

Conclusion

1. *Transport Bulletin,* Aug. 1942, 10; Kramer, 35 (Zander quote); Shaffer, 315–16; *Government Employee Relations Reporter,* Nov. 18, 1991, 1502–3.

2. *Government Employee Relations Reporter,* Nov. 18, 1991, 1504; Troy, 9–10; Kearney, 16–17 (2,866,000 federal workers in 1980; 13,383,000 state and local government workers), 19, citing *Reynolds v. Sims,* 377 U.S. 533 (1964), 35–36 (the NEA in 1997 claimed 2.2 million members); Dubofsky, *State and Labor,* 208; Advisory Commission on Intergovernmental Relations, *Labor Management Policies for State and Local Government* (Washington, D.C., 1975), 5; P. Johnston, 5–6; Najita and Stern, 4–5.

3. P. Johnston, 26; see, e.g., Gregory Saltzman, "Bargaining Laws as a Cause and a Consequence of the Growth of Teacher Unionism," *Industrial and Labor Relations Review* 38 (1985): 335–51.

4. Spero, 221 (quoting *New York Times,* May 30, 1946). For the modern era, see Shaffer.

5. International City Managers Association, *Municipal Personnel Administration* (Chicago, 1950), 283. See, e.g., Tomlins, *State and the Unions;* Klare, "Judicial Deradicalization of the Wagner Act"; Atleson; Stone, "The Post-War Paradigm."

6. *Government Employee Relations Report* (BNA), July 9, 2002, 691; Kearney, 58–59, 62, 66. The laws are hard to catalogue. In some contrast to Kearney's count, Najita and Stern, 6–8, estimate that in 1999 there were "over ninety" public sector statutes; thirty-four states had laws covering "some or all occupational groups," six states "authorized other forms of representation and bargaining," and ten had "no such authorizations." For older but more comprehensive treatments of state laws, see Leibig and Kahn; Schneider. For Virginia, see *Abbott v. Virginia Beach,* 879 F.2d 132, 134, 136 (4th Cir. 1989), cert. denied, 493 U.S. 1051 (1990); *Commonwealth v. County Board of Arlington,* 217 Va. 558 (1977).

7. *Commonwealth v. County Board of Arlington; Moreau v. Klevenhagen,* 508 U.S. 22 (1993), 31–35, interpreting 29 U.S.C. sec. 207(o)(2)(A). The pertinent regulation stated in part that "the representative need not be a formal or recognized bargaining agent as long as the representative is designated by the employees"; 29 C.F.R. sec. 553.23(b).

8. Dubofsky, *State and Labor,* chap. 8.

9. Joel Rogers, "Divide and Conquer: Further 'Reflections on the Distinctive Character of American Labor Laws,'" *Wisconsin Law Review,* 1990, 119–44; Paul Weiler, *Governing the Workplace: The Future of Labor and Employment Law* (Cambridge: Harvard University Press, 1990).

10. Tomlins, *State and the Unions;* Stone, "The Post-War Paradigm"; Klare, "Labor Law as Ideology." Klare, like James Atleson, is more open to the idea that judicial interpretation of the NLRA, rather than the statute itself, is to blame. Klare, "Labor Law as Ideology"; Klare, "Judicial Deradicalization of the Wagner Act."

11. Dubofsky and Tomlins had a running debate on the value of the NLRA. Dubofsky's *State and Labor* is in part an attempt to rebut the critique of this law in Tomlins's *State and the Unions.*

12. A few variations in public sector laws favor unions. Some state statutes are more liberal about allowing supervisory employees to form unions, and there is no "permanent replacement" of those public employees allowed to strike. See Kearney; Leibig and Kahn;

Schneider. Perhaps the private sector, and those who study it, could learn from such practices.

13. Joel Rogers, "In the Shadow of the Law: Institutional Aspects of Postwar U.S. Union Decline," in *Labor Law in America: Historical and Critical Essays*, ed. Christopher Tomlins and Andrew King (Baltimore: Johns Hopkins University Press, 1992), 283–302.

14. Sanford Jacoby, "American Exceptionalism Revisited: The Importance of Management," in Jacoby; Kearney, 11; Sexton. For a revealing look at modern anti-union practices, see Martin Levitt, *Confessions of a Union Buster* (New York: Crown, 1993). The ratio of those illegally fired to those organizing was 1:6 in 1990, as opposed to 1:183 in 1955, 1:44 in 1970, and 1:13 in 1980; National Labor Relations Board, *NLRB Annual Report 20* (Washington, D.C., 1955), 9; idem, *NLRB Annual Report 35* (Washington, D.C., 1970), 7–15; idem, *NLRB Annual Report 45* (Washington, D.C., 1980), 3, 9; idem, *NLRB Annual Report 55* (Washington, D.C., 1990), 198–225.

15. Lichtenstein, 185. For modern practice in the private sector, see Sexton; Rogers; Levitt. Some claim that public employers offer less resistance mainly because they are less concerned about the "bottom line" than are private employers. In the modern era of tax cuts and downsizing and privatization in government, this argument can easily be exaggerated. Nor should the anti-union animus of some public employers be underestimated. See Berkeley and Canak.

16. See Archer; Julie Greene, *Pure and Simple Politics: The American Federation of Labor and Political Activism, 1881–1917* (New York: Cambridge University Press, 1998); Thomas Clark, "Law, Rights, and Local Labor Politics in California, 1901–11: Reflections on Recent Labor Law Historiography," *Studies in American Political Development* 11 (1997): 325–46. Christopher Tomlins, "The Heavy Burden of the State: Revisiting the History of Labor Law in the Interwar Period," *Seattle University Law Review* 23 (2000): 606–11, helped clarify some points in this section.

17. For example, public sector unions, especially AFSCME and the SEIU, were crucial in electing the relatively progressive John Sweeney to the presidency of the AFL-CIO.

18. As to politics in the present, see, e.g., Shaffer; Marick Masters, "AFSCME as a Political Union," *Journal of Labor Research* 19 (1998): 313–349. On voluntarism in the past, see Kenneth Casebeer, "The Workers Unemployment Insurance Bill: American Social Wage, Labor Organization, and Legal Ideology," in Tomlins and King, 231–59.

19. P. Johnston, 4.

20. Public sector unions were also subject to the conditions that inhibited private sector labor from forming such a party. The red scares after both wars and continuing anticommunism hurt leftists in all unions. The "first past the post" system of electing candidates that exists in the United States makes it much more difficult for radical or third parties of any kind to succeed, as does the diffuse separation of powers in a federalist system. Racial divisions appeared in the public sector as well. For example, the NEA excluded blacks for many years (the AFT did not).

21. David Noble, *America by Design: Science, Technology, and the Rise of Corporate Capitalism* (New York: Oxford University Press, 1977), 272; *CIO News*, Mar. 3, 1941, 3.

22. Jerry Wurf, among others, used this term; Goulden, xv.

Selected Bibliography

Periodicals, convention proceedings, and annual reports are not listed here; please see notes for these sources.

Manuscript Collections

The American Federation of Labor and the Unions: National and International Union Records from the Samuel Gompers Era. Sanford, N.C.: Microfilming Corporation of America, 1981.

American Federation of Teachers Collection. Walter Reuther Archives. Wayne State University.

Communications to Edwin U. Curtis Regarding the Boston Police Strike, 1919. Special Collections. Boston Public Library.

Calvin Coolidge Collection. Massachusetts State House Library, Boston.

Court Archives, Suffolk County. Boston, Mass.

Walter Kohler Archives. State Historical Society of Wisconsin, Madison.

Local 382 SEIU Collection. Tamiment Library, New York University.

Microfilm Records of the BSEIU. Walter Reuther Archives. Wayne State University, Detroit.

Gaylord Nelson Archives. State Historical Society of Wisconsin, Madison.

Seattle Public School Archives and Records Management Center.

Dietrich Schmitz Collection. University of Washington Archives, Seattle.

Transport Workers Union Collection. Tamiment Library, New York University.

Washington State Archives. Central Branch, Ellensburg.

Wisconsin Legislative Reference Bureau, Madison.

Printed Works

Advisory Commission on Intergovernmental Relations. *Labor Management Policies for State and Local Government.* Washington, D.C., 1975.

American Federation of Labor. *American Federation of Labor: History, Encyclopedia, Reference Book.* Washington, D.C., 1919.

Anderson, Arvid. "Wisconsin: A Pioneer in Labor Relations Law." In *State and Social Legislation: A Symposium in Honor of Elizabeth Brandeis Raushenbush.* Madison: Industrial Relations Research Institute, 1966.

Ansell, Christopher, and Arthur Burris. "Bosses of the City Unite! Labor Politics and Political Machine Consolidation, 1880–1910." *Studies in American Political Development* 11 (1997): 1–43.

Archer, Robin. "Unions, Courts, and Parties: Judicial Repression and Labor Politics in Late Nineteenth Century America." *Politics and Society* 26 (1998): 391–422.

Arnesen, Eric. "Up from Exclusion: Black and White Workers, Race, and the State of Labor History." *Reviews in American History* 26 (1998): 146–74.

Atleson, James. *Values and Assumptions in American Labor Law.* Amherst: University of Massachusetts Press, 1983.

Avery, Dianne. "Images of Violence in Labor Jurisprudence: The Regulation of Picketing and Boycotts, 1894–1921." *Buffalo Law Review* 37 (1989): 1–117.

Bates, Frank, and Oliver Field. *State Government.* New York: Harper and Bros., 1939.

Beadling, Tom, Pat Cooper, Grace Palladino, and Peter Pieragostini. *A Need for Valor: The Roots of the Service Employees International Union, 1902–1992.* Washington, D.C.: SEIU, 1992.

Bean, Ron. "Police Unrest, Unionization, and the 1919 Strike in Liverpool." *Journal of Contemporary History* 15 (1980): 633–53.

Befort, Stephen. "Labor and Employment Law at the Millennium: A Historical Review and Critical Assessment." *Boston College Law Review* 43 (2002): 351–460.

Berkeley, Miller, and William Canak. "There Should Be No Blanket Guarantee: Employer Opposition to Public Employee Unions." *Journal of Collective Negotiations in the Public Sector* 24 (1995): 17–36.

Bernstein, Irving. *A Caring Society: The New Deal, the Worker, and the Great Depression.* Boston: Houghton Mifflin, 1985.

——. *The Lean Years: A History of the American Worker, 1920–1933.* Baltimore: Penguin, 1966.

——. *The Turbulent Years: A History of the American Worker, 1933–1941.* Boston: Houghton Mifflin, 1969.

Biles, Roger, *Big City Boss in Depression and War: Mayor Edward J. Kelly of Chicago.* De Kalb: Northern Illinois University Press, 1984.

Billings, Richard, and John Greenya. *Power to the Public Worker.* Washington, D.C.: Robert Luce, 1974.

Bopp, William. *The Police Rebellion: A Quest for Blue Power.* Springfield, Ill.: Charles Thomas, 1971.

The Boston Police Strike: Two Reports. New York: Arno Press, 1971.

Brandeis, Louis. "The Living Law." *Illinois Law Review* 10 (1916): 463–71.

Braverman, Harry. *Labor and Monopoly Capital.* New York: Monthly Review Press, 1974.

Brigham, Jay. "Public Power and Progressivism in the 1920s." Ph.D. diss., University of California, Riverside, 1992.

Brody, David. *Steelworkers in America: The Nonunion Era.* Cambridge: Harvard University Press, 1960.

——. *Workers in Industrial America.* New York: Oxford University Press. 1980.

Burpo, John. *The Police Labor Movement: Problems and Perspectives.* Springfield, Ill.: Charles Thomas, 1971.

Cammack, Paul. "Bringing the State Back In?" *British Journal of Political Science* 19 (1989): 261–90.

Casebeer, Kenneth. "The Workers Unemployment Insurance Bill: American Social Wage, Labor Organization, and Legal Ideology." In *Labor Law in America: Historical and Critical Essays,* ed. Christopher Tomlins and Andrew King. Baltimore: Johns Hopkins University Press, 1992.

Chicago, City of. *Chicago's Report to the People, 1933–46.* 1947.

Clark, Thomas. "Law, Rights, and Local Labor Politics in California, 1901–11: Reflections on Recent Labor Law Historiography." *Studies in American Political Development* 11 (1997): 325–46.

Cling, Edward. "Industrial Labor Relations Policies and Practices in Municipal Government, Milwaukee, Wisconsin." Ph.D. diss., Northwestern University, 1957.

Cole, Peter. "Shaping Up and Shipping Out: The Philadelphia Waterfront during and after the IWW Years, 1913–1940." Ph.D. diss., Georgetown University, 1997.

Cole, Stephen. *The Unionization of Teachers: A Case Study of the UFT.* New York: Praeger, 1969.

Commons, John. *Labor and Administration.* New York: Macmillan, 1913.

Cooper, Frank. *State Administrative Law.* Vol. 1. Indianapolis: Bobbs-Merrill, 1965.

Crain, Marion. "Between Feminism and Unionism: Working Class Women, Sex Equality, and Labor Speech." *Georgetown University Law Journal* (1994): 1903–2001.

Crouch, Winston. *Organized Civil Servants.* Berkeley: University of California Press, 1978.

Davis, Kenneth C. *Administrative Law.* St. Paul: West Publishing, 1951.

——. *Administrative Law Text.* 3d ed. St. Paul: West Publishing, 1972.

——. *Administrative Law Treatise.* Vol. 1. 2d ed. San Diego: K. C. Davis, 1978.

Dubofsky, Melvyn. *The State and Labor in Modern America.* Chapel Hill: University of North Carolina Press, 1994.

——. *We Shall Be All: A History of the IWW.* Chicago: Quadrangle Books, 1969.

Dulles, Foster, and Melvyn Dubofsky. *Labor in America: A History.* 4th ed. Arlington, Ill.: Harlan Davidson, 1984.

Eaton, William. *The American Federation of Teachers, 1916–1961.* Carbondale: Southern Illinois University Press, 1975.

Ernst, Daniel. "Law and American Political Development, 1877–1938." *Reviews in American History* 26 (1998): 205–19.

——. *Lawyers against Labor: From Individual Rights to Corporate Liberalism.* Urbana: University of Illinois Press, 1995.

——. "The Yellow Dog Contract and Liberal Reform, 1917–32." *Labor History* 30 (1989): 251–274.

Fabricant, Solomon, and Robert Lipsey. *The Trend of Government Activity in the United States since 1900.* New York: National Bureau of Economic Research, 1952.

Fink, Leon. *Workingmen's Democracy: The Knights of Labor and American Politics.* Urbana: University of Illinois Press, 1983.

Foner, Philip. *History of the Labor Movement in the United States.* Vol. 8: *Postwar Struggles, 1918–20.* New York: International Publishers, 1987.

Forbath, William. *Law and the Shaping of the American Labor Movement.* Cambridge: Harvard University Press, 1991.

Fox, Neil. "PATCO and the Courts: Public Sector Labor Law as Ideology." *Illinois Law Review* (1985): 245–314.

Frank, Dana. *Purchasing Power: Consumer Organizing, Gender, and the Seattle Labor Movement, 1919–1929.* New York: Cambridge University Press, 1994.

Frankfurter, Felix. "Hours of Labor and Realism in Constitutional Law." *Harvard Law Review* 29 (1916): 353–73.

Frankfurter, Felix, and Nathan Greene. *The Labor Injunction.* New York: Macmillan, 1930.

Freeman, Joshua. *In Transit: The Transport Workers Union in New York City, 1933–1966.* New York: Oxford University Press, 1989.

Freeman, Richard, and Casey Ichniowski. *When Public Sector Workers Unionize.* Chicago: University of Chicago Press, 1988.

Friedman, Lawrence. *American Law in the Twentieth Century.* New Haven: Yale University Press, 2002.

Gammage, Allen, and Stanley Sachs. *Police Unions.* Springfield, Ill.: Charles Thomas, 1972.

Godine, Morton. *The Labor Problem in the Public Service.* Cambridge: Harvard University Press, 1951.

Gompers, Samuel. *Seventy Years of Life and Labor: An Autobiography.* 2d ed. New York: E. P. Dutton, 1967.

Gordon, Robert. "Critical Legal Histories." *Stanford Law Review* 36 (1984): 57–125.

——. "The Past as Authority and as Social Critic: Stabilizing and Destabilizing Functions of History in Legal Argument." In *The Historic Turn in the Human Sciences,* ed. Terrence McDonald. Ann Arbor: University of Michigan Press, 1996.

Goulden, Joseph. *Jerry Wurf: Labor's Last Angry Man.* New York: Atheneum, 1982.

Grant, Daniel, and H. C. Nixon. *State and Local Government in America.* Boston: Allyn and Bacon, 1968.

Greene, Julie. *Pure and Simple Politics: The American Federation of Labor and Political Activism, 1881–1917.* New York: Cambridge University Press, 1998.

Grubbs, Frank. *Samuel Gompers and the Great War: Protecting Labor's Standards.* Wake Forest, N.C.: Meridional Press, 1982.

Haferbecker, Gordon. *Wisconsin Labor Laws.* Madison: University of Wisconsin Press, 1958.

Halperin, Rick, and Jonathan Morris, eds. *American Exceptionalism? U.S. Working Class Formation in an International Context.* New York: St. Martin's Press, 1997.

Hanslowe, Kurt. "The Emerging Law of Labor Relations in Public Sector Employment." In *Labor Relations Law in the Public Sector: Cases and Materials,* ed. Harry Edwards, R. Theodore Clark, and Charles Craver. 4th ed. Charlottesville, Va.: Michie, 1991.

Hattam, Victoria. *Labor Visions and State Power: The Origins of Business Unionism in the United States.* Princeton: Princeton University Press, 1993.

Hazard, Joseph. *Pioneer Teachers of Washington.* Seattle: Seattle Retired Teachers Association, 1955.

Henkel, Jane. "Wisconsin Legislative Council Report No. 3: Legislation Relating to Municipal Collective Bargaining." Wisconsin State Historical Society, Madison, 1981.

Horwitz, Morton. *The Transformation of American Law, 1780–1860.* Cambridge: Harvard University Press, 1977.

——. *The Transformation of American Law, 1870–1960: The Crisis of Legal Orthodoxy.* New York: Oxford University Press, 1992.

Houlihan, William. "Interest Arbitration and Municipal Employee Bargaining: The Wisconsin Experience." In *Collective Bargaining in the Public Sector: The Experience of Eight States,* ed. Joyce Najita and James Stern. Armonk, N.Y.: M. E. Sharpe, 2001.

Hoxie, Robert. *Trade Unionism in the United States.* New York: D. Appleton, 1923.

Hurst, James Willard. *Law and the Conditions of Freedom in the Nineteenth Century United States.* Madison: University of Wisconsin Press, 1956.

International Association of Chiefs of Police Bulletin. *Police Unions.* Washington, D.C.: IACP, 1958.

International City Managers Association. *Municipal Personnel Administration.* Chicago, 1950.

Jacoby, Sanford, ed. *Masters to Managers: Historical and Comparative Perspectives on American Employers.* New York: Columbia University Press, 1991.

Jentz, John. "Citizenship, Self-Respect, and Political Power: Chicago's Flat Janitors Trailblaze the Service Employees International Union, 1912–21." *Labor's Heritage* 9 (1997): 4–23.

——. "Labor, the Law, and Economics: The Organization of the Chicago Flat Janitors' Union, 1902–1917." *Labor History* 38 (1998): 413–31.

Johnson, Ed. "Emerging Problems in Labor Relations in Wisconsin Cities and Villages." In *Papers on Bargaining Relationships and Practices.* Madison: League of Wisconsin Municipalities, 1968.

Johnston, Edna. "Rendering a Permanent Service: Organized Labor and the Federal Civil Service, 1900–32." Forthcoming Ph.D. diss., University of Virginia.

Johnston, Paul. *Success While Others Fail: Social Movement Unionism and the Public Workplace.* Ithaca, N.Y.: Cornell University Press, 1994.

Kasalow, Everett. "Recent Developments in Collective Bargaining for Public Employees." In *Collective Bargaining for Public Employees,* ed. Jack Triplett. Eugene: University of Oregon Press, 1966.

Katznelson, Ira. "The 'Bourgeois' Dimension: A Provocation about Institutions, Politics, and the Future of Labor History." *International Labor and Working Class History* 46 (1994): 7–32.

Kazin, Michael. "Struggling with Class Struggle: Marxism and the Search for a Synthesis of U.S. Labor History." *Labor History* 28 (1987): 497–514.

Kearney, Richard, and David Carnevale. *Labor Relations in the Public Sector.* 3d ed. New York: Marcel Dekker, 2001.

Keller, William, ed. *International Labor and Employment Laws.* Vol. 1. Washington, D.C.: BNA Books, 1997.

Kelly, Brian. *Race, Class, and Power in the Alabama Coalfields, 1908–21.* Urbana: University of Illinois Press, 2001.

Kessler-Harris, Alice. "Treating the Male as 'Other': Defining the Parameters of Labor History." *Labor History* 34 (1993): 190–204.

Kessner, Thomas. *Fiorello H. LaGuardia and the Making of Modern New York.* New York: McGraw-Hill, 1989.

Kheel, Theodore. "Introduction: Background and History." In *Public Employee Unions: A Study of the Crisis in Public Sector Labor Relations,* ed. Lawrence Chickering. San Francisco: Institute for Contemporary Studies, 1976.

Kienast, Philip. "Police and Firefighter Employee Organizations." Ph.D. diss., Michigan State University, 1972.

Kimmeldorf, Howard. "Bringing Unions Back In (or Why We Need a New Old Labor History)." With comments by Michael Kazin, Alice Kessler-Harris, David Montgomery, Bruce Nelson, Daniel Nelson, and a response by Kimmeldorf. *Labor History* 32 (1991): 91–129.

Klare, Karl. "Judicial Deradicalization of the Wagner Act and the Origins of Modern Legal Consciousness: 1937–1941." *Minnesota Law Review* 62 (1978): 265–339.

——. "Labor Law as Ideology: Towards a New Historiography of Collective Bargaining Law." *Industrial Relations Law Journal* 4 (1981): 450–82.

Koss, Frederick. "The Boston Police Strike." Ph.D. diss., Boston University, 1966.

Kramer, Leo. *Labor's Paradox: The American Federation of State, County, and Municipal Employees, AFL-CIO.* New York: Wiley, 1962.

Krause, Robert. "The Short, Troubled History of Wisconsin's New Labor Law." *Public Administration Review* 25 (1965): 302–7.

Kropp, Steven. "Reflections on Law, Economics, and Policy in Public Sector Labor Relations in Canada, the United States, and the United Kingdom." *Law and Policy in International Business* 27 (1996): 825–51.

Lambert, J. Bartlett. "The Right to Strike in American Political Development: Labor, the State, and Social Policy." Ph.D. diss., University of Wisconsin, 1998.

Lawrence, Elliot. *Little Flower: The Life and Times of Fiorello LaGuardia.* New York: Morrow, 1983.

Leibig, Michael, and Wendy Kahn. *Public Employee Organizing and the Law.* Washington, D.C.: BNA Books, 1987.

Levinson, Harold. *Collective Bargaining by British Local Authority Employees.* Ann Arbor: University of Michigan Press, 1971.

Levitt, Martin. *Confessions of a Union Buster.* New York: Crown, 1993.

Lewin, David, Peter Feuille, Thomas Kochan, and John Thomas Delaney, eds. *Public Sector Labor Relations: Analysis and Readings.* Lexington, Mass.: Lexington Books, 1988.

Lichtenstein, Nelson. *State of the Union: A Century of American Labor.* Princeton: Princeton University Press, 2002.

Maier, Mark. *City Unions: Managing Discontent in New York City.* New Brunswick, N.J.: Rutgers University Press, 1987.

Margalioth, Sharon. "The Significance of Worker Attitudes: Individualism as a Cause for Labor's Decline." *Hofstra Labor and Employment Law Journal* 16 (1998): 133–65.

Marx, Fritz, ed. *Elements of Public Administration.* New York: Prentice-Hall, 1946.

Masters, Marick. "AFSCME as a Political Union." *Journal of Labor Research* 19 (1998): 313–349.

McBride, John, Thomas Touhey, and Barbara McBride. *Government Contracts: Law, Administration, Procedure.* Vol. 1. New York: Matthew Bender, 1984.

McCurdy, Charles. "The Roots of Liberty of Contract Reconsidered: Major Premises in the Law of Employment, 1867–1932." *Supreme Court Historical Society Yearbook* (1984): 20–33.

McGinley, James. *Labor Relations in the New York Rapid Transit Systems, 1904–1944.* New York: King's Crown Press, 1949.

McKusko, M. Brady. *Carriers in a Common Cause: A History of Letter Carriers and the NALC.* Washington, D.C.: NALC, 1986.

Meany, George. "Union Leaders and Public Sector Unions—AFL-CIO." In *Public Employee Unions: A Study of the Crisis in Public Sector Labor Relations,* ed. Lawrence Chickering. San Francisco: Institute for Contemporary Studies, 1976.

Montgomery, David. *The Fall of the House of Labor: The Workplace, the State, and American Labor Activism, 1865–1925.* New York: Cambridge University Press, 1987.

Mosher, W. E., J. D. Kingsley, and O. G. Stahl. *Public Personnel Administration.* New York: Harper, 1950.

Murphy, Marjorie. *Blackboard Unions: The AFT and the NEA, 1900–1980.* Ithaca: Cornell University Press, 1990.

Murray, Robert. *Red Scare: A Study in National Hysteria, 1919–1920.* Minneapolis: University of Minnesota Press, 1955.

Myers, Frederic. *The State and Government Employee Unions in France.* Ann Arbor: University of Michigan Press, 1971.

Najita, Joyce, and James Stern. "Introduction and Overview." In *Collective Bargaining in the Public Sector: The Experience of Eight States,* ed. Joyce Najita and James Stern. Armonk, N.Y.: M. E. Sharpe, 2001.

National Labor Relations Board. *Legislative History of the National Labor Relations Act of 1935.* Vol. 2. Washington, D.C.: Government Printing Office, 1949.

Nelson, Bruce. *Good Schools: The Seattle Public School System, 1901–30.* Seattle: University of Washington Press, 1988.

Nesbitt, Murray. *Labor Relations in the Federal Government Service.* Washington, D.C.: BNA Books, 1976.

New York Labor Relations Board Report, 1937–42. Albany: J. B. Lyons, 1942.

Noble, David. *America by Design: Science, Technology, and the Rise of Corporate Capitalism.* New York: Oxford University Press, 1977.

Novick, Peter. *That Noble Dream: Objectivity and the American Historical Profession.* Cambridge: Cambridge University Press, 1988.

Oestreicher, Richard. "Urban Working-Class Political Behavior and Theories of American Electoral Politics, 1870–1940." *Journal of American History* 74 (1988): 1257–86.

O'Neil, Hugh. "The Growth of Municipal Employee Unions." In *Unionization of Municipal Employees,* ed. Robert Connery and William Farr. New York: Academy of Political Science, 1971.

Orren, Karen. *Belated Feudalism: Labor, the Law, and Liberal Development in the United States.* New York: Cambridge University Press, 1991.

Ozanne, Robert. *The Labor Movement in Wisconsin.* Madison: State Historical Society of Wisconsin, 1984.

Palmer, Bryan. *Descent into Discourse: The Reification of Language and the Writing of Social History.* Philadelphia: Temple University Press, 1990.

Perlman, Selig. *A Theory of the Labor Movement.* New York: Macmillan, 1928.

Pois, Joseph, Edward Martin, and Lyman Moore. *The Merit System in Illinois.* Chicago: Joint Committee on the Merit System, 1935.

Posey, Rollin. "Employee Organizations in the United States Public Service." *Public Personnel Review,* October 1956, 238–45.

Rains, Harry. "Collective Bargaining in Public Employment." *Labor Law Journal* 8 (August 1957): 548–50.

Repas, Robert. "Collective Bargaining Problems in Federal Employment." In *Collective Bargaining in the Public Service,* ed. Daniel Kruger and Charles Schmidt. New York: Random House, 1969.

Reppetto, Thomas. *The Blue Parade.* New York: Free Press, 1978.

Rhyne, Charles. *Labor Unions and Municipal Employee Law.* Washington, D.C.: National Institute of Municipal Law Offices, 1946.

Rogers, Joel. "Divide and Conquer: Further 'Reflections on the Distinctive Character of American Labor Laws.'" *Wisconsin Law Review,* 1990, 1–147.

———. "In the Shadow of the Law: Institutional Aspects of Postwar U.S. Union Decline."

In *Labor Law in America: Historical and Critical Essays,* ed. Christopher Tomlins and Andrew King. Baltimore: Johns Hopkins University Press, 1992.

Russell, Francis. *A City in Terror: The 1919 Boston Police Strike.* New York: Viking, 1975.

Saltzman, Gregory. "Bargaining Laws as a Cause and a Consquence of the Growth of Teacher Unionism." *Industrial and Labor Relations Review* 38 (1985): 335–51.

Schatz, Ronald. "From Commons to Dunlop: Rethinking the Field and Theory of Industrial Relations." In *Industrial Democracy in America,* ed. Nelson Lichtenstein and Howell Harris. Cambridge: Cambridge University Press, 1993.

Schiller, Reuel. "From Group Rights to Individual Liberties: Post-War Labor Law, Liberalism, and the Waning of Union Strength." *Berkeley Journal of Employment and Labor Law* 20 (1999): 1–73.

Schneider, Krista. *Public Employees Bargain for Excellence: A Compendium of State Public Sector Labor Relations Laws.* Washington, D.C.: AFL-CIO Public Employee Department, 1993.

Schrag, Zachary. "Nineteen-Nineteen: The Boston Police Strike in the Context of American Labor." A.B. honors thesis, Harvard University, 1992.

Scott, Joan. "On Language, Gender, and Working Class History." *International Labor and Working Class History* 31 (1987): 1–13.

Sexton, Patricia. *The War on Labor and the Left: Understanding America's Unique Conservatism.* Boulder: Westview Press, 1991.

Shaffer, Robert. "Where Are the Organized Public Employees? The Absence of Public Employee Unionism from U.S. History Textbooks, and Why It Matters." *Labor History* 43 (2002): 315–34.

Shefter, Martin. *Political Parties and the State: The American Historical Experience.* Princeton: Princeton University Press, 1994.

Skocpol, Theda. "Bringing the State Back In: Strategies of Analysis in Current Research." In *Bringing the State Back In,* ed. Peter Evans, Dietrich Rueschmeyer, and Theda Skocpol. New York: Cambridge University Press, 1985.

Skocpol, Theda, and Kenneth Finegold. "Explaining New Deal Labor Policy." With comments by Michael Goldfield. *American Political Science Review* 84 (1990): 1297–1315.

Skowronek, Stephen. *Building a New American State: The Expansion of National Administrative Capacities, 1877–1920.* New York: Cambridge University Press, 1982.

Slater, Joseph. "The Court Does *Not* Know 'What a Labor Union Is': How State Structures and Judicial (Mis)Constructions Deformed Public Sector Labor Law." *Oregon Law Review* 79 (2000): 981–1032.

———. "Down by Law: Public Sector Unions and the State in America, World War I to World War II." Ph.D. diss., Georgetown University, 1998.

———. "Petting the Infamous Yellow Dog: The Seattle High School Teachers Union and the State, 1928–31." *Seattle University Law Review* 23 (2000): 485–501.

———. "Public Workers: Labor and the Boston Police Strike of 1919." *Labor History* 38 (1997): 7–27.

———. "The Rise of Master-Servant and the Fall of Master Narrative: A Review of *Labor Law in America.*" *Berkeley Journal of Employment and Labor Law* 15 (1994): 141–71.

Speiser, Karen. "Labor Arbitration in Public Agencies: An Unconstitutional Delegation of Power or the 'Waking of a Sleeping Giant'?" *Journal of Dispute Resolution,* 1993, 333–47.

Spero, Sterling. *Government as Employer.* New York: Remsen Press, 1948.

Spero, Sterling, and John Capozolla. *The Urban Community and Its Unionized Bureau-cracies: Pressure Politics in Local Government Labor Relations.* New York: Dunellen, 1973.

Stieber, Jack. *Public Employee Unionism: Structure, Growth, Policy.* Washington, D.C.: Brookings Institution, 1973.

Stone, Katherine. "The Legacy of Industrial Pluralism: The Tension between Individual Employment Rights and the New Deal Collective Bargaining System." *University of Chicago Law Review* 59 (1992) 575–644.

———. "The Post-War Paradigm in American Labor Law." *Yale Law Journal* 90 (1981): 1509–80.

Swoboda, Larry, and Gail Schneider. "The Impact and Effect of the Municipal Employee Collective Bargaining Law upon Wisconsin's Public Elementary and Secondary Educa-tion Environment: Its Historical Context and Political Perspective." Wisconsin Legisla-tive Reference Bureau, Madison, 1988.

Taft, Philip. *The AFL in the Time of Gompers.* New York: Harper and Bros., 1957.

Tager, Jack. *Boston Riots: Three Centuries of Social Violence.* Boston: Northeastern Uni-versity Press, 2001.

Thompson, E. P. *The Making of the English Working Class.* New York: Vintage, 1966.

———. *The Poverty of Theory and Other Essays.* New York: Monthly Review Press, 1978.

Thompson, William. *The History of Wisconsin: Continuity and Change, 1940–65.* Vol. 6. Madison: State Historical Society of Wisconsin, 1988.

Tomlins, Christopher. "The Heavy Burden of the State: Revisiting the History of Labor Law in the Interwar Period." *Seattle University Law Review* 23 (2000): 605–29.

———. *Law, Labor, and Ideology in the Early American Republic.* New York: Cambridge University Press, 1993.

———. *The State and the Unions: Labor Relations, Law, and the Organized Labor Move-ment in America, 1880–1960.* New York: Cambridge University Press, 1985.

Tomlins, Christopher, and Andrew King, eds. *Labor Law in America: Historical and Critical Essays.* Baltimore: Johns Hopkins University Press, 1992.

Torpey, W. G. *Public Personnel Management.* New York: Van Nostrand, 1953.

Troy, Leo. *The New Unionism in the New Society: Public Sector Unions in the Redistrib-utive State.* Fairfax, Va.: George Mason University Press, 1994.

Uphoff, Walter. *Kohler on Strike: Thirty Years of Conflict.* Boston: Beacon Press, 1966.

Urban, Wayne. *Why Teachers Organized.* Detroit: Wayne State University Press, 1982.

Urofsky, Melvyn. "State Courts and Protective Legislation during the Progressive Era: A Reevaluation." *Journal of American History* 72 (June 1985): 63–91.

U.S. Bureau of the Census. *Historical Statistics of the United States from Colonial Times to 1970.* 2 parts. Washington, D.C.: Government Printing Office, 1975.

———. "State and Local Government Quarterly Employment Survey." Washington, D.C., March 29 and October 22, 1940.

Wachs, Roy. "How to Organize to Deal with Employee Groups." In *Papers on Bargain-ing Relationships and Practices.* Madison: League of Wisconsin Municipalities, 1968.

Walsh, John. *Labor Struggle in the Post Office: From Selective Lobbying to Collective Bargaining.* Armonk, N.Y.: M. E. Sharpe, 1992.

Weiler, Paul. *Governing the Workplace: The Future of Labor and Employment Law.* Cambridge: Harvard University Press, 1990.

Weisenfeld, Allen. "Collective Bargaining by Public Employees in the U.S.," in *Collective Bargaining in the Public Service,* ed. Gerald Somers. Milwaukee: Industrial Relations Research Association, 1966.

Wellington, Harry, and Ralph Winter Jr. *The Unions and the Cities.* Washington, D.C.: Brookings Institution, 1971.

Westbrook, James. "The Use of the Nondelegation Doctrine in Public Sector Labor Law: Lessons from Cases That Have Perpetuated an Anachronism." *St. Louis University Law Journal* 30 (1986): 331–84.

White, Jonathan. "A Triumph of Bureaucracy: The Boston Police Strike and the Ideological Origins of the American Police Structure." Ph.D. diss., Michigan State University, 1982.

Wrigley, Julia. *Class Politics and Public Schools: Chicago, 1900–50.* New Brunswick, N.J.: Rutgers University Press, 1982.

Wyman, Henry. "Opinion of Sept. 11, 1919." In *Official Opinions of the Attorneys General of the Commonwealth of Massachusetts.* Vol. 5: *1917–1920.* Boston: Wright and Potter, 1922.

Zieger, Robert. *The CIO, 1935–1955.* Chapel Hill: University of North Carolina Press, 1995.

Ziskind, David. *One Thousand Strikes of Government Employees.* New York: Columbia University Press, 1940.

Zweig, Michael. *The Working Class Majority: America's Best Kept Secret.* Ithaca: Cornell University Press, 2002.

Cases

Abbott v. Virginia Beach, 879 F.2d 132 (4th Cir. 1989), cert. denied, 493 U.S. 1051 (1990).

Adair v. United States, 208 U.S. 161 (1908).

Adkins v. Children's Hospital, 261 U.S. 525 (1923).

AFSCME Local 201 v. City of Muskegon, 369 Mich. 384, 120 N.W.2d 197 (1963).

Alden v. Maine, 527 U. S. 706 (1999).

Amalgamated Ass'n of Street, Electric Railway & Motor Coach Employees v. WERB, 340 U.S. 383 (1951).

Andresen v. Rice, 277 N.Y. 271, 14 N.E.2d 65 (1938).

Atkins v. City of Charlotte, 296 F. Supp. 1068 (W.D.N.C. 1969).

Barhelmess v. Cuckor, 231 N.Y. 435, 132 N.E. 140 (1921).

Beverly v. City of Dallas, 292 S.W.2d 172 (Tex. Civ. App. 1956), writ refused, n.r.e.

Board of Regents v. Roth, 408 U.S. 564 (1972).

Board of Trustees. v. Garrett, 531 U. S. 356 (2001).

Carpenters & Joiners Union of America, Local 213 v. Ritter's Café, 149 S.W.2d 694 (Tex. Civ. App. 1940), aff'd 315 U.S. 722 (1942).

Carter v. Thompson, 164 Va. 312, 180 S.E. 410 (1935).

CIO v. City of Dallas, 198 S.W.2d 143 (Tex. Civ. App. 1946), writ refused, n.r.e.

City of Cleveland v. Division 268, Amalgamated Association of Street, Electric Railway and Motor Coach Employees of America, 57 Oh. Abs. 173, 90 N.E.2d 711 (C.P. 1949).

City of Jackson v. McLeod, 199 Miss. 676, 24 So.2d 319 (1946), cert. denied, 328 U.S. 863 (1946).

City of Los Angeles v. Los Angeles Building and Trades Council, 94 Cal.App.2d 36, 210 P.2d 305 (1949).

City of New Orleans v. Police Association of Louisiana, 369 So.2d 188 (La. Ct. App.), cert. denied, 376 So.2d 1269 (La. 1979).

In the Matter of the City of New York, acting by the Board of Transportation of the City of New York and Transport Workers Union of America, New York State Labor Relations Board Dec. No. 56 (Jan. 22, 1938). Reprinted in *Decisions and Orders of the N.Y. State Labor Relations Board* (Albany, 1938), 219–21.

City of Springfield v. Clouse, 356 Mo. 1239, 206 S.W.2d 539 (1947).

City Policemen's Union No. 16718 v. Commissioners of the District of Columbia, Equity No. 37142 (D.C., Sept. 4, 1919).

Commonwealth v. County Board of Arlington, 217 Va. 558, 232 S.E.2d 30 (1977).

Commonwealth v. Hunt, 4 Met. 111 (Mass. 1842).

Cook v. United States, 91 U.S. 389 (1875).

Coppage v. Kansas, 236 U.S. 1 (1915).

Fraternal Order of Firemen v. Harris, 306 Mich. 68 (1943), cert. denied, 321 U.S. 784 (1944).

Fraternal Order of Police v. Lansing Board of Police & Fire Commissioners, 306 Mich. 68, 10 N.W.2d 310 (1943).

Frederick v. Owens, 25 Oh. Cir. Ct. Rpt. 581 (Ct. App. 1915), error dismissed, Owens v. Board of Education, 95 Oh. 407, 116 N.E. 1085 (1916).

Fursman v. City of Chicago, 278 Ill. 318, 116 N.E. 158 (1917).

Garcia v. San Antonio Metropolitan Transit Authority, 469 U.S. 528 (1985).

Goldfinger v. Feintuch, 276 N.Y. 281, 11 N.E.2d 910 (1937).

Government and Civic Employees Organizing Committee, CIO v. Windsor, 262 Ala. 285, 78 So.2d 646 (1955).

Hammer v. Dagenhart, 247 U.S. 251 (1918).

Hogan v. Petrucci, 5 Misc.2d 480, 27 N.Y.S.2d 718 (1941).

Hutchinson v. Magee, 278 Pa. 119, 122 A. 234 (1923).

Keyeshian v. Board of Regents, 385 U.S. 589 (1967).

Kimel v. Florida Bd. of Regents, 528 U.S. 62 (2000).

King v. Priest, 357 Mo. 68, 206 S.W.2d 547 (1947), app. dismissed, 333 U.S. 852, reh. denied., 333 U.S. 878 (1948).

Levasseur v. Wheeldon, 79 S.D. 442, 112 N.W.2d 894 (1962).

Lindsay-Strathmore Irrigation District v. Bekins, 304 U.S. 27 (1938).

Local 891, Operating Engineers, and Local 74, BSEIU, New York State Labor Relations Board, case SU-4254 (Nov. 1940).

Local 1226, Rhinelander City Employees, AFSCME v. City of Rhinelander, 35 Wis.2d 209, 151 N.W.2d 30 (1967).

Lochner v. New York, 198 U.S. 45 (1905).

Louisiana v. Pilsbury, 105 U.S. 278 (1881).

Lowe v. Lawlor, 298 U.S. 274 (1908).

Matter of the Board of Rapid Transit Railroad Commissioners, 197 N.Y. 81, 90 N.E. 456 (Ct. App. 1909).

McAuliffe v. Mayor of New Bedford, 155 Mass. 216, 29 N.E. 517 (1892).

McInnes v. Police Commissioner of the City of Boston, No. 16836, Law (Suffolk County, Mass. 1919).

McLaughlin v. Tilendis, 398 F.2d 287 (7th Cir. 1967).

McNatt v. Lawther, 223 S.W. 503 (Tex. Ct. App. 1920).

Miami Water Works Local 654 v. City of Miami, 157 Fla. 445, 26 So.2d 194 (1946).

Moreau v. Klevenhagen, 508 U.S. 22 (1993).

Morehead v. New York ex. rel. Tipaldo, 298 U.S. 587 (1936).

Mugford v. Mayor of Baltimore, 185 Md. 266, 44 A.2d 745 (1945).

In re Municipal Government, City of Newark, N.J., and SCMWA Local 277 (CIO);

Board of Transportation of the City of New York and TWU (CIO) and TWU Local 100 (CIO); Metropolitan Utilities District, Omaha, Neb., and AFSCME Local 431 (AFL), 5 War Labor Reports 286 (Dec. 24, 1942).

In re New York State Labor Relations Board, 37 N.Y.S.2d 304 (1942), aff'd, 267 App. Div. 763, 45 N.Y.S.2d 942 (1943), aff'd, 293 N.Y. 671, 56 N.E.2d 263 (1944).

NLRB v. Jones & Laughlin Steel Corp., 301 U.S. 1 (1937).

Norwalk Teachers' Association v. Bd. of Education, 138 Conn. 269, 83 A.2d 482 (1951).

Nutter v. Santa Monica, 74 Cal.App.2d 292, 168 P.2d 741 (Ct. App. 1946).

Perez v. Board of Police Commissioners of the City of Los Angeles, 78 Cal.App.2d 638, 178 P.2d 537 (1947).

Pickering v. Board of Education, 391 U.S. 563 (1968).

Potts v. Hay, 104 Ark. 438, 318 S.W.2d 826 (1958).

Railway Mail Ass'n v. Murphy, 180 Misc. 868, 44 N.Y.S.2d 601 (1943), rev'd on other grounds sub nom. Railway Mail Association v. Corsi, 267 App. Div. 470 (1944), aff'd, 293 N.Y. 315, 56 N.E.2d 721 (Ct. App. 1944), aff'd, 326 U.S. 88 (1945).

Reynolds v. Sims, 377 U.S. 533 (1964).

San Antonio Firefighters' Union v. Bell, 223 S.W. 506 (Tex. Ct. App. 1920).

Schechter Poultry Corp. v. United States, 295 U.S. 495 (1935).

Seattle High School Teachers Chap. 200 v. Sharples, Case No. 209483 (Super. Ct., King County, Wash., May 28, 1928).

Seattle High School Teachers Chap. 200 v. Sharples, 159 Wash. 424, 293 P. 994 (1930).

State Bd. of Dry Cleaners v. Thrift-D-Lux Cleaners, Inc., 40 Cal.2d 436, 254 P.2d 29 (1953).

State ex rel. Brister v. Weston, 241 Wis. 584, 6 N.W.2d 648 (1942).

State ex rel. Cooper v. Baumann, 231 Wis. 607, 286 N.W. 76 (Wis. 1939).

State v. Kreutzberg, 114 Wis. 530, 90 N.W. 1098 (1902).

United Public Workers v. Mitchell, 330 U.S. 75 (1946).

United States v. Darby, 312 U.S. 100 (1941).

United States v. United Mine Workers, 330 U.S. 258 (1947).

Weinstein v. New York City Transit Authority, 49 Misc.2d 170, 267 N.Y.S.2d 111 (Sup. Ct. 1966).

Index

Katznelson, Ira, 5
Kearney, Richard, 80, 194
Kelly, Brian, 10
Kelly, Edward, 102, 105–8
Kelly, Michael, Jr., 122
Kennedy, John F., 190, 195
Kessner, Thomas, 134
Kimmeldorf, Howard, 10
King, Andrew, 7
King v. Priest, 83, 85, 89
Klare, Karl, 6, 238 n.10
Kohler, Walter, Jr., 168, 171–73, 175
Kramer, Leo, 164
Kuehn, Philip, 185–86, 190

Labor history, 95, 194–97; exclusion of
  public sector employees, 1–7; law and society approach, 6–7; legal realism, 72, 74;
  linguistic turn and, 4–5, 10, 81–82; new
  labor history, 3–4, 10–11; old labor history, 2–3; periodization of, 1–2; postmodern approaches, 4–5, 10–11; Sombart
  question, 6, 12, 200–201, 208–9 n.30
Labor News (Washington State), 42–45,
  47, 52, 55, 58–61, 64, 68
LaFollette, Philip, 167, 168
LaGuardia, Fiorello, 100, 129, 131–32,
  145–46; dues issue and, 137–38, 143;
  memorandum of understanding, 144–45;
  NWLB and, 149–51; view of labor,
  133–34
Landes, Bertha, 44
Landrum-Griffin Act of 1959, 158
Language, construction of reality, 4–5, 7,
  81–82
Lawton, John, 10, 169–70, 173–74, 176–79,
  178, 181–82, 184–85, 187, 234 n.41
Lehman, Herbert, 131–32
Leiserson, William, 167
Levine, David, 46–47, 50, 64, 67
Lewis, John L., 126–27, 131, 135
Lichtenstein, Nelson, 5, 199
Linville, Henry, 50, 56
"Little Steel" decision, 147–49, 155
Lloyd-LaFollette Act of 1912, 19, 21, 90,
  92, 210 n.19, 222 n.81
Loeb rule, 41, 53, 73
Long, Richard, 34
Ludvigsen, Alfred, 180

MacMahon, Arthur, 151
MacMahon, Douglas, 128, 151

Madison Square Garden rallies, 125–26,
  139–40, 153
Making of the English Working Class, The
  (Thompson), 11
Massachusetts Federation of Labor, 32
McAuliffe v. Mayor of New Bedford, 53,
  65, 80–81
McCarthy, Frank, 26–27, 31, 33, 35, 37
McConnell, Francis, 151
McFetridge, William, 98, 100, 102, 104,
  107–8, 110, 118, 120, 122
McInnes, John, 10, 25–26, 31
McNatt v. Lawther, 73, 86–88
Meany, George, 91, 130, 157, 232 n.66
Merit system, 91, 117, 127, 131, 134
*Miami Water Works Local 654 v. City of
  Miami*, 85–86
Miliken, W. Earl, 41, 45, 52–55
Missouri constitution, section 29, 83–84
Mitchell, John, 66
Montgomery, David, 14
Moriarty, Charles, 46
Morrow, Lewis, 42, 51, 57–58, 217 n.60
Morse, Wayne, 148–49, 151
Mugford v. Mayor of Baltimore, 77
Murphy, Marjorie, 69
Murphy, Vincent, 147–48
Murray, Philip, 135, 137–38, 141–42, 151;
  telegrams to LaGuardia, 144–45

National Civil Service League, 156, 161, 163
National Education Association (NEA), 3,
  41, 57, 95, 216 n.56
National Federation of Federal Employees
  (NFFE), 18–19, 126, 150, 229 n.2
National Labor Relations Act (NLRA), 6,
  70, 71, 74, 81, 109, 169, 195; deficiencies, 197–98; exclusion of government
  workers, 90–91, 95, 97, 176; transportation workers and, 140–41
National Recovery Act, 109–10
National War Labor Board (NWLB), 92,
  147–52, 232 nn.66, 68
Nelson, Gaylord, 179, 183, 185–86
Nesbitt, Murray, 79
New York City board of transportation,
  125–26, 129–30, 135–36, 139, 145–46;
  criticism of, 153–55; inflexibility of,
  150–51, 154; proprietary function and,
  129, 140, 142–43; union dues and,
  137–38, 142–43; work rules and, 146–47
New York City Transit System: BMT and